50% OFF Online PCCN Prep Course!

Dear Customer,

We consider it an honor and a privilege that you chose our PCCN Study Guide. As a way of showing our appreciation and to help us better serve you, we have partnered with Mometrix Test Preparation to offer you **50% off their online PCCN Prep Course.** Many PCCN courses are needlessly expensive and don't deliver enough value. With their course, you get access to the best PCCN prep material, and **you only pay half price.**

Mometrix has structured their online course to perfectly complement your printed study guide. The PCCN Prep Course contains **in-depth lessons** that cover all the most important topics, **100+ video reviews** that explain difficult concepts, over **900 practice questions** to ensure you feel prepared, and more than **940 digital flashcards**, so you can study while you're on the go.

Online PCCN Prep Course

Topics Covered:

- Clinical Judgement
  - Cardiovascular
  - Respiratory
  - Endocrine
  - Hematology/Immunology/Oncology
  - Neurological
  - Gastrointestinal
  - Renal
  - Musculoskeletal
  - Multisystem
  - Behavioral/Psychosocial
- Professional Caring and Ethical Practice
  - Advocacy
  - Caring Practices
  - Response to Diversity
  - Facilitation of Learning
  - Systems Thinking
  - Therapeutic Relationships
  - Clinical Inquiry
  - Interdisciplinary Collaboration

Course Features:

- PCCN Study Guide
  - Get content that complements our best-selling study guide.
- 4 Full-Length Practice Tests
  - With over 900 practice questions, you can test yourself again and again.
- Mobile Friendly
  - If you need to study on the go, the course is easily accessible from your mobile device.
- PCCN Flashcards
  - Their course includes a flashcard mode consisting of over 940 content cards to help you study.

To receive this discount, visit their website: mometrix.com/university/pccn/ or simply scan this QR code with your smartphone. At the checkout page, enter the discount code: **TPBPCCN50**

If you have any questions or concerns, please don't hesitate to contact Mometrix at support@mometrix.com.

SCAN HERE

FREE Test Taking Tips Video/DVD Offer

To better serve you, we created videos covering test taking tips that we want to give you for FREE. **These videos cover world-class tips that will help you succeed on your test.**

We just ask that you send us feedback about this product. Please let us know what you thought about it—whether good, bad, or indifferent.

To get your **FREE videos**, you can use the QR code below or email freevideos@studyguideteam.com with "Free Videos" in the subject line and the following information in the body of the email:

   a. The title of your product

   b. Your product rating on a scale of 1-5, with 5 being the highest

   c. Your feedback about the product

If you have any questions or concerns, please don't hesitate to contact us at info@studyguideteam.com.

Thank you!

PCCN Study Guide 2024-2025
3 Practice Tests and PCCN Review Book for Certification Prep [3rd Edition]

Lydia Morrison

Interested in buying more than 10 copies of our product? Contact us about bulk discounts: bulkorders@studyguideteam.com

ISBN 13: 9781637752449

Table of Contents

Welcome *1*
   FREE Videos/DVD OFFER 1

Quick Overview *2*

Test-Taking Strategies *3*

Bonus Content *7*

Introduction to the PCCN Exam *8*

Study Prep Plan for the PCCN Exam *10*

Clinical Judgment *15*
   Cardiovascular 15
   Practice Quiz 67
   Answer Explanations 68

Respiratory *69*
   Practice Quiz 108
   Answer Explanations 109

Endocrine/Hematology/Neurology/Gastrointestinal/ Renal
.... *110*
   Practice Quiz 163
   Answer Explanations 164

Musculoskeletal/Multisystem/Psychosocial *165*
   Practice Quiz 187
   Answer Explanations 188

Professional Caring and Ethical Practice *189*
   Advocacy/Moral Agency 189

Caring Practices 190

Response to Diversity 193

Facilitation of Learning 195

Collaboration 199

Systems Thinking 200

Clinical Inquiry 201

Practice Quiz 203

Answer Explanations 204

PCCN Practice Test #1 205

Answer Key and Explanations 232

PCCN Practice Test #2 253

Answer Key and Explanations #2 279

PCCN Practice Test #3 304

Welcome

Dear Reader,

Welcome to your new Test Prep Books study guide! We are pleased that you chose us to help you prepare for your exam. There are many study options to choose from, and we appreciate you choosing us. Studying can be a daunting task, but we have designed a smart, effective study guide to help prepare you for what lies ahead.

Whether you're a parent helping your child learn and grow, a high school student working hard to get into your dream college, or a nursing student studying for a complex exam, we want to help give you the tools you need to succeed. We hope this study guide gives you the skills and the confidence to thrive, and we can't thank you enough for allowing us to be part of your journey.

In an effort to continue to improve our products, we welcome feedback from our customers. We look forward to hearing from you. Suggestions, success stories, and criticisms can all be communicated by emailing us at info@studyguideteam.com.

Sincerely,
Test Prep Books Team

FREE Videos/DVD OFFER

Doing well on your exam requires both knowing the test content and understanding how to use that knowledge to do well on the test. We offer completely FREE test taking tip videos. **These videos cover world-class tips that you can use to succeed on your test.**

To get your **FREE videos**, you can use the QR code below or email freevideos@studyguideteam.com with "Free Videos" in the subject line and the following information in the body of the email:

     a. The title of your product
     b. Your product rating on a scale of 1-5, with 5 being the highest
     c. Your feedback about the product

If you have any questions or concerns, please don't hesitate to contact us at info@studyguideteam.com.

Quick Overview

As you draw closer to taking your exam, effective preparation becomes more and more important. Thankfully, you have this study guide to help you get ready. Use this guide to help keep your studying on track and refer to it often.

This study guide contains several key sections that will help you be successful on your exam. The guide contains tips for what you should do the night before and the day of the test. Also included are test-taking tips. Knowing the right information is not always enough. Many well-prepared test takers struggle with exams. These tips will help equip you to accurately read, assess, and answer test questions.

A large part of the guide is devoted to showing you what content to expect on the exam and to helping you better understand that content. In this guide are practice test questions so that you can see how well you have grasped the content. Then, answer explanations are provided so that you can understand why you missed certain questions.

Don't try to cram the night before you take your exam. This is not a wise strategy for a few reasons. First, your retention of the information will be low. Your time would be better used by reviewing information you already know rather than trying to learn a lot of new information. Second, you will likely become stressed as you try to gain a large amount of knowledge in a short amount of time. Third, you will be depriving yourself of sleep. So be sure to go to bed at a reasonable time the night before. Being well-rested helps you focus and remain calm.

Be sure to eat a substantial breakfast the morning of the exam. If you are taking the exam in the afternoon, be sure to have a good lunch as well. Being hungry is distracting and can make it difficult to focus. You have hopefully spent lots of time preparing for the exam. Don't let an empty stomach get in the way of success!

When travelling to the testing center, leave earlier than needed. That way, you have a buffer in case you experience any delays. This will help you remain calm and will keep you from missing your appointment time at the testing center.

Be sure to pace yourself during the exam. Don't try to rush through the exam. There is no need to risk performing poorly on the exam just so you can leave the testing center early. Allow yourself to use all of the allotted time if needed.

Remain positive while taking the exam even if you feel like you are performing poorly. Thinking about the content you should have mastered will not help you perform better on the exam.

Once the exam is complete, take some time to relax. Even if you feel that you need to take the exam again, you will be well served by some down time before you begin studying again. It's often easier to convince yourself to study if you know that it will come with a reward!

Test-Taking Strategies

1. Predicting the Answer

When you feel confident in your preparation for a multiple-choice test, try predicting the answer before reading the answer choices. This is especially useful on questions that test objective factual knowledge. By predicting the answer before reading the available choices, you eliminate the possibility that you will be distracted or led astray by an incorrect answer choice. You will feel more confident in your selection if you read the question, predict the answer, and then find your prediction among the answer choices. After using this strategy, be sure to still read all of the answer choices carefully and completely. If you feel unprepared, you should not attempt to predict the answers. This would be a waste of time and an opportunity for your mind to wander in the wrong direction.

2. Reading the Whole Question

Too often, test takers scan a multiple-choice question, recognize a few familiar words, and immediately jump to the answer choices. Test authors are aware of this common impatience, and they will sometimes prey upon it. For instance, a test author might subtly turn the question into a negative, or he or she might redirect the focus of the question right at the end. The only way to avoid falling into these traps is to read the entirety of the question carefully before reading the answer choices.

3. Looking for Wrong Answers

Long and complicated multiple-choice questions can be intimidating. One way to simplify a difficult multiple-choice question is to eliminate all of the answer choices that are clearly wrong. In most sets of answers, there will be at least one selection that can be dismissed right away. If the test is administered on paper, the test taker could draw a line through it to indicate that it may be ignored; otherwise, the test taker will have to perform this operation mentally or on scratch paper. In either case, once the obviously incorrect answers have been eliminated, the remaining choices may be considered. Sometimes identifying the clearly wrong answers will give the test taker some information about the correct answer. For instance, if one of the remaining answer choices is a direct opposite of one of the eliminated answer choices, it may well be the correct answer. The opposite of obviously wrong is obviously right! Of course, this is not always the case. Some answers are obviously incorrect simply because they are irrelevant to the question being asked. Still, identifying and eliminating some incorrect answer choices is a good way to simplify a multiple-choice question.

4. Don't Overanalyze

Anxious test takers often overanalyze questions. When you are nervous, your brain will often run wild, causing you to make associations and discover clues that don't actually exist. If you feel that this may be a problem for you, do whatever you can to slow down during the test. Try taking a deep breath or counting to ten. As you read and consider the question, restrict yourself to the particular words used by the author. Avoid thought tangents about what the author *really* meant, or what he or she was *trying* to say. The only things that matter on a multiple-choice test are the words that are actually in the question. You must avoid reading too much into a multiple-choice question, or supposing that the writer meant something other than what he or she wrote.

3

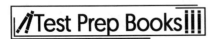

5. No Need for Panic

It is wise to learn as many strategies as possible before taking a multiple-choice test, but it is likely that you will come across a few questions for which you simply don't know the answer. In this situation, avoid panicking. Because most multiple-choice tests include dozens of questions, the relative value of a single wrong answer is small. As much as possible, you should compartmentalize each question on a multiple-choice test. In other words, you should not allow your feelings about one question to affect your success on the others. When you find a question that you either don't understand or don't know how to answer, just take a deep breath and do your best. Read the entire question slowly and carefully. Try rephrasing the question a couple of different ways. Then, read all of the answer choices carefully. After eliminating obviously wrong answers, make a selection and move on to the next question.

6. Confusing Answer Choices

When working on a difficult multiple-choice question, there may be a tendency to focus on the answer choices that are the easiest to understand. Many people, whether consciously or not, gravitate to the answer choices that require the least concentration, knowledge, and memory. This is a mistake. When you come across an answer choice that is confusing, you should give it extra attention. A question might be confusing because you do not know the subject matter to which it refers. If this is the case, don't eliminate the answer before you have affirmatively settled on another. When you come across an answer choice of this type, set it aside as you look at the remaining choices. If you can confidently assert that one of the other choices is correct, you can leave the confusing answer aside. Otherwise, you will need to take a moment to try to better understand the confusing answer choice. Rephrasing is one way to tease out the sense of a confusing answer choice.

7. Your First Instinct

Many people struggle with multiple-choice tests because they overthink the questions. If you have studied sufficiently for the test, you should be prepared to trust your first instinct once you have carefully and completely read the question and all of the answer choices. There is a great deal of research suggesting that the mind can come to the correct conclusion very quickly once it has obtained all of the relevant information. At times, it may seem to you as if your intuition is working faster even than your reasoning mind. This may in fact be true. The knowledge you obtain while studying may be retrieved from your subconscious before you have a chance to work out the associations that support it. Verify your instinct by working out the reasons that it should be trusted.

8. Key Words

Many test takers struggle with multiple-choice questions because they have poor reading comprehension skills. Quickly reading and understanding a multiple-choice question requires a mixture of skill and experience. To help with this, try jotting down a few key words and phrases on a piece of scrap paper. Doing this concentrates the process of reading and forces the mind to weigh the relative importance of the question's parts. In selecting words and phrases to write down, the test taker thinks about the question more deeply and carefully. This is especially true for multiple-choice questions that are preceded by a long prompt.

4

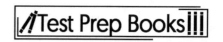

9. Subtle Negatives

One of the oldest tricks in the multiple-choice test writer's book is to subtly reverse the meaning of a question with a word like *not* or *except*. If you are not paying attention to each word in the question, you can easily be led astray by this trick. For instance, a common question format is, "Which of the following is...?" Obviously, if the question instead is, "Which of the following is not...?," then the answer will be quite different. Even worse, the test makers are aware of the potential for this mistake and will include one answer choice that would be correct if the question were not negated or reversed. A test taker who misses the reversal will find what he or she believes to be a correct answer and will be so confident that he or she will fail to reread the question and discover the original error. The only way to avoid this is to practice a wide variety of multiple-choice questions and to pay close attention to each and every word.

10. Reading Every Answer Choice

It may seem obvious, but you should always read every one of the answer choices! Too many test takers fall into the habit of scanning the question and assuming that they understand the question because they recognize a few key words. From there, they pick the first answer choice that answers the question they believe they have read. Test takers who read all of the answer choices might discover that one of the latter answer choices is actually *more* correct. Moreover, reading all of the answer choices can remind you of facts related to the question that can help you arrive at the correct answer. Sometimes, a misstatement or incorrect detail in one of the latter answer choices will trigger your memory of the subject and will enable you to find the right answer. Failing to read all of the answer choices is like not reading all of the items on a restaurant menu: you might miss out on the perfect choice.

11. Spot the Hedges

One of the keys to success on multiple-choice tests is paying close attention to every word. This is never truer than with words like almost, most, some, and sometimes. These words are called "hedges" because they indicate that a statement is not totally true or not true in every place and time. An absolute statement will contain no hedges, but in many subjects, the answers are not always straightforward or absolute. There are always exceptions to the rules in these subjects. For this reason, you should favor those multiple-choice questions that contain hedging language. The presence of qualifying words indicates that the author is taking special care with their words, which is certainly important when composing the right answer. After all, there are many ways to be wrong, but there is only one way to be right! For this reason, it is wise to avoid answers that are absolute when taking a multiple-choice test. An absolute answer is one that says things are either all one way or all another. They often include words like *every*, *always*, *best*, and *never*. If you are taking a multiple-choice test in a subject that doesn't lend itself to absolute answers, be on your guard if you see any of these words.

12. Long Answers

In many subject areas, the answers are not simple. As already mentioned, the right answer often requires hedges. Another common feature of the answers to a complex or subjective question are qualifying clauses, which are groups of words that subtly modify the meaning of the sentence. If the question or answer choice describes a rule to which there are exceptions or the subject matter is complicated, ambiguous, or confusing, the correct answer will require many words in order to be expressed clearly and accurately. In essence, you should not be deterred by answer choices that seem

5

excessively long. Oftentimes, the author of the text will not be able to write the correct answer without offering some qualifications and modifications. Your job is to read the answer choices thoroughly and completely and to select the one that most accurately and precisely answers the question.

13. Restating to Understand

Sometimes, a question on a multiple-choice test is difficult not because of what it asks but because of how it is written. If this is the case, restate the question or answer choice in different words. This process serves a couple of important purposes. First, it forces you to concentrate on the core of the question. In order to rephrase the question accurately, you have to understand it well. Rephrasing the question will concentrate your mind on the key words and ideas. Second, it will present the information to your mind in a fresh way. This process may trigger your memory and render some useful scrap of information picked up while studying.

14. True Statements

Sometimes an answer choice will be true in itself, but it does not answer the question. This is one of the main reasons why it is essential to read the question carefully and completely before proceeding to the answer choices. Too often, test takers skip ahead to the answer choices and look for true statements. Having found one of these, they are content to select it without reference to the question above. Obviously, this provides an easy way for test makers to play tricks. The savvy test taker will always read the entire question before turning to the answer choices. Then, having settled on a correct answer choice, he or she will refer to the original question and ensure that the selected answer is relevant. The mistake of choosing a correct-but-irrelevant answer choice is especially common on questions related to specific pieces of objective knowledge. A prepared test taker will have a wealth of factual knowledge at their disposal, and should not be careless in its application.

15. No Patterns

One of the more dangerous ideas that circulates about multiple-choice tests is that the correct answers tend to fall into patterns. These erroneous ideas range from a belief that B and C are the most common right answers, to the idea that an unprepared test-taker should answer "A-B-A-C-A-D-A-B-A." It cannot be emphasized enough that pattern-seeking of this type is exactly the WRONG way to approach a multiple-choice test. To begin with, it is highly unlikely that the test maker will plot the correct answers according to some predetermined pattern. The questions are scrambled and delivered in a random order. Furthermore, even if the test maker was following a pattern in the assignation of correct answers, there is no reason why the test taker would know which pattern he or she was using. Any attempt to discern a pattern in the answer choices is a waste of time and a distraction from the real work of taking the test. A test taker would be much better served by extra preparation before the test than by reliance on a pattern in the answers.

6

Bonus Content

We host multiple bonus items online, including all 3 practice tests in digital format. Scan the QR code or go to this link to access this content:

testprepbooks.com/bonus/pccn

The first time you access the tests, you will need to register as a "new user" and verify your email address.

If you have any issues, please email support@testprepbooks.com.

Introduction to the PCCN Exam

Function of the Exam

The Progressive Care Certified Nurse (PCCN®) exam is required to obtain the PCCN® specialty certification, which is one of several specialty certifications offered to nurses by the AACN Certification Corporation. The PCCN® certification is designed for progressive care nurses who provide nursing care for adult patients who are acutely ill. Although most of the patients that progressive care nurses will provide care for are moderately stable, the patients are at an elevated risk of becoming unstable. Accordingly, progressive care nurses, who typically work in progressive care units, need to deliver high-intensity, specialized care to their patients with a high degree of vigilance. Care may be focused on a specific system, such as renal, cardiac, or pulmonary, or it may be more generalized, geared toward multisystem, systemic issues.

Progressive care nurses who are seeking PCCN® certification typically work in progressive care settings and may be involved in immediate and emergency care, step-down care, direct observation, telemetry, and transitional care units.

The PCCN® exam is designed based on a job analysis, which examines the practice and skills of registered nurses (RNs) or advanced practice registered nurses (APRNs) who provide direct care to adult patients who are acutely ill. This process occurs at least every five years and helps determine and validate the abilities, skills, and knowledge needed to work with this patient population. An expert PCCN® panel then works to ensure the exam is designed to reflect the findings of the job analysis and clinical practice.

Exam candidates must have a current, unencumbered RN or APRN license. Additionally, one of the following two clinical practice requirements must be met prior to sitting for the exam:

- At least 1,750 hours providing direct care to acutely ill adult patients over the previous two years as an RN or APRN, with at least 875 of those hours obtained in the most recent year

- At least 2,000 hours providing direct care to acutely ill adult patients over the previous five years as an RN or APRN, with at least 144 of those hours obtained in the most recent year

It should be noted that orientation hours do not count towards minimum hour requirements unless the candidate was the assigned nurse who was providing direct care to adult patients with acute illnesses during those hours.

Test Administration

Candidates can register online or via a paper application for the exam. After receiving an approval-to-test email, they can schedule their exam administration. The exam is offered twice daily, Monday through Friday, and some Saturdays, at more than 300 PSI/AMP testing locations around the United States. The exam is offered in computer and paper-and-pencil format. Scores are provided immediately after submitting the computer-based version, and are received three to four weeks after sitting for the paper version. The exam may be retaken, but a fee will be incurred.

8

Test Format

The PCCN® exam contains 125 multiple-choice questions, of which, 100 are scored. The remaining 25, which are randomly scattered throughout the exam, are used to gauge their worth for inclusion in future versions. Test takers are given 150 minutes to complete the exam. Clinical Judgment comprises 80% of the questions, while Professional Caring and Ethical Practice topics contribute 20% of the questions. The following table provides the domains of the exam and the breakdown of their percentage contributions to the total:

Domain	Percentage of Exam
Clinical Judgement	80%
Cardiovascular	20%
Respiratory	14%
Endocrine/Hematology/Immunology/Oncology/Neurology/ Gastrointestinal/Renal	27%
Musculoskeletal/Multisystem/Psychosocial	20%
Professional Caring and Ethical Practice	20%

Scoring

A panel of subject matter and exam experts establish the passing score of the PCCN®. The passing score is established via the modified Angoff, a criterion-referenced process for setting standards. Each test taker's PCCN® performance is compared to the predetermined standard to determine their passing status. The difficulty rating of each question also impacts the value of answering a question correctly. The passing score is said to be established to identify those candidates who possess an acceptable level of knowledge and skill in providing care to acutely ill adult patients. Candidates who successfully pass the exam receive a certificate denoting their specialty certification within three to four weeks after passing the test.

Study Prep Plan for the PCCN Exam

1 **Schedule** - Use one of our study schedules below or come up with one of your own.

2 **Relax** - Test anxiety can hurt even the best students. There are many ways to reduce stress. Find the one that works best for you.

3 **Execute** - Once you have a good plan in place, be sure to stick to it.

One Week Study Schedule		
Day 1	Clinical Judgment
Day 2	Pulmonary
Day 3	Endocrine/Hematology/Neurology/Gastrointestinal/Renal
Day 4	Musculoskeletal/Multisystem/Psychosocial
Day 5	Practice Test #1
Day 6	Practice Tests #2 & #3
Day 7	Take Your Exam!

Two Week Study Schedule			
Day 1	Clinical Judgment	Day 8	Musculoskeletal/Multisystem/Psychosocial
Day 2	Dysrhythmias	Day 9	Behavioral/Psychosocial
Day 3	Hypertensive Crisis	Day 10	Professional Caring and Ethical Practice
Day 4	Pulmonary	Day 11	Practice Test #1
Day 5	Respiratory Depression	Day 12	Practice Test #2
Day 6	Endocrine/Hematology/Neurology/Gastrointestinal/Renal	Day 13	Practice Test #3
Day 7	Gastrointestinal	Day 14	Take Your Exam!

10

One Month Study Schedule						
Day 1	Clinical Judgment	Day 11	Respiratory Depression	Day 21	Response to Diversity
Day 2	Acute Inflammatory Disease	Day 12	Thoracic Surgery	Day 22	Facilitation of Learning
Day 3	Cardiac Surgery	Day 13	Endocrine/Hematology/ Neurology/ Gastrointestinal/Renal	Day 23	Collaboration
Day 4	Dysrhythmias	Day 14	Hematology/ Immunology/Oncology	Day 24	Practice Test #1
Day 5	Genetic Cardiac Disease	Day 15	Neurology	Day 25	Answer Explanations #1
Day 6	Hypertensive Crisis	Day 16	Gastrointestinal	Day 26	Practice Test #2
Day 7	Septal Defects	Day 17	Renal	Day 27	Answer Explanations #2
Day 8	Pulmonary	Day 18	Musculoskeletal/ Multisystem/ Psychosocial	Day 28	Practice Test #3
Day 9	COPD Exacerbation	Day 19	Behavioral/Psychosocial	Day 29	Answer Explanations #3
Day 10	Pulmonary Embolism	Day 20	Professional Caring and Ethical Practice	Day 30	Take Your Exam!

Build your own prep plan by visiting:
testprepbooks.com/prep

11

As you study for your test, we'd like to take the opportunity to remind you that you are capable of great things! With the right tools and dedication, you truly can do anything you set your mind to. The fact that you are holding this book right now shows how committed you are. In case no one has told you lately, you've got this! Our intention behind including this coloring page is to give you the chance to take some time to engage your creative side when you need a little brain-break from studying. As a company, we want to encourage people like you to achieve their dreams by providing good quality study materials for the tests and certifications that improve careers and change lives. As individuals, many of us have taken such tests in our careers, and we know how challenging this process can be. While we can't come alongside you and cheer you on personally, we can offer you the space to recall your purpose, reconnect with your passion, and refresh your brain through an artistic practice. We wish you every success, and happy studying!

Clinical Judgment

Cardiovascular

Cardiovascular issues can be life threatening. Any condition that impedes circulation has the potential to damage the **myocardium**, or heart muscle. A damaged myocardium may be unable to meet the oxygen demands of the body. It is important to quickly identify any patient exhibiting symptoms indicative of such emergencies so that they can receive prompt treatment to prevent further cardiovascular injury or death. Every patient presenting with possible cardiovascular symptoms should immediately be given a focused assessment followed by a history and physical. Simultaneously, an intravenous (IV) line should be established, an electrocardiogram (ECG) performed, and laboratory and radiographic studies obtained. The triage, assessment, diagnostics, and treatment of such patients must be prioritized to preserve cardiac function and, ultimately, life.

Upon completion of a focused health history, the nurse should examine the patient for signs and symptoms of cardiovascular compromise, including chest pain, palpitations, paresthesia, cold extremities, and edema. In general, the nurse should note overall appearance (e.g., demeanor, posture, and gait); examine skin tone (e.g., pink, pallor, red, or cyanotic); look for skin abnormalities (e.g., rashes and lesions); and assess nail beds (e.g., color and capillary refill). A through assessment of the patient's pain should be completed, including exacerbating and relieving factors. If edema is noted, the nurse should use the assessment scale for pitting edema to note specifics, which ranges from 1+ for slight pitting to 4+ for very deep pits lasting 2–5 minutes.

The nurse should palpate carotid pulses and assess range of motion in the neck. Using a pulse scale rated from 0-4+, with 0 meaning absent and 4+ meaning strong and bounding, the nurse should assess the following pulse points: temporal, apical, brachial, radial, ulnar, femoral, popliteal, posterior tibial, and dorsal pedis. The nurse should auscultate the **aortic area**, which is found at the second right intercostal space and right sternal border; the **pulmonic area**, which is found second to the left intercostal space and left sternal border; the **tricuspid area**, which is located at the fourth left intercostal space and the left sternal border; and finally, the **mitral area**, which spans the fifth left intercostal space and the midclavicular line.

The **electrocardiogram** (ECG) captures a graphic record of the depolarization and repolarization of the atria and ventricles to understand the direction and magnitude of the electrical activity and determine a diagnosis. Before ECG lead placement, there are some basic considerations for the nurse to understand. First, the nurse should count the intercostal spaces starting right below the clavicle and working down to the nipple, or just below the breast for patients with large breasts. Second, the nurse should ensure a clean working space; this means the skin should be prepped to be dry, hair-free, and oil free to ensure a strong read. Third, the nurse should have a baseline understanding of the patient's status, including vital signs and oxygenation, before obtaining an ECG reading. Once the patient is ready, the nurse should assist them to a supine or semi-Fowler's position with arms relaxed by their side if tolerated.

If possible, the nurse should ensure that the patient's shoulders are relaxed and legs are uncrossed, while quietly resting in a still position. Additionally, the nurse should ensure that mobile devices are removed, as they can interfere with the reading by producing artifact. Placement of the electrodes is key to receiving an accurate read, so the nurse should take great care in applying fresh pads with moist gels over the appropriate sites, ensuring bones and areas of greatest muscle movement are avoided.

Most patients with simple cardiac concerns are placed on **telemetry monitoring**, which involves five leads (1 precordial lead, along with 4 extremity leads: RL, RA, LL, LA). This intervention provides continuous information regarding the patient's cardiac rhythm by offering views of much of the electrical activity. However, the 5-lead system is inferior to the 12-lead system and the rarely used 15-lead system that both offer details regarding ST information. When the information gathered from five leads is deemed insufficient because a critical event is suspected, the care team should opt to increase the views by applying additional electrodes. If cardiac ischemia is suspected, a 12-lead ECG should be performed.

The results will help to reveal if the patient has experienced a **STEMI** (ST-elevation myocardial infarction), which is one of the most serious types of **myocardial infarction** (MI). When working with a 12-lead cardiac monitoring system, the nurse should review changes to determine the affected area of the heart. If changes are noted in leads I, aVL, V5, and V6, the patient is suffering from lateral wall ischemia, injury, or infarction. If changes are noted in leads II, III, and aVF, the patient is suffering from inferior wall ischemia, injury, or infarction. If changes are noted in leads V1 and V2, the patient is suffering from septal wall ischemia, injury, or infarction. Finally, if changes are noted in leads V3 and V4, the patient is suffering from anterior wall ischemia, injury, or infarction.

Electrocardiograph (ECG) electrode placement sites:

- V1: Fourth intercostal space, right of sternum
- V2: Fourth intercostal space, left of sternum
- V3: Between V2 and V4, midway
- V4: Fifth intercostal space, midclavicular line
- V5: Fifth intercostal space, anterior axillary line
- V6: Fifth intercostal space, midaxillary line
- RL (green): Right leg, between right ankle and torso
- RA (white): Right arm, between right shoulder and wrist
- LL (red): Left leg, between left ankle and torso
- LA (black): Left arm, between left shoulder and wrist
- aVR: Right shoulder
- aVL: Left shoulder
- aVF: Umbilicus

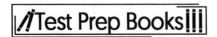

If electing to use a 15-lead placement system, the V4, V5, and V6 electrodes are instead placed posteriorly on the patient's left scapula and referred to as V7, V8, and V9. For quick recall when placing a 5-lead system, the nurse can remember the mnemonic "smoke over fire," which represents black above red, and "snow over grass," which represents white above green. The nurse ensures to note any clinical manifestations present during the ECG reading to provide a thorough clinical picture of activity.

In addition to cardiac monitoring, the nurse should review the homeostatic state of the patient to include primary diagnosis, comorbidities, and lifestyle. Hemodynamic parameters to monitor include blood pressure, heart rate, respiratory rate, cardiac output, mean arterial perfusion, systemic vascular resistance, systolic time intervals, and lung congestion. When electing to use noninvasive monitoring systems, the nurse should detect cardiovascular homeostasis via external applications of automated or manual detection devices including the following: manual blood pressure cuff, stethoscope, automated blood pressure cuff with pulse detection, and pulse oximetry. The nurse should also assess capillary refill for color and timing, skin temperature through a thermometer and via physical assessment, and quality of pulse.

Invasive hemodynamic monitoring may be necessary if the care team deems that a highly accurate and reliable reading is necessary for the severity of the patient's vulnerable condition. Invasive monitoring typically takes place in critical care environments and includes devices such as pulmonary artery catheter and arterial line. The need to monitor via invasive devices typically centers on obtaining precisely accurate measurements of blood pressure and cardiac function when early intervention is crucial to avoid devastating outcomes. Some examples of conditions that may warrant invasive monitoring include myocardial injury, ischemic stroke, renal injury, and myocardial infarction, along with the postoperative period following cardiac surgeries such as coronary bypass.

An **arterial line** is a catheter placed in a patient's artery to continuously monitor the patient's internal blood pressure. Arterial lines may be placed in the radial or femoral artery and are generally indicated when the patient is at high risk of becoming hemodynamically unstable. In addition to monitoring the patient's blood pressure, nursing management of an arterial line involves maintenance of the line, monitoring for signs of infection or infiltration, and, in some cases, drawing blood from the arterial line. The arterial line setup requires a 500 mL bag of saline, placed in a pressure bag maintained at 300 mmHg. All air bubbles should be removed from the line when priming and prior to hooking the line up to the patient. Initial setup and maintenance require zeroing of the arterial line. This means the nurse must place the transducer at the **phlebostatic axis** of the patient, turn off the stopcock to the patient, and press the "zero" button on the monitor. This allows the arterial line system to check the patient's blood pressure in comparison to the outside atmospheric pressure for accurate readings. If the nurse notices any signs of infection or infiltration, the provider should be notified immediately to determine the possibility of discontinuing the arterial line, initiating a new arterial line at a different site, and/or treating the potential infection or infiltration.

Once homeostasis has been maintained and the patient is stable, the care team may opt to return to less invasive monitoring, such as mechanical or manual blood pressure readings and pulse oximetry. The frequency and continuity of these external monitors usually depend on the stability and potential risk of decompensation of the patient. Most patients in the progressive care unit will be on continuous telemetry monitoring to monitor for potential arrythmias. However, continuous pulse oximetry may be limited to patients with specific cardiac or respiratory conditions. Additionally, the frequency of blood pressure recording may depend on the patient's determined stability. Nursing management of these systems involves initiation of monitoring, troubleshooting potential issues with the monitoring, interpretation of vital signs, advocating for the appropriate level of monitoring based on nursing assessment, and reporting to the provider any abnormal vital signs that may require intervention.

The nurse implements care plans with evolving interventions that follow unique changes to hemodynamic status.

Acute Coronary Syndromes

Acute coronary syndrome (ACS) is the term used to describe the clinical symptoms caused by the sudden reduction in blood flow to the heart, but it is also known as **acute myocardial ischemia**. This syndrome presents as one of the following: unstable angina (UA), non-ST-elevation myocardial infarction (NSTEMI), or ST-elevation myocardial infarction (STEMI), which is shown in the figure below.

All three categories can occur with increased oxygen demand in the heart tissue, such as that caused by exercise and emotional distress.

In any of the three cases, major determining factors for tissue damage include how severe the blockage of the arteries is, how long the arteries are blocked, how much of the heart is affected, how high the demand for oxygen is in the heart, and how well the heart can compensate for the oxygen loss.

Common symptoms of a patient presenting with ACS include:

- Chest pain or discomfort in the upper body that radiates to the arms, back, neck, jaw, or stomach, as shown in the image below:

Typical Pain Radiation Patterns of Acute Coronary Syndrome

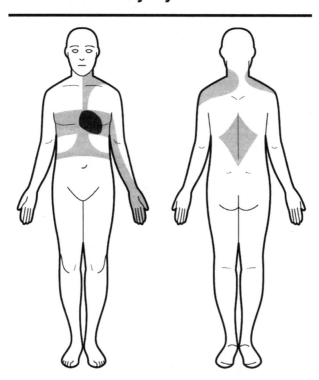

- Dizziness, syncope, or changes in the level of consciousness (LOC), which are common presentations in the geriatric population

- Nausea or vomiting

- Palpitations or tachycardia

- Shortness of breath (SOB) or dyspnea

- Unusual fatigue

A patient may be experiencing a different condition than acute coronary syndrome, such as uncontrolled anxiety or acid reflux, that may mimic the same signs and symptoms. The clinician must be aware of this when making a clinical judgment. An accurate assessment will be made based on patient history, clinical presentation, and events leading up to the current symptoms.

The most common symptom that signals acute coronary syndrome is chest pain. The chest pain of a heart attack has been described as "crushing pressure," "heavy weight," "tightness," and/or "fullness" in the chest area above the heart. Other accompanying symptoms include a shooting pain radiating down one or both arms, along the jawline, or even in the back or abdomen. The patient may present with complaint of "not being able to catch their breath," breathing rapidly, or shallow breathing. Dizziness, lightheadedness, nausea, and profuse sweating may be part of the patient's presentation.

It is important to note that gender plays a role in how patients may present with a heart attack. Considering that heart disease is the leading cause of death for women in the United States, the nurse should be aware that women may not exhibit the classic signs of a heart attack. A woman is more likely to have non-chest-related symptoms, such as nausea, anxiety, and radiating pain in the upper or lower back and jaw region. These symptoms may occur weeks before the actual attack, making correct diagnosis even more difficult to pinpoint. Knowing that there may be a different presentation will help the nurse make the correct clinical judgment regarding the situation, considering all involved factors.

Non-ST-Segment Elevation Myocardial Infarction

A **Non-ST-Segment Elevation Myocardial Infarction** (NSTEMI) does not produce changes in the ST segment of the ECG cycle. However, troponin levels are positive. Patients with a confirmed NSTEMI are hospitalized. Treatment includes aspirin and nitroglycerin (if not compromised hemodynamically). Morphine can be administered as needed for severe pain. Oxygen is not routinely recommended for the ACS patient unless the patient's oxygen saturation is ≤94 or the patient is in respiratory distress. Additional pharmacological agents for treatment are beta-blockers, ACE inhibitors, statins, and antiplatelet medications. Coronary angiography and revascularization may be necessary.

The primary difference between UA and an NSTEMI is whether the ischemia is severe enough to damage the myocardium to the extent that cardiac markers indicative of injury are released and detectable through laboratory analysis. A patient is diagnosed with an NSTEMI when the ischemia is severe enough to cause myocardial damage and the release of a myocardial necrosis biomarker into the circulation (usually cardiac-specific troponins T or I). In contrast, a patient is diagnosed with UA if such a biomarker is undetectable in their bloodstream hours after the ischemic chest pain's initial onset.

ST Segment Elevation Myocardial Infarction

An **ST-Segment Elevation Myocardial Infarction** (STEMI) is the most serious form of MI. It occurs when a coronary artery is completely blocked and unable to receive blood flow. Emergent revascularization is needed either through angioplasty or a thrombolytic medication.

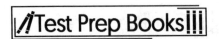

UA and NSTEMIs generally indicate a partial-thickness injury to the myocardium, but a STEMI indicates injury across the full thickness of the myocardium, as shown in the image below. The etiology behind ischemia is partial or full occlusion of coronary arteries.

Differentiation Between Non-ST and ST MIs

Transverse section of the heart

Partial thickness damage

Full thickness damage

Angina

Angina is the term used to describe chest pain caused by decreased blood flow to the myocardium. The two primary categories of angina are stable or unstable, with stable angina being more common. It presents in a predictable pattern for patients, responds quickly to cessation of exertion or medication, and while it increases the likelihood of a future heart attack, it is not necessarily indicative of such an event occurring imminently. Unstable angina is often more frequent and severe. It may occur without physical exertion and be unresponsive to medication or activity cessation. It should be treated as an emergency and can signal an imminent heart attack.

Treatment for angina depends on the severity of the symptoms and can range from lifestyle modifications to surgical intervention. Pharmacological treatments for angina include beta-blockers, calcium channel blockers (CCBs), long- and short-acting nitrates, angiotensin-converting enzyme (ACE) inhibitors, statins, and antiplatelet medications. These medications treat the symptoms related to angina by lowering blood pressure (BP), slowing heart rate (HR), relaxing blood vessels, reducing strain on the heart, lowering cholesterol levels, and preventing blood clot formation. The most common risk factors for the development of angina include:

- Diabetes
- Dietary deficiency (fruits and vegetables)
- Excessive alcohol consumption
- Family history of early coronary heart disease

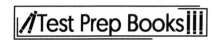

- Hypertension (HTN)
- High LDL (low-density lipoprotein)
- Low HDL (high-density lipoprotein)
- Male gender
- Obesity
- Old age
- Sedentary lifestyle

Stable Angina

Atherosclerotic buildup generally occurs slowly over time. Because the buildup is gradual, the heart can usually continue to meet the body's oxygen demands despite the narrowing lumen of the vessel. However, in situations with increased oxygen demand, such as exercise or stress, the myocardium may not be able to meet the increased demands, thereby causing angina. **Stable angina** is predictable (e.g., occurs in association with stress or certain activities), subsides with rest, and does not increase in intensity or worsen over time. Nitroglycerine is effective in the treatment of stable angina because it dilates the blood vessels, reduces resistance to blood flow, and decreases the demand on the myocardium. Lifestyle modifications, such as smoking cessation and routine exercise, are needed to slow atherosclerotic buildup.

Unstable Angina

Unstable angina (UA) is a more severe form of heart disease than stable angina. The angina associated with UA is generally related to small pieces of atherosclerotic plaque that break off and cause occlusions. The occlusions suddenly decrease blood flow to the myocardium, resulting in angina, without causing an actual MI. The pain associated with UA occurs suddenly without a direct cause, worsens over a short period of time, and may last 15 to 20 minutes. Dyspnea (shortness of breath) and decreased blood pressure are also common. Because this type of angina is related to an acute decrease in blood flow, rest does not alleviate symptoms. Generally, UA does not respond to the vasodilatory effect of nitroglycerine. Laboratory values are typically negative for cardiac enzymes related to cardiac damage, but they can be slightly elevated. Therefore, a comprehensive history and physical exam that properly identify pertinent risk factors are critical for early diagnosis and treatment.

Depending on the severity of symptom presentation, pharmacological treatment for UA will include one or more antiplatelet medications and a cholesterol medication. In addition, medications to treat hypertension, arrhythmias, and anxiety may be necessary. The recommended intervention is angioplasty with coronary artery stenting. A **coronary artery bypass grafting** (CABG) surgery may be necessary in the case of extensive occlusion of one or more of the coronary arteries.

A coronary artery bypass graft (CABG) is a cardiac surgery in which a coronary artery blockage is bypassed by grafting a blood vessel onto the artery in order to redirect the blood around the blockage. The traditional surgical procedure requires a large incision to the chest. However, with the minimally invasive method, a small incision is made between the ribs, and the CABG is performed using laparoscopy. This procedure is indicated for patients experiencing an acute myocardial infarction that cannot be improved with a simple cardiac catheterization.

Patients presenting with an acute myocardial infarction indicating possible need for a CABG may present with chest pain, jaw pain, shortness of breath, diaphoresis, nausea and vomiting, and altered mental status or loss of consciousness. Electrocardiograms for patients requiring a CABG will often show ECG

23

abnormalities (like an ST elevation), and their troponin will often be elevated. These findings may continue for the first few days following the CABG while the heart is healing following the procedure. The definitive diagnostic to determine if blockage is significant enough to require a CABG is cardiac angiography.

Following a CABG, patients will generally be placed on antiplatelet therapy with low-dose aspirin and clopidogrel to reduce the risk of further thrombus formation. These patients are often also placed on a beta-blocker for rate management, blood pressure medications (such as ACE inhibitors), and lipid-lowering medications to reduce the risk of further myocardial infarction.

Nursing management prior to any CABG (minimal or otherwise) requires early identification of myocardial infarction. While most of these patients may come through the emergency room, the progressive care nurse should know that inpatients are at increased risk of clot formation and be able to quickly identify signs of myocardial infarction so that early intervention can take place. This requires cardiac monitoring, review of laboratory results (such as troponin), and intervening quickly if the patient shows signs and symptoms of myocardial infarction. Following the CABG, nursing management involves continued cardiac monitoring in case of arrythmia or new myocardial infarction. The nurse should also provide education to the patient on their new medication regimen and the need to follow up regularly with cardiology. Finally, patients with a recent myocardial infarction are at increased risk of future myocardial infarction, so the nurse should provide patient education on when to be seen again for a potential medical emergency.

Treatment and Risk Scoring

Treatment for UA and NSTEMI is planned according to a risk score using the **Thrombolysis in Myocardial Infarction** (TIMI) tool. In the presence of UA or an NSTEMI, seven categories are scored: age, risk factors, a prior coronary artery stenosis, ST deviation on ECG, prior aspirin intake, presence and number of angina episodes, and elevated creatinine kinase (CK-MB) or troponins. In the presence of a STEMI, the TIMI tool scores eleven categories: age, angina history, hypertension, diabetes, systolic BP, heart rate, Killip class, weight, anterior MI in an ECG, left bundle branch block (LBBB) in an ECG, and a treatment delay after an attack. The **Global Registry of Acute Coronary Events** (GRACE), or ACS risk calculator, is a common tool used to predict the probability of death upon admission and six months post-discharge following a diagnosis of Acute Coronary Syndrome (ACS).

ACS can be life threatening; therefore, treatment and survival are time-dependent. Quick recognition by the nurse followed by a thorough focused assessment that includes evaluation of pain type, location, characteristic, and onset is essential. The American Heart Association algorithm for Acute Coronary Syndrome should be followed immediately. The nurse should obtain a family, social, and lifestyle assessment to identify high-risk patients. An evaluation of recent medical history is imperative since most ACS patients experience prodromal symptoms a month or more prior to the acute event. Establishing IV access is paramount for rapid administration of medications. Obtaining and reviewing an ECG and labs, including troponins, CK-MB, complete blood count (CBC), C-reactive protein (CRP), electrolytes, and renal function, will provide critical diagnostic data. A chest x-ray and echocardiogram will also add to the differential diagnosis. Immediate and long-term complications of ACS are cardiac dysrhythmia, heart failure (HF), and cardiogenic shock. Education should be provided to each patient about the diagnosis, risk factors, lifestyle modifications, and medications once the acute event has stabilized.

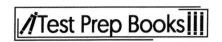

Acute Inflammatory Disease

Myocarditis

Myocarditis is inflammation of the myocardium, or the central muscle tissue that forms the heart. This inflammation can be caused by reactions of the immune system, such as infections (usually viral, but may also be bacterial or fungal) or autoimmune conditions, such as lupus. Myocarditis can also be caused by medications, including chemotherapy as well as some antidepressants and antipsychotics. Finally, myocarditis can be caused by drug use (e.g., cocaine) and exposure to toxins, such as spider or snake bites. Regardless of the cause, myocarditis can lead to both acute and chronic cardiac conditions, making its identification and prompt treatment vital to improving patient outcomes.

A patient with myocarditis may present with the following symptoms:

- Chest pain
- Shortness of breath
- Increased fatigue
- Syncope
- Tachycardia or other arrhythmias
- Signs of poor peripheral perfusion (e.g., cool extremities or peripheral edema)
- Signs of infection (e.g., fever)

As with most patients presenting with these signs and symptoms, initial diagnosis will likely start with laboratory testing, an electrocardiogram (ECG), and imaging. Laboratory tests will likely include the following:

- Complete blood count (CBC) to check for signs of infection or anemia
- Metabolic panel (CMP) to check for electrolyte abnormalities
- Cardiac enzymes (e.g., troponin) to look for stress on the cardiac muscle
- B-type natriuretic peptide (BNP) to check for signs of heart failure
- Potentially other samples to find a source of suspected infection (e.g., viral panels, streptococcus testing, or blood cultures).

ECG results will generally show tachycardia and/or T wave changes but may also reveal prolonged QT or other abnormalities, depending on the location of the inflammation and the progression of the disease process. Initial imaging will likely be x-ray, which may show an enlarged heart in the patient with myocarditis. Additional imaging may include a cardiac computed tomography (CT) scan to rule out blocked arteries, magnetic resonance imaging (MRI) to show a more detailed image of the cardiac inflammation, and an echocardiogram to evaluate the heart's ability to pump efficiently and to find any possible abnormalities in valves or heart chambers. These diagnostics will allow the treatment team to identify the presence of myocarditis, find a potential cause, and help determine necessary treatment.

Treatment of myocarditis depends on its cause, severity, and any other resulting sequelae of the condition. If myocarditis is found to be caused by an infection, initial treatment will likely involve administration of antivirals, antibacterials, or antifungals. If the cause is determined to be medication, the treatment team may have to determine the risks and benefits of holding, changing, or decreasing the medication. For example, it may not be possible to stop a specific chemotherapy drug; however, other medications such as steroids may be added to decrease inflammation. If the cause is recreational drug use, the patient will likely be given resources and education on drug cessation. If the cause is some

25

other toxin, treatment will vary based on the specific toxin and what resources are available to either counter the toxin (e.g., antivenom) or symptomatically treat the patient.

If the myocarditis progresses into other heart conditions, those will also need to be treated. For example, myocarditis can lead to heart failure and valve abnormalities. These may require blood pressure medications, rate control medications, diuretics, and potentially surgical intervention. Arrythmias may need to be treated depending on the rhythm and stability of the patient. If the arrythmias become chronic, the patient may also require placement of a pacemaker or implantable cardioverter-defibrillator device (ICD). In the most severe cases of myocarditis, the patient may even require **extracorporeal membrane oxygenation (ECMO)**.

Nursing management of patients with myocarditis involves continued assessment of the patient for signs of worsening cardiovascular symptoms. These may include the following: worsening chest pain or shortness of breath; changes in mental status; changes to peripheral vascular perfusion (e.g., edema or decreased perfusion); changes in cardiac monitoring (e.g., life-threatening arrhythmias); and changes in monitoring of laboratory values. Nursing management also requires providing patient education throughout the disease process. The nurse should educate patients on ways to prevent myocarditis, such as taking antibiotics when they have strep throat or cessation of recreational drugs. For those who have been diagnosed, the nature of the condition should be thoroughly explained, including potential complications and treatment expectations depending on the patient's individual needs. For example, if the patient's myocarditis progresses into heart failure, the patient should be educated on diuretic and cardiac medication usage as well as what signs and symptoms may imply an exacerbation of their condition that requires further treatment (e.g., worsening extremity swelling, shortness of breath, and/or chest pain).

Endocarditis

By definition, **endocarditis** is the inflammation of the endocardium, or innermost lining of the heart chambers and valves. It is also called **infective endocarditis**, or **bacterial endocarditis**.

To review, there are three layers of tissue that comprise the heart. A double-layer serous membrane, known as the **pericardium**, is the outermost layer. The pericardium forms the pericardial sac that surrounds the heart. The middle and largest layer is the **myocardium**. Since an MI occurs when the heart muscle is deprived of oxygen, the myocardial layer of the heart is where the damage due to lack of oxygen occurs. The innermost layer that lines the heart chambers and the heart valves is called the **endocardium**. Endocarditis occurs when the endocardial layer and heart valves become infected and inflamed.

The most common cause of endocarditis is a bloodstream invasion of bacteria. *Staphylococci* and *Streptococci* account for the majority of infective endocarditis occurrences. During medical or dental procedures—such as a colonoscopy, cystoscopy, or professional teeth cleaning—bacteria may enter the bloodstream and travel to the heart. Inflammatory bowel disease and sexually transmitted diseases also foster bacterial transmission to the bloodstream, ultimately leading to the heart.

Risk factors for the development of endocarditis include valve and septal defects of the heart, an artificial heart valve, a history of endocarditis, an indwelling long-term dialysis catheter, parenteral nutrition or central lines in the right atrium, IV drug use, and body piercings. Patients taking steroids or immunosuppressive medications are susceptible to fungal endocarditis. Regardless of the source, the bacteria infect the inside of the heart chambers and valves. Clumps of infective bacteria, or vegetation, develop within the heart at the site of infection. The heart valves are a common infection site, which often results in incomplete closure of the valves.

The classic symptoms of endocarditis are fever, cardiac murmur, and petechial lesions of the skin, conjunctiva, and oral mucosa. However, symptoms can range in severity. Flu-like symptoms, weight loss, and back pain may be present. Dyspnea and swelling of the feet and ankles may be evident. Endocarditis caused by **Staphylococcus** has a rapid onset, whereas **Streptococcus** occurs gradually with a prolonged course.

Layers of the Heart Wall

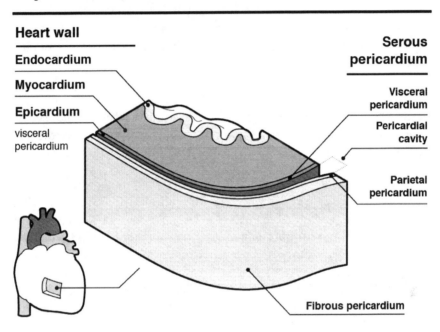

Antimicrobial treatment for four to six weeks is the standard of care. In some cases, two antimicrobials are used to treat the infection and prevent drug resistance. The objective of treatment is to eradicate the infection and treat complications. Surgery may be required for persistent recurring infections, one or more embolic occurrences, or if heart failure develops.

Left untreated, endocarditis can result in stroke or organ damage, as the vegetation breaks off, travels through the bloodstream, and blocks circulation. The spread of infection and subsequent formation of abscesses throughout the body may also occur. Heart failure may develop when the infection hampers the heart's ability to pump effectively or with perforation of a valve.

A complete history and physical that includes inquiry about medications, recent surgeries, screening, and diagnostic testing may provide the crucial piece of information that identifies endocarditis in the face of otherwise vague symptom presentation. The nurse should anticipate the order for blood cultures, an erythrocyte sedimentation rate (ESR), a CBC, an ECG, a chest x-ray, and a transthoracic or transesophageal echocardiogram (TEE) to identify the location of the infected area.

A **transesophageal echocardiogram (TEE)** is an echocardiogram (ultrasound of the heart) that is accessed through the esophagus. This diagnostic procedure requires procedural sedation and is indicated if a standard echocardiogram does not produce sufficient imaging. The patient will need to be NPO for at least 6 hours to prevent aspiration while under sedation. One of the most severe potential complications of this procedure is an upper gastrointestinal (GI) bleed from trauma to the esophagus. Because of this, nursing management may involve verifying if blood thinning medications should be held prior to and possibly after the procedure. Nurses should also monitor for signs of a GI bleed, such as hematemesis or melena, changes to vital signs, pallor, increased fatigue or shortness of breath, and altered mental status.

An in-depth patient interview and assessment by the nurse are essential. Diagnostic and laboratory results coupled with data from the patient interview will aid in early recognition and treatment of endocarditis. Because an incident of endocarditis places one at a higher risk for future infections, patient teaching should include informing all providers and dentists prior to treatment. Antibiotic prophylaxis may be indicated.

Pericarditis

Pericarditis is inflammation of the pericardium, which forms the pericardial sac that surrounds the heart. The pericardial sac consists of two layers. The **pericardium**, or outer layer of the heart wall, is a two-layer membrane that forms the pericardial sac, which envelops the heart.

The **visceral** (inner) layer of the pericardium is a double-layered membrane. One layer is affixed to the heart. The second layer lines the inside of the parietal layer (outer layer). The small space between the parietal and visceral layers is the pericardial space. The space normally contains between 15 and 50 milliliters of pericardial fluid. The pericardial fluid lubricates the membranes and allows the two layers to slide over one another as the heart beats.

The **parietal** (outer) layer of the pericardium is made of tough, thickened fibrous tissue. This layer is attached to the mid-diaphragm and to the back of the sternum.

These attachments keep the heart in place during acceleration or deceleration. The fibrous nature of the parietal layer prevents cardiac distention into the mediastinal region of the chest. It separates the heart from the surrounding structures, and it protects the heart against infection and inflammation from the lungs. The pericardium contains pain receptors and mechanoreceptors, both of which prompt reflex changes in the BP and HR.

Pericarditis can be either acute or chronic in presentation. Causes are varied and include an acute MI; bacterial, fungal, and viral infections; certain medications; chest trauma; connective tissue disorders such as lupus or rheumatic fever; metastatic lesions from lung or breast tumors; and a history of radiation therapy of the chest and upper torso. Frequent or prolonged episodes of pericarditis can lead to thickening and scarring of the pericardium and loss of elasticity. These conditions limit the heart's ability to fill with blood, and therefore limit the amount of blood being pumped out to the body. The result is a decrease in cardiac output (CO). Pericarditis can also cause fluid to accumulate in the pericardial cavity, known as pericardial effusion.

A characteristic symptom of pericarditis is chest pain. The pain is persistent, sharp, pleuritic, felt in the mid-chest, and aggravated by deep inhalation. Pericarditis may also cause ST elevation, thereby mimicking an acute MI, or it may be asymptomatic.

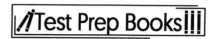

A pericardial friction rub is diagnostic of pericarditis and characterized by a creaky or scratchy sound heard at the end of exhalation. The rub is best heard when the patient is sitting and leaning forward. Stethoscope placement should be at the left lower sternal border in the fourth intercostal space. The rub is audible on auscultation and synchronous to the heartbeat. A pericardial friction rub is differentiated from a pleural friction rub by having patients hold their breath. The pericardial friction rub will remain constant with the heartbeat. Other presenting symptoms include a mild fever, cough, and dyspnea. Common laboratory findings are elevated white blood cell (WBC), ESR, or CRP levels.

The diagnosis of pericarditis is based on history, signs, and symptoms. Treatment goals are to determine the cause, administer therapy for treatment and symptom relief, and detect signs of complications. A thorough medical and surgical history will identify patients at risk for developing pericarditis. The physical assessment should evaluate the reported pain level during position changes, inspiration, expiration, coughing, swallowing, and breath holding. In addition, flexion, extension, and rotation of the neck and spine should be assessed for their influence on reported pain.

Aneurysm

An **aneurysm** is an abnormal bulge or ballooning that can form on an artery wall, as seen in the image below. Depending on the location, the rupture of an aneurysm can result in hemorrhage, stroke, or death. The most common places for the formation of an aneurysm are the left ventricle (LV) of the heart, the aorta, the brain, and the spleen.

Blood Vessel with an Aneurysm and Rupture

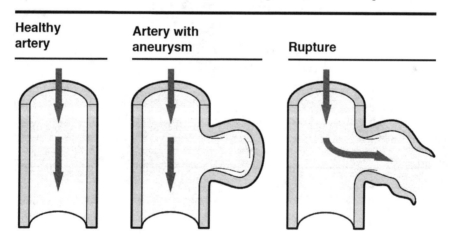

Generally, arteries carry oxygenated blood away from the heart to the organs and tissues of the body. The largest artery is the aorta, which receives blood directly from the LV of the heart. Oxygen-carrying

29

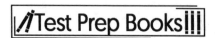
blood continues to travel down the arterial system through successively smaller arteries that supply organs, ending with the arterioles that empty into the capillary bed.

Pulmonary and Systemic Circulation

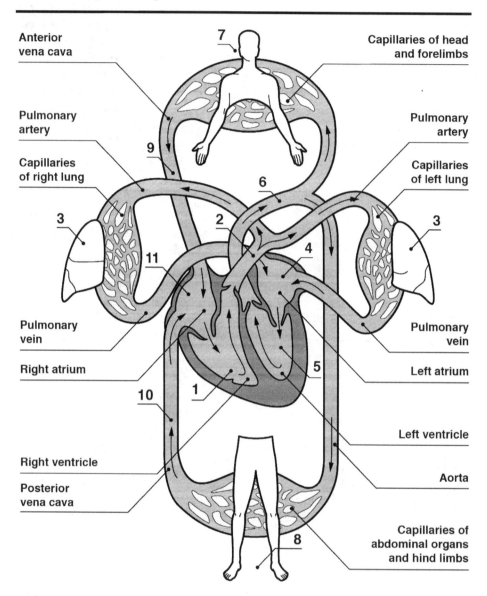

The capillary beds are drained on their opposite side by the venules, which return the now-deoxygenated blood back to the right atrium through progressively larger veins, ending in the great veins of the heart, known as the superior and inferior vena cava. The deoxygenated blood from the great veins moves into the right atrium, then the right ventricle, which pumps the blood to the lungs via the pulmonary artery to become oxygenated once again. The oxygenated blood flows from the pulmonary veins into the left atrium, then the left ventricle, and into the aorta to repeat the cycle.

There are three tissue layers in the structure of arteries and veins. The **endothelium**, or **tunica intima**, forms the inner layer. The middle layer, the **tunica media**, contains elastin and smooth muscle fibers, and connective tissue forms the outside coating, called the **tunica externa**.

Arteries have a thicker elastin middle layer that enables them to withstand the fluctuations in pressure, which result from the high-pressure contractions of the LV. **Arterioles** regulate blood flow into the capillary bed through constriction and dilation, so they are the primary control structures for blood pressure regulation. Meanwhile, the venous side of circulation operates under very low pressures, so **veins** have no elastin in their structure; instead, they use valves to prevent backflow in those vessels working against gravity, as shown in the image below.

Structure of an Artery and Vein

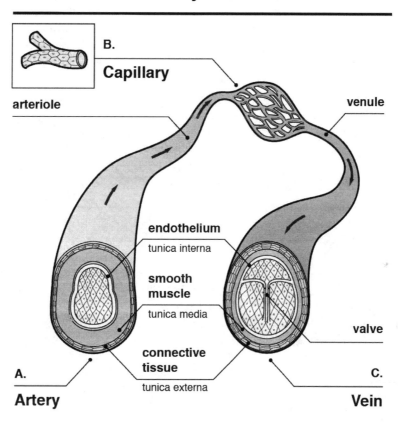

The aorta stretches from the LV through the diaphragm into the abdomen and pelvis. In the groin, the aorta separates into two main arteries that supply blood to the lower trunk and the legs. An aneurysm can occur anywhere along the aorta; an **abdominal aortic aneurysm** (AAA) is the most common. Atherosclerosis, hypertension, diabetes, infection, inflammation, and injuries (e.g., a fall or motor vehicle crash) are frequent causes. The most common presenting symptoms with an AAA are chest pain and back pain. The clinician may be able to palpate a pulsating bulge in the abdomen. Nausea and vomiting may be present. Other symptoms include lightheadedness, confusion, dyspnea, tachypnea, sweating, numbness, and tingling. When an AAA develops slowly over a period of years, it is less likely to rupture, in which case the patient should be regularly monitored with ultrasound imaging. Aneurysms greater than 2 inches (5.5 centimeters) will generally require surgical repair.

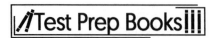

A **thoracic aortic aneurysm** occurs in the stretch of the aorta that lies within the chest cavity. The critical size for surgical intervention of a thoracic aortic aneurysm is 2.3 inches (6 centimeters). As with all surgeries in such close proximity to the heart, the risk-to-benefit ratio must be carefully weighed.

A **left ventricular aneurysm** (LVA) is a bulge or ballooning of a weakened area of the LV, commonly caused by an MI. While large cases may cause symptoms (e.g., fatigue, shortness of breath, and arrythmias), there are often no symptoms of a small LVA, and diagnosis occurs with an echocardiogram and angiogram. Monitoring will be used in the case of small LVAs to ensure that they do not require treatment. However, clot formation is a common occurrence with LVAs. In the body's attempt to repair the aneurysm, the inflammatory process and the clotting cascade are initiated, both of which increase the propensity for clot formation. Most patients are prescribed anticoagulants. Rapid treatment for an MI reduces the incidence of LVA formation.

A patient experiencing a sudden onset of tearing chest pain may be experiencing a rupture or dissection of an aortic aneurysm. Aortic aneurysms may occur at the top of the aorta, right after exiting the heart, termed **thoracic aortic aneurysms**. Aortic aneurysms may also occur farther down the aorta, then called either **thoracoabdominal aortic aneurysms** or **abdominal aortic aneurysms**. An aneurysm is any ballooning or enlargement of a blood vessel, often caused by atherosclerosis. When an aneurysm suddenly tears apart, massive amounts of the patient's blood surge out with each heartbeat, resulting in an immediate medical emergency. A patient experiencing an aortic aneurysm dissection needs immediate surgical repair followed by intensive cardiac and hemodynamic monitoring until stabilized.

Patients with unruptured aortic aneurysms may be completely asymptomatic. Detection of an aortic aneurysm occurs through ultrasonography, abdominal CT, echocardiography, and/or transesophageal echocardiography (TEE). Treatment for aortic aneurysms that have not ruptured includes elective surgical repair along with encouragement to quit smoking, which is a major cause of atherosclerosis, and drug therapy, including antilipids and blood pressure control.

Risk factors for aneurysms include genetic factors, family history of aneurysm, arteriovenous malformation (AVM) at the circle of Willis, polycystic kidney disease (PKD), and Marfan syndrome. Poor lifestyle choices, such as smoking and cocaine use, greatly increase the risk for aneurysm formation. There is also a higher risk for women, individuals over 40 years of age, patients who have experienced a traumatic head injury, and patients with hypertension.

Dissection vs. Rupture

Dissection is a condition in which the layers of the arterial wall become separated and blood leaks in between the layers of the vessel, as shown in the image below. A dissection represents damage through at least the first layer of an artery. It is a more serious form of aneurysm because all of the layers are compromised.

A dissection is different from a rupture. With a dissection, blood leaks in and through the layers of an artery, but the artery remains structurally intact, albeit weakened. Blood is still contained within the vessel. When a **rupture** occurs, it is similar to the popping of a balloon. The integrity of the artery is disrupted, and blood leaks out of the artery. Dissections increase the risk of rupture. Medical management with beta-blockers is the treatment of choice for stable aortic dissections.

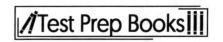

Summary

Symptoms of an aneurysm or dissection may be absent, vague, or difficult to identify. The consequences of a rupture are life-threatening. The expert clinician will ascertain a thorough patient and family history, including social factors and lifestyle choices. Autoimmune disorders, age, gender, a sedentary lifestyle, smoking, and drug or alcohol abuse are contributing factors to the development of an aneurysm. Rapid assessment, diagnosis, and treatment are essential. Therefore, the patient's vital signs, neurological status, overall presentation should be closely monitored.

Cardiac Surgery

The postoperative course for a patient following the insertion of a coronary artery bypass graft (CABG) is influenced by the patient's preoperative baseline health status and level of cardiac function; the vessel chosen for the graft, which is commonly the internal mammary artery or the great saphenous vein; whether or not the extracorporeal pump was used, and if used, the length of time that was required to complete the procedure; and the extent of the inflammatory response that can occur as a result of the circulating blood volume being perfused through the non-endothelialized surface of the bypass pump. Commonly, 48 hours postoperatively, patients are sufficiently stable to be transferred to a progressive care medical unit (commonly referred to as "step-down" unit). The nursing care of these patients is then focused on continued surveillance for changes that signal the onset of possible complications that include, but are not limited to, infection, occlusion of the graft, bleeding, acute inflammation or thrombophlebitis of the peripheral veins, acute kidney injury, alterations in respiratory function, dysrhythmias, and myocardial infarction or other cardiac events. In addition, the patient requires expert pain management, identification and management of elevated cardiac biomarkers (e.g., troponin and creatine kinase MB fraction [CK-MB]), and patient and family discharge teaching.

Cardiac Tamponade

Cardiac tamponade, or **pericardial tamponade**, is a syndrome caused by the excessive accumulation of blood or fluid in the pericardial sac, resulting in the compression of the myocardium and reduced ventricular filling. It is a medical emergency with complications of pulmonary edema, shock, and death, if left untreated.

A **pericardial effusion** develops when excess blood or fluid accumulates in the pericardial sac. If the effusion progresses, a pericardial tamponade will ensue. Because the fibrous parietal layer prevents cardiac distention, the pressure from the excessive blood or fluid is exerted inward, compressing the myocardium and reducing space for blood to fill the chambers. The normally low-pressure right ventricle and atrium are the first structures to be impacted by tamponade. Therefore, signs of right-sided heart failure, such as jugular vein distention, edema, and hepatomegaly, may be present.

Symptoms of a pericardial tamponade include dyspnea, chest tightness, dizziness, tachycardia, hypotension, muffled heart sounds, jugular vein distention, and restlessness. **Beck's triad**, a cluster of clinical signs associated with cardiac tamponade, refers specifically to the combination of distended neck veins, muffled heart sounds, and hypotension. **Pulsus paradoxus** is an important clinical finding in tamponade; it represents an abnormal BP variation during the respiration cycle and is evidenced by a decrease of 10 mmHg or more in systolic BP during inspiration. Pulsus paradoxus represents decreased diastolic ventricular filling and reduced volume in all four chambers of the heart.

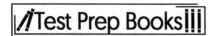

Removal of the pericardial fluid via pericardiocentesis is the definitive therapy. A **pericardiocentesis** is an emergent procedure in which a needle is inserted into the pericardial sac, aspirating the leaked blood and subsequently relieving pressure surrounding the heart. Fluid removed during the procedure is analyzed to determine the cause of the effusion. Malignancies, metastatic disease, and trauma are major causes of the development of pericardial effusions.

Although pericardiocentesis may be required in an emergent situation (e.g., cardiac tamponade) or in a non-emergent situation (e.g., pericardial effusion from a chronic condition), the procedure and nursing management before and after will be similar. In most cases, the patient will not require sedation for the procedure, only receiving local anesthesia. Therefore, the patient will not need to limit oral intake prior to the procedure. Both before and after the procedure, the nurse should monitor telemetry for signs of arrythmias caused by the fluid buildup (prior to the procedure) or irritation to the heart (caused by the insertion of the needle into the heart). The nurse should also monitor for signs of other potential complications, such as infection at the insertion site, pericarditis, and pneumothorax (which could happen with misplacement of the needle).

Identification and treatment of a tamponade requires emergent medical intervention. A rapid focused assessment of heart sounds and BP, including assessing for pulsus paradoxus, is a critical first step. An in-depth medical and surgical history can aid in identifying etiology.

Cardiac/Vascular Catheterization

A progressive care nurse is well acquainted with the **cardiac catheterization** procedure, as it is a powerful and frequently used tool to determine if a patient has cardiac disease. The test involves the threading of a small, thin catheter through peripheral arteries or veins up to the heart, obtaining information about the chambers, valves, and structures therein, as well as about the pulmonary artery, the coronary arteries, and the veins. A sheath functions as a protective covering while placing or advancing a cardiac catheter. Depending on the procedure, a sheath can be used to protect an artery, a vein, or at times both.

There are two different approaches to cardiac catheterization: left heart and right heart. **Left heart catheterization** is commonly used to determine anatomy of the heart, blood pressure in the aorta, or to assess aortic or mitral valve function. If the cardiologist wishes to use this approach, they will access the radial or femoral artery and enter the heart through the aorta on the left side. The radial artery is gaining more acceptance as the gold-standard due to the reduced risk of post-procedural bleeding and increased patient comfort.

For **right heart catheterization**, the venous system is accessed. The heart is approached from the right side, entering through the right atrium where venous blood is returning. Right heart cardiac catheterization is used to determine the pressures in the right atria, right ventricle, and pulmonary arteries, as well as the pulmonary artery occlusion pressure (PAOP). Common venous access sites used for right heart catheterization are the femoral, subclavian, internal jugular, or antecubital veins.

The method of visualization used in cardiac catheterization is through the injection of radiopaque contrast into the heart chambers and surrounding structures while x-ray images are taken to produce images. This is called **angiography**. Another visualization technique uses tiny ultrasound transducers placed at the end of the catheter to produce images. Angiography and ultrasonography can be used at the same time.

Patients with kidney disease may not be good candidates for undergoing a cardiac catheterization due to the contrast that is used. When this dye is injected into the heart, it must be metabolized by the kidneys, which can lead to further damage in a compromised kidney. Patients with active infections, fever, heart failure, heart arrhythmias, and coagulopathies may also be poor candidates for cardiac catheterizations, at the discretion of the physician.

There are two uses for cardiac catheterization: diagnostic and interventional. The diagnostic approach means the cardiologist is looking to assess the anatomy of the heart, determine its functioning ability, and evaluate disease states. Common diagnostic uses of cardiac catheterization include angiography, intravascular ultrasonography, measuring of cardiac output, biopsy of tissues within the heart, shunt detection, and measurement of the heart's metabolic function.

The second approach to cardiac catheterization is interventional, often occurring during a diagnostic procedure. A problem is seen, and action is taken to correct it. Common interventions during cardiac catheterization are percutaneous transluminal coronary angioplasty and stent insertion.

The tip of the cardiac catheter is a tiny balloon that can be inflated to open occluded arteries, a procedure termed **angioplasty**. After balloon inflation, the cardiologist may choose to insert a **stent** into the reopened artery to maintain patency of the vessel, as shown in the image below. Stent placement is used often in the case of acute MI. This intervention helps restore blood flow to areas of ischemia in the heart following a coronary artery occlusion.

Illustration of catheter insertion, balloon inflation, and stent placement during cardiac catheterization

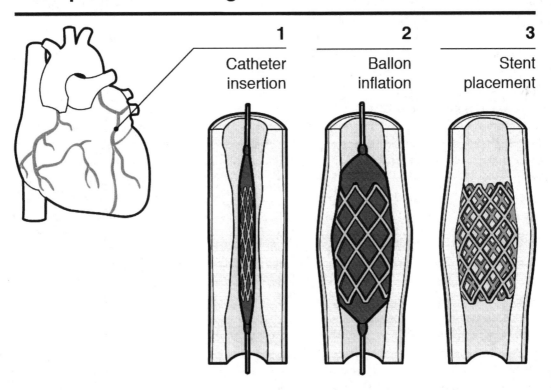

1	2	3
Catheter insertion	Ballon inflation	Stent placement

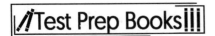

To prepare for a cardiac catheterization, the patient will be kept NPO for 4 to 6 hours prior to the procedure. During the procedure, the patient will be given medication to help them relax but will not be put under general anesthesia. While conducting the cardiac catheterization, the cardiologist can then determine if the patient will need percutaneous coronary intervention (PCI), which can be done using the cardiac catheter, or if the patient has a blockage that requires a coronary artery bypass graft (CABG).

Cardiac catheterization may be done emergently if the patient is determined to be having an ST-elevation myocardial infarction (STEMI). For these patients, nursing care may include administration of medications such as aspirin and/or heparin to prevent worsening thrombosis, maintaining the patient's NPO status, continuous monitoring of the patient's vital signs and mental status, placing defibrillation pads in place in anticipation of possible cardiac arrest, and ensuring the patient is prepared for the catheterization lab (e.g., changing the patient into a gown and preparing access sites). If not already completed, the nurse should also advocate for informed consent to be obtained by the physician. These STEMI patients should be transported for cardiac catheterization as quickly as possible to prevent worsening ischemia to the heart, which can lead to life-threatening arrhythmias.

Cardiac catheterization may also be competed on a less emergent basis for patients with unstable angina or non-ST-elevation myocardial infarctions (NSTEMI). For these patients, nursing care involves continuous cardiac monitoring, frequent vital sign monitoring, and assessing for signs of worsening ischemia (e.g., worsening chest pain, increasing serum troponin, ECG changes). These patients should also be kept NPO for at least 8 to 12 hours prior to the procedure. The nurse may also expect to administer a heparin drip or nitroglycerin drip depending on the patient's condition and cardiologist orders.

After a cardiac catheterization, the patient's insertion site should be closely monitored for a minimum of four hours, checking for hematoma or bleeding at the site as well as signs of good circulation below the site (e.g., color, pulses, paresthesia/paralysis, and capillary refill). If patients have an episode of coughing or vomiting, the nurse should check the site immediately. If bleeding is noted, pressure should be held to the puncture site until hemostasis can be achieved. Patients' vital signs and cardiac rhythm should also be closely observed, notifying the provider of abnormalities. Nursing care post-cardiac catheterization with sheath placement includes the administration of anticoagulant and antithrombotic medication. Since this medication increases the risk of bleeding, the nurse will continue to monitor for signs and symptoms of hematoma formation or hemorrhage. Additional care considerations include monitoring the sheath site for inflammation, obtaining vital signs and pedal pulses, and assessing for chest pain or shortness of breath. Laboratory testing for coagulation, along with a complete blood count, assists in determining when the patient is ready for sheath removal, which is then performed by a specially trained nurse or a physician. After the sheath is removed, the nurse will very closely monitor vital signs along with femoral and pedal pulses, especially during the first 24 hours after the procedure.

With **arterial sheath removal**, the main goal is to restore hemostasis. The traditional gold standard of restoring hemostasis following sheath removal is manual compression. Manual compression requires the nurse to apply prolonged pressure to the site (typically 5-10 minutes). Vascular closure devices are an alternative that can reduce downtime and bedrest requirements following a cardiac catheterization. A **vascular closure device** is used to close the puncture site on the artery used for angiography or cardiac catheterization. These devices may be sutures, metal clamps, or collagen and have the main purpose of stopping bleeding from the artery. Regardless of the site or form of closure device, the nurse's main priority is to monitor for signs of uncontrolled bleeding. If the patient starts bleeding from the site, strong, direct pressure should be applied immediately until the bleeding stops. If the nurse is unable to control the bleeding, the physician should be notified immediately. If the access site is the femoral artery, the patient will need to remain flat for at least 1 hour following the procedure and should not walk for around 2 to 4 hours after the procedure.

If the patient is remaining in the hospital, the nurse should continue to monitor the site for signs of bleeding or infection. Additionally, since the patient is at increased risk of future myocardial infarction, the nurse should continue assessment of any changes in their vital signs, ECG, or condition. Upon discharge, the patient should be provided with instructions on care of the site, when to return emergently (e.g., uncontrolled bleeding or signs of myocardial infarction), and when to follow up for possible vascular closure device removal.

Cardiogenic Shock

The clinical definition of **cardiogenic shock** is decreased CO and evidence of tissue hypoxia in the presence of adequate intravascular volume. It is a medical emergency and the most severe expression of LV failure. Cardiogenic shock is the leading cause of death following an MI, with mortality rates between 70 and 90 percent without aggressive treatment. When a large area of the myocardium becomes ischemic, the heart cannot pump effectively. Therefore, SV, CO, and BP drastically decline, with the result of endpoint hypoperfusion and organ failure. Characteristics of cardiogenic shock include ashen, cyanotic, or mottled extremities; distant heart sounds; and rapid and faint peripheral pulses. Additional signs of hypoperfusion, such as altered mental status and decreased urine output, may also be present.

Cardiogenic shock often occurs following an acute MI. The ischemia that results from this condition causes the heart to fail in its ability to adequately circulate blood in the body. Mortality rates for cardiogenic shock are high if swift, aggressive intervention is not provided as soon as possible.

Cardiogenic shock is an emergency, and the patient must be treated immediately to prevent death. Admission to an ICU is likely, where the patient may have a central line placed to ensure rapid volume replacement and allow for multiple infusions of medicines to help maintain BP and cardiac output.

A **central line** is an intravenous catheter placed by a qualified medical practitioner (usually a physician or advanced practice provider) that reaches the patient's heart. This allows for medication to circulate more directly within the patient's bloodstream. Central lines may be placed in the internal jugular vein, the subclavian vein, or the femoral vein. Types of central lines include single-lumen (meant for rapid fluid resuscitation or blood transfusion) or triple-lumen (which allows for multiple medications to be administered at once). Central lines are generally indicated for patients who require frequent IV access, those who require multiple continuous intravenous medications and lack sufficient peripheral IV access, and those who are hemodynamically unstable.

Nursing management of the central line mainly revolves around maintaining the safety and health of the patient. Central line placement increases the patient's risk of infection, which can both affect the heart and become systemic, leading to **sepsis**. Because of this, nurses should maintain sterile technique when using a central line. The nurse must clean the hub thoroughly prior to administration of any medication into the central line and prior to drawing blood from the line. Unused lines should remain clamped and (if available at the facility) should have an antiseptic cap applied to the hub. **Central line dressings** should also be changed using sterile technique per facility protocol and whenever they become soiled. Any signs of infection or misplacement of the central line should be immediately reported to the physician. Finally, in order to decrease infection risk, the nurse should advocate for removal of the central line as soon as its use is no longer indicated.

The patient may also have an arterial line placed for continuous blood pressure monitoring while treatment is managed. Pharmacologic therapy will likely include drugs to improve cardiac contractility, such as dopamine, and diuretics to maintain volume and prevent volume overload during fluid resuscitation. If dopamine does not do an adequate job of maintaining BP, a stronger option would be norepinephrine, a potent vasoconstrictor. Any electrolyte abnormalities, such as acidosis, hypokalemia, or hypomagnesemia, should also be corrected.

Some patients will have an intra-aortic balloon pump inserted in the aorta to assist the heart's function. When the heart pumps, during **systole**, the balloon is deflated. When the heart rests, during **diastole**, the balloon inflates. While inflation helps push blood into the coronary arteries to restore adequate perfusion, deflation allows for more space in the aorta and thus more blood to flow out to the body and the tissues needing oxygen.

Patients in cardiogenic shock are likely candidates for a percutaneous intervention (PCI) or coronary artery bypass graft (CABG) surgery to immediately correct the issue. Research has shown that a PCI is most effective within 90 minutes of patient presentation to prevent mortality and long-term damage.

Percutaneous coronary intervention (PCI) uses cardiac catheterization to access the cardiac arteries and open up stenosis or blockages. In PCI, a stent is placed into the affected coronary artery. Depending on the indication for the procedure, PCI may be performed emergently or non-emergently. Following PCI, the nurse should monitor for signs of bleeding or infection at access points. Since the patient is also at increased risk of future myocardial infarction, the nurse should continue to assess for signs and educate the patient on the need for follow-up and return for emergency care if symptoms recur.

Obstructive Shock

Obstructive shock occurs when the heart or the great vessels are mechanically obstructed. A cardiac tamponade or massive PE is a frequent cause of obstructive shock. Systemic circulatory collapse occurs because blood flow in or out of the heart is blocked. Generalized treatment goals for shock are to identify and correct the underlying cause. In the case of obstructive shock, the goal is to remove the obstruction.

Treatment begins simultaneously with evaluation. Stabilization of the airway, breathing, and circulation are the primary interventions, followed by fluid resuscitation to increase BP. Vital signs, urine output, and mental status (e.g., using the Glasgow Coma Scale [GCS]) should be monitored. Shock patients must be kept warm, and serial measurements of renal and hepatic function, electrolyte levels, and ABGs should be monitored.

Summary

Shock is characterized by inadequate circulatory perfusion to meet the oxygen demands of vital organs. The management goal for shock is to restore oxygen delivery to the tissues and reverse the perfusion deficit. This is accomplished through fluid resuscitation, increasing CO with inotropes, and raising the systemic vascular resistance (SVR) with vasopressors.

Cardiomyopathies

A **cardiomyopathy** is any condition in which the heart muscle is diseased. There are three main categories of cardiomyopathy that will be discussed: dilated, hypertrophic, and restrictive cardiomyopathy.

Dilated

Dilated cardiomyopathy is the most common form of cardiomyopathy. Usually both ventricles will be affected (e.g., dilating, thinning, and becoming hypertrophic), causing systolic dysfunction. Mitral and tricuspid regurgitation often develop because of dilation. When the left ventricle is affected, the patient will have exertional dyspnea and fatigue because the left ventricular diastolic pressure rises, and cardiac output is lowered. When the right ventricle is affected, the patient may present with edema of the legs and arms along with jugular vein distention. The symptoms of dilated cardiomyopathy will vary in severity and presentation based on the etiology. The most common etiologies for dilated cardiomyopathy include ischemia, certain infectious diseases, substance abuse (e.g., cocaine and alcohol abuse), inherited syndromes, rheumatological disorders, and extreme stress (e.g., Takotsubo cardiomyopathy or broken heart syndrome). Dilated cardiomyopathy can also be idiopathic, meaning there is no known etiology.

Ischemic dilated cardiomyopathy is primarily seen in patients with atherosclerosis. The inadequate perfusion results in ischemia within the myocardium, tissue damage, and increased risk for a cardiac event. **Non-ischemic dilated cardiomyopathy** has several different potential causes, including viral infections, substance abuse, inherited syndromes, and autoimmune reactions. Viral infections are a well-known cause of dilated cardiomyopathy, with over twenty different viruses identified, such as human immunodeficiency virus (HIV) infection.

Takotsubo cardiomyopathy, also known as **acute apical ballooning cardiomyopathy** or **broken heart syndrome**, is triggered by a sudden and extreme amount of emotional distress. The patient may have experienced the loss of a loved one or some other catastrophic life event, which set in motion a hyperadrenergic state in the body. *Takotsubo* is a Japanese word for a fishing pot used for capturing octopuses, which is what the left ventricle has been said to look like during this type of cardiomyopathy. Patients typically present in a similar manner to those experiencing an ischemic event, with dyspnea, chest pain, nausea, and vomiting, among other symptoms. This type of heart failure is typically reversible, requiring acute hemodynamic support and similar treatment to patients with acute coronary syndrome. While Takotsubo cardiomyopathy is technically deemed an unclassified form of cardiomyopathy, there is left ventricular dilation and systolic heart failure present, making it most similar to dilated cardiomyopathy.

A patient with dilated cardiomyopathy will be diagnosed using a chest x-ray, which will show the enlargement of the heart, called **cardiomegaly**. The chest film may also show pleural effusions, a result of ventricular failure. Serological markers such as troponin may be elevated in dilated cardiomyopathy. Tissue samples from the heart muscle may be obtained for biopsy in some cases. ECG and imaging studies, such as echocardiography and cardiac magnetic resonance imaging (MRI), will also be used to make a diagnosis of dilated cardiomyopathy.

Patients with dilated cardiomyopathy will be treated with angiotensin-converting enzyme (ACE) inhibitors, beta blockers, angiotensin-receptor blockers (ARBs), diuretics, and digoxin, among other pharmacologic therapies. These drugs are often used in heart failure with a lowered ejection fraction.

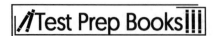

Ejection fraction is a term of measurement used to quantify the percentage of blood leaving the heart with each beat. A patient with systolic heart failure will have a much lower ejection fraction than normal. A normal ejection fraction is around 50 to 70 percent. The patient with dilated cardiomyopathy may also require pacemaker therapy and/or an implantable cardioverter-defibrillator.

Hypertrophic

Hypertrophic cardiomyopathy is an inherited condition due to a genetic mutation. In rare cases, this type of cardiomyopathy may be acquired, as is the case in patients with acromegaly. **Hypertrophy** refers to a thickening of the cardiac muscle, often becoming stiff and noncompliant. Ejection fraction in patients with hypertrophic cardiomyopathy may be elevated as the smaller heart chamber empties completely with each beat to maintain cardiac output.

This type of cardiomyopathy often occurs in athletes, frequently causing sudden death and the official diagnosis made upon autopsy. Symptoms are similar to an acute coronary artery occlusion, such as chest pain, dyspnea, and syncope. Patients will be diagnosed using echocardiography or cardiac MRI, where the heart structures are visualized and the severity of the hypertrophy is analyzed.

Family history of sudden death or patient history of unexplained syncope are clues that the patient may have this type of cardiomyopathy.

The treatment plan for a patient diagnosed with hypertrophic cardiomyopathy usually includes beta-blockers, such as metoprolol, and calcium channel blockers, such as verapamil. Beta-blockers and calcium channel blockers help with this type of cardiomyopathy because they slow the heart rate, decrease contractility, and prolong the time that the heart chambers can fill between beats. Nitrates, diuretics, and ACE inhibitors should be avoided because they reduce preload, which worsens the condition. Implantable cardioverter-defibrillator (ICD) is recommended to prevent death in patients with a history of cardiac arrest and syncope.

Restrictive

A cardiomyopathy characterized by noncompliant heart walls that are resistant to filling during the diastolic period is termed **restrictive cardiomyopathy**. The etiology of restrictive cardiomyopathy can be related to a foreign substance infiltrating the myocardium (typically the protein amyloid), inflammatory diseases, cardiotoxicity related to medical interventions, or genetic predispositions. One or both ventricles of the heart may be affected. Restrictive cardiomyopathy is much less common than dilated and hypertrophic cardiomyopathies.

A patient with restrictive cardiomyopathy may present with fatigue and exertional dyspnea, like the other cardiomyopathic presentations. This is due to decreased cardiac output and oxygen delivery to the tissues and organs of the body. The resistance to diastolic filling results in an increased filling pressure, followed by pulmonary venous hypertension.

A patient will be diagnosed with restrictive cardiomyopathy using echocardiography to visualize the ventricles and other structures of the heart. Cardiac MRI, heart catheterization, and biopsy may also be used to confirm the diagnosis.

A patient diagnosed with restrictive cardiomyopathy has a poor prognosis, unfortunately, as diagnosis is often made in the later stages of the disease. The cause will be treated, if possible, along with supportive treatment for symptoms. Diuretics will be used to relieve pulmonary vascular congestion if appropriate.

Illustration comparing a normal heart muscle with dilated, hypertrophic, and restrictive cardiomyopathies

Normal	Dilated	Hypertrophic	Restrictive

Dysrhythmias

Dysrhythmia, also known as **arrhythmia**, is abnormal electrical activity of the heart. The abnormal heartbeat may be irregular, too fast, or too slow.

Normally, the electrical conduction system of the heart begins with an impulse known as the **action potential** at the pacemaker sinoatrial (SA) node. The impulse travels across the right and left atria before activating the atrioventricular (AV) node.

Cardiac Conduction Cycle

A.

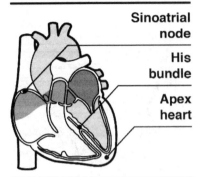

Sinoatrial
node

His
bundle

Apex
heart

An electrical impulse travels
from the sinoatrial node to the
walls of the atria, causing
them to contract.

B.

Atrioventricular
node

The impulse reaches the
atrioventricular node, which
delays it by about 0.1 second.

C.

Bundle branches carry signals
from the atrioventricular node
to the heart apex.

D.

The signal spreads through
the ventricular walls, causing
them to contract.

42

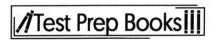

The pathway from the SA to the AV node is visualized on the ECG as the P wave. From the AV node, the impulse continues down the septum along cardiac fibers. These fibers are known as the **bundle of His**. The impulse then spreads out and across the ventricles via the **Purkinje fibers**, represented on the ECG as the QRS complex. The T wave represents the **repolarization** or recovery of the ventricles.

Electrical Events of the Cardiac Cycle

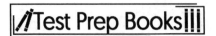
Cardiac cells have four important properties: excitability, conductivity, contractility, and automaticity. **Excitability** allows the heart to respond to stimuli and maintain homeostasis. **Conductivity** is the ability to transfer the electrical impulse initiated at the SA node across cardiac cells. **Contractility** is the cardiac cells' ability to transform an action potential into the mechanical action of contraction and relaxation. **Automaticity** is the ability of cardiac cells to contract without direct nerve stimulation; in other words, the heart initiates its own impulse. If the SA node fails to initiate the impulse, the AV node will fire the impulse at a slower rate. If neither the SA nor the AV node fires the impulse, the cells within the bundle of His and the Purkinje fibers will fire to start the impulse at an even slower rate.

The action potential is a representation of the changes in voltage of a single cardiac cell. Action potentials are formed as a result of ion fluxes through cellular membrane channels, most importantly, the sodium (Na+), potassium (K+), and calcium (Ca+) channels. Electrical activity requires an action potential. Contraction of the cardiac muscle fibers immediately follows electrical activity.

Phases of an Action Potential

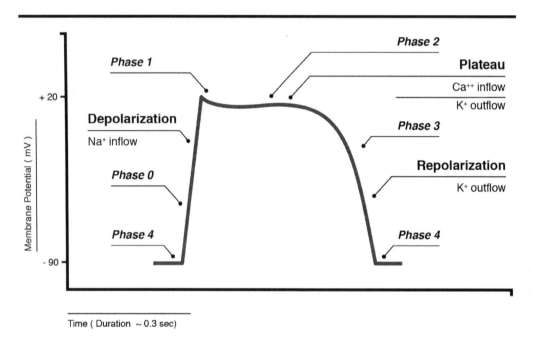

Time (Duration ~ 0.3 sec)

Phase 0: Depolarization

- Rapid Na+ channels are stimulated to open.

- The cardiac cell is flooded with Na+ ions, which change the transmembrane potential.

- The shift in potential is reflected by the initial spike of the action potential.

- Depolarization of one cell triggers the Na+ channels in surrounding cells to open, which causes the depolarization wave to propagate cell by cell throughout the heart.

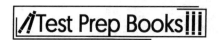

Phases 1 – 3: Repolarization phases

- During these phases, represented as the plateau, Ca^{2+} and some K^+ channels open.

- Ca^{2+} flows into the cells, and K^+ flows out.

- The cell remains polarized, and the increased Ca^{2+} within the cell triggers contraction of the cardiac muscle.

Phase 4: Completion of repolarization

- Ca2+ channels close.

- K+ outflow continues.

- The cardiac cell returns to its normal state.

The cardiac cycle of **depolarization-polarization-depolarization** is represented on the ECG by the P wave, QRS complex, and T wave. A dysrhythmia can occur anywhere along the conduction system. It can result when an impulse from between the nodes or fibers is delayed or blocked. Arrhythmias also occur when an ectopic focus initiates an impulse, thereby disrupting the normal conduction cycle. Additional sources of damage to the conduction system include MIs, hypertension, coronary artery disease (CAD), and congenital heart defects.

Overview of Dysrhythmias

Abnormalities in the electrical conduction system of the heart may occur at the SA node, the AV node, or the His-Purkinje system of the ventricles. Careful evaluation of the ECG will aid in determining the location and subsequent cause of the dysrhythmia.

Dysrhythmias that occur above the ventricles in either the atria or the SA/AV nodes are known as **supraventricular dysrhythmias**. Common arrhythmias in this category are sinus bradycardia, sinus tachycardia, atrial fibrillation, atrial flutter, junctional rhythm, and supraventricular tachycardia (SVT). **Atrioventricular (AV) blocks**, known as heart blocks, occur when the impulse is delayed or blocked at the AV node. The three types of **heart block** are first degree, second degree, and third degree, with first degree being the least severe and third degree being the most severe.

Ventricular dysrhythmias can be life-threatening because they severely impact the heart's ability to pump and maintain adequate cardiac output (CO). A bundle branch block (BBB), premature ventricular complexes (PVCs), sustained ventricular tachycardia (V-tach), ventricular fibrillation (V-fib), Torsades de pointes, and digoxin-induced ventricular dysrhythmias are the most common ventricular arrhythmias.

Atrial Fibrillation

Atrial fibrillation is the most common sustained dysrhythmia. It is caused when multiple foci in the atria fire randomly, thereby stimulating various parts of the atria simultaneously. The result is a highly irregular atrial rhythm, while the ventricular rate may be rapid or normal. Fatigue, lightheadedness, chest pain, dyspnea, and hypotension may be present. Treatment goals are to improve ventricular pumping and prevent stroke. Beta-blockers and CCBs impede conduction through the AV node, thereby

45

controlling ventricular rates, so they are the medications of choice. Cardioversion and ablation are also treatment options.

Cardioversion is a cardiac procedure in which the patient is administered a synchronized shock in order to restore their cardiac rhythm. This is most commonly used as a treatment for patients with supraventricular tachycardia (SVT), atrial fibrillation, and atrial flutter when pharmacological interventions have been unsuccessful or when the patient has become unstable (e.g., hypotensive, altered mental status). Ideally, the patient will receive conscious sedation and pain management prior to receiving the shock. Prior to the procedure, the nurse should place the defibrillator pads on the patient as well as continuous cardiac monitoring, including frequent blood pressures and capnography. Additionally, the nurse should ensure that additional staff, including the physician, respiratory therapists, and additional hands, are present in case the cardioversion is unsuccessful and puts the patient into a life-threatening arrhythmia (e.g., ventricular fibrillation or pulseless ventricular tachycardia). Depending on the medications given and hospital policy, the nurse or physician may administer the sedation. The nurse should monitor for hypotension and record the cardioversion, noting the time and the strength of the shock. Once the procedure is complete, the nurse should remain with the patient and continue to monitor vitals until the sedation has fully worn off. The patient should remain on cardiac monitoring to ensure that they do not return to the unstable arrhythmia.

An **ablation** is a cardiac procedure in which the cardiologist creates scarring on the heart tissue in order to correct a symptomatic arrythmia that has been poorly controlled with medications. Some examples of these arrythmias are symptomatic atrial fibrillation, recurrent supraventricular tachycardia (SVT), and Wolff-Parkinson-White syndrome. Ablations are generally performed in the cardiac catheterization lab under sedation. Therefore, the patient should be placed NPO for approximately 8 hours prior to the procedure to prevent aspiration. Following the procedure, the nurse should place the patient on continuous cardiac monitoring and look for signs of pericardial effusion, cardiac tamponade, pneumothorax, and uncontrolled bleeding. It is possible that the patient's serum troponin levels will be slightly elevated after the ablation due to stress or trauma placed on the cardiac muscles. However, abnormal results should still be reported to the cardiologist to determine if further intervention is necessary. It is also likely that the patient will be placed on a blood thinning medication, such as warfarin or apixaban, at least temporarily following the ablation. The nurse should educate the patient on risks of bleeding while on these medications and the importance of regularly following up with cardiology.

The patient with atrial fibrillation should always be treated with antithrombotic therapy, unless contraindicated.

Atrial Fibrillation and Flutter ECG Tracings

Atrial Fibrillation

fibrillatory waves

Atrial Flutter

sawtooth pattern

Atrial Flutter

Atrial flutter is caused by an ectopic atrial focus that fires between 250 and 350 times a minute. The AV node is unable to transmit impulses at that speed, so typically only one out of every two impulses reach the ventricles. Cardioversion is the treatment of choice to convert atrial flutter back to a sinus rhythm. Calcium channel blockers (CCBs) and beta-blockers are used to manage ventricular rates.

Junctional Dysrhythmias

If either the SA node slows or its impulse is not properly conducted, the AV node will become the pacemaker. The heart rate for an impulse initiated at the AV junction will be between 40 and 60 bpm. The P wave will be absent or inverted on an ECG, referred to as a junctional rhythm. The suggested treatment is similar to that of sinus bradycardia: transcutaneous pacing, atropine, and epinephrine.

Bradydysrhythmias

Sinus bradycardia occurs when the SA node creates an impulse at a slower-than-normal rate—less than 60 beats per minute (bpm). Causes include metabolic conditions, calcium channel blockers (CCB) and beta-blocker medications, MIs, and increased intracranial pressure. If symptomatic, treatment involves transcutaneous pacing and atropine.

Conduction Defects and Blocks

Heart Block

In **first-degree heart block**, the impulse from the SA node is slowed as it moves across the atria. On an ECG, the P and R waves will be longer and flatter. First-degree block is often asymptomatic.

Second-degree heart block is divided into two categories known as Mobitz type I and Mobitz type II. In **Mobitz type I** (also known as Wenckebach), the impulse from the SA node is increasingly delayed with each heartbeat until eventually a beat is skipped entirely. On an ECG, this is visible as a delay in the PR

47

interval. The normal PR interval is 0.12–0.20. The PR interval will get longer until the QRS wave doesn't follow the P wave. Patients may experience mild symptoms with this dysrhythmia.

When some of the impulses from the SA node fail to reach the ventricles, the arrhythmia is a **Mobitz type II** heart block. Some impulses move across the atria and reach the ventricles normally, and others do not. On an ECG, the QRS follows the P wave at normal speed, but some QRS complexes are missing because the signal is blocked. Patients experiencing this dysrhythmia usually need a pacemaker.

A **third-degree heart block** is also known as **complete heart block**, or **complete AV block**. The SA node may continue to initiate the impulses between 80 and 100 bpm, but none of the impulses reach the ventricles. The automaticity of cardiac cells in the Purkinje fibers will prompt the ventricles to initiate an impulse; however, beats initiated in this area are between 20 and 40 bpm. The slower impulses initiated from the ventricles are not coordinated with the impulses from the SA node. Therefore, third-degree heart block is a medical emergency that requires a temporary to permanent pacemaker. The nursing care of a patient with a pacemaker will depend on the specific type (e.g., single chamber, dual-chamber, or biventricular).

A **pacemaker** is a device implanted in the patient's chest that provides shocks to ensure that the patient's cardiac rhythm remains life-sustaining. Pacemakers are usually used to treat bradycardia and heart block, but in some cases can also be used to regulate tachycardia. **Single-chamber pacemakers** have a single electrical lead that goes into either the right atrium or the right ventricle. If the pacemaker lead is in the atrium, the nurse should note pacer spikes just prior to the P wave on the electrocardiogram (ECG). If the pacemaker lead is in the ventricle, the nurse should notice pacer spikes just prior to the QRS complex, and the QRS complex may be widened and appear inverted. In a **dual-chamber pacemaker**, the leads are in both the right atrium and the right ventricle. On an ECG, the nurse should expect two pacer spikes for each beat, one at the P wave and one at the QRS complex with widening. **Biventricular pacemakers** are placed in both the right and left ventricle and are mainly indicated for patients with severe heart failure and cardiomegaly. Their purpose is less to correct an abnormal rhythm and more to ensure that the heart's ventricles are contracting sufficiently in systole and diastole. The expected ECG finding for biventricular pacing is a pacer spike just before the QRS complex with some widening to the QRS (no inversion) and possibly an inverted T wave.

Bundle Branch Block
A **bundle branch block** (BBB) occurs when there is a delay or defect in the conduction system within the ventricles; a BBB may be designated as "left" or "right" to specify the ventricle at fault or as "complete" or "partial." The QRS complex will be widened or prolonged. Treating the underlying cause is the goal.

Premature Ventricular Complex
A **premature ventricular complex** (PVC) occurs when a ventricular impulse is conducted through the ventricle before the next sinus impulse. This may be caused by cardiac ischemia, heart failure, hypoxia, or hypokalemia. Treatment is to correct the cause, and long-term treatment is not indicated unless the patient is symptomatic.

Treatment Related Dysrhythmias
The use of an **implantable cardiac device** (ICD) is associated with three forms of arrhythmias: inappropriate shocks, appropriate shocks, and "phantom shocks." There are two concerns related to the frequency of the ICD shocks. First, any time that the ICD fires, there is a risk of stimulating a life-threatening rhythm. Second, reports of depression, anxiety, and pain related to these shocks are noted

in more than 75 percent of patients with an ICD. An **inappropriate shock** occurs when the ICD delivers the shock for any rhythm other than ventricular tachycardias. The most common cause is the presence of a supraventricular tachycardia because the rate of the dysrhythmia is within the programmed range of the ICD. The rate of appropriate shocks, and thereby the patient's concerns, are kept to a minimum with the use of antiarrhythmic therapy; however, these medications can affect the defibrillation threshold of the ICD and are used with caution. **Phantom shocks** are sensed by the patient when no shock was delivered. This abnormal sensation most often decreases over time.

DDD Pacemakers

The **DDD pacemaker** (dual-chamber activity sensing and response pacemaker) is associated with three specific dysrhythmic events. **Crosstalk** occurs when the pacemaker senses a signal as an R wave, thereby interrupting the signal to the ventricle, inhibiting output, and resetting the timing of the next signal. If the pacemaker fails to fire for any reason, the failure can result in a "native tachycardia," which inhibits the pacemaker action until the tachycardia subsides. Pacemaker-mediated tachycardias are associated with native atrial tachycardias, retrograde transmission, or endless-loop tachycardias. These conditions are commonly asymptomatic in patients with normal AV conduction but may be lethal with any degree of AV block.

Digoxin-Induced Ventricular Dysrhythmias

Digoxin is a cardiac glycoside medication that increases the strength and regularity of the cardiac rhythm. It has a very narrow therapeutic range, and toxicity occurs when therapeutic levels are exceeded. Digoxin toxicity can mimic all types of dysrhythmias. Digoxin acts by increasing automaticity in the atria, ventricles, and the His-Purkinje system. It also decreases conduction through the AV node. Therefore, an AV block is the most common form of presenting dysrhythmia in patients with **digoxin toxicity**. Among the elderly, chronic toxicity is common as well, as it can be easily caused by drug-to-drug interactions and declining renal function.

Lethal Ventricular Dysrhythmias

There are four lethal dysrhythmias that originate in the ventricles: ventricular tachycardia, ventricular fibrillation, Torsades de pointes, and asystole.

Ventricular Tachycardia

Ventricular tachycardia (V-tach) occurs from a single, rapidly firing ectopic ventricular focus that is typically at the border of an old infarct (MI). This dysrhythmia is usually associated with CAD. Ventricular rates can be 150 to 250 bpm; however, the heart cannot pump effectively at those increased rates. Immediate cardioversion is the treatment of choice. Antidysrhythmic medications such as amiodarone, lidocaine, or procainamide may be given. An implantable cardioverter defibrillator (ICD) may be necessary.

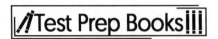
Ventricular Tachycardia and Fibrillation ECG Tracings

Ventricular Fibrillation

Ventricular fibrillation (V-fib) is a life-threatening emergency that requires immediate treatment. It is caused by multiple ventricular ectopic foci firing simultaneously, which forces the ventricles to contract asynchronously. Coordinated ventricular contraction is impossible in this scenario. The result is reduced cardiac output, and defibrillation is required. Lidocaine, amiodarone, and procainamide may be used.

Defibrillation is the administration of an unsynchronized electric shock to a patient's heart that is in an arrhythmia that is not life-sustaining. The two rhythms that are compatible with defibrillation are pulseless ventricular tachycardia (pVT) and ventricular fibrillation (VF). If the nurse finds that the patient is unresponsive or not breathing, the cardiac monitor shows one of these rhythms, and the patient has no pulse, defibrillation is indicated and should be administered as quickly as possible. If a defibrillator is not present in the room, the nurse should activate the code team and start CPR immediately. Following defibrillation, CPR should be continued immediately for at least 2 minutes before rechecking the patient's pulse and heart rhythm, unless the patient shows obvious signs of a **return of spontaneous circulation** (ROSC). If the code team achieves ROSC, cardiac monitoring should continue, and the patient may be moved to a higher level of care for further treatment, depending on the suspected cause of cardiac arrest.

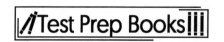

Torsade de Pointes

Torsade de pointes is an atypical, rapid, undulating ventricular tachydysrhythmia. This rhythm has a prolonged QT interval; however, a variety of drugs can also cause QT-interval prolongation. The treatment is intravenous magnesium and cardioversion for sustained V-tach.

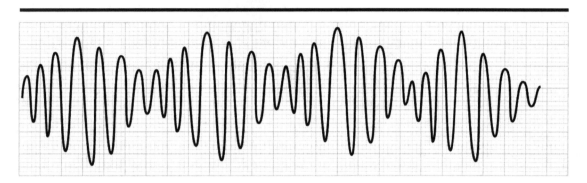

Asystole

Asystole is defined as sudden cardiac arrest (SCA) or death (SCD) that is manifested by a lack of electrical activity of the cardiac muscle resulting in an isoelectric ECG pattern. In monitored patients, asystole is most commonly preceded by ventricular dysrhythmias; however, bradyarrhythmias also may result in asystole. These lethal dysrhythmias often occur after a period of increasing premature ventricular activity. The most common cause of asystole is coronary artery disease; however, SCD is also associated with heart failure, structural heart diseases (e.g., myocarditis and cardiomyopathy), and primary electrical diseases (e.g., Brugada syndrome and Wolff-Parkinson-White syndrome). In addition, non-cardiac events such as traumatic injuries, hemorrhage, recreational drug intoxication, head injuries, and sudden airway obstruction due to disease or drowning may result in asystole.

Tachydysrhythmias
Supraventricular Tachycardia

Sustained **supraventricular tachycardia** (SVT) is usually caused by an AV nodal reentry circuit. Heart rate can increase to 150 to 250 bpm. Interventions that increase vagal tone, such as the Valsalva maneuver or carotid massage, may slow the heart rate. Beta-blockers and CCBs may be given intravenously for immediate treatment or may be taken orally to prevent recurrence.

Sinus Tachycardia

Sinus tachycardia occurs when the SA node creates an impulse at a faster-than-normal rate, also characterized as a rate greater than 100 bpm. Causes include physiological stress such as shock, volume loss, and heart failure, as well as medications and illicit drugs. Sinus tachycardia is typically treated by treating the underlying cause.

Summary

Dysrhythmias range from asymptomatic to life-threatening. They can be divided into three major groups: supraventricular dysrhythmias, heart block, and ventricular dysrhythmias. Treatment is necessary when ventricular pumping and cardiac output are impacted. There are two phases of treatment. The first is to terminate the dysrhythmia using medications, defibrillation, or both. The second is long-term suppression with medications and/or lifestyle changes.

A complete medical history with an emphasis on current medications, comorbidities, and family history is paramount. Immediate nursing priorities include establishing IV access, monitoring vital signs, and administering oxygen as needed. Evaluation of the ECG, chest x-ray, and both laboratory and diagnostic values is required. Defibrillation, cardioversion, and transcutaneous pacing are other possibilities.

Genetic Cardiac Disease

Long QT Syndrome

Long QT syndrome occurs when the QT segment of the ECG wave form is prolonged, representing the electrical activity in the ventricles. This hereditary and rare disorder usually occurs in healthy adults and children and is characterized by fainting episodes, feelings of "fluttering" in the chest, and abnormal heart rate or rhythm. Diagnosis occurs with ECG and stress testing. Long QT syndrome may be fatal, as it could potentially cause sudden cardiac arrest. A treatment plan for long QT syndrome may include beta-blockers, avoiding drugs that aggravate the syndrome, and possible implantation of an ICD or pacemaker.

Brugada Syndrome

Brugada syndrome is the result of an inherited defect in the cardiac sodium channels gene. It is characterized by an ECG pattern of right bundle branch block with ST-segment elevation in leads V1, V2, and V3. This syndrome is associated with a significant risk of sudden cardiac arrest (SCA), with or without syncopal episodes, which is most often preceded by polymorphic ventricular ectopy. Two additional conditions, agonal nocturnal respiration and **sudden unexpected nocturnal death syndrome** (SUNDS), are also associated with the risk of SCA, characterized by similar ECG patterns, and related to a genetic defect in a cardiac sodium channel. SUNDS was first studied in a population of young men in Thailand where researchers proposed that the incidence of SCA was also related to the presence of hypokalemia. The treatment for Brugada includes antiarrhythmic therapy, ICD placement, and the avoidance of calcium channel blocker medications.

Structural Defects

The most common types of heart defects occur in developing fetuses and are often diagnosed prenatally or shortly after the child is born. Some common types of congenital defects are **atrial septal defects** (ASDs), **patent foramen ovale** (PFO), patent ductus arteriosus (PDA), coarctation of the aorta, and tetralogy of Fallot.

ASD and PFO are similar in that there is a hole between the two atria of the heart, and oxygen-rich blood leaks from the left chamber to the right. In ASD, the tissue never forms, and in PFO, the hole that is normally there does not close after birth as it should. An ASD hole is generally larger than a PFO.

Patent ductus arteriosus (PDA) occurs when the **ductus arteriosus**, the vessel that connects the pulmonary artery and the aorta, does not close as it should after birth. The ductus arteriosus is vital for fetal development, but if it remains open after birth, the oxygen-rich blood of the aorta that is meant for body circulation gets mixed with the oxygen-poor blood of the pulmonary artery, resulting in increased pulmonary pressures and stress on the heart.

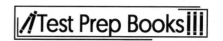

A narrowing of the aorta in a baby is called **coarctation of the aorta** and results in hypertension and heart damage.

Tetralogy of Fallot is a complex congenital heart defect involving four defects: a hole between the two ventricles called a **ventricular septal defect** (VSD), pulmonary valve stenosis, an aorta that is located between the two ventricles and above the VSD, and hypertrophy, or a thickening of the right ventricle due to working harder because of the pulmonary valve stenosis. Patients with tetralogy of Fallot must have open heart surgery to repair the defects.

Structural Heart Defects

Structural heart defects occurring in adulthood include valvular disease. There are four valves in the heart: mitral, tricuspid, aortic, and pulmonary. These valves control the flow of blood between the chambers of the heart, the lungs for oxygenation, and the body for circulation. Valvular defects occur because of normal aging and degeneration, infections, hypertension, atherosclerosis, ischemic conditions such as heart attack, tumors, radiation, and even some medications. Valve dysfunctions can include stiffening, in which blood is forced backward rather than forward, or weakening, in which blood leaks inappropriately between chambers. The severity of the valve dysfunction determines the number of symptoms and the amount and type of treatment needed. Patients with valvular disease may experience palpitations, fatigue, dizziness, and/or chest pain. Diagnosis is made with an ECG, stress tests, chest x-rays, echocardiograms, and/or cardiac catheterization. Management and treatment options can include encouragement of smoking cessation, antithrombotics or anticoagulants, and possible surgery to repair the valves.

Heart Failure

Mechanism

Defined as the inability of the heart to meet the metabolic demands of the body, **heart failure** (HF) is a general term that refers to the failure of the heart as a pump. Heart failure is a syndrome with diverse clinical features and various etiologies. The syndrome is progressive and often fatal. It may involve one or both sides of the heart (right and/or left). Based on an ejection fraction (EF), it can be further categorized as diastolic or systolic HF.

Left-sided HF is also referred to as **congestive heart failure** (CHF) because the congestion occurs in the pulmonary capillary beds. As mentioned previously, oxygenated blood flows from the pulmonary veins into the left atrium, then the left ventricle, and into the aorta for distribution through the systemic circulation.

Once the oxygenated blood has been delivered to end-point tissues and organs, it arrives at the capillary bed. The now-deoxygenated blood begins the return journey back to the heart by passing from the capillary beds into small veins that feed into progressively larger veins and, ultimately, into the superior and inferior vena cava. The vena cava empties into the right atrium. From the right atrium, blood flows into the right ventricle and then into the pulmonary system for oxygenation.

When the RV is impaired in **right-sided HF**, it cannot effectively pump blood forward into the pulmonary system. The ineffective forward movement of blood causes an increase in venous pressure. When venous pressure rises, the blood backs up and leaks into the tissues and the liver. The end result is edema in the extremities and congestion within the liver.

When the LV is impaired, it cannot effectively pump blood forward into the aorta for systemic circulation. The ineffective forward movement of blood causes an increase in the pulmonary venous blood volume, which forces fluids from the capillaries to back up and leak into the pulmonary tissues. This results in pulmonary edema, impaired oxygenation, and can ultimately lead to right-sided heart failure over time.

Ejection fraction (EF) is the percentage of blood volume pumped out by the ventricles with each contraction. The normal EF is 50 to 70 percent. An EF of 60 percent means that 60 percent of the available blood volume was pumped out of the LV during contraction. It is an important measurement for diagnosing and tracking the progression of HF. The EF also differentiates between diastolic and systolic HF.

Diastolic HF is currently referred to as **HF with normal ejection fraction** (HFNEF). The heart muscle contracts normally, but the ventricles do not adequately relax during ventricular filling. In **systolic HF**, or **heart failure with reduced ejection fraction** (HFrEF), the heart muscle does not contract effectively, so less blood is pumped out to the body.

There are several variables that both impact and are impacted by HF. A review of these variables will provide the backdrop for a closer look at the classification, sequelae, symptoms, and treatment of HF.

Cardiac output (CO, or Q) is the volume of blood being pumped by the heart in one minute. It is the product of heart rate multiplied by stroke volume. $CO = HR \times SV$

Stroke volume (SV) is the amount of blood pumped out of the ventricles per beat. Normal CO is between 4-8 liters per minute. Both CO and SV are reduced in HF.

Systemic vascular resistance (SVR) is related to the diameter and elasticity of blood vessels and the viscosity of blood. For example, narrow and stiff vessels and/or thicker blood will cause an increase in SVR. An increase in SVR causes the LV to work harder to overcome the pressure at the aortic valve. Conversely, larger and more elastic vessels and/or thin blood will decrease SVR and reduce cardiac workload.

Pulmonary vascular resistance (PVR) is the resistance level the blood must push against within the pulmonary vasculature. It is the difference between the mean pulmonary arterial pressure and the left atrial filling pressure. Resistance and blood viscosity impact both SVR and PVR. However, pulmonary blood flow, lung volume, and hypoxic vasoconstriction are unique to the pulmonary vasculature.

Preload is defined as the amount of ventricular stretch at the end of diastole, or when the chambers are filling. In other words, preload is the amount of pressure from the blood that is being exerted against the inside of the LV. It is also known as **left ventricular end-diastolic pressure** (LVEDP) and reflects the amount of stretch of cardiac muscle sarcomeres. **Afterload** is the amount of resistance the heart must overcome to open the aortic valve and push the blood volume into the systemic circulation.

Sequelae

Heart failure may have an acute or chronic onset, but it is progressive. When CO is diminished, tissues are not adequately perfused, and organs will ultimately fail. When the LV works harder because of increased preload or afterload, its muscular walls become thick and enlarged, resulting in ventricular hypertrophy. **Ventricular hypertrophy** causes ventricular remodeling (**cardiac remodeling**), which is a change to the heart's size, shape, structure, and physiological function.

The sympathetic nervous system responds to a diminished CO by increasing the heart rate, constricting arteries, and activating the **renin-angiotensin-aldosterone system** (RAAS). Elevated angiotensin levels raise BP and afterload, thereby prompting the heart to work harder. The reduced CO caused by HF can diminish blood flow to the kidneys. The kidneys respond to the decreased perfusion by secreting renin and activating the RAAS. As a result, the increase in aldosterone signals the body to retain Na^+ and water. Retained Na^+ and water leads to volume overload, pulmonary congestion, and hypertension. The body's response to reduced CO caused by HF can perpetuate a downward spiral. However, there are naturally occurring natriuretic peptides that are secreted in response to elevated pressures within the heart. These peptides counteract fluid retention and vasoconstriction.

Atrial natriuretic peptide (ANP) is secreted by the atria. **B-type natriuretic peptide** (BNP) is secreted by the ventricles. Both ANP and BNP cause diuresis, vasodilation, and decreased aldosterone secretion, thereby balancing the effects of sympathetic nervous system response and RAAS activation. Elevated levels of BNP are a diagnostic indication of HF.

Acute Exacerbations

Either an MI or a dysrhythmia can precipitate HF. The clinical presentation reflects congestion in the pulmonary and/or systemic vasculature. Treatment depends on the clinical stage of the disease. Common symptoms include:

- Dyspnea on exertion
- Fatigue
- Pulmonary congestion, which causes a cough and difficulty breathing when lying down
- Feelings of suffocation and anxiety that are worse at night
- Peripheral edema

Heart failure symptoms may vary based on the side of the heart affected. Symptoms of left-sided HF include tachycardia, shortness of breath, and the expectoration of frothy pink sputum. Pitting edema is symptomatic of right-sided HF and increased venous pressure that backs up into the tissues, causing peripheral edema. Ascites is a result of diffuse congestion in the liver caused by the increased venous pressure that characterizes right-sided heart failure.

The most common cause of HF exacerbation is fluid overload due to nonadherence to sodium and water restrictions. Patient education is crucial to avoid and manage exacerbations. Congestive heart failure is a core measure that is tied to patient satisfaction, patient education, subsequent readmissions in a defined period of time, and ultimately reimbursements.

Chronic

HF is strongly associated with chronic hypertension, CAD, and diabetes mellitus. **The New York Heart Association (NYHA) classification tool** is most frequently used to categorize the stages and symptom progression of HF as it relates to heart disease.

- Stage I: Cardiac disease; no symptoms during physical activity
- Stage II: Cardiac disease; slight limitations on physical activity
- Stage III: Cardiac disease; marked limitations during physical activity
- Stage IV: Cardiac disease; unable to perform physical activity; symptoms at rest

Therapy for HF focuses on three primary goals: reduction of preload, reduction of afterload (SVR), and inhibition of the RAAS and vasoconstrictive mechanisms of the sympathetic nervous system. Pharmacotherapy includes ACE inhibitors, angiotensin II receptor blockers (ARBs), diuretics, beta-blockers, vasodilators, and cardiac glycosides.

The ACE inhibitors and ARBs interfere with the RAAS by preventing the body's normal mechanism to retain fluids and constrict blood vessels. Diuretics decrease fluid volume and relieve both pulmonary and systemic congestion. Beta-blockers and cardiac glycosides slow the HR and strengthen the myocardium to improve contractility. Vasodilators decrease SVR. In addition to a thorough physical exam and complete medical history, a clinical work-up will include a chest x-ray, a BNP and other laboratory values, an ECG, and an echocardiogram or MUGA scan to measure EF.

HF is a common debilitating syndrome characterized by high mortality, frequent hospitalizations, multiple comorbidities, and poor quality of life. A partnership between providers, nurses, and patients is paramount to managing and slowing disease progression. Patient education should include a discussion of the disease process, prescribed medications, diet restrictions, and weight management. Patients

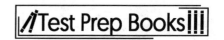

should know which symptoms require immediate medical care. Self-care can be the most important aspect of HF management. The nurse as educator performs an essential role in this and all disease management.

Hypertension

Hypertension (HTN) is an abnormally high BP (140/90 mmHg or higher). The diagnosis is based on two or more accurate readings that are elevated. HTN is known as the **silent killer**; while some patients may experience symptoms (e.g. severe headaches and vision changes), others will be asymptomatic. Several variables impact BP and understanding them is essential.

Variables

BP is the product of CO multiplied by SVR; $BP = CO \times SVR$. CO is the volume of blood being pumped by the heart in one minute. It is the product of HR multiplied by SV; $HR \times SV = CO$. SV is the amount of blood pumped out of the ventricles per beat.

SVR is related to the diameter of blood vessels and the viscosity of blood. The narrower the vessels or the thicker the blood, the higher the SVR. Conversely, larger-diameter vessels and thinner blood decrease SVR.

Mechanism

For HTN to develop, there must be a change in one or more factors affecting SVR or CO and a problem with the control system responsible for regulating BP. The body normally maintains and adjusts BP by either increasing the HR or the strength of myocardial contraction or by dilating or constricting the veins and arterioles.

When veins are dilated, less blood returns to the heart, and subsequently, less blood is pumped out of the heart. The result is a decrease in CO. Conversely, when veins are constricted, more blood is returned to the heart, and CO is increased. The arterioles also dilate or constrict. An expanded arteriole reduces resistance, and a constricted arteriole increases resistance. The veins and arterioles impact both CO and SVR. The kidneys contribute to the maintenance and adjustment of BP by controlling Na^+, chloride, and water excretion and through the RAAS. Management of HTN will focus on one or more of the factors that regulate BP. Those regulatory factors are SVR, fluid volume, and the strength and rate of myocardial contraction.

Classification

HTN is classified as primary or secondary depending on the etiology. In **primary HTN**, the cause is unknown, but the key factors include problems related to the natriuretic hormones, RAAS, or electrolyte disturbances. Primary HTN is also known as essential or idiopathic HTN.

In **secondary HTN**, there is an identifiable cause. Associated disease states include kidney disease, adrenal gland tumors, thyroid disease, congenital blood vessel disorders, alcohol abuse, and obstructive sleep apnea. Products associated with secondary HTN are nonsteroidal anti-inflammatory drugs (NSAIDs), birth control pills, decongestants, cocaine, amphetamines, and corticosteroids.

HTN normally increases with age, and it is more prominent among African Americans.

BP is classified according to treatment guidelines as normal, elevated blood pressure (prehypertension), Stage 1 HTN, and Stage 2 HTN. **Normal blood pressure** is a systolic reading of <120 mmHg AND diastolic reading of <80 mmHg. Elevated blood pressure (referred to as **prehypertension**) is defined as a systolic reading ranging from 120 to 129 mmHg AND a diastolic reading maintaining <80 mmHg. **Stage 1 HTN** includes either a systolic reading ranging from 130 to 139 mmHg OR a diastolic reading ranging from 80 to 89 mmHg. In the more severe **Stage 2 HTN**, the systolic reading is 140 mmHg or higher OR the diastolic reading is 90 mmHg or higher.

Sequelae
Systolic pressure is the amount of pressure exerted on arterial walls immediately after ventricular contraction and emptying. This represents the highest level of pressure during the cardiac cycle. **Diastolic pressure** is the amount of pressure exerted on arterial walls when the heart is filling. This represents the lowest pressure during the cardiac cycle. In general, hypertension increases the risk of cardiovascular disease; however, **diastolic hypertension** specifically poses the greatest risk.

Prolonged HTN damages the delicate endothelial layer of vessels. The damaged endothelium initiates the inflammatory response and clotting cascade. As mentioned, the diameter of veins, arterioles, and arteries changes SVR. When SVR is increased, the heart must work harder to pump against the increased pressure. In other words, the pressure in the LV must be higher than the pressure being exerted on the opposite side of the aortic valve by systemic vascular pressure. The ventricular pressure must overcome the aortic pressure for contraction and ventricular emptying to occur. When the myocardium works against an elevated systemic pressure for a prolonged period of time, the LV will enlarge, and HF may ensue.

Risk Factors
There are both modifiable and nonmodifiable risk factors associated with the development of HTN. Modifiable risk factors include obesity, a sedentary lifestyle, tobacco use, a diet high in sodium, dyslipidemia, excessive alcohol consumption, stress, sleep apnea, and diabetes. Age, race, and family history are nonmodifiable risk factors.

Treatment
First-line treatments include lifestyle changes and pharmacologic therapy.

Initial therapy includes diuretics, CCBs, ACE inhibitors, and ARBs. Diuretics decrease fluid volume, while CCBs decrease myocardial contractility. Both ACE inhibitors and ARBs interfere with the RAAS by preventing the normal mechanism that retains fluids and narrows blood vessels. The result is decreased volume and SVR.

Summary
The astute nurse will conduct an in-depth patient interview to identify prescribed and illicit drug use, alcohol and tobacco use, family history, sleep patterns, and dietary habits. Patient education should include information about the **Dietary Approach to Stop Hypertension (DASH) diet** and alcohol in moderation with a limit of one to two drinks per day. Aerobic exercise and resistance training three to four times weekly for an average of 40 minutes is recommended. Information about prescribed hypertensive medications should also be reviewed with the patient.

Hypertensive Crisis

A **hypertensive crisis** is defined as a BP higher than 180/120 mmHg. BP must be lowered quickly to prevent end organ damage. Pregnancy, an acute MI, a dissecting aortic aneurysm, and an intracranial hemorrhage are associated with a hypertensive crisis. The therapeutic goal is to reduce the BP by 25 percent within the first hour of treatment, with a continual reduction over the following 2 to 6 hours and an ongoing reduction to the target goal over a period of days. Short-acting antihypertensive medications administered intravenously is the primary treatment.

Structural Heart Procedures

Transcatheter Aortic Valve Replacement/Implantation (TAVR/TAVI)
A **transcatheter aortic valve replacement** (TAVR) or **transcatheter aortic valve implantation** (TAVI) is a minimally invasive cardiac procedure where a replacement valve is placed within the aorta. The valve is placed either through the femoral artery or through a laparoscopic site in the chest to enter an artery (often the subclavian) into the heart. TAVR/TAVI is indicated for patients with severe aortic stenosis, especially elderly patients who do not qualify for surgical valve replacement, such as those with severe heart failure.

Severe aortic stenosis may first be identified based on symptoms such as chest pain, fatigue, shortness of breath, and edema to extremities. The nurse or physician may also hear a murmur when auscultating the patient's heart. An ECG and x-ray imaging will likely be performed and may show signs of hypertrophy or pulmonary edema, but this may not appear for all patients. An echocardiogram is the definitive diagnostic indicator of severe aortic stenosis and the need for a TAVR/TAVI.

Directly before and after the procedure, TAVR/TAVI patients are likely to be placed on an antibiotic, such as a cephalosporin or vancomycin, to prevent infection from the procedure itself. These patients will also likely be placed on antiplatelet therapy, such as aspirin or clopidogrel, long-term to prevent the formation of thrombus at the site of the valve replacement. It is also possible that the patient will need to continue their medications for their aortic stenosis, such as diuretics and blood pressure medications.

Nursing management of TAVR/TAVI is dependent upon whether the patient is awaiting the procedure or has already had the procedure. Prior to the procedure, they will need to be NPO for at least 8 hours (due to risk of aspiration during sedation), placed on continuous cardiac monitoring, and provide informed consent. While nurses may assist in educating the patient on what to expect during and after the procedure, the physician performing the procedure should provide definitive education and obtain informed consent. Following the procedure, the nurse will continue to monitor the patient's vitals and ECG, as the patient is at an increased risk of arrhythmia. If the femoral artery was used for access, the nurse should monitor for signs of bleeding to the site and apply pressure to the area as needed. Although elevated troponin levels may be expected directly following the procedure, these should be reported to the physician in case they are a sign of ischemia. Upon discharging the patient, the nurse should provide patient education on their new medications and the need to have regular follow-up with cardiology.

Transcatheter Mitral Valve Repair (TMVr)
A **transcatheter mitral valve repair** (TMVr) is a minimally invasive cardiac procedure in which a catheter is inserted through the femoral vein into the heart to place a clip on the mitral valve, allowing the valve to close properly. TMVr is indicated in patients with severe **mitral valve regurgitation**, which is caused

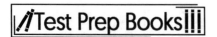

by a backup of blood in the heart due to an inability of the mitral valve to close sufficiently. Mitral valve regurgitation can lead to atrial fibrillation and heart failure.

Patients with mitral valve regurgitation that may indicate the need for a TMVr will often present signs of heart failure or uncontrolled atrial fibrillation, such as fatigue, chest pain, shortness of breath, palpitations, and extremity swelling. Auscultation of the heart may reveal a heart murmur. An ECG may show the patient in atrial flutter or atrial fibrillation, while an x-ray may show cardiomyopathy and/or pulmonary edema. If the patient is in heart failure, their BNP may be elevated. Echocardiography is the definitive diagnostic tool for determining if the patient's condition indicates that a TMVr would be beneficial.

Directly before and after the procedure, TMVr patients are likely to be placed on an antibiotic, such as a cephalosporin or vancomycin, to prevent risk of infection related to the procedure. These patients will also likely be placed on anticoagulant therapy, such as warfarin, long-term to prevent the formation of thrombus at the site of the valve replacement. It is also possible that the patient will need to continue their medications for their mitral valve regurgitation, such as diuretics, rate control medications, and blood pressure medications.

Similar to the TAVR/TAVI patient, preparation of the TMVr patient includes remaining NPO for at least 8 hours prior, continuous cardiac monitoring, and ensuring informed consent is obtained by the physician. Following the procedure, care is also performed in a similar manner of monitoring the patient's vitals and ECG (as the patient is at an increased risk of arrhythmia) and for signs of bleeding if the femoral artery was used (applying pressure to the area as needed). Likewise, elevated troponin levels directly following the procedure are expected but should still be reported to the physician. Upon discharging the patient, the nurse should provide patient education on their new medications (especially if being placed on an anticoagulant) and the need to have regular follow-up with cardiology. TMVr patients are also at increased risk of thrombus formation; therefore, education should include signs of stroke and myocardial infarction as well as when to seek care for these symptoms.

Valvular Heart Disease

Stenosis and insufficiency due to regurgitation are the two most common processes associated with valvular heart disease.

Valvular stenosis is described as a stiffening of the valvular leaflets which increases the pressure required to move the blood through the valve, leading to enlargement of the cardiac chambers and decreased cardiac output. Common causes of stenosis include congenital abnormalities, rheumatic heart disease, and calcification of the valve leaflets due to altered mineral metabolism and atherosclerosis.

Valvular insufficiency occurs when the valvular leaflets do not close completely, allowing regurgitation of the blood back to the original chamber, which eventually decreases cardiac output. Insufficiency is most often due to congenital defects, rheumatic fever, endocarditis, and coronary artery disease. The patient with mild valvular dysfunction may be asymptomatic; however, valvular disease is most often progressive, resulting in the eventual onset of fatigue, dyspnea, syncope, and chest tightness. Open and percutaneous valve repair or replacement procedures are considered based on the individual patient and the specific defect.

Aortic

Aortic stenosis may be caused by a congenital defect or acquired. The most common congenital defect of the aortic valve is an alteration in the number of valvular leaflets. The resulting anatomical shape of the valve increases the bending motion of the valve during systole, which restricts the opening of the valve and increases friction on the valve as it closes. The resulting damage to the endothelium and the formation of fibrotic areas results in symptomatic disease in younger patients. The most common acquired defect is the calcification of the valve leaflets that appears to be associated with the development of atherosclerosis and calcification in other areas of the cardiac vasculature.

Aortic regurgitation or insufficiency may be caused by endocarditis with vegetative growth on the valve leaflets, rheumatic fever, collagen vascular diseases, chest trauma, or damage related to the use of a left ventricular assist device (LVAD).

A **ventricular assist device** (VAD) is a device that is surgically attached to the heart and assists in pumping blood from the left ventricle, into the aorta, and out to the body's circulation. A VAD is indicated for patients who have severe heart failure, either as a permanent solution or as a temporary treatment while the patient awaits a heart transplant. Following the surgery to implant the device, the patient will likely be transferred to an intensive care unit (ICU). The progressive care nurse may see patients with a VAD after they have recovered sufficiently to leave the ICU or if they are being admitted and already have the device implanted.

Patients with a VAD require frequent vial sign monitoring, continuous cardiac monitoring in case of arrhythmias, and assessment for worsening heart failure. Signs of worsening heart failure include chest pain, shortness of breath, orthopnea, crackles in lung sounds, edema, sudden weight gain, and BNP elevation. Additionally, these patients will likely be placed on anticoagulation therapy (to prevent the formation of a thrombus in the device) and on antihypertensive medications (to maintain the patient's blood pressure). With the anticoagulation therapy in place, the nurse should monitor for signs of uncontrolled bleeding as well as signs that the therapy has been insufficient, such as deep vein thrombosis, myocardial infarction, pulmonary embolism, or stroke. The nurse should also closely monitor the patient's blood pressure, maintaining a mean arterial pressure (MAP) between 60 and 90 mmHg. This is to ensure that the patient achieves sufficient perfusion while avoiding an elevated blood pressure that could overwhelm or damage the device. Discharge instructions should include bleeding precautions from the anticoagulation and how to monitor for the following at home: blood pressure, signs of worsening heart failure (daily weights), and signs of increased edema.

Mitral

Mitral valve stenosis can be caused by rheumatic fever, or more rarely by a congenital defect. The condition evolves slowly with the gradual deposition of vegetative growths that eventually thicken and calcify the leaflets, resulting in the narrowing of the pathway from the left atria to the left ventricle.

Mitral valve insufficiency occurs as a result of mitral valve prolapse, endocarditis, rheumatic disease, or ischemic heart disease. The regurgitation of the blood from the left ventricle to the left atrium results from any alteration in the valve structure. This condition often develops gradually; however, rapid onset of the insufficiency is common when occurring concurrently with left-sided heart failure.

Mitral valve prolapse results from enlargement of the bicuspid leaflets and redundancy of the chordae tendineae that attach to the ventricular endocardium. This process may be the result of an inherited disorder, Marfan syndrome, hyperthyroidism, or alterations in the autonomic nervous system. The condition is more prevalent in women.

Vascular Disease

Peripheral vascular disease (PVD) refers to diseases of the blood vessels that are outside the heart and brain. The term PVD is commonly used interchangeably with **peripheral arterial disease** (PAD), but there should be a clear understanding of the difference in the two conditions. While PVD refers to any vasculature that is outside of the heart and brain, PAD is specific to only peripheral arterial—most commonly the lower extremities. The primary factor for the development of both PVD and PAD is the narrowing of peripheral vessels caused by atherosclerosis; however, PVD can also be caused by venous insufficiency, a DVT, and some infections or inflammatory processes. The narrowing can be compounded by emboli or thrombi. Limb ischemia due to reduced blood flow can result in the loss of limb or life.

PVD encompasses several conditions: atherosclerosis, Buerger's disease, chronic venous insufficiency, deep vein thrombosis (DVT), Raynaud's phenomenon, thrombophlebitis, and varicose veins.

CAD, atrial fibrillation, cerebrovascular disease, and renal disease are common comorbidities. Risk factors include smoking, phlebitis, injury, surgery, and hyperviscosity of the blood. Autoimmune disorders and hyperlipidemia are also common factors. The two major complications of PVD are limb complications or loss and the risk for stroke or heart attack.

Intermittent claudication (cramping pain in the leg during exercise) may be the sole manifestation of early symptomatic PVD. It occurs with exercise and stops with rest. Physical findings during examination may include the classic **five P's**: pulselessness, paralysis, paresthesia, pain, and pallor of the extremity.

The most critical symptom of PVD is **critical limb ischemia** (CLI), which is pain that occurs in the affected limb during rest. Manifestations of PVD may include the following symptoms:

- Feet that are cool or cold to the touch
- Aching or burning in the legs that is relieved by sitting
- Pale color when legs are elevated
- Redness when legs are in a hanging-down (dependent) position
- Brittle, thin, or shiny skin on the legs and feet
- Loss of hair on feet
- Nonhealing wounds or ulcers over pressure points
- Loss of muscle or fatty tissue
- Numbness, weakness, or heaviness in muscles
- Reddish-blue discoloration of the extremities
- Restricted mobility
- Thickened, opaque toenails

The **ankle-brachial index** (ABI) should be measured. The ABI is the systolic pressure of the ankle, divided by the systolic pressure of the arm. It is a specific and sensitive indicator of peripheral artery disease (PAD). The **Allen test** looks for an occlusion of either the radial or ulnar arteries; the test is performed by applying compression to these arteries in the hand, followed by the release of pressure to restore blood flow and observation of the length of time required for reperfusion. A Doppler ultrasonography flow study can determine the patency of peripheral arteries.

The patient should be assessed for heart murmurs, and all peripheral pulses should be evaluated for quality and bruit. An ECG may reveal an arrhythmia. Because the presence of atherosclerosis initiates an inflammatory response, inflammatory markers such as the D-dimer, CRP, interleukin 6, and homocysteine may be present. Blood urea nitrogen (BUN) and creatinine levels may provide indications of decreased organ perfusion. A lipid profile may reveal the risk for atherosclerosis. A stress test or angiogram may be necessary.

The two main goals for treatment of PVD are to control the symptoms and halt the progression to lower the risk of heart attack and stroke. Specific treatment modalities depend on the extent and severity of the disease, the patient's age, overall medical history, clinical signs, and their preferences. Lifestyle modifications include smoking cessation, improved nutrition, and regular exercise. Aggressive treatment of comorbidities can also aid in stopping the progression. Pharmacotherapy may include anticoagulants and vasodilators.

Carotid Artery Stenosis

Carotid artery stenosis is a subcategory of peripheral vascular insufficiency involving the arteries of the neck that supply the brain with nutrient-filled blood. This condition may exist long before symptoms occur, as the narrowing may not be severe enough to significantly reduce blood flow to the brain. Stenosis, the narrowing of a blood vessel, in this case is most often caused by atherosclerosis. This entails the building up of a fatty substance called **plaque** inside the artery walls, which leads to reduced blood flow.

An acute condition involving carotid artery stenosis is when a clot occurs at the site of the stenosis, interrupting blood flow completely. This leads to a **transient ischemic attack** (TIA), or worse, a **cerebrovascular accident** (CVA), commonly referred to as a **stroke**. A TIA is an episode that mimics stroke symptoms, such as slurring of speech, drooping of face, and other neurologic deficits, and lasts for less than an hour but greater than 5 minutes. There is no long-term damage, as the episode is transient enough that no brain tissue is injured. A TIA may be the first clue to signal that the patient has carotid artery stenosis, as there may be few to no symptoms beforehand.

Risk factors for developing carotid artery stenosis include alcohol abuse, hypertension, smoking, hyperlipidemia, diabetes, obesity, stress, heart disease, drug abuse (especially cocaine and amphetamines), vascular inflammation, history of stroke, and old age. Smoking cessation information should be given to the patient to encourage them to quit.

Carotid artery stenosis is most commonly diagnosed with carotid ultrasound, using sonography to visualize the arterial structures in the neck. Other tests that may be ordered include carotid angiography, magnetic resonance angiography, and computerized tomography angiography (CTA).

The arteries may be stented or partially removed to correct the stenosis. Antiplatelet and anticoagulant therapies will be used to prevent future blood clots.

Minimally Invasive Interventions

Endografts

Peripheral vascular disease is broadly defined as atherosclerotic alterations in the vasculature outside of the heart; however, the general understanding of the term refers to occlusive disease of the arms or legs that most commonly affects the aortic-iliac segment, the femoropopliteal segment, and the tibial arteries. The manifestations are related to the progressive decrease in the arterial circulation to the legs

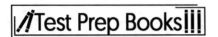

and may include intermittent claudication, pain at rest, development of arterial ulcers, pallor, and diminished peripheral pulses. The most common risk factors associated with the development of the disease are hypertension, smoking, male gender, history of the disease in a first-degree relative, obesity, atherosclerosis with abnormal cholesterol levels, diabetes, and chronic renal failure.

The disease can compromise circulation to the extremities by gradually decreasing the lumen of the vessels due to plaque formation or by sudden total occlusion due to thrombus formation. The manifestations are associated with the etiology and the extent of the available collateral circulation to the limb. Treatment is aimed at eliminating or treating the risk factors and restoring the arterial blood supply. Angioplasty with the placement of a peripheral **endograft** in the occluded artery is a common choice. The vessel is expanded to allow normal blood flow, and the endograft is placed to maintain the patency of the vessel. Continued surveillance of the integrity of the endograft is necessary to identify and treat possible leakage from that area.

Peripheral stents
Peripheral stents are another option to attempt to open occluded arteries in a patient with **peripheral arterial disease** (PAD). Stent placement occurs at the same time as angioplasty, in which a small thin catheter is threaded into the affected blood vessel, and a tiny balloon is inflated to "pop" open the lumen of the blood vessel. Then, stent placement can occur.

The stent is, in most cases, a tiny metal, mesh-like tube that provides a scaffolding or support structure to keep a blood vessel open. The stent remains in the patient's blood vessel permanently, although it is possible to remove a stent if absolutely necessary.

Antiplatelet and antithrombotic therapies are used in the postoperative period to reduce the risk of stent thrombosis.

Peripheral Arterial Occlusions
When an artery or vein is blocked by a clot, the occlusion is termed a **thrombosis**. Clot formation is a normal hemostatic adjustment that occurs in a healthy individual to prevent excessive bleeding and promote wound healing. Inappropriate clotting, however, can interrupt critical blood flow and thus oxygen delivery to the tissues of the body. Interruption in oxygen delivery, if not corrected, will lead to tissue damage and death.

Occlusion of an artery may sometimes occur because of **atherosclerosis**, in which fatty deposits, called **plaques**, build up over time, sticking to the walls of the vessels. These fatty deposits are composed of lipids, inflamed smooth muscle cells, and a connective tissue matrix composed of thrombi in various stages, as well as calcium deposits.

A person may not know that they have atherosclerosis until a plaque bursts or occludes blood flow, causing ischemic conditions such as stroke or heart attack.

Persons who smoke should be encouraged to cease, as smoking is one of the greatest risk factors for developing atherosclerosis. Nicotine and other chemicals found in cigarettes or cigar smoke are toxic to the inner lining of blood vessels. These toxins inflame and scar the vascular endothelium, not only increasing the risk of plaque accumulation, but also causing vasoconstriction. Vasoconstriction in already narrowed blood vessels increases BP and puts the smoker in danger of other life-threatening events.

Other risk factors for atherosclerosis include hyperlipidemia, diabetes, family history, sedentary lifestyle, obesity, and hypertension.

To confirm a diagnosis of atherosclerosis, the affected blood vessels need to be visualized by imaging techniques such as angiography or ultrasonography.

Modifications in lifestyle such as diet, exercise, and smoking cessation will be encouraged for the patient with atherosclerosis. Drug therapy will include antiplatelets (e.g., aspirin at 100 mg daily) and statins for targeting lipids (e.g., atorvastatin at 40–80 mg daily).

Peripheral Surgical Interventions
Femoropopliteal bypass
A **femoropopliteal bypass graft** (fem pop bypass) is a surgical procedure that reroutes blood in the leg past an occluded section of artery, caused by atherosclerosis. The patient's own vein may be used, or an artificial vein will be used, though this presents a risk for narrowing over time. The vein bypasses the occlusion starting at the femoral artery and ending at the popliteal artery in the knee.

Femoropopliteal Bypass

Blockage

Graft being sewn into place

This procedure is used for patients with severe claudication. **Claudication** is a word of Latin origin, originally meaning "limp," but in this case, it means severe pain in the legs caused by restricted blood supply. Claudication may occur in the feet or, most commonly, in the calves. The patient may also be experiencing sores that will not heal or gangrene due to restricted blood flow. The bypass will reinstate healthy blood flow to previously ischemic areas, hopefully alleviating symptoms.

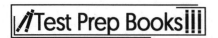

Patients should be encouraged to quit smoking before the procedure to prevent complications and promote overall health. Smoking cessation information and resources should be shared early and often.

Patients will be anesthetized for the procedure. Blood transfusion is a distinct possibility to maintain volume and replace blood loss. The incision made by the surgeon is generally 4 to 8 inches in length, in the groin area where the femoral artery is located. Internal stitches will be made to secure the graft in place. The patient may be in surgery anywhere from 1 to 6 hours depending on the complexity of the surgery.

Following the procedure, the nurse will need to monitor the incision site for infection, bleeding, and/or hematoma. Hemodynamic monitoring will be in place to watch for hypotension, which could indicate bleeding, or hypertension, which could put added pressure on the healing graft. The patient will be started on antiplatelet and antithrombotic therapy to prevent clotting and restenosis of the vessels.

Peripheral Venous Thrombosis

A common venous occlusion is a **deep vein thrombosis** (DVT). Although DVTs may be asymptomatic, the common presentation is redness, pain, and swelling over the site of the clot. Common sites for DVT are the lower extremities, specifically the superficial femoral, popliteal, posterior tibial, or peroneal veins in the calves. Formation of DVTs occurs due to impaired venous return, an injury to the endothelium such as leg fractures, or in states of hypercoagulability, in which the body is more apt to form clots. Impaired venous return is common in immobile patients. Therefore, early ambulation is encouraged as well as mobility exercises while the patient is still in bed, to prevent clots.

DVTs in the lower extremities have a high correlation with patients also developing pulmonary embolisms (PEs), or blood clots that travel to the lungs. This is a life-threatening situation. Other complications of DVTs include a chronic insufficiency of the veins and post-thrombotic (postphlebitic) syndrome, in which a patient feels aching, cramping, pain, and other symptoms in the legs that worsen with walking or standing and are relieved by resting.

A **D-dimer** is the test used to help diagnose a DVT. A negative result rules out a DVT, while a positive is not 100 percent conclusive. A positive D-dimer requires further testing, usually ultrasonography, to confirm the diagnosis. History and physical examination are also helpful in determining the probability of a DVT.

If left untreated, there is a risk that the patient will develop a life-threatening PE; therefore, prompt detection and treatment are vital. Treatment is usually with anticoagulants, such as subcutaneous heparin for a short period, followed by a longer period of oral warfarin. Pain control with acetaminophen may be included in the treatment plan, along with leg elevation with pillows while the patient is at rest, being careful to avoid venous compression, which could lead to clot dislodgement.

Practice Quiz

1. What emergency surgery is necessary to relieve cardiac tamponade?
   a. Thoracentesis
   b. Pericardiocentesis
   c. Left heart cardiac catheterization
   d. Open heart surgery

2. A progressive care nurse is caring for a patient who is being treated with a DDD pacemaker. Which of the following ECG findings is the nurse's main concern?
   a. The interval between the pacing spike and the R wave is consistent.
   b. The R wave of the captured beats is a negative complex.
   c. The patient's native rhythm is a second-degree AV degree block.
   d. Every complex has a 0.20 second PR interval.

3. The nurse is aware that the congenital and acquired alterations in the mitral and aortic valves have a significant impact on the function of the valves. Which of the following statements correctly identifies the resulting pathology?
   a. A tricuspid aortic valve causes stenosis but does not result in regurgitation.
   b. A unicuspid mitral valve has five leaflets, which causes heart failure in the elderly.
   c. Acquired alterations are symptomatic earlier than congenital alterations.
   d. Endocarditis results in the deposition of vegetative complexes that prevent valve closure.

4. What is the pathway of oxygenated blood from the lungs?
   a. Lungs to the left atrium, through the mitral valve into the left ventricle, pumped into the aorta upon contraction, then dispersed to tissues via a network of arteries and capillaries
   b. Lungs to the right atrium, through the mitral valve into the right ventricle, pumped into the aorta upon contraction, then dispersed to tissues via a network of arteries and veins
   c. Lungs to the left atrium, directly to the right aorta, then dispersed to tissues via a network of arteries and capillaries
   d. Lungs to the left atrium, through the septum valve, stored in the left ventricles, then dispersed to tissues via a network of arteries and capillaries

5. Which procedure uses a small, inflated balloon to treat arterial blockages?
   a. Coronary bypass surgery
   b. Defibrillation
   c. Coronary angioplasty
   d. Laparoscopy

See answers on the next page.

Answer Explanations

1. B: Pericardiocentesis is indicated in the emergent situation of cardiac tamponade. A needle is inserted, and the hemorrhaging blood is aspirated from the pericardial sac. Thoracentesis, or pleural tap, can be used for hemothorax or pneumothorax, making Choice *A* incorrect. Left cardiac catheterization is used in acute myocardial infarctions to open obstructed coronary vessels, making Choice *C* incorrect. Open heart surgery can be performed in emergency situations involving thoracic trauma, but not specifically for cardiac tamponade, making Choice *D* incorrect.

2. B: The function of the DDD pacemaker can result in asystole if the patient has an underlying AV block because any R wave that is incorrectly identified by the pacemaker inhibits ventricular output and resets the refractory period. In this instance, the atrial pacemaker is functioning properly, but the signals from the atria are blocked in the diseased AV pathways. Choices *A* and *C* are normal patterns for paced rhythms. Choice *D* represents a normal sinus rhythm, rather than a paced rhythm.

3. D: Endocarditis results in areas of inflammation along the surface of the valve that support vegetative growth, which eventually occupies space thereby preventing the adequate closure of the valve leaflets. Alterations in the number of cusps in the mitral or aortic valves are associated with both stenosis and regurgitation because the anatomical shape of the valve is distorted. The repeated bending of the misshapen valve and the resulting stress on the chordae tendineae can affect either the diameter of the open valve (leading to stenotic changes), or incomplete closure of the valve (leading to regurgitation), making Choice *A* incorrect. A unicuspid mitral valve has one cusp, which results in heart failure in the neonate, making Choice *B* incorrect. Congenital valve defects are most commonly diagnosed before adulthood depending on the characteristics of the alteration. Acquired defects are associated with progressive vascular events such as atherosclerosis and the effects of diabetes. Therefore, Choice *C* is incorrect.

4. A: This path correctly describes where blood flows after leaving the lungs in order to reach the tissues of the body. The other paths listed are incorrect, out of order, and list fictitious structures.

5. C: Coronary angioplasty inflates a small balloon inside the blocked artery to break down the blockages and widen the pathway through which blood can flow. A coronary bypass surgery, Choice *A*, reroutes blood from unhealthy vessels to healthier ones. Defibrillation, Choice *B*, tries to reset the electrical rhythm of the heart. Laparoscopy, Choice *D*, refers to surgical procedures that take place in the torso.

Respiratory

Working in tandem with the cardiovascular system is the respiratory (also referred to as pulmonary) system, composed of the two lungs and the airway. Airway and breathing are part of the airway, breathing, circulation (ABC) mnemonic representing the patient's most vital functions. While each bodily system serves a unique and vital function, the respiratory system represents two of the three priority assessments in an emergent situation—following the ABC mnemonic.

The nursing assessment of the respiratory system is multifaceted and includes an in-depth review of the patient's overall pulmonary status. First, the nurse should assess the depth of respirations and note if breaths are shallow or deep, and then assess the rhythm and note whether it is even or uneven. Next, the nurse should assess the level of effort needed to breathe. Continuing on, the nurse should note chest expansion (including symmetry), along with any presence of a cough (productive or nonproductive). Finally, the nurse should auscultate the lungs to assess air exchange throughout and determine the presence of adventitious, absent, lowered, diminished, or distant sounds.

Various patterns of respiration exist; therefore, the nurse must closely examine the patient to ensure accuracy in the assessment. Normal respirations for a resting adult are regular, comfortable, and at a rate of 12-20 breaths per minute. If the rate is lower than 12 breaths per minute, the patient is displaying **bradypnea**; if the rate is higher than 20 breaths per minute, the patient is displaying **tachypnea**. **Hyperventilation** is when the rate is higher than 20 breaths per minute, accompanied by deep breathing. Similar to hyperventilation, **hyperpnea** also encompasses deep, rapid breathing, but is typically in response to an increase in oxygen demand—therefore not altering blood gases. **Cheyne-Stokes respiration** involves varying periods of increased depth, alternating with periods of **apnea**, which is breathlessness. **Kussmaul respirations** involve rapid, deep, and labored breaths. **Biot respirations** (also referred to as cluster breathing) are irregular and disorganized respirations with random periods of apnea.

In order to measure the oxygen level of the blood, the nurse should place a **pulse oximeter** on the patient's finger; this device provides an indirect reading that displays how well oxygen is reaching peripheral areas of the body, noted as SpO_2. The pulse oximetry must be interpreted, and then appropriate action must take place, including determining the patient's need for continuous or intermittent monitoring. When additional information is warranted, such as during periods of alterations from normal (e.g., outside of either the reference range or the patient's usual baseline), an invasive measurement can be obtained via laboratory blood work. This method is used to gather direct arterial oxygen saturation levels (SaO_2). While both laboratory analysis and pulse oximetry display the arterial oxygen saturation level, noting the finding through the use of SpO_2 terminology simply denotes that the level was obtained via pulse oximetry rather than via arterial blood gas sampling. **End-tidal carbon dioxide** ($ETCO_2$) monitoring, also called **capnography**, is a noninvasive technique used to measure the amount of CO_2 at the end of exhalation, which is displayed as a plateau waveform in terms of mmHg. Measured with a nasal prong device equipped with sensors, the normal range value for capnography is 5–6 percent CO_2, or 35-45 mmHg. These values are important for understanding cardiac output and pulmonary blood flow. While capnography can adequately measure ventilation, there is no indication of oxygenation status. Capnography can provide an earlier detection of hypoventilation, including the impending poor oxygenation, sooner than pulse oximetry.

A two-step system should be used when assessing **arterial blood gases (ABGs)**. First, the care team should check the pH level to determine if an imbalance exists; however, it is important to note that even if the pH is normal, the patient may still be suffering from a disturbance, as the system attempts to compensate to maintain homeostasis. Review of various levels, including pH, $PaCO_2$, PaO_2, HCO_3-, and O_2 saturation, helps the care team to understand a complete clinical picture of acid-base manifestations.

If **acidosis** is present, the pH will be below 7.35; alternatively, a pH above 7.45 is indicative of **alkalosis**, as normal blood pH is around 7.4. If an imbalance is detected, the care team must determine the primary cause of the disturbance. The nurse should look to the primary abnormal lab value to determine the cause of the acid-base imbalance. For a respiratory imbalance, the $PaCO_2$ or serum CO_2 will be abnormal. For a metabolic imbalance, the HCO_3- will be abnormal. The body can respond with either partial or full compensation. If a metabolic disturbance is occurring, the respiratory system will likely compensate; if a respiratory imbalance is occurring, the renal system will likely compensate.

Arterial blood gases are drawn using a heparinized syringe. The blood should not come into contact with room air and should be transported to the lab immediately. In the event of a delay in the transfer or inability of the lab to process the blood sample immediately, the sample should be placed on ice. Simple hypoxia may be seen in acute respiratory distress and pneumonia. Acidosis is seen in chronic obstructive pulmonary disease (COPD), lung edema, shock, and diabetes mellitus. Alkalosis is seen in anxiety disorders, vomiting, and diuretic use. The nurse must understand that hypoventilation may lead to respiratory acidosis, while hyperventilation may lead to respiratory alkalosis. Alterations in acid-base status are closely monitored and fluctuations in ABGs are reported to the care team and the patient.

Normal ABG values:

- pH: 7.35-7.45
- $PaCO_2$: 35-45 mm Hg
- PaO_2: 75-100 mm Hg
- HCO_3-: 22-26 mEq/L
- O_2 sat: 95%-100%

Venous blood gases (VBG) are a measurement of the patient's venous pH, partial pressure of oxygen (pO_2), partial pressure of carbon dioxide (pCO_2), and bicarbonate (HCO_3-). Venous blood gases are used to determine the effectiveness of the body's perfusion of O_2 and CO_2, along with determining if the patient may be in compensated or uncompensated acidosis or alkalosis. A low pH would indicate uncompensated acidosis. If this is related to respiratory distress, the patient may require a higher level of oxygen supplementation, such as high-flow oxygen, BiPAP, or even intubation. If the acidosis is metabolic, the patient may require pharmacologic intervention to correct the metabolic cause. For example, a patient with diabetic ketoacidosis may require an insulin drip to lower their blood sugar and treat ketosis. Other patients may require a sodium bicarbonate infusion to increase their pH level. On the other hand, patients with an elevated pH (alkalosis) may require interventions such as treating metabolic electrolyte imbalances and, if the cause is respiratory, treating the cause of hyperventilation.

Normal VBG values:

- pH: 7.31-7.41
- pO2: 35-45 mmHg
- pCO2: 41-51 mmHg

- HCO_3^-: 22-26 mmol/L

Acute Respiratory Distress Syndrome

Acute respiratory distress syndrome (ARDS) is the widespread inflammation of the lungs and capillaries of the alveoli and results in the rapid development of pulmonary system failure. It can occur in both adults and children and is considered the most severe form of acute lung injury. Presence of the syndrome is determined by:

- Timing: Onset of symptoms within one week of inciting incident
- Chest x-ray: Bilateral lung infiltrates not explained by consolidation, atelectasis, or effusions
- Origin of edema: Not explained by heart failure or fluid overload
- Severity of hypoxemia

It should be noted that the severity of hypoxemia is based on PaO_2/FiO_2 ratio while on 5 cm of continuous positive airway pressure (CPAP). PaO_2 is the partial pressure of oxygen, while FiO_2 is the fraction of inspired oxygen. Categories are:

- Mild (PaO_2/FiO_2 = 200–300)
- Moderate (PaO_2/FiO_2 = 100–200)
- Severe ($PaO_2/FiO_2 \leq 100$)

ARDS has a high mortality rate (30–40 percent), which increases with advancing age and severity of disease. It also leads to significant morbidity because of its association with extended hospital stays, frequent nosocomial (hospital-acquired) infections, muscle weakness, significant weight loss, and functional impairment. The most common cause of ARDS is sepsis, a life-threatening bacterial infection of the blood. Other common causes include:

- Severe pneumonia
- Inhalation of toxic fumes
- Trauma (such as falls, bone fractures, motor vehicle accidents, near drowning, and burns)
- Massive blood transfusion

It should also be noted that, for one in five patients with ARDS, there will be no identifiable risk factors. Therefore, the cause of ARDS may not be evident.

The onset of ARDS symptoms is fairly rapid, occurring 12 to 48 hours after the inciting incident. Many of the signs and symptoms of ARDS are nonspecific. Signs and symptoms of ARDS can include:

- Dyspnea (initially with exertion, but rapidly progressing to occurring even at rest)
- Hypoxia
- Tachypnea
- Tachycardia
- Fever
- Bilateral rales
- Cyanosis
- Hypotension
- Fatigue

The diagnosis of ARDS is clinical since there is no specific test for the condition. Diagnosing ARDS is done by exclusion, ruling out other diseases that mimic its signs and symptoms. Tests used to diagnose ARDS can include:

- Chest x-ray: by definition, should reveal bilateral lung infiltrates
- ABGs: usually reveal extreme hypoxemia and respiratory alkalosis or metabolic acidosis
- CBC with differential: can reveal leukocytosis, leukopenia, and/or thrombocytopenia
- Plasma B-type natriuretic peptide (BNP): level < 200 pg/mL favors ARDS rather than CHF, which can be much higher (alterations in BNP increase mortality risk in the ARDS patient)
- CT scan: to provide detailed views of the heart and lungs
- Echocardiography: helpful in excluding CHF (cardiogenic pulmonary edema)
- **Bronchoscopy** with bronchoalveolar lavage (BAL): helpful in excluding lung infections
    - o Nursing management for the preoperative patient:

        As bronchoscopy is a procedure that requires sedation, the nurse should ensure that the patient remains NPO for at least 6 to 12 hours prior to the procedure. This is to decrease the patient's risk of aspiration while sedated. The nurse should also hold NSAIDs, aspirin, and blood thinners prior to the procedure to decrease the risk of uncontrolled bleeding during and after the procedure. Although the bronchoscopy may be performed for a variety of pulmonary indications, the nurse should maintain continuous cardiac and respiratory monitoring to ensure that the patient remains stable prior to the procedure. Finally, before the patient has a bronchoscopy, the physician should obtain informed consent from the patient or the patient's medical power of attorney. The nurse should ensure that this is complete.

    - o Nursing management for postoperative patient:

        Following a bronchoscopy, the patient may still be drowsy as they recover from sedation. The patient may have a sore throat and hoarse voice initially. Fluids and food may be advanced as tolerated, depending on physician orders. The nurse should continue cardiac and respiratory monitoring and assess the patient for signs of complications, such as bleeding, pneumothorax, laryngospasm, and bronchospasm. Bleeding may be frank (seen in coughing or emesis) or may be insidious, with varying symptoms depending on the originating location of the bleeding. Pneumothorax may present with shortness of breath, chest pain, and absent breath sounds. Laryngospasm may present as shortness of breath and upper airway wheezing, while bronchospasm may present as shortness of breath and lower airway wheezing. Any of these symptoms should be reported to the physician immediately for further intervention.

Medications such as corticosteroids, inhaled nitric oxide, and inhaled prostaglandins have been used for the treatment of ARDS, but specific treatment will be based on patient comorbidities and severity of disease. Treating the underlying symptoms of ARDS and providing supportive care are the most crucial components of therapy in the beginning stages of treatment. The most consistent therapy found to improve survival in ARDS is intubation and mechanical ventilation using low tidal volumes (6 mL/kg of ideal body weight). Because sepsis, an infection, is the most common etiology of ARDS, early administration of a broad-spectrum antibiotic is crucial.

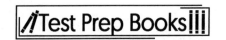

Treatment also includes fluid management and nutritional support. For individuals with shock secondary to sepsis, initial aggressive fluid resuscitation is administered, followed by a conservative fluid management strategy. It is best to institute nutritional support within 48 to 72 hours of initiation of mechanical ventilation. Positional changes may also be indicated for the ARDS patient. As opposed to the supine or seated positions, prone positioning allows for improved oxygenation through enhanced gas exchange throughout all lung fields. Contraindications may be patient specific, but one of the more common medical contraindications is a spinal cord injury. Nursing interventions for the prone patient include routine eye care (as most patients will require an eye pad or cover); frequent assessment of the endotracheal tube and any invasive lines; and positional changes (micro-turns if hemodynamically unstable) every two hours to relieve pressure from facial area and bony prominences. Pulse oximetry and arterial blood pressure readings should be monitored while the patient is in a prone position to ensure adequate oxygenation and perfusion.

Important preventative measures include DVT prophylaxis with enoxaparin; stress ulcer prophylaxis with sucralfate or omeprazole; turning and skin care to prevent decubitus ulcers; and elevating the head of the bed and using a subglottic suction device to help prevent ventilator-associated pneumonia.

Severe Asthma

Status asthmaticus is an acute episode of worsening asthma that is unresponsive to treatment with bronchodilators. Even after increasing their bronchodilator use to every few minutes, individuals will not experience relief of symptoms. Status asthmaticus represents a respiratory emergency that can lead to respiratory failure. Airway inflammation, bronchospasm, and mucus plugging highlight the condition. Common triggers include exposure to an allergen or irritant, viral respiratory illness, and exercise in cold weather.

The main symptoms of status asthmaticus are wheezing, cough, and dyspnea; however, severe airway obstruction can result in a "**silent chest**" without audible wheezes. This can be a sign of impending respiratory failure. Other signs and symptoms of status asthmaticus include:

- Chest tightness or pain
- Tachypnea
- Tachycardia
- Cyanosis
- Use of accessory respiratory muscles
- Inability to speak more than one or two words at a time
- Altered mental status
- Pulsus paradoxus >20mm Hg
- Syncope
- Hypoxemia
- Hypercapnia
- Retractions and the use of abdominal muscles to breathe
- Diminished breath sounds
- Hypertension
- Seizures (late sign)
- Bradycardia (late sign)
- Hypotension (late sign)

- Agitation (late sign)

Useful tests for the diagnosis of status asthmaticus include:

- Chest x-ray (for the exclusion of pneumonia, pneumothorax, and CHF)

- ABG analysis can be diagnostic as well as therapeutic (tracking response to treatment measures). Assess cost/benefit for children due to pain associated with ABG sampling.

- CBC with differential can reveal an elevated WBC count with left shift (possible indication of a microbial infection).

- Peak flow measurement can be diagnostic as well as therapeutic (tracking response to treatment measures).

- Pulse oximetry provides continuous measurement of O_2 saturation. Reading is affected by decreased peripheral perfusion, anemia, and movement.

- Blood glucose levels, stress, and therapeutic medications can lead to hyperglycemia. Younger children may exhibit hypoglycemia.

- Blood electrolyte levels (therapeutic medications can lead to hypokalemia)

Intubation and mechanical ventilation should be used with extreme caution in individuals with status asthmaticus. It's usually considered a therapy of last resort due to its inherent dangers—air trapping leading to an increased risk for barotrauma (especially pneumothorax); decreased cardiac output; and increasing bronchospasm. Mechanical ventilation of individuals with status asthmaticus often requires controlled hypoventilation with low tidal volumes, prolonged exhalation times, low respiratory rates, and tolerance of permissive hypercapnia. The majority of individuals needing mechanical ventilation can be extubated within 72 hours.

Supportive Treatment
- O_2 therapy to maintain O_2 saturation > 92%; non-rebreather mask can deliver 98% O_2
- Hydration
- Correction of electrolyte abnormalities
- Antibiotics only with evidence of concurrent infective process

Pharmacological Agents Used for Acute Asthma
Various classes of pharmacological agents are used for the treatment and control of status asthmaticus. The following discussion concentrates on pharmacological agents to treat and control acute asthma rather than chronic asthma. Urgent care of asthma can include the following:

Beta-2 Adrenergic Agonists (Beta-2 Agonists)
Short-acting preparations of Beta-2 agonists relax the muscles in the airways, resulting in **bronchodilation** (expanding of the bronchial air passages) and increased airflow to the lungs. It is important to remember that one of the underlying factors in asthma is bronchoconstriction. Albuterol is the most commonly used short-acting Beta-2 agonist. Adverse effects of albuterol include tachycardia, tremors, and anxiety. Another short-acting Beta-2 agonist used to treat acute asthma is levalbuterol (Xopenex). This medication is related to albuterol and has the same result, but without the adverse

effects. However, it must be noted that the frequent use of adrenergic agents prior to receiving emergency care can decrease a patient's response to these medications in a hospital setting.

Anticholinergics

Anticholinergics block the action of the neurotransmitter acetylcholine which, in turn, causes bronchodilation. Anticholinergics can also increase the bronchodilation effect of short-acting Beta-2 agonists. The most commonly used anticholinergic is ipratropium, which is used in combination with short-acting Beta-2 agonists for the treatment of status asthmaticus. Adverse effects can include dry mouth, blurred vision, and constipation.

Corticosteroids

Corticosteroids are potent anti-inflammatory medications that fight the inflammation accompanying asthma. Corticosteroids commonly used in the treatment of status asthmaticus include prednisone, prednisolone, and methylprednisolone. Methylprednisolone is typically administered once intravenously (IV) in cases of status asthmaticus and then followed by a taper of oral prednisone over seven to ten days. The intravenous administration of corticosteroids is equal in effectiveness to oral corticosteroid administration. Corticosteroids have numerous adverse effects, and they should not be used for more than two weeks. Adverse effects of long-term corticosteroid use can include weight gain, osteoporosis, thinning of skin, cataracts, easy bruising, and diabetes. Therefore, it is necessary to monitor blood glucose routinely and use regular insulin on a sliding scale. Electrolytes (particularly potassium) must also be monitored.

Methylxanthines

Methylxanthines are used as bronchodilators and as adjuncts to Beta-2 agonists and corticosteroids in treating status asthmaticus. The primary methylxanthines are theophylline and aminophylline. At therapeutic doses, methylxanthines are much weaker bronchodilators than Beta-2 agonists. The adverse effects of methylxanthines can include nausea, vomiting, tachycardia, headaches, and seizures. As a result, therapeutic monitoring is mandatory. Therapeutic levels of theophylline range from 10 mcg/mL to 20 mcg/mL. Methylxanthines aren't frequently used to treat status asthmaticus because of their possible adverse effects and the need for close monitoring of drug blood levels.

Magnesium Sulfate

Magnesium sulfate is a calcium antagonist that relaxes smooth muscle in the lung passages, leading to bronchodilation. Clinical studies indicate it can be used as an adjunct to Beta-2 agonist therapy during status asthmaticus. Intravenous magnesium sulfate is given slowly to prevent adverse effects, such as bradycardia and hypotension. The administration of magnesium sulfate is controversial due to varying clinical studies of effectiveness, but its use (inhaled or intravenously administered) may be considered as an adjunct treatment for the asthmatic patient.

Leukotriene Inhibitors

Leukotriene inhibitors target inflammation related to asthma. Typically used for the long-term control of asthma, this class of medication can be helpful for a minority of individuals with status asthmaticus. The primary leukotriene inhibitors used in the treatment of asthma are montelukast and zafirlukast. Adverse effects of leukotriene inhibitors include headache, rash, fatigue, dizziness, and abdominal pain.

Medication Monitoring

Beta-2 agonists used for pulmonary system support, such as albuterol and terbutaline, can cause side effects that include tremor, dizziness, and palpitations. Nursing interventions include ensuring the correct dosing and contacting the prescriber if the prescribed dose becomes ineffective for the patient. Prolonged corticosteroid use can induce **Cushing's syndrome**, which includes the following signs and symptoms: fat loss from arms and legs, muscle weakness, anxiety, moon face, diaphoresis, fatty deposits around upper back, and abdominal weight gain. Corticosteroids should be weaned following a gradual titration, as abrupt discontinuation may trigger an adrenal insufficiency crisis. Theophylline, a methylxanthine, can cause arrhythmias and seizures. The nurse must carefully monitor vital signs and provide patient education on maintenance, which should include taking the medication at regular intervals during the day.

COPD Exacerbation

Chronic Obstructive Pulmonary Disease (COPD) is characterized by an airflow obstruction that is not fully reversible. It is usually progressive and associated with an abnormal inflammatory response in the lungs. As one of the leading causes of death in the United States, the primary cause of COPD is exposure to tobacco smoke. COPD includes chronic bronchitis, emphysema, or a combination of both. Although asthma is part of the classic triad of obstructive lung diseases, it is not technically considered to be part of the definition of COPD. However, someone with COPD can have an asthma component to their disease. **Chronic bronchitis** is described as a chronic productive cough for three or more months over the course of two consecutive years. **Emphysema** is the abnormal enlargement of **alveoli** (air sacs) with accompanying destruction of their walls. Signs and symptoms of COPD can include:

- Dyspnea
- Wheezing
- Cough (usually worse in the morning and that produces sputum/phlegm)
- Cyanosis
- Chest tightness
- Fever
- Tachypnea
- Orthopnea
- Use of accessory respiratory muscles
- Elevated jugular venous pressure (JVP)
- Barrel chest
- Pursed lip breathing
- Altered mental status

As smoking is the most common cause of COPD, smoking cessation should be encouraged to decrease exacerbations and slow the progression of the disease. Over the course of several years, the disease will worsen, starting with a productive cough and leading to trouble with breathing. Patients with COPD will often complain of a recurring headache in the morning. Their chest may become barrel-like in appearance due to hyperinflation of the lungs. Weight loss and muscle wasting are common signs of advanced disease. The patient may breathe with their lips pursed, a sign of intrinsic PEEP or "gas trapping". By pursing their lips, the patient has more control over their respirations and can keep their airway open longer, allowing them to prevent or reduce hypercapnia. As the disease progresses, their

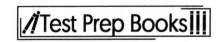

exacerbations will increase. A COPD exacerbation occurs when, for a reason that may be unknown, the patient's symptoms worsen, and hospitalization often follows.

A diagnosis of COPD can be made through **pulmonary function tests** (PFTs), a chest x-ray, blood chemistries, ABG analysis, or a CT scan. A formal diagnosis of COPD can be made through a PFT known as **spirometry**, which measures lung function. PFTs measure the ratio of forced expiratory volume in one second over **forced vital capacity** (FEV_1/FVC) and should normally be >70%. Values below 70% usually indicate a respiratory problem. The other diagnostic tests mentioned are useful in determining the acuity and severity of exacerbations of the disease. In acute exacerbations of COPD, ABG analysis can reveal respiratory acidosis, hypoxemia, and hypercapnia. Generally, a pH less than 7.3 indicates acute respiratory compromise. Compensatory metabolic alkalosis may develop in response to chronic respiratory acidosis. A chest x-ray can show flattening of the diaphragm and increased retrosternal air space (both indicative of hyperinflation); cardiomegaly; and increased bronchovascular markings. Blood chemistries can suggest sodium retention or hypokalemia. A CT scan is more sensitive and specific than a standard chest x-ray for diagnosing emphysema.

Treatment for acute exacerbations of COPD can include oxygen supplementation, short-acting Beta-2 agonists, anticholinergics, corticosteroids, and antibiotics. Oxygen should be titrated to achieve an oxygen saturation of 88-92%, but a specific target range may be patient or facility specific. Low-flow oxygen is used, while the nurse understands that patients with chronically high CO_2 levels may be triggered to cease respirations when given pure oxygen. Taking that into consideration, the priority intervention for the patient experiencing an acute COPD exacerbation is restoring adequate oxygenation. Short-acting Beta-2 agonists (albuterol or levalbuterol) administered via nebulizer can improve dyspnea associated with COPD. The anticholinergic medication ipratropium, administered via nebulizer, can be added as an adjunct to Beta-2 agonists (ipratorpium-albuterol is commonly used). Short courses of corticosteroids can be given orally or intravenously. In clinical trials, the administration of oral corticosteroids in the early stage of a COPD exacerbation decreased the need for hospitalization. Also in clinical trials, the use of antibiotics was found to decrease the risk of treatment failure and death in individuals with a moderate to severe exacerbation of COPD. If the patient has a PaO_2 that is less than 55 mmHg, the patient may be discharged on home oxygen therapy. Discharge education should include how to use home oxygen safely, benefits of smoking cessation, importance of avoiding airway infections, and demonstration of diaphragmatic and pursed-lip breathing techniques.

Minimally Invasive Thoracic Surgery

Video-Assisted Thoracoscopic Surgery (VATS)

Video-assisted thoracoscopic surgery (VATS) is a laparoscopic surgery used to diagnose and treat conditions within the chest cavity. This minimally invasive procedure can be used to collect tissue for biopsy, drain excess fluids from different organs (e.g., heart or lungs), or repair damage to organs (e.g., esophagus or diaphragm). It can even be used for cardiac procedures, such as valve replacement and pacemaker placement. Some specific procedures that may use VATS include lobectomy, repair of recurrent pneumothorax, repair of chest trauma, treatment of empyema, evacuation of hemothorax, repair of fistulas within the chest cavity, and biopsy of tumors.

Because the indications for VATS are so varied, the specific diagnostic tests used may vary from patient to patient. However, most patients will likely have some form of imaging (e.g., x-ray, CT scan, or PET scan) and laboratory work that would indicate a need for invasive diagnostics or surgical intervention. For example, those requiring repair of recurrent pneumothorax or evacuation of a hemothorax will likely have had a chest x-ray to confirm diagnosis as well as a chest CT scan to determine the extent of the condition. Additionally, an ECG can be used to determine if the patient requires a pacemaker placement. Since this is an invasive surgery that requires anesthesia, most patients will have similar testing completed again prior to the procedure to ensure that they meet stability requirements and prepare for any potential adverse events during or after the procedure. This means that most patients will have basic labs drawn (e.g., CBC and CMP), an ECG, and a type and screen (in case transfusion is needed for hemorrhage). Those at risk of excess bleeding (e.g., those on anticoagulants or with clotting disorders) may also have their clotting factors tested.

Because the specifics of the procedure performed using VATS may vary, specific nursing management before and after may also vary. For example, a patient requiring pneumothorax repair may have a chest tube in place. On the other hand, a patient with a pacemaker may require percutaneous pacing prior to the procedure. However, some management will be the same for all VATS patients. As the procedure requires anesthesia, the patient will need to remain NPO for at least 8 to 12 hours prior to undergoing VATS. The patient should also be on continuous cardiac and respiratory monitoring before and after the procedure. Finally, the nurse should watch for signs of potential complications, such as arrythmias, pneumothorax, hemorrhage, and infection.

Sleep Apnea

Apnea refers to temporary pauses in breath in which the lung volume stagnates. The musculature involved in respiration temporarily ceases function. Apnea can be caused by distress, laughing, trauma, or neurological disease. It is also a common sleep condition, in which a patient can stop breathing up to thirty times per hour.

Obstructive Sleep Apnea

Obstructive sleep apnea is the most common type of sleep apnea, with the less common types being central sleep apnea and complex sleep apnea. It occurs when the muscles in the throat and soft palate relax during sleep, blocking the passage of air. While loud snoring is a classic symptom, headaches upon waking, excessive daytime sleepiness, and waking up abruptly with a gasp or choke are also common.

Risk factors include excessive weight, smoking, asthma or breathing disorders, male sex, and hypertension. Without detection or treatment, sleep apnea can greatly tax the cardiovascular system and lead to cardiac events, due to the long periods of time without oxygen circulation. Sleep apnea is often an undetected condition. The condition can be treated with a mouthpiece to thrust the jaw forward or a CPAP machine, which helps keep a patent airway.

A nurse caring for an acutely ill patient should be especially vigilant in monitoring for signs or symptoms of sleep apnea, especially after that patient has been given anesthesia or pain medication. This may include close observation, including continuous SpO_2 monitoring, of a patient the first time they have been given a new medication that could cause respiratory distress. Continuous SpO_2 monitoring can quickly detect an oxygen desaturation, but the nurse should be aware of the potential complications and limitations. While rare, continuous SpO_2 monitoring can potentially cause skin integrity damage— most often related to poor perfusion or burns in the event of an MRI. The nurse can provide intervention by routinely rotating continuous pulse oximetry sites (which can also improve accuracy of readings) and briefly removing the sensor for a patient getting an MRI. Limitations of continuous SpO_2 monitoring include the inability to account for the oxyhemoglobin dissociation curve; inability to distinguish molecules outside of hemoglobin and oxygenated hemoglobin (e.g., carboxyhemoglobin with

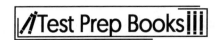

carbon monoxide—resulting in falsely high readings of oxygenation); and possibility of inaccurate readings (e.g., nail polish, poor circulation, or uncontrolled movements causing artifact).

Central Sleep Apnea

Central sleep apnea is a disorder in which the patient's brain sends incorrect signals to the respiratory system during sleep, leading to periods of apnea. Some potential causes of central sleep apnea are damage or disease of the brain stem, narcotic use, sleeping at high altitudes, and continuous positive airway pressure (CPAP) use for obstructive sleep apnea. Signs of central sleep apnea include excessive fatigue, the patient feeling that they did not sleep well, and an observation by others of abnormal breathing patterns while sleeping. The nurse may note that the patient becomes hypoxic when asleep, requiring supplemental oxygen, but will return to their baseline oxygen saturation when awake. However, definitive diagnosis of central sleep apnea is performed through a sleep study.

Treatment for central sleep apnea generally includes the administration of supplemental oxygen and/or positive airway therapy, such as CPAP or bilevel positive airway pressure (BiPAP). If these interventions are ineffective or insufficient, the doctor may prescribe medications, such as acetazolamide, to help stimulate respirations. Finally, the patient's central sleep apnea may require treatment with a phrenic nerve stimulator meant to send signals to the diaphragm. It should be noted that patients with phrenic nerve stimulators either may not be able to receive MRI or may require specific modifications to the stimulator, depending on the specific model.

Nursing management of patients with central sleep apnea involves continuous cardiac and pulse oximetry monitoring, especially when the patient is asleep. The nurse may administer supplemental oxygen or assist in the setup and management of the positive airway therapy. Education should be provided on the risks of cardiovascular disease, heart failure, and arrhythmias should the patient not maintain proper treatment of their central sleep apnea.

Pleural Space Complications

Pneumothorax

Pneumothorax is the abnormal presence of air in the **pleural cavity**, which is the space between the parietal and visceral pleurae.

Pneumothorax can be categorized as:

- **Primary Spontaneous Pneumothorax**: This occurs in individuals with no history of lung disease or inciting event. Those at risk for primary spontaneous pneumothorax are typically young (teenage–mid 30s), tall, thin, and smokers. There's also a familial tendency for primary spontaneous pneumothorax.

- **Secondary Spontaneous Pneumothorax**: This occurs in individuals with an underlying lung disease, such as COPD, cystic fibrosis, asthma, tuberculosis (TB), or lung cancer.

- **Traumatic Pneumothorax**: This occurs as a result of blunt or penetrating trauma to the chest wall. The trauma disrupts the parietal and/or visceral pleura(e). Examples of inciting events include: gunshot or stab wounds; air bag deployment in a motor vehicle accident; acute respiratory distress syndrome (ARDS); and medical procedures such as mechanical ventilation, lung biopsy, thoracentesis, needle biopsy, and chest surgery.

- **Tension Pneumothorax**: This is the trapping of air in the pleural space under positive pressure. It causes a mediastinal shift toward the unaffected lung and a depression of the hemidiaphragm on the side of the affected lung. Shortly after, the event is followed by severe cardiopulmonary compromise. Tension pneumothorax can result from any of the conditions or procedures listed for spontaneous and traumatic pneumothorax.

Signs and symptoms of pneumothorax depend on the degree of lung collapse (partial or total) and can include:

- Chest pain
- Dyspnea
- Cyanosis
- Tachypnea
- Tachycardia
- Hypotension
- Hypoxia
- Anxiety
- Adventitious breath sounds
- Unilateral distant or absent breath sounds
- Jugular venous distention (JVD)
- Tracheal deviation away from the affected side (with tension pneumothorax)

While pneumothorax may be suspected using clinical judgement (based on signs and symptoms), confirmation of the diagnosis can involve an upright posteroanterior (PA) chest x-ray, chest CT scan (the most reliable imaging for diagnosis), ABG analysis, and ultrasonography of the chest.

Treatment of a pneumothorax depends on the severity of the condition and can include:

- Supplemental oxygen

- **Thoracostomy** (chest tube): standard treatment for all large, symptomatic pneumothoraces

  - As thoracostomy can be completed with local anesthetics, the patient may not be required to remain NPO prior to the procedure, unless it will be completed in the operating room due to other complications that caused the pneumo/hemothorax. The nurse should place the patient on continuous cardiac and respiratory monitoring to ensure patient stability. Additionally, the nurse should monitor for signs of tension pneumothorax that could develop prior to the thoracostomy due to worsening pressure from the pneumothorax. Finally, the nurse should have supplemental oxygen available as needed, along with suction and the chest drainage system ready to be attached to the patient's chest tube.

  - Following thoracostomy, relief should be noticeable in the patient's shortness of breath and chest pain. The nurse should make note of the depth at which the chest tube was secured and assess for possible misplacement should the depth change during the patient's care. The chest tube may be hooked up to a water seal chamber and/or to suction, depending on the doctor's orders. The nurse should monitor for any signs of chest drainage system malfunction and ensure that the patient's symptoms do not

80

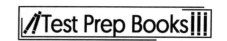

worsen, as this could be a sign of system malfunction, chest tube misplacement, or infection.

- Observation: a reasonable option for small asymptomatic pneumothoraces, requiring multiple series of chest x-rays until resolution

- **Thoracentesis**: removal of air or fluid from the pleural space

  o Nursing management for the preoperative patient:

  Thoracentesis is a procedure that can typically be performed without sedating a patient, requiring only local anesthetics. Because of this, the patient may be permitted to eat and drink up until the procedure. However, because this procedure is conducted to drain excess fluid from the pleural cavity, the nurse should place the patient on continuous cardiac and respiratory monitoring to watch for signs of worsening shortness of breath and decompensation. In order to prevent uncontrolled bleeding, anticoagulants may need to be held prior to the procedure. Finally, the nurse should ensure that the physician has obtained informed consent prior to the start of the procedure.

  o Nursing management for the postoperative patient:

  Following thoracentesis, the nurse should maintain continuous cardiac and respiratory monitoring as well as monitor for signs of complications from the procedure, such as pneumothorax, bleeding, and infection. Because the procedure involves puncturing the chest wall, it is possible that a lung may become punctured, resulting in a pneumothorax. Signs of this complication would include chest pain, shortness of breath, and absent lung sounds. Bleeding may also occur, causing compression of the lung or hypotension, and can be potentially life-threatening. Should the nurse suspect either of these complications or note adverse changes to cardiac monitoring or vitals, the physician should be notified immediately for further intervention.

Because they can quickly cause life-threatening cardiopulmonary compromise, the standard of treatment for all tension pneumothoraces is an emergent needle thoracostomy. **Pleural drains** are placed in order to allow for drainage of excess fluid within the lungs. They may be indicated for pneumothorax, pleural effusion, empyema, or following other surgeries that require incision near the pleural cavity. Depending on the indication, the pleural drain may be in the form of a chest tube requiring a water seal chamber and suction, or it may be a permanent catheter device that can be intermittently drained using the negative pressure of bulb suction.

If the patient has a **chest tube** in place, the nurse should first make note of the depth at which the chest tube was placed to monitor for potential misplacement. Chest tube dressings may require changing if they become soiled. The nurse should also monitor the output from the chest tube drainage system, notifying the physician of any unexpected findings. Additionally, the nurse should monitor for signs of system malfunction, such as kinks, blockages, or leaks. If the patient has a **permanent catheter device**, the nurse should also make note of placement and ensure that the device is not dislodged. Furthermore, the nurse should change the dressing around the catheter regularly, and if it becomes soiled, while also educating the patient on how to do so. The nurse should drain the catheter device regularly and monitor the patient's output, reporting any unexpected findings. For both forms of pleural drain, the nurse should be on the lookout for worsening shortness of breath and signs of infection.

Hemothorax

Hemothorax, the presence of blood in the pleural space, is most commonly the result of blunt or penetrating chest trauma. The **pleural space** lies between the parietal pleura of the chest wall and the visceral pleura of the lungs. A large accumulation of blood in the pleural space can restrict normal lung movement and lead to hemodynamic compromise. Common signs and symptoms of hemothorax include chest pain, dyspnea, and tachypnea. When there is substantial systemic blood loss, tachycardia and hypotension can also be present.

Diagnosis of hemothorax primarily involves a chest x-ray, which reveals blunting at the costophrenic angle on the affected side of the lung. A helical CT scan has a complementary role in the management of hemothorax, and it can localize and quantify the retention of blood or clots within the pleural space.

Small hemothoraces usually require no treatment but need close observation to ensure resolution. Tube thoracostomy drainage is the mainstay of treatment for significant hemothoraces. Needle aspiration is rarely used in the management of a hemothorax. Blood transfusions can be necessary for those with significant blood loss or hemodynamic compromise. Complications from hemothorax can include **empyema** (secondary bacterial infection of a retained clot) or **fibrothorax** (fibrosis of the pleural space, which can trap lung tissue and lead to decreased pulmonary function).

Pleural Effusion

A **pleural effusion** is an abnormal accumulation of fluid in the pleural space, located between the parietal and visceral pleura of each lung. The **parietal pleura** covers the inner surface of the chest cavity, while the **visceral pleura** surrounds the lungs. Approximately 10 milliliters of pleural fluid is maintained by oncotic and hydrostatic pressures as well as lymphatic drainage; this is necessary for normal respiratory function. Pleural effusions can be categorized as transudates or exudates.

Transudative pleural effusions result from an imbalance between oncotic and hydrostatic pressures, so they are characterized by low protein content. The transudates are often the result of congestive heart failure (CHF), cirrhosis, low albumin blood levels, nephrotic syndrome, and peritoneal dialysis.

Exudative pleural effusions result from decreased lymphatic drainage or inflammation of the pleura, so they are characterized by high protein content. The exudates are often the result of malignancy, pancreatitis, pulmonary embolism, uremia, infection, and certain medications.

The main symptoms of a pleural effusion include dyspnea, cough, and chest pain. Diagnosis of a pleural effusion can include chest x-ray, chest CT scan, ultrasonography, and thoracentesis. Thoracentesis can provide pleural fluid for analysis, such as lactate dehydrogenase (LD), glucose, pH, cell count and differential, culture, and cytology. Pleural fluid should be distinguished as either transudate or exudate based on the **Light's criteria**. In the event of one or more of the following being true, the fluid will be deemed exudative:

- Ratio of pleural fluid to serum protein > 0.5
- Ratio of pleural fluid to serum LD > 0.6
- Pleural fluid LD > 0.67 of the upper limit of normal serum value

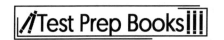

Treatment of a pleural effusion is usually dictated by the underlying etiology; however, the treatment of a very large pleural effusion can include:

- Thoracentesis (typically indicated for smaller pleural effusions)
- Chest tube (also known as tube thoracostomy)
- Indwelling tunneled pleural catheters
- **Pleurodesis** (instillation of an irritant to cause inflammation and subsequent fibrosis to obliterate the pleural space), which is typically reserved for patients with recurring or refractory pleural effusions

Empyema

In patients with pneumonia, thoracic surgery, or chest trauma, the development of empyema may be a complication. Empyema occurs when pathogens enter the pleural area and form pus. The resulting exudate is usually protein rich and can hinder lung expansion. *Streptococcus pneumoniae* and *Staphylococcus aureus* are the two most commonly found pathogens that result in an empyema; this is due to these types of bacteria being the most common culprits for pneumonia and pneumonia being the most common cause of empyema. Patients already in the hospital on appropriate antibiotics who show worsening chest x-rays should be evaluated for empyema, unless another diagnosis fits the patient's clinical picture. On a physical exam, percussion of the area with the empyema will sound dull, with breath sounds decreased. Patients may also present with elevated temperature, dyspnea, and productive cough. Once an empyema has been visualized on a chest x-ray, patients may either undergo CT or ultrasonography to assess the empyema further and decide on an approach to treatment. Most patients with a moderate to large empyema will undergo a diagnostic thoracentesis, which can be done concurrently with therapeutic thoracentesis if drainage is considered necessary for relieving symptoms. Prior to sending a patient for thoracentesis, the nurse should assess that the consent has been completed and that the patient (or responsible caregiver) understands the procedure with verbal reiteration of the education provided.

If the patient is on blood thinner medication, the nurse should discuss with the provider if this should be held or administered. Fluid gathered from thoracentesis should be sent for cell count with differential, cytology, and microbiology. Some patients will require that the tube for drainage be left in place as a tube thoracostomy (chest tube). If so, follow-up chest CT or x-ray is usually done immediately to assess the placement of the tube. The chest tube and drainage must be frequently assessed and documented, including color and amount of drainage volume and any redness, bleeding or leaking around the site. The provider should be notified immediately of any change in respiratory status, especially dyspnea or chest pain. If patients develop a new fever, this should also be reported. If the patient fails to improve with drainage and antibiotics, other treatments may be considered, including video-assisted thoracoscopy (VATS).

Chylothorax

Chylothorax involves an accumulation of lymph formed in the digestive system (**chyle**) in the pleural cavity. This complication typically arises from trauma (including surgical procedures), malignancy, aortitis, filariasis, tuberculosis lymphadenitis, or is found as a congenital condition potentially co-occurring with other malformations of the lymphatic system. As chylothorax is a lymphatic flow disorder impacting the space between the lung and chest wall, development of shortness of breath, chest heaviness, and cough is typical. Nursing care targets symptom resolution via the delivery of parenteral nutrition, including a dietician consult to implement a therapeutic dietary plan. If these interventions

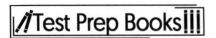
fail, the patient and care team may consider surgical interventions. In the case of surgery to perform ligation of the thoracic duct, insert a shunt, or otherwise directly target the trauma or malformation, preoperative supportive nursing care may include medication management, patient comfort, and respiratory support.

Pulmonary Embolism

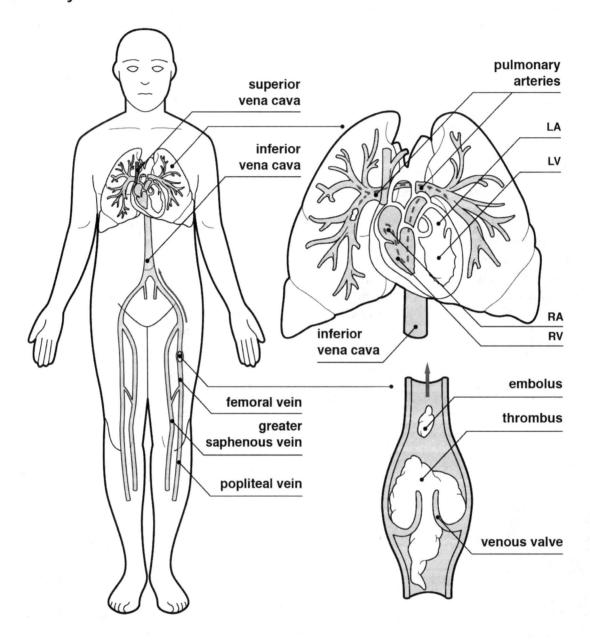

A **pulmonary embolism** (PE) is the abnormal presence of a blood clot, or thromboembolism, that travels to the lungs and causes a blockage in the pulmonary arteries. Although the clot can originate in other locations, the most common cause of PE is a complication of thromboembolism formation in the venous system of one of the lower extremities, which is termed deep venous thrombosis (DVT). Both PEs and

DVTs are a type of **venous thromboembolism** (VTE). Other rarer causes of PEs are thromboembolisms arising in the veins of the kidneys, pelvis, upper extremities, or the right atrium of the heart. Occasionally, other matter besides blood clots can cause pulmonary emboli, such as fat, air, and septic (infected with bacteria) emboli. PE is a common and potentially fatal condition.

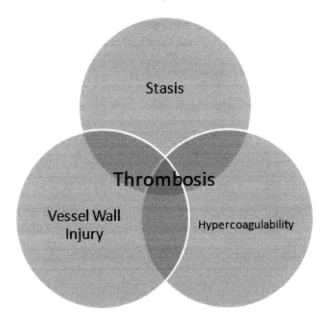

The primary influences on the development of DVT and PE are shown in **Virchow's triad**: blood hypercoagulability, endothelial injury/dysfunction, and stasis of blood. Risk factors for DVT and PE include:

- Cancer
- Heart disease, especially congestive heart failure (CHF)
- Prolonged immobility (such as prolonged bedrest or lengthy trips in planes or cars)
- Surgery (one of the leading risk factors, accounting for up to 15 percent of all postoperative deaths)
- Overweight/obesity
- Smoking
- Pregnancy
- Supplemental estrogen from birth control pills or estrogen replacement therapy (ERT)

Types of Pulmonary Embolism

There are three categories of PEs based on severity: small, submassive, and massive. **Small PEs** may exist without any symptoms. **Submassive PEs** may slightly impair right ventricular function, but hypotension is absent. A **massive PE** impairs the function of the right ventricle, causes a hypotensive crisis, and presents a serious risk of death for the patient.

While both submassive and massive PEs can be referred to as an acute PE, the main difference is the sustained hypotension with the massive PE. A PE can also be chronic, meaning the embolus doesn't dissolve or move further and can worsen over time. A **chronic PE** can lead to chronic thromboembolic pulmonary hypertension (CTEPH).

A **saddle PE** is a particularly dangerous type of clot in which the pulmonary embolus has lodged itself in the bifurcation between the main pulmonary artery and the left and right pulmonary arteries—blocking blood flow to both lungs. Saddle PEs usually impair right ventricular function with or without hypotension.

Clinical Presentation and Diagnostics

The signs and symptoms of PE are nonspecific, which often presents a diagnostic dilemma and a delay in diagnosis. Nearly half of all individuals with PE are asymptomatic. The signs and symptoms of PE can vary greatly depending on the size of the blood clots, how much lung tissue is involved, and an individual's overall health. Signs and symptoms of PE can include:

- Pleuritic chest pain
- Dyspnea
- Cough
- Tachypnea
- Hypoxia
- Fever
- Diaphoresis
- Rales
- Cyanosis
- Unilateral lower extremity edema (symptom of DVT)

The diagnosis of PE can be a difficult task. Many clinicians support determining the clinical probability of PE before proceeding with diagnostic testing. This process involves assessing the presence or absence of the following manifestations:

- Pulmonary signs: tachypnea, rales, cyanosis, SOB, inability to take or hold a deep breath

- Cardiac signs: tachycardia, S3 or S4 gallop, attenuated second heart sound, cardiac murmur, chest pain

- Systemic signs: fever, diaphoresis, signs of thrombophlebitis, lower extremity edema

Once the clinical probability of PE has been determined, diagnostic testing ensues. **Duplex ultrasonography** is the standard for diagnosing a DVT. While **pulmonary angiography** maintains the benchmark for testing due to its high specificity and sensitivity, the **computed tomography pulmonary angiogram** (CTPA) has become the more common diagnostic tool for a PE. Pulmonary angiography is an invasive procedure and more costly, making CTPA more practical. **Ventilation-perfusion (V/Q) scanning** is another common testing modality for a pulmonary embolism. Magnetic resonance imaging (MRI) is usually reserved for pregnant women and individuals with a contraindication to the administration of intravenous contrast material. A D-dimer blood test is most useful for individuals with a low or moderate pretest probability of PE, since levels are typically elevated with PE. Arterial blood gas (ABG) analysis usually reveals hypoxemia, hypocapnia, and respiratory alkalosis.

A chest x-ray, though not diagnostic for PE since its findings are typically nonspecific, can exclude diseases that mimic PE, as can an echocardiogram. Electrocardiography is also useful because it can assess right ventricular heart function and serve as a prognostic indicator, since there is a 10 percent death rate from PE with right ventricular dysfunction. Lastly, transesophageal echocardiography (TEE) can reveal central PE.

Treatment

The first step in treating a PE is determining the patient's stability. Patients with hypotension are categorized as unstable, while patients without hypotension are generally considered stable. For hemodynamically unstable patients presenting with a PE, treatment should focus on stabilizing the patient, including vasopressors or intubation if needed. Treatment of PE should begin immediately to prevent complications or death. PE treatment is focused on preventing an increase in size of the current blood clot(s) and the formation of new blood clots. Supportive care treatment of PE can include:

- Supplemental oxygen to ease hypoxia/hypoxemia
- Norepinephrine or dobutamine administered via IV for related hypotension
- Conservative IV fluid therapy for hypotension
- Cardiac monitoring in the case of associated arrhythmias or right ventricular dysfunction
- Intubation and mechanical ventilation

While pharmacological therapy will be tailored to the specific patient, medications involved in treatment can include thrombolytics or clot dissolvers (e.g., tissue plasminogen activator (tPA), alteplase, urokinase, streptokinase, or reteplase). These medications are reserved for individuals with a diagnosis of acute PE and associated hypotension (systolic BP < 90 mmHg) but are not given concurrently with anticoagulants. In cases where anticoagulation therapy is needed, medications will be carefully selected based on the patient's current clinical presentation, comorbidities, and healthcare setting. Options include low molecular weight heparin (LMW heparin), fondaparinux, unfractionated heparin (UFH), oral factor Xa inhibitors, and direct thrombin inhibitors. Warfarin, a vitamin K antagonist, is also an option as an adjunct therapy for initial treatment and long-term anticoagulation. UFH and warfarin are prescribed with caution as they will both require routine lab monitoring.

An **embolectomy** (removal of emboli via catheter or surgery) is reserved for individuals with a massive PE and contraindications to thrombolytics or anticoagulants. Vena cava filters, also called **inferior vena cava (IVC) filters**, are only indicated in the following situations:

- In a patient with an absolute contraindication to anticoagulants
- In a patient who has survived a massive PE with potential for a recurrent PE that would be fatal
- In a patient with a documented recurrent PE

Pulmonary Fibrosis

Pulmonary fibrosis is an interstitial lung disease that results in scarring and thickening of lung tissue over time. Specifically, the condition stiffens the connective tissue and alveoli sacs of the lungs, hindering their normal ability to expand and perform oxygen delivery to the rest of the body. With decreased lung expansion, the patient will experience increased difficulty in breathing and performing activities of daily living without shortness of breath.

Risk factors for pulmonary fibrosis include cigarette smoking, older age, male gender, occupational dust or fume exposure, and radiation exposure. However, the most common form of the condition is idiopathic pulmonary fibrosis, meaning there is not a specific causative factor. Symptoms of pulmonary fibrosis include shallow breathing, dry cough, fatigue, shortness of breath, and weight loss; with advanced disease, clubbing of the nails and cyanosis may be present. In addition to being based on symptoms and physical exam, diagnostic indicators include laboratory tests (e.g., ABGs), pulmonary function tests (PFTs), and radiology studies (e.g., chest x-ray and CT scan) to evaluate the severity of the illness and rule out other conditions. To further confirm diagnosis, a lung biopsy may be performed.

Since the disease is chronic in nature and currently without a cure, the patient's condition will continue to progress in severity over time. The available treatment options support the goal to slow disease progression (e.g., pirfenidone and nintedanib) and improve patient comfort (e.g., oxygen therapy and pulmonary rehabilitation programs). In some cases, lung transplant may be recommended. The nurse should work with the interdisciplinary team of providers and respiratory therapists to create an individualized plan of care. Additional nursing responsibilities include vital sign and oxygen saturation monitoring, medication administration, supplemental oxygen management, and reporting of any concerning findings to the provider. Patient education should emphasize medication and treatment compliance along with reporting of symptoms that may require emergency care.

Pulmonary Hypertension

When the pressure in the pulmonary circulation rises, it is termed **pulmonary hypertension** (PH). The blood vessels within the pulmonary beds of circulation become constricted and sometimes even obstructed. This resulting hypertension may cause failure of the right ventricle of the heart. While causes of pulmonary hypertension may be idiopathic, factors such as left heart failure, diastolic dysfunction, parenchymal lung disease, and a PE have been known to raise the pulmonary pressures.

A patient with pulmonary hypertension may complain of exertional dyspnea and chronic fatigue, experience loss of consciousness, and feel chest discomfort. Diagnosis is made via echocardiography, which estimates the pressures, and confirmed by right heart catheterization.

Pulmonary hypertension can be treated through use of vasodilators and diuretics. Sildenafil is an example of a phosphodiesterase inhibitor used to treat pulmonary hypertension and is helpful in increasing blood flow in the lungs. Amlodipine is an example of a calcium channel blocker, a class of drugs that may be helpful for pulmonary hypertension. Epoprostenol is a drug specifically formulated for use in patients with pulmonary hypertension. Single or double lung transplantation may be an option in advanced disease states.

A specific form of pulmonary hypertension, **pulmonary artery hypertension** (PAH), refers to elevated blood pressure in the arteries of the lungs, which causes arterial stenosis and decreases perfusion through the lungs. This in turn causes added strain on the heart in order to send the blood to the rest of the body. PAH can be idiopathic, genetic, or caused by damage to the lung vasculature from lesions, drug use, and chemical exposure.

Patients with PAH may present with similar symptoms to patients with heart failure, including chest pain, palpitations, shortness of breath, fatigue, and edema. PAH patients may also have a systolic murmur. Additionally, because PAH presents similarly to other cardiovascular conditions, diagnostics often begin with exclusion of other conditions. Laboratory tests will likely include a CBC, BNP, troponin, liver enzymes, HIV testing, and thyroid levels. An ECG may show stress to the right side of the heart, while an echocardiogram may reveal increased pressure to the pulmonary arteries.

Treatment of PAH will depend on the severity of the disease process, with many patients requiring long-term supplemental oxygen. PAH patients may also be placed on diuretic medications to assist in

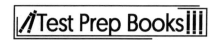

decreasing both the blood volume and resulting pressure to the pulmonary arteries. Anticoagulants may also be started, as these patients can be at increased risk of thrombosis. In more severe cases, a lung transplant may be indicated.

Nursing management of the PAH patient involves maintaining the patient's oxygen saturation levels and monitoring for signs of worsening cardiac function. This includes watching for changes in cardiac rhythm, increased peripheral edema, and decreased activity tolerance. Patient education should include the importance of strict medication compliance, follow-up with their physician, and signs that indicate a need for emergency care.

Connective Tissue Disorders

Sarcoidosis
Sarcoidosis is an immune disease in which the body has an overreactive inflammatory response, resulting in the formation of granulomas within organs. These inflammatory clusters can form within the heart, eyes, lungs, skin, and nervous system. Specific symptoms of sarcoidosis are dependent on which organs are affected. For example, the most common locations of granulomas are the skin and lungs, which can cause growths under the skin and shortness of breath, respectively. Similarly, specific diagnostics to determine if a patient has sarcoidosis may depend on the location of the granulomas. A CT scan may identify granulomas in the lungs or lymph nodes, and echocardiography may identify them in the heart; however, biopsy may be required to distinguish the inflammatory clusters from cancerous lesions.

Treatment of sarcoidosis is based on both symptom management and reducing the size, number, and impact of the granulomas. Nonsteroidal anti-inflammatory drugs (NSAIDs) may be recommended for pain management as needed. Those with significant granulomas in the lungs may require supplemental oxygen. Patients may also be prescribed oral steroids to decrease inflammation and immunosuppressants to decrease the formation of granulomas.

Nursing management for the patient with sarcoidosis requires ongoing assessment of symptoms and vital signs to ensure that appropriate symptomatic management is provided. The nurse should also be mindful that patients on immunosuppressants are at greater risk of infection. Patients should be educated on infection prevention and possible lifestyle changes. Since patients on steroids may have metabolic changes, such as elevated blood sugar levels, it is important to promote a balanced diet and exercise.

Rheumatoid Arthritis
Rheumatoid arthritis (RA) is an autoimmune disease in which the body attacks connective tissue, particularly in the joints. In addition to attacking the joints, the immune system may attack the eyes, lungs, skin, heart, and blood vessels. The most common symptoms of RA are joint pain, swelling, and fatigue. However, depending on the other organs affected, the patient may also have loss of vision, difficulty breathing, and cardiac conditions, such as arrythmias, myocardial infarction, and heart failure.

Since RA can affect multiple systems, specific diagnostics may vary from patient to patient. It is common for the CBC of an RA patient show anemia. Those suspected to have RA may also have a serum rheumatoid factor drawn to check for antibodies specific to RA. MRI can also be used for diagnosis and may be repeated throughout the patient's care to monitor for changes caused by the disease.

Treatment of the RA patient will be specific to the body systems affected by the disease. Medication options that may be utilized include the following: NSAIDs for pain relief and to decrease inflammation; steroids to further decrease inflammation; and immunosuppressants to decrease the body's autoimmune response. Surgery, such as joint repair, may also be indicated.

Nursing management of the RA patient involves the following: maintaining patient comfort; assessing for potentially worsening symptoms (e.g., heart or lung dysfunction); maintaining patient safety (e.g., infection prevention); and educating the patient on self-care upon discharge (e.g. infection prevention and diet/exercise maintenance).

Systemic Sclerosis

Systemic sclerosis is an autoimmune disease in which connective tissue is affected, causing fibrosis and tissue hardening. This disease can affect most systems of the body, including the skin, heart, lungs, joints, kidneys, and the gastrointestinal system. The skin of the patient with systemic sclerosis may be tough and shiny with development of calcifications in the subcutaneous layer. Additionally, joints may become arthritic and contracted. The lungs may develop fibrosis, leading to difficulty breathing or respiratory failure, while the heart may develop pericarditis, heart failure, and arrythmias. The disease's effect on the gastrointestinal system may cause dysphagia, malabsorption, peritonitis, and cirrhosis. Diagnosis of systemic sclerosis is primarily based on clinical manifestations along with antibody testing.

Treatment of systemic sclerosis is dependent upon the organs affected and progression of damage to each system. In general, patients with systemic sclerosis may be prescribed NSAIDs for pain and inflammation relief. As with other autoimmune diseases, steroids and immunosuppressants are commonly prescribed to decrease the immune system's attack on the body systems. Should the heart be affected, drugs may be prescribed to treat heart failure, hypertension, pericarditis, and arrythmias. Kidney failure may require hemodialysis and kidney transplant, while respiratory fibrosis may require supplemental oxygen and eventually lung transplant.

Nursing management of systemic sclerosis requires thorough head-to-toe assessment, including cardiac and respiratory monitoring. Nurses should monitor for ECG changes, laboratory results (e.g. those indicating heart, kidney, or liver failure), and for clinical manifestations of worsening progression of the disease. Nurses should also be mindful of infection prevention for patients on immunosuppressants, as they are at greater risk of developing sepsis.

Sjögren's Syndrome

Sjögren's syndrome is an autoimmune disorder that affects the mucous membranes, most commonly causing severely dry eyes and mouth. These patients can later have damage to other organs, such as the kidneys, liver, lungs, and nervous system. Diagnostics for Sjögren's include blood tests for antibodies, x-ray or nuclear medicine imaging of the salivary glands, and mucous membrane biopsy. Treatment involves medications to improve eye and mouth hydration, antifungals to prevent yeast infection to the mucous membranes, and systemic immunosuppressants to decrease the overall effects on the body. Nursing management involves providing supportive care for symptoms, such as ensuring sufficient hydration and pain control. The nurse should also be mindful that patients on immunosuppressants are at increased risk of infection. Therefore, careful hand hygiene and standard precautions are especially important. Any signs of infection should be immediately reported to the patient's physician, as these patients are at increased risk of sepsis.

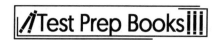

Myositis

Myositis is an autoimmune disorder that attacks the patient's muscles. In most cases, it will attack the muscles of the trunk, arms, and legs. However, in some cases, the esophagus, eyes, and even the diaphragm may be affected. Diagnostics include MRI, muscle biopsy, and electromyography. Treatment, as with other autoimmune disorders, involves immune suppression through the use of steroids and immunosuppressants. In addition, these patients may benefit from physical therapy to help regain lost muscle strength. If the disorder affects the patient's esophagus, the patient may have difficulty swallowing or digesting food and require external assistance receiving nourishment. This may involve placement of a nasogastric tube or a gastric tube to allow for tube feeding. Should the disorder attack the patient's diaphragm, the patient may be unable to breathe sufficiently and require mechanical ventilation. The nurse should look for signs of difficulty swallowing (in case of aspiration) and difficulty breathing. However, specific care interventions may differ among patients, depending on which muscles are affected and the level of assistance required with activities of daily living. The nurse should also be mindful that patients on immunosuppressants are at increased risk of infection. Therefore, careful hand hygiene and standard precautions are especially important. Any signs of infection should be immediately reported to the patient's physician, as these patients are at an increased risk of sepsis.

Respiratory Depression

Respiratory depression, also referred to as **hypoventilation**, occurs when the amount of inhaled air or tidal volume is insufficient for normal gas exchange at the alveolar membrane. If hypoventilation is severe or prolonged, the saturation of oxygen in the circulating blood volume falls, while the carbon dioxide level rises. This results in tissue hypoxia and subsequent depression of the respiratory drive, due to the onset of respiratory acidosis. The most common causes of hypoventilation include narcotic, barbiturate, and benzodiazepine medication overdoses; however, if the specific agent is not known, the **naloxone protocol** is used to determine the if a narcotic medication is the source of the hypoventilation.

Depressed respiratory function can also result from any traumatic brain injury (TBI), hemorrhagic or occlusive event that damages the brainstem, increased intracranial pressure or status epilepticus, or rarely from adult congenital central hypoventilation syndrome. Direct injury to the brainstem results in damage to the chemoreceptors that control respiration, and the brain stem is also adversely affected by the decreased blood pressure and ischemia associated with increased intracranial pressure. Anxiety and restlessness, which can occur before any overt signs of respiratory depression, are associated with the onset of hypoventilation, which may be rapid or slowly progressive. Depending on the patient's baseline health status and the cause of the hypoventilation, the treatment includes the elimination of the cause and ventilatory support.

SaO₂ Monitoring

If the SaO_2 obtained via blood analysis is greater than 94%, this means that the partial pressure of arterial blood oxygen (PaO_2) is greater than 70 mmHg and no immediate action aside from continued intermittent monitoring is required. When the SaO_2 is between 90% and 94%, this represents a PaO_2 that falls within 60–70 mmHg; in this case, the progressive care nurse should reposition the probe to ensure accuracy and continue intermittent or continuous monitoring, depending on the patient's overall pulmonary status and pattern of results. If the SaO_2 is between 85% and 90% while the PaO_2 is within 55–60 mmHg, the nurse should expect orders to administer non-invasive oxygen therapy, place the patient in prone position, and instruct the patient to take slow, deep breaths. If this does not raise the

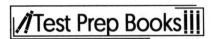

SaO_2 or if the SaO_2 drops below 85% (PaO_2 drops below 55 mmHg), the nurse should notify the provider immediately as more invasive therapies may be necessitated.

Respiratory Failure

Any case in which oxygen exchange in the alveoli of the lungs is impaired, whether due to impaired respiration, weakness of respiratory effort, or obstruction of the airway, is called **respiratory failure**. Though respiratory arrest and cardiac arrest are two different events, one always leads to another if the problem is left untreated. Lack of oxygen will cause permanent damage to vital organs if respiratory arrest goes on for longer than around five minutes. For the progressive care nurse, a patient may present with **acute (short term) respiratory failure**, which can develop very quickly from respiratory or non-respiratory causes and require emergency care. However, a great number of patients cared for in progressive care units suffer from **chronic (long term) respiratory failure**, which comes on slowly and is usually the result of a lung disease requiring ongoing, long-term care. Patients with diseases such as COPD, asthma, and cystic fibrosis are at a much higher risk of developing chronic respiratory failure.

Patients with central nervous system deficits may have decreased respiratory effort, leading to respiratory failure. Examples of this include brain stem injuries, as is the case with strokes and tumors. An adverse medication effect may cause decreased respiratory effort. Alcohol, opioids, and sedatives are all examples of drugs that can depress respiratory effort to the point of failure. Respiratory failure can also occur because of an upper or lower airway obstruction. Upper airway obstructions include blood, mucus, foreign objects, tumors, inflammation, or edema. Lower airway obstructions include aspiration, bronchospasm, pneumonia, pulmonary edema or hemorrhage, or drowning. Hypoglycemia and hypotension are examples of metabolic disorders that may weaken respiratory effort.

Timely nursing assessments are critical for recognizing a patient in respiratory distress who is progressing into respiratory failure. A focused respiratory assessment includes assessing for hypoxia, tachypnea, tachycardia, and mottled extremities. The nurse should recognize any anxiety, irritability, and confusion as a potential sign of hypoxia. The nurse should also monitor for signs of respiratory distress, such as nasal flaring, intercostal retractions, profuse sweating, lowered respiratory effort, difficulty breathing, unconsciousness, cyanosis, and decreased pulse oximetry readings. It is imperative that the progressive care nurse maintain the patient's airway to prevent progression from respiratory distress to arrest. Interventions to support the patient's airway include optimal positioning; performing the **head tilt-chin lift** maneuver to help with occlusions; removing and minimizing sputum or other airway secretions; and early assessment, intervention, and reporting of respiratory distress to the provider. Most hospitals also have a rapid response team (RRT) which should be called as soon as symptoms of respiratory distress appear.

Diagnosis of respiratory failure will be based on clinical observation, and treatment will depend on finding and reversing the cause. If there is an obstruction present, it will need to be removed. If failure was caused by an adverse drug effect, an antidote may be given if appropriate. Titration of oxygen and non-invasive ventilation may be tried, but if those are unsuccessful, or if the patient is in extreme distress, intubation and mechanical ventilation may be necessary to prevent impending cardiac arrest. Oxygenation and ventilation are the high priorities at this point.

Considering that the goals are to maintain airway patency and ensure adequate oxygenation, nursing responsibilities in respiratory management involve understanding when and how to use oxygen delivery devices, along with monitoring for effectiveness. Oxygen delivery systems that the progressive care nurse should be prepared to use include the nasal cannula, simple face mask, partial rebreather mask, non-rebreather mask, Venturi mask, high-flow nasal cannula, BiPAP, and CPAP.

Device	Image of Device	Max Flow Rate	FiO2	Indications	Nursing Management
Nasal cannula		6 L/min	24–44%	For patients requiring a smaller amount of O2 through their nose to maintain sufficient oxygen saturation	- Monitor for skin breakdown and dry mucous membranes. This can be remedied with use of humidity or nasal ointments. - Evaluate if appropriate for patient needs.
Simple face mask		10 L/min	40–60%	For patients who are mouth breathers or require 5-10 L/min of oxygen and therefore cannot use a nasal cannula	- Minimum flow rate is 5 L/min - Monitor for skin breakdown. - Offer assistance with meals or supplementation.
Venturi mask		Blue: 3 L/min White: 6 L/min Yellow: 12 L/min Red: 15 L/min Green: 15 L/min	Blue 24% White 28% Yellow 35% Red 40% Green 60%	For patients requiring less than 5 L/min of oxygen (but nasal cannulas are ineffective) or who need tighter control of FiO2 and flow rate	- Valve colors correspond to different FiO2 and flow rates - Offer assistance with meals or supplementation.

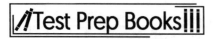

Partial rebreather mask		10 L/min	60–80%	For patients with low blood oxygen levels for whom non-rebreathers are not safe	- Allows for some rebreathing and decreases the risk of suffocation that non-rebreather masks may have
Non-rebreather mask		15 L/min	60–90%	For patients who have low blood oxygen levels, such as due to COPD, carbon monoxide poisoning, and smoke inhalation	- Use with caution since patient may suffocate from carbon dioxide inhalation. In order to prevent this, the minimum flow rate is 10 L/min. - If needed, change to a simple mask or a partial rebreather to decrease the risk of suffocation.
High-flow nasal cannula	360° Smooth Rotatable	60 L/min	100%	For patients with respiratory distress for whom nasal cannula and masks have not supplied sufficient oxygenation	- Patients requiring high-flow are at greater risk of decompensating; use continuous cardiac/respiratory monitoring. - Monitor blood gases to determine effectiveness of treatment. - As the oxygen is delivered at such a high rate, this route can be incredibly uncomfortable. This can be remedied with heated and humidified oxygen.

				For patients requiring increased positive end-expiratory pressure (PEEP) For stable patients with sleep apnea who require different inhalation and exhalation pressures	- Contraindicated for patients who are unconscious or at risk of aspiration due to inability to control secretions or emesis - Ensure proper seal on patient's face. - Monitor blood gases and patient tolerance to determine effectiveness or need to return to less invasive method of oxygen.
BiPAP	**Bilevel Positive Airway Pressure (BPAP)**	30 cm H₂O	35–100%		
CPAP		15 cm H₂O	>90%	For patients who require assistance with opening their airway, such as in acute pulmonary edema or stable patients with sleep apnea	- Should not be used for patients with aspiration risk who are unable to control their secretions or emesis - Ensure proper seal on patient's face. Some models only cover the nose, while others include the mouth.

Failure to Wean

In the event that a patient requires invasive oxygen therapy through mechanical ventilation, the patient will typically be transferred to an intensive care unit. While the progressive care nurse can play a vital role in all steps of ventilator care, the most common scenario is ventilator weaning once the patient has been stabilized and is deemed medically appropriate to extubate. Sedation and neuromuscular blocking agents are reduced while weaning, which is the process of decreasing ventilator support. However, if the patient is unable to remain hemodynamically stable and maintain their respiratory function independently, the medications are increased.

A **spontaneous breathing trial** (SBT) is used to assess the patient's ability to breathe on their own once the underlying condition causing the respiratory failure is thought to have been resolved. If the weaning attempt fails, the nurse continues to provide supportive care, including assessing sleep quality, handgrip strength, and diaphragmatic function. As the ultimate goal is to successfully wean off mechanical ventilation, the nurse monitors patient readiness to engage in another spontaneous breathing trial. Typical criteria include adequate cough, reduction of tracheobronchial secretions, stable cardiovascular status, adequate hemoglobin level, afebrile, and a tidal volume greater than 5 mL/kg.

Failure to wean can be related to multiple factors including respiratory/ventilatory issues, cardiac dysfunction, psychological/neurological dysfunction, and malnutrition. Medical interventions for a patient that has failed to wean off mechanical ventilation include the following:

- Reevaluate timing, duration, and method of SBTs
- Ensure adequate positioning during SBT
- Provide suctioning and any appropriate bronchodilators prior to SBT
- Providing physical therapy for respiratory muscles
- Tracheostomy placement for the refractory patient (multiple failed SBTs with medical interventions provided for underlying cause)

Tracheostomy Care

A patient may require the establishment of a **tracheostomy** if long-term care via invasive mechanical ventilation is warranted. Tracheostomy care responsibilities for the progressive care nurse include ensuring the stoma remains clean, patent, and free from infection; assessing lung fields; and suctioning secretions. For patients vulnerable to decreased oxygen levels, such as those receiving mechanical ventilation, the nurse provides suction for shorter, more frequent durations to avoid hypoxia. Nursing documentation involves detailed assessment of the color, amount, and consistency of secretions; site and dressing condition; and respiratory status. The nurse should understand the length of time since the tracheostomy was placed, along with the type and size of the tracheostomy tube. The correct sized obturator, additional tube, lubricant, and syringe should always be readily available at the bedside—especially for a tracheostomy tube that has been in place less than seven days, as it is not considered mature. While the patient is under sedation and unable to verbally respond, the nurse should also be cognizant of the patient's potential to be present for the interventions and verbally explain the process to the patient to reduce anxiety, maintain dignity, and provide patient-centered care.

Ventilator Management

A **mechanical ventilator** is a machine that assists a patient with breathing. The ventilator may provide all inspiration and expiration efforts for the patient, or it may work with the patient's spontaneous breathing pattern to ensure sufficient respiration. For example, a BiPAP may provide positive pressure to increase a fluid-overloaded patient's lung capacity with spontaneous breaths, but a patient in a traumatic coma may require full mechanical ventilation if they are unable to breathe on their own. While these are both examples of emergent use of mechanical ventilation, some patients require chronic ventilators to continue breathing sufficiently upon discharge. Some indications for chronic ventilators are neuromuscular diseases (e.g., amyotrophic lateral sclerosis); end-stage chronic lung conditions (e.g., chronic obstructive pulmonary disease); recovery from an extended hospital stay requiring mechanical ventilation (e.g., severe pneumonia or trauma); and other chronic conditions that may obstruct breathing (e.g., severe obesity). Some of these patients may eventually be weaned from the mechanical ventilator to breathe independently, but those with progressive illness may maintain mechanical ventilation for the rest of their lives.

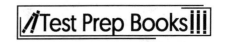

In general, there are two main forms of mechanical ventilation. **Noninvasive ventilation** involves the application of a face mask and is generally used temporarily or only as needed (such as at night). This form of ventilation is usually either BiPAP or CPAP and may be used for temporary exacerbations of respiratory symptoms. In most chronic cases, however, this form of ventilation is used for patients with sleep apnea, who require positive pressure ventilation assistance due to periods of apnea in their sleep. **Chronic invasive ventilation** is usually administered through a tracheostomy and is generally used continuously. The tracheostomy allows the patient to be awake and interact with their surroundings while ventilated. Mechanical ventilators provide a variety of settings: respiratory rate (fully in control of the patient's breathing or supplemental to spontaneous breathing); **tidal volume** (TV, or volume of air moving in and out); **peak inspiratory pressure** (PIP, or the amount of pressure applied to the lung during exhalation); **positive end-expiratory pressure** (PEEP, or the amount of positive pressure in the lungs after exhalation); flow (the amount of oxygen administered per minute); and fraction of inspired oxygen (FiO_2, or the percentage of oxygen in the room air being administered). The specific settings used will be dependent upon the patient and their specific respiratory needs.

Diagnostics that indicate the need for chronic ventilation involve assessment of the patient's respiratory status without mechanical ventilation. The patient may go into respiratory distress or have clinical and laboratory signs of ineffective respiration and gas exchange within the lungs. The patient may require periodic blood gas testing to ensure that current ventilator settings are sufficient. Chest x-rays may be utilized to ensure that adverse effects, such as pneumonia or barotrauma, have not been caused by the continuous mechanical ventilation.

Nursing management of the patient with a chronic ventilator often involves close work with the respiratory therapy team and attending physician. Generally, they will be the providers determining if the ventilator settings need to be modified. However, the nurse should make note of the patient's baseline ventilator settings and monitor for signs of respiratory distress, ventilator errors, and alarms. While each home ventilator may be slightly different, it is important for the nurse to become familiar with its basic functions to assist in troubleshooting any alarms. Should the ventilator stop working entirely, the nurse should be prepared to provide **bag-valve-mask ventilation** (BVM) until the resuscitation team arrives. The nurse may also be responsible for maintaining the patient's airway through routine and as needed suctioning. The patient should be provided with supplemental oxygenation prior to suctioning of the airway, and suctioning should last no longer than 15 seconds to prevent hypoxia. Finally, upon discharge, the patient and any caregivers should be educated on how to use and monitor the ventilator at home.

Respiratory Infections

Upper Respiratory Infections

Epiglottitis

Epiglottitis (also known as **supraglottitis**) is inflammation of the epiglottis. The **epiglottis** is the small piece of cartilage that's pulled forward to cover the windpipe when a person swallows. The cause of the condition is usually bacterial, with *Haemophilus influenzae* type B being the most common. Other bacterial causes include *Streptococcus pneumoniae*, *Streptococcus* groups A, B, and C, and non-typeable *Haemophilus influenzae*. The disease is most diagnosed in children but can be seen in adolescents and adults. A decline in the number of cases of epiglottitis has been noted since the introduction of the *Haemophilus influenzae* type B (Hib) vaccine in the 1980s.

Epiglottitis is usually accompanied by the classic triad of symptoms: dysphagia, drooling, and respiratory distress. Other signs and symptoms can include:

- Fever
- Sore throat
- Inability to lay flat
- Voice changes (can be muffled or hoarse)
- **Tripod breathing position** (a position said to optimize the mechanics of breathing where an individual sits up on their hands, with their head leaning forward and tongue protruding)
- Tachypnea
- Hypoxia
- Agitation
- Cyanosis

Direct visualization of the epiglottis via nasopharyngoscopy/laryngoscopy is the gold standard for diagnosing epiglottitis since an infected epiglottis has a cherry red appearance.

Epiglottitis is a potentially life-threatening medical emergency and should be treated promptly. It can quickly progress to total obstruction of the airway and death. Treatment of the condition can include:

- IV antibiotics (after blood and epiglottic cultures have been obtained)

- Analgesic-antipyretic agents such as aspirin (for adults), acetaminophen, and nonsteroidal anti-inflammatory drugs (NSAIDs, such as ibuprofen)

- Intubation with mechanical ventilation, tracheostomy, or needle-jet insufflation (options for immediate airway management, if needed)

Laryngitis

Laryngitis is inflammation to the larynx. This inflammation can be caused by overuse of the vocal cords, irritation from external toxins or allergens, or infection. Typical signs and symptoms of laryngitis include sore throat, hoarseness when vocalizing, fatigue, fever, cough, and swollen lymph nodes. Diagnosis of laryngitis is typically done through clinical manifestations. However, the provider may order laboratory testing and imaging to determine the cause of the laryngitis and severity of the illness.

Since laryngitis is typically caused by a viral infection, treatment is usually supportive based on symptoms. Hydration and voice rest are typically recommended to relieve larynx discomfort and improve recovery. Antitussives may be prescribed to decrease coughing. If the cause is suspected to be bacterial, the physician may prescribe an antibiotic. Laryngitis is usually self-limiting, and the patient will generally recover within two to three weeks. If symptoms last longer, the laryngitis may be chronic and require follow-up with an otolaryngologist.

Nursing management of the patient with laryngitis mainly involves providing supportive care for the patient's symptoms. Along with pushing fluids, the nurse may provide humidified air to relieve larynx discomfort. The nurse should monitor for signs of airway obstruction and respiratory distress. In immunocompromised populations, laryngitis could turn into sepsis, which the nurse should be aware of and recognize for early treatment.

Pharyngitis

Pharyngitis refers to inflammation of the pharynx and is typically caused by a viral or bacterial infection of the throat or tonsils. Signs and symptoms of pharyngitis can include sore throat, fever, fatigue, cough, swollen lymph nodes, and tonsillar exudate. Diagnosis tends to be based on a combination of clinical presentation and laboratory tests. A swab of the tonsils may be done to determine if the pharyngitis is caused by *Group A Streptococcus*, commonly known as **strep throat**. If swelling is severe, a CT scan of the patient's head and neck may be done to determine the extent of the swelling and other potential causes (e.g., cancerous lesions).

Treatment of pharyngitis is dependent upon the cause and extent of the illness. If the patient is found to have strep throat, an antibiotic will be prescribed to treat the infection and decrease the patient's risk of developing rheumatic fever, which can cause pericarditis. Regardless of the cause, treatment will include maintaining airway patency, rest, and fluids.

Nursing management of the patient with pharyngitis prioritizes monitoring airway patency, cardiac status (especially with strep throat), and providing supportive care for the patient's symptoms. Antipyretics may be given for fever, and fluids should be encouraged to decrease throat irritation and promote healing. If the patient is discharged on antibiotics, the nurse should provide education on the importance of completing the regimen to decrease the risks of developing worsening infection or pericarditis. Should pharyngitis be recurrent, the patient may require follow-up with an otolaryngologist.

Sinusitis

Sinusitis is inflammation of the sinuses that is typically viral but can also be caused by bacterial infection or allergies. Signs and symptoms of sinusitis can include rhinorrhea, congestion, headache, fever, fatigue, cough, and pressure to the sinus areas. Diagnosis is typically based on clinical presentation. However, if symptoms are severe and include altered mental status, nuchal rigidity, or are reoccurring, laboratory testing and imaging (e.g., CT scan) may be done to find a specific cause and rule out sepsis.

Treatment is usually supportive based on symptoms. The patient may be given a saline nasal spray or decongestants to assist with congestion and a steroid to assist with inflammation. If a bacterial infection is suspected, the patient may be prescribed an antibiotic. If the sinusitis becomes recurrent or complex, an otolaryngologist may be involved for further evaluation and treatment.

Nursing management of the patient with sinusitis is largely supportive. Along with pain management, the nurse may administer nasal sprays to assist with congestion. The nurse should also encourage rest and fluid intake. Warm compresses can be applied to help relieve pressure and congestion. Should the nurse suspect worsening infection or the development of sepsis, the physician should be notified immediately for early intervention.

Lower Respiratory Infections

Bronchitis

Bronchitis is inflammation of the bronchial tubes (bronchi), which extend from the trachea to the lungs. It is one of the top five reasons for visits to healthcare providers and can take between ten days and three weeks to resolve. Common causes of bronchitis include respiratory viruses (such as influenza A and B), RSV, parainfluenza, adenovirus, rhinovirus, and coronavirus. Bacterial causes include *Mycoplasma species, Streptococcus pneumoniae, Chlamydia pneumoniae, Haemophilus influenzae,* and

Moraxella catarrhalis. Other causes of bronchitis are irritants such as chemicals, pollution, and tobacco smoke.

Signs and symptoms of bronchitis can include:

- Cough (most common symptom) with or without sputum
- Fever
- Sore throat
- Headache
- Nasal congestion
- Rhinorrhea
- Dyspnea
- Fatigue
- Myalgia
- Chest pain
- Wheezing

Bronchitis is typically diagnosed by exclusion, which means tests are used to exclude more serious conditions such as pneumonia, epiglottitis, or COPD. Useful diagnostic tests include a CBC with differential, a chest x-ray, respiratory and blood cultures, PFTs, bronchoscopy, laryngoscopy, and a procalcitonin (PCT) test to determine if the infection is bacterial.

Treatment of bronchitis is primarily supportive and can include:

- Bedrest
- Cough suppressants, such as codeine or dextromethorphan
- Beta-2 agonists, such as albuterol for wheezing
- Nonsteroidal anti-inflammatory drugs (NSAIDs) for pain
- Expectorants, such as guaifenesin

Although bronchitis should not be routinely treated with antibiotics, there are exceptions to this rule. It's reasonable to use an antibiotic when an existing medical condition poses a risk of serious complications. Antibiotic use is also reasonable for treating bronchitis in elderly patients who have been hospitalized in the past year, have been diagnosed with congestive heart failure (CHF) or diabetes, or are currently being treated with a steroid.

Bronchiolitis

Bronchiolitis is inflammation of the **bronchioles** (the small airways in the lungs) and is most commonly caused by **respiratory syncytial virus** (RSV). It typically affects children under the age of two, with a peak onset of three to six months of age. The disease is spread through direct contact with respiratory droplets. Bronchiolitis results in hospitalization of approximately 2 percent of children, the majority of which are under six months of age. Criteria for hospitalization can include prematurity, under three months of age, diagnosis of a congenital heart defect, respiratory rate >70–80 bpm, inability to maintain oral hydration, and cyanosis.

Signs and symptoms of bronchiolitis include:

- Difficulty feeding
- Fever
- Congestion
- Cough
- Dyspnea
- Tachypnea
- Nasal flaring
- Tachycardia
- Wheezing
- Fine rales
- Hypoxia
- Retractions
- Apnea

A diagnosis of bronchiolitis is usually established through a clinical examination. The most common diagnostic tests for the disease are: a rapid, viral antigen test of nasopharyngeal secretions for RSV; white blood cell (WBC) count with differential; ABG analysis; a chest x-ray; and a test of C-reactive protein (CRP, a marker of inflammation).

Although highly contagious, the disease is self-limiting and typically resolves without complication in one to two weeks. Treatment of bronchiolitis is supportive and can include oxygen supplementation, maintenance of hydration, fever reducers, nasal and oral suctioning, and intubation and mechanical ventilation.

Pneumonia

Pneumonia is an infection that affects the functional tissue of the lung. Microscopically, it is characterized by consolidated lung tissue, with exudate, fibrin, and inflammatory cells filling the alveoli (air sacs). Pneumonia can represent a primary disease or a secondary disease (e.g., post-obstructive pneumonia due to lung cancer), and the most common causes of pneumonia are bacteria and viruses. Other causes of pneumonia include fungi and parasites.

Pneumonia can be categorized according to its anatomic distribution on a chest x-ray or the setting in which it is acquired.

Pneumonia categorized according to its anatomic distribution on chest x-ray can be:

- **Lobar pneumonia**: Affects one or more lobes of the lungs. It can affect more than one lobe on the same side (unilateral multilobar pneumonia) or bilateral lobes ("double" pneumonia).

- **Bronchopneumonia**: Scattered diffusely throughout the lungs

- **Interstitial pneumonia**: Involves areas between the alveoli

Pneumonia categorized according to the setting in which it is acquired can be:

- **Community-Acquired Pneumonia** (CAP): Pneumonia in an individual who hasn't been recently hospitalized, or its occurrence in less than 48 hours after admission to a hospital.

- **Hospital-Acquired (Nosocomial) Pneumonia**: Pneumonia acquired during or after hospitalization for another ailment with onset at least 48 hours or more after admission.

- **Aspiration Pneumonia**: Pneumonia resulting from the inhalation of gastric or oropharyngeal secretions.

Common causes of community-acquired pneumonia (CAP) include:

- *Streptococcus pneumoniae*

- *Haemophilus influenzae*

- *Moraxella catarrhalis*

- Atypical organisms (such as *Legionella* species, *Mycoplasma pneumoniae*, and *Chlamydia pneumoniae*)

- *Staphylococcus aureus*

- Respiratory viruses

Streptococcus pneumonia (also known as **S. pneumonia** or **pneumococcal pneumonia**) is a gram-positive bacterium and the most common cause of CAP. Due to the introduction of a pneumococcal vaccine in 2000, cases of pneumococcal pneumonia have decreased. However, medical providers should be aware there is now evidence of increasing antibiotic-resistant strains of the organism. Signs and symptoms of pneumococcal pneumonia can include:

- Cough productive of rust-colored sputum (mucus)
- Fever with or without chills
- Dyspnea
- Wheezing
- Chest pain
- Tachypnea
- Altered mental status
- Tachycardia
- Rales over involved lung
- Increase in tactile fremitus
- Egophony ("E" to "A" change)
- Hypotension
- Lung consolidation

Diagnosis of pneumococcal pneumonia can include:

- CBC with differential
- Chest x-ray
- CT scan (if underlying lung cancer is suspected)
- Sputum gram stain and/or culture
- Blood cultures
- Procalcitonin (PCT) and C-reactive protein (CRP) blood level tests

- Sputum, serum, and/or urinary antigen tests
- Immunoglobulin studies
- Bronchoscopy with bronchoalveolar lavage (BAL)

Treatment of pneumococcal pneumonia can include:

- Antibiotics, such as ceftriaxone plus doxycycline, or azithromycin
- Respiratory quinolones, such as levofloxacin, moxifloxacin, or gemifloxacin
- Supplemental oxygen
- Beta-2 agonists, such as albuterol via nebulizer or metered-dose inhaler (MDI), as needed for wheezing
- Analgesics and antipyretics
- Chest physiotherapy
- Active suctioning of respiratory secretions
- Intubation and mechanical ventilation

Mycoplasma pneumonia, also known as **M. pneumoniae**, is a bacterium that causes atypical CAP. It is one of the most common causes of CAP in healthy individuals under the age of forty. The most common symptom of mycoplasma pneumonia is a dry, nonproductive cough. Other signs and symptoms can include diarrhea, earache, fever (usually ≤ 102 °F), sore throat, myalgias, nasal congestion, skin rash, and general malaise. Chest x-rays of individuals with mycoplasma pneumonia reveal a pattern of bronchopneumonia. Cold agglutinin titers in the blood can be significantly elevated (> 1:64). Serology, sputum cultures, and polymerase chain reaction (PCR) tests are the most common confirmatory tests for mycoplasma pneumonia. PCR is becoming more commonly used due to the rapid results but is typically used in conjunction with additional diagnostics.

Treatments for mycoplasma pneumonia are no different than for CAP, except for antibiotic choices, which include:

- Macrolide antibiotics, such as erythromycin, azithromycin, clarithromycin
- Doxycycline (a tetracycline antibiotic derivative)

Community-Acquired Methicillin-Resistant Staphylococcus Aureus (CA-MRSA), while not as common, has emerged as a concerning form of CAP. It also remains a significant cause of hospital-acquired pneumonia with a high mortality rate (ranging from 30–40 percent or as high as 63 percent in some studies). The at-risk population for CA-MRSA can vary drastically, but includes prolonged hospitalization, recent or prolonged antibiotic usage, history of MRSA colonization, recurring hemodialysis, injection drug use, athletes (frequent skin-to-skin contact increases risk for MRSA infection), and crowded living situations. Symptoms are usually identical to those seen with other causes of CAP. Chest x-ray typically reveals multilobar involvement with or without cavitation/necrosis. Gram staining of sputum and/or blood can reveal gram-positive bacteria in clusters. Other diagnostic tests are nonspecific and do not aid in the diagnosis of CA-MRSA pneumonia.

Treatment of CA-MRSA should be prompt due to the high mortality rate. Supportive measures are needed as in other cases of CAP. CA-MRSA is notoriously resistant to most antibiotics, with the exception of vancomycin and linezolid.

Viral pneumonia is more common at the extremes of age (young children and the elderly). It accounts for the majority of cases of childhood pneumonia. Common causes of viral pneumonia in children, the elderly, and the immunocompromised are the influenza viruses (most common), RSV, parainfluenza virus, and adenovirus.

Signs and symptoms of viral pneumonia largely overlap those of bacterial pneumonia and can include:

- Cough (nonproductive)
- Fever/chills
- Myalgias
- Fatigue
- Headache
- Dyspnea
- Tachypnea
- Tachycardia
- Wheezing
- Cyanosis
- Hypoxia
- Decreased breath sounds
- Respiratory distress

Viral pneumonia is diagnosed via a chest x-ray and viral cultures. The chest x-ray usually reveals bilateral lung infiltrates, instead of the lobar involvement commonly seen in bacterial causes. Viral cultures can take up to two weeks to confirm the diagnosis. Molecular testing, specifically the polymerase chain reaction (PCR) test, is commonly used to shorten the lag time in confirming the diagnosis.

Treatment of viral pneumonia is usually supportive and can include:

- Supplemental oxygen
- Rest
- Antipyretics
- Analgesics
- Intravenous fluids
- Parenteral nutrition
- Intubation and mechanical ventilation

Thoracic Surgery

In certain conditions of the lung, **thoracic surgery** may be considered. A thoracic surgeon is one who specializes in operations on the thoracic region of the body, involving the organs of the chest. The heart and lungs are the primary targets of these surgical procedures.

Surgeries may be performed to remove cancerous tumors of the lung. Possible procedures a patient would undergo for this purpose would be a pneumonectomy, lobectomy, wedge resection, or sleeve resection. **Pneumonectomy** removes the entire lung, while **lobectomy** removes the entire lobe that is diseased. **Wedge resection** removes part of the affected lobe. **Sleeve resection** refers to "trimming" the affected part of the airway and sewing it back together, like cutting a stain off a sleeve and reattaching the upper and lower portions.

If a thoracic surgeon wishes to visualize the interior of the chest wall and surrounding tissues, they may opt to perform a **thoracoscopy**. During this procedure, small incisions are made into the chest wall, and a thin tube with a camera at the end, called a *scope*, is inserted. The surgeon then explores the interior cavity and visualizes the area they wish to view. This procedure may be used to biopsy tissue for histological analysis. A more invasive procedure used to visualize the interior chest cavity is called a **thoracotomy**, where the chest is opened directly.

Thoracic surgery involves either percutaneous or open incisions into the thorax for the purpose of removing cancerous or benign lesions, diseased tissue that may result from tuberculosis or other infections, or non-functioning tissue that increases the respiratory effort in patients with chronic obstructive pulmonary disease (COPD). The choice of the exact procedure is dependent on the type, size, and location of the lesion.

There are two basic approaches to the removal of the tissue, including an anatomic approach and a nonanatomic approach. Anatomic approaches include the pneumonectomy, lobectomy, segmentectomy, and the sleeve resection, which require ligation and attachment of the "feeding vessels" and the airways to a portion of unresected lung tissue. A nonanatomic wedge resection is considered a nonanatomic approach, as a large piece of anatomical tissue is not removed.

Lobectomy

A **lobectomy** refers to the removal of an entire lobe of one lung with ligation of its vasculature and lobular bronchi. Lobectomy is most commonly performed for the treatment of primary and metastatic lung cancer, bronchiectasis, and traumatic injury.

The specific surgical approach is based on a rigorous preoperative evaluation and risk assessment and may be either an open procedure, or a minimally invasive procedure such as video-assisted thoracoscopic surgery (VATS), or robotic-assisted thoracoscopic surgery (RATS). Video-assisted thoracoscopic surgery (VATS) results in fewer hospital days and a quicker recovery as compared to the open approach. In addition, the VATS approach has gained wider acceptance than the RATS approach due to the expense of the system and accessibility of equipment. Video-assisted thoracoscopic surgery (VATS) uses a small video camera called a thoracoscope to diagnose and treat chest conditions. The camera is inserted into the chest via one or more small incisions. The surgeon is guided through the procedure via chest images projected onto the video screen. This technique may be performed to assist with multiple surgical procedures, such a lung biopsy, hiatal hernia repair, or thymus gland removal, among many other chest-related issues.

Possible complications include hemorrhage, nerve damage, and pneumonia. Compared with more invasive options such as thoracotomy, VATS may improve outcomes by reducing complications and shortening recovery time. Nursing care involves frequent respiratory and cardiac monitoring, pain assessment and management, and patient education regarding condition-specific care. Wound assessment and management are conducted to reduce post-operative risk for infection and bleeding. As VATS is used to support the investigation and treatment of a large variety of chest conditions, additional care considerations should be tailored to the underlying reason for the VATS, along with condition-specific discharge planning.

Post-operative care following any type of lobectomy is focused on providing pain management, treating the underlying cause, and maintenance of optimal respiratory function.

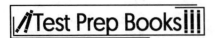

Pneumonectomy

A **left pneumonectomy** is the removal of both the upper and lower lobes, while a **right pneumonectomy** refers to the removal of the upper, middle and lower lobes. Indications for pneumonectomy include stage I and II primary tumors, selected metastatic lesions, pulmonary TB, fungal infections, and traumatic tracheobronchial injuries. Pneumonectomy is an anatomic approach to thoracic surgery that requires securing the fragile pulmonary vasculature and the pulmonary airway structures to maintain the integrity of the surviving lung. The preoperative evaluation for pneumonectomy includes a comprehensive risk assessment that compares all elements of the patient's pulmonary and constitutional status to the projected outcome of the surgical procedure. In addition, all imaging studies will be completed and repeated if necessary.

Currently, pneumonectomy commonly requires an open surgical approach that corresponds to the anatomical position of the disease; however, in patients with small growths that are favorably positioned, the use of VATS, a minimally invasive approach, may be an option. The less invasive surgical approach is associated with improved patient outcomes and decreased length of stay, which offsets the initial expenses of the VATS technology.

After thoracic surgery, use of an incentive spirometer is usually encouraged during a patient's postoperative recovery. **Incentive spirometry** promotes maximal inspiratory volume and lung expansion to prevent atelectasis. The progressive care nurse can also use incentive spirometry readings to assess patients for signs of atelectasis, along with watching for decreased breath sounds, shallow respirations, and changes in vital signs and respiratory rate or depth. This process provides identification of respiratory conditions that impede breathing and also supports healthy respiratory function. The nurse must take great care to consider discontinuation of incentive spirometry use if the patient is uncooperative or if hypoxia develops secondary to the interruption of other prescribed therapies. After educating the patient on the procedure, the nurse assists them to an upright position and uses pillows for splinting support when necessary. The nurse instructs the patient to exhale, and then inhale slowly to full lung capacity while maintaining sealed lips around the spirometry mouthpiece. At this point, the nurse instructs the patient to hold their breath for three to five seconds and notes the highest level the volume indicator reaches to gather the **inspiratory capacity**.

Nursing care for pneumonectomy or lobectomy involves assisting with ambulation and cardiopulmonary therapies as indicated. **Air leaks** are significant post-operative complications requiring expiratory chest tube management, while prolonged air leaks lasting a week may require subsequent surgical intervention to correct. The nurse should focus on respiratory assessment to discover early warning signs of complications and proactively support healing to reduce the risk of atelectasis, mucous plugging, and pneumonia. Patient education should involve the importance of smoking cessation and strategies for goal attainment, which should ideally be initiated pre-operatively and continued in the post-operative period. Chest physiotherapy, antibiotic treatment, and pain management techniques should be included as needed. Additional complications vary by procedure specifics, which may include pulmonary edema, cardiac herniation, hemothorax, bronchopleural fistula, wound infection, chylothorax, hemorrhage, and nerve injury.

The progressive care nurse should closely watch for early complications and report abnormal findings to the care team for continued monitoring and diagnosis, which may involve imaging, laboratory assessment, and invasive procedures. Length-of-stay and discharge instructions are dependent on the particular procedure performed and the patient's individual response to it. The nurse should prioritize adequate patient ventilation, which is evidenced by smooth, non-labored respirations; normal respiratory rate (within the patient's typical baseline or normal baseline for the specific condition); and breath sounds present in all lobes prior to discharge.

Practice Quiz

1. Apnea and loss of normal oxygenation during a spontaneous breathing trial are signs that what should occur?
   a. Sedation should be increased.
   b. The breathing trial should continue for a few more minutes.
   c. An antidote for respiratory distress should be administered.
   d. Mechanical ventilation should continue.

2. Which of the following procedures confirms a diagnosis of pulmonary hypertension?
   a. Transesophageal echocardiography
   b. Right cardiac catheterization
   c. Left cardiac catheterization
   d. Lung transplantation

3. Pulmonary hypertension will likely be treated with all but which of the following drug therapies?
   a. Sildenafil
   b. Amlodipine
   c. Epoprostenol
   d. Diazepam

4. Which of the following terms refers to severe bronchoconstriction with wheezing that does not respond to the usual bronchodilation treatment?
   a. Delirium tremens
   b. Status asthmaticus
   c. Pulsus paradoxus
   d. Febre rubra

5. Which of the following is a more invasive procedure performed by a thoracic surgeon involving opening the chest wall to visualize the interior structures?
   a. Thoracotomy
   b. Thoracentesis
   c. Thoracobronchotomy
   d. Thoracoscopy

See answers on the next page.

Answer Explanations

1. D: If a patient becomes apneic and oxygenation level decreases during a spontaneous breathing trial, it is a sign that the patient should be placed back on mechanical ventilation, as they are not ready to breathe on their own. Increasing sedation will worsen the patient's breathing function, making Choice *A* incorrect. Continuing the breathing trial will lead to organ damage due to lack of oxygenation and perfusion, making Choice *B* incorrect. Choice *C* is incorrect, as an antidote is not appropriate in this scenario.

2. B: Right cardiac catheterization is a procedure that will confirm a diagnosis of pulmonary hypertension. Transesophageal echocardiography is useful in visualizing the back side of the heart but does not fit with this specific scenario, making Choice *A* incorrect. Left cardiac catheterization enters the opposite side of the heart and is not helpful in confirming diagnosis, making Choice *C* incorrect. Lung transplantation is a surgical procedure used to treat severe cases of pulmonary hypertension, making Choice *D* incorrect.

3. D: Diazepam is an anxiolytic that is not specifically used for the treatment of pulmonary hypertension. Diuretics, calcium channel blockers, and vasodilators may all be used to treat pulmonary hypertension. Sildenafil is an example of a phosphodiesterase inhibitor and is helpful in increasing blood flow in the lungs, making Choice *A* incorrect. Amlodipine is an example of a calcium channel blocker, a class of drugs that may be helpful for pulmonary hypertension, making Choice *B* incorrect. Epoprostenol is a drug specifically formulated for use in patients with pulmonary hypertension, making Choice *C* incorrect.

4. B: Status asthmaticus is the Latin term for a severe asthma attack, characterized by wheezing and bronchoconstriction, that is unresponsive to the usual therapy of bronchodilators. Delirium tremens is the set of symptoms experienced by an alcoholic in withdrawal, making Choice *A* incorrect. Pulsus paradoxus is defined as a drop in the systolic blood pressure by ten points and a decrease in the amplitude of pulse waves during inspiration. This phenomenon can be observed during cardiac tamponade, making Choice *C* incorrect. Choice *D* is incorrect, as febre rubra is the Latin term for scarlet fever.

5. A: A thoracotomy is the opening of the chest by a thoracic surgeon to visualize the interior structures and tissue of the chest. Thoracentesis is procedure where small incisions are made in the chest wall with the purpose of removing air or fluid and potentially inserting a chest tube to drain, making Choice *B* incorrect. Thoracentesis is also called a pleural tap. Thoracobronchotomy, or thoracic bronchotomy, is a procedure where an incision is made into the bronchus and thorax, usually to remove a tumor or foreign object, making Choice *C* incorrect. Thoracoscopy is a less invasive procedure involving small incisions and the insertion of a thin tube with a camera affixed to the end, called a scope, to visualize the interior structure and tissues of the chest, making Choice *D* incorrect.

Endocrine/Hematology/Neurology/Gastrointestinal/ Renal

The progressive care nurse will encounter several conditions affecting the hormonal regulation of the human body, the blood and its unique chemistry, the digestive tract, the kidneys and their filtration processes, and the largest organ of the body, the skin, which protects the interior of the body from the exterior environment. This section comprises a discussion of those body systems, including the endocrine, hematological, neurological, gastrointestinal, and renal systems.

Endocrine

The hormones of the body play a key role in metabolism and the regulation of body processes. Each hormone, produced in various glands throughout the body, has a specific target tissue that it acts upon, producing a specific result. Dysfunction of hormonal regulation can lead to disease states.

The endocrine system is maintained through homeostatic balance of a variety of hormones. To ensure proper maintenance and detection of disease, laboratory values are monitored via individualized, patient-centered treatment plans regarding frequency and response to results. If medication management is initiated in response to laboratory and clinical findings, repeat laboratory values should be assessed on an individualized basis to provide follow-up response to treatment.

Major Human Endocrine Glands and Some of Their Hormones

Gland		Hormone	Chemical Class	Representative Actions	Regulated By
Hypothalamus		Hormones released from the posterior pituitary and hormones that regulate the anterior pituitary *see below*			
Posterior pituitary gland *Releases neurohormones made in hypothalamus*		Oxytocin	Peptide	Stimulates contraction of uterus and mammary gland cells	Nervous system
		Antidiuretic hormone ADH	Peptide	Promotes retention of water by kidneys	Water/salt balance
Anterior pituitary gland		Growth hormone GH	Protein	Stimulates growth (especially bones) and metabolic functions	Hypothalamic hormones
		Prolactin PRL	Protein	Stimulates milk production and secretion	Hypothalamic hormones
		Follicle-stimulating hormone FSH	Glycoprotein	Stimulates production of ova and sperm	Hypothalamic hormones
		Luteinizing hormone LH	Glycoprotein	Stimulates ovaries and testes	Hypothalamic hormones
		Thyroid-stimulating hormone TSH	Glycoprotein	Stimulates thyroid gland	Hypothalamic hormones
		Adrenocorticotropic hormone ACTH	Peptide	Stimulates adrenal cortex to secrete glucocorticoids	Hypothalamic hormones
Thyroid gland		Triiodothyrocine T_3 Thyroxine T_4	Amine	Stimulate and maintain metabolic processes	TSH
		Calcitonin	Peptide	Lowers blood calcium level	Calcium in blood
Parathyroid glands		Parathyroid hormone PTH	Peptide	Raises blood calcium level	Calcium in blood
Pancreas		Insulin	Protein	Lowers blood calcium level	Glucose in blood
		Glucagon	Protein	Raises blood calcium level	Glucose in blood
Adrenal glands	Adrenal medulla	Epinephrine Norepinephrine	Amines	Raises blood glucose level; Increases metabolic activities; Constrict certain blood vessels	Nervous system
	Adrenal cortex	Glucocorticoids	Steroid	Raises blood glucose level	ACTH
		Mineralocorticoids	Steroid	Promote reabsorbtion of Na^+ and excretion of K^+ in kidneys	K^+ in blood; angiotensin II
Gonads	Testes	Androgens	Steroid	Support sperm formation; Promote development and maintenance of male secondary sex characteristics	FSH LH
	Ovaries	Estrogens	Steroid	Stimulate uterine lining growth; Promote development and maintenance of female secondary sex characteristics	FSH LH
		Progestins	Steroid	Promote uterine lining growth	FSH and LH
Pineal gland		Melatonin	Amine	Involved in biological rhythms	Light/dark cycles

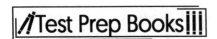
Diabetes Mellitus

Diabetes mellitus is a condition that affects how the body responds to the presence of glucose. Glucose is needed for cell functioning. All consumable calories eventually are converted to glucose in the body. A hormone produced by the pancreas, called **insulin**, is needed to break down food and drink into glucose molecules. In patients with **type 1 diabetes**, the pancreas fails to produce insulin, leading to high levels of glucose in the bloodstream. This can lead to organ damage, organ failure, or nerve damage. Patients with type 1 diabetes receive daily insulin injections or have a pump that can be programmed to release insulin continuously and/or as needed based on the patient's specific needs and blood glucose levels. **Type 2 diabetes** can be an issue with insulin production and/or impairment of insulin sensitivity, also known as **insulin resistance**. Patients with type 2 diabetes typically need to manage their condition through lifestyle changes, such as losing weight and eating fewer carbohydrate-rich and sugary foods. There are also some medications that help the body use the insulin that is present in the bloodstream.

Gestational diabetes is a form of diabetes that some women develop during the second to third trimester of pregnancy, when their systems temporarily become resistant to insulin—typically due to hormonal shifts and potential weight gain. High blood sugar in a pregnant woman can affect fetal growth and influence the baby's risk of becoming obese. Pregnant women with gestational diabetes are encouraged to exercise daily, avoid excessive weight gain, and carefully monitor their diet. Gestational diabetes is similar to type 2 diabetes in the way symptoms present and in treatment options.

Medication management will vary depending on the type of diabetes mellitus and the patient's current medical condition. Diabetes mellitus type I is an autoimmune condition that requires insulin therapy for disease management, as these patients do not produce insulin. Diabetes mellitus type II often requires oral agents for disease management; however, as the disease progresses, patients may require insulin therapy, as they do not respond to insulin effectively and later struggle to produce insulin.

Nursing considerations for insulin administration include ensuring the correct route, either subcutaneous or intravenous (regular insulin). For subcutaneous administration, the injection angle should be at 45–90 degrees, and sites should be rotated to prevent the development of lipohypertrophy. When not in use, insulin vials are stored in the refrigerator once open. If the patient's blood sugar level is well maintained using **mixed insulin**, the care team typically continues this treatment plan, which requires the nurse to first draw up the short-acting insulin and then the long-acting insulin into the syringe. The insulin should not be diluted unless ordered by the provider. Fast-acting insulin should be injected approximately fifteen minutes before meals. Nursing care considerations include thorough knowledge of common hypoglycemic agents, including types, peak, and duration. Before administering hypoglycemic agents, the progressive care nurse should review the indications and directions approved for each medication, as wide variation exists. In general, oral agents typically peak within an hour to several hours, with the onset of action one hour for fast-acting, two to four hours for intermediate-acting, and four to six hours for long-acting insulin therapies.

Diabetic Ketoacidosis (DKA)

A patient diagnosed with diabetes mellitus may be prone to a complication of this condition called **diabetic ketoacidosis** (DKA), which is a medical emergency. While DKA can develop in both type 1 and type 2 diabetes mellitus, it is more common for the type 1 diabetic. The process of developing DKA is a complex metabolic pathway in which the body seeks alternative energy sources to glucose, resulting in an acidotic state.

At the beginning of DKA, the body is in a state of insulin deficiency. This at times happens because of diabetes mellitus, and the body must compensate in attempts to restore homeostasis. The body begins to metabolize triglycerides and amino acids to create energy. In a normal state, the body breaks down glucose as an energy source. However, when insulin is deficient and blood glucose supply is constantly in flux, as is the case with diabetes mellitus, the body searches for an alternative, more stable energy source.

The breakdown of triglycerides and amino acids then causes an increase in serum levels of glycerol and free fatty acids as a byproduct of **lipolysis**, or fat breakdown. Serum alanine also rises, as a byproduct of muscle breakdown, to provide another energy source when the body cannot find enough glucose. This rise in alanine and glycerol stimulates the liver to produce its own glucose as an energy source. Glucagon, which is produced in the pancreas and used as an emergency source of energy when outside glucose sources drop, rises to excessive levels and stimulates free fatty acids to be converted to ketones. This process is called **ketogenesis** and is normally blocked by sufficient levels of insulin. Ketogenesis results in ketoacids, such as acetone, which create the acidic environment of DKA. Acetone is released from the body by way of respiration, which is why a patient with DKA has a "fruity" smell to their breath.

When the blood sugar rises during DKA, it causes substantial amounts of fluids to be excreted through the urine, called **osmotic diuresis**. This leads to fluid and electrolyte imbalances. Potassium levels must be carefully monitored during DKA. They may not initially fall in serum tests because, despite great loss of potassium through the urine, there is also a great release of potassium from the cells into the bloodstream. Potassium will be ushered back into the cells when insulin levels return to normal.

Presenting symptoms of DKA include polyuria, polydipsia, nausea, abdominal pain, fruity breath odor, confusion, and hyperglycemia. Diagnosis will be made based on symptoms and measurements of arterial blood gases. Presence of ketones in the bloodstream (ketonemia) or urine (ketonuria), hyperglycemia, and an anion gap of >20 mEq/L are considered positive diagnostic signs of DKA. Metabolic acidosis, as evidenced by hypocapnia and arterial pH <7.3, can also be diagnostic signs for DKA.

During diabetic ketoacidosis management, the progressive care nurse provides care to reduce unpleasant symptoms while closely monitoring blood glucose levels, intake and output, diabetic diet, vital signs, and level of orientation. Emergency treatment of DKA will include insulin administration, correction of fluid and electrolyte imbalances (especially potassium), and possibly bicarbonate to correct severe cases of acidosis. Most facilities have policies in place for DKA, with the key components including isotonic saline, potassium to replace deficit, and IV insulin at low doses once potassium is within normal range. Frequent blood sugars and ABGs will be drawn per institution protocol. Monitoring serum sodium, potassium, and chloride are also crucial in the medical management of the DKA patient.

Titrating an IV insulin drip is a vital component for the progressive care nurse. The progressive care nurse should feel adequately trained in hospital policy and always have a second nurse verify the insulin drip protocol order and pump settings. Often, once potassium levels are deemed appropriate, an initial bolus of 0.1 units/kg of regular insulin is given and then a continuous drip of 0.1 units/kg/hr is usually started. From there, titrations occur per protocol based on recent blood glucose levels, which should be checked every 1–2 hours during IV insulin administration and PRN with any symptoms of hypoglycemia.

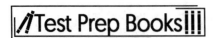
Hyperosmolar Hyperglycemic State (HHS)

A patient with type 2 diabetes has an impaired response to insulin, as the cells have developed a resistance to insulin. When blood sugar rises to unhealthy levels, it stimulates the kidneys to excrete large amounts of urine, a condition called **polyuria**. The blood volume is thus depleted, causing a state of dehydration and abnormal serum concentration. Concentration of the blood creates a hyperosmolar state in the bloodstream. When the blood is concentrated yet not acidotic as a result of fat cells breaking down, it is called **hyperosmolar hyperglycemic state** (HHS).

HHS can result from a patient not taking their prescribed diabetic medications appropriately, causing a hyperglycemic state. At other times, an infection or illness unrelated to diabetes mellitus may cause a hyperglycemic state. Corticosteroids are known to cause a rise in blood sugar; thus, their use must be administered with caution in high-risk individuals. If the patient also suffers from high blood sugar and has been prescribed diuretics, a hyperosmolar state may result. Unlike DKA that typically develops quickly, HHS can gradually progress over days. While hyperglycemia is commonplace for both DKA and HHS, the patient with HHS will have severe hyperglycemia—potentially exceeding 1000 mg/dL.

The concentrated blood of HHS will primarily cause neurological deficits such as confusion, disorientation, drowsiness, and even coma. Certain patients will experience seizures or stroke-like syndromes. Death may occur if HHS is left untreated.

HHS will be diagnosed based on symptoms of confusion and blood tests to look for hyperosmolarity of the blood, as well as decreased blood volume signaling dehydration. Treatment will occur via intravenous (IV) therapy to correct fluid and electrolyte imbalances. Treatment of HHS is very similar to treatment of DKA.

Syndrome of Inappropriate Antidiuretic Hormone Diabetic Secretion (SIADH)

Syndrome of inappropriate antidiuretic hormone secretion (SIADH) is a condition in which too much antidiuretic hormone (ADH) is produced. ADH is a hormone produced in the hypothalamus that assists in controlling urine production and sodium excretion. An increase in ADH causes a decrease in urine production in the kidneys. Possible causes of SIADH include the following: central nervous system disturbances (e.g., brain tumor or abscess, traumatic brain injury, stroke); neurological diseases (e.g., multiple sclerosis, Guillain-Barré syndrome); infections (e.g., meningitis, Rocky Mountain spotted fever, HIV); and certain medications (e.g., antidepressants, antipsychotics, anticonvulsants, pain medications). Signs and symptoms of SIADH are generally related to hyponatremia, as there is an excess of fluid in the blood. These include concentrated or low urinary output, nausea, vomiting, headache, confusion, seizures, and loss of consciousness.

Along with the presence of clinical manifestations, the diagnosis of SIADH mainly involves laboratory testing with further investigation (such as imaging) to assist in determining the cause. A CMP will likely show that the patient is hyponatremic. The patient may also have elevated creatinine, indicating acute kidney injury.

Specific treatment of a patient with SIADH is dependent on the cause, as correcting the underlying issue should correct the disorder. However, the initial treatment includes limiting fluid intake to gradually restore electrolyte imbalances. In some cases, fluid restriction will improve the patient's serum sodium levels. In more severe cases, the patient may require an infusion of hypertonic saline along with furosemide to increase both serum sodium and fluid excretion. However, hyponatremia correction should be gradual to decrease the risk of developing central pontine myelinolysis from the rapid shift in fluid and electrolyte balances.

Nursing management of the patient with SIADH requires close monitoring for worsening electrolyte imbalances and continuous cardiac monitoring for the development of arrythmias. The patient should also have regular neurological assessments as well as strict intake and output measurements.

Diabetes Insipidus (DI)

Diabetes insipidus (DI) is a condition in which the body produces an excess of urine. DI can be either central or nephrogenic. Central DI is generally caused by damage or illness of the pituitary gland or hypothalamus in the brain, which impairs the production or release of antidiuretic hormone (ADH). Nephrogenic DI occurs due to damage in the kidneys and how they respond to ADH. This can be due to an infection, serum electrolyte imbalances, certain medications, or an inherited condition. Regardless of the cause, patients generally present with excessive thirst, excessive urination, and signs of hypernatremia (e.g., muscle weakness, restlessness, seizures, decreased level of consciousness).

Diagnosis of a patient with DI is dependent upon the specific cause. However, the DI patient will have elevated serum sodium levels and highly diluted urine. The patient may also have imaging (e.g., CT scan or MRI) of the brain and kidneys to help determine the likely cause.

The primary goal of treating the patient with DI is to correct fluid and electrolyte imbalances. The patient will likely receive hypotonic saline initially to prevent dehydration while gradually decreasing serum sodium levels. Patients with central DI may be treated with an ADH supplement (desmopressin) to promote kidney excretion of sodium. Those with nephrogenic DI, however, will not respond to desmopressin. These patients will require decreased sodium intake and may be placed on a diuretic (such as hydrochlorothiazide) to assist in excretion of sodium.

Nursing management of the DI patient requires continuous monitoring for signs of worsening electrolyte imbalances. Along with recording the patient's intake and output, the nurse should educate the patient on maintaining a low-sodium diet. The nurse should also watch for signs of neurological changes through regular neurological assessments and for signs of cardiovascular changes through continuous cardiac monitoring.

Hypoglycemia and Hyperglycemia

In the body, a normal amount of blood glucose is necessary as an energy source for metabolic processes. The brain relies on glucose as an energy source to perform vital functions. When the body has too little or too much glucose, the metabolic dysfunction can result in organ damage, electrolyte imbalance, neurological impairments, and even life-threatening medical emergencies. The term "**blood sugar**" refers to the amount of glucose circulating in one's blood at any given time. A normal fasting blood sugar for a non-diabetic individual ranges from 70–99 mg/dL (diabetic patients can range from 80–130 mg/dL). Postprandial blood sugar for the non-diabetic will be higher but should be no more than 140 mg/dL two hours after a meal (diabetic patients should aim to be below 180 mg/dL). When the blood glucose level falls below 70 mg/dL, the person is hypoglycemic, meaning they are in a state of low blood sugar.

Hypoglycemia may occur with or without symptoms. The body has several regulatory activities that are performed to correct low blood sugar. As a compensatory mechanism, the levels of glucagon and epinephrine may rise, and growth hormone and cortisol levels may increase. These regulatory mechanisms may occur and correct hypoglycemia before any noticeable symptoms arise.

Symptoms of hypoglycemia are reflective of the autonomic activity occurring within the body. The patient may be sweating, feel warm, or experience nausea, anxiety, and/or palpitations. The patient may tremble, complain of headache, experience blurry or double vision, become confused, slur their speech, or even begin to have a seizure or enter a comatose state. Many of these symptoms are caused by the lack of blood glucose in the brain, resulting in neurological effects.

The cause of an acute hypoglycemic state is almost always drug-induced, especially if the patient is receiving insulin therapy. Overtreatment with insulin without proper balance with the patient's mealtime schedule will result in hypoglycemia. Patients in the hospital setting often fall victim to hypoglycemia due to an ever-changing schedule of tests, procedures, and periods of time where they are required to fast.

Treatment of hypoglycemia usually includes administration of dextrose or some other form of sugar. Oral glucagon is an option for the alert patient who can swallow. Symptoms should be corrected upon normalization of blood sugar.

When the blood glucose level rises above 125 mg/dL while fasting or 180 mg/dL 2 hours postprandial, the person is hyperglycemic, meaning they are in a state of excess blood sugar. Symptoms of **hyperglycemia** include polyuria, polydipsia, blurred vision, and dry mouth. The cause of hyperglycemia can include insulin resistance, pancreatic dysfunction, illness, chronic or acute stress, certain medications (including steroids), and improper management of diabetes mellitus (e.g., poor insulin therapy or noncompliance with lifestyle alterations).

Treatment of hyperglycemia includes lifestyle changes (e.g., dietary changes and increased physical activity), oral hypoglycemic medications, insulin therapy, and routine monitoring of serum glucose to prevent recurring events.

Metabolic Syndrome

Metabolic syndrome refers to the presence of comorbid cardiovascular and insulin-related conditions. Patients diagnosed with metabolic syndrome must have three or more of the following conditions: hypertension, elevated fasting blood glucose levels, low HDL cholesterol, high triglycerides, and excess belly fat. This syndrome is believed to result from insulin resistance, causing high blood glucose, insulin, and lipid levels. Patients with metabolic syndrome tend to be overweight or obese and at an increased risk of organ failure, heart attacks, and strokes. They often suffer from another underlying condition, such as diabetes or polycystic ovary syndrome, that leads to metabolic syndrome. Metabolic syndrome is often treated with prescription medications that lower cholesterol and blood pressure, but diet and exercise changes are strongly recommended. Weight loss is a key component in managing metabolic syndrome.

Adrenal Disorders

Conn's syndrome, also known as **primary aldosteronism**, is the primary hypersecretion of the hormone aldosterone often in response to an aldosterone-producing adrenal adenoma, genetic predisposition, adrenal hyperplasia, or idiopathic cause. Sodium retention leads to hypertension, while potassium loss leads to muscle weakness. Laboratory assessment of fluid and electrolyte balance is necessary for analysis. The progressive care nurse monitors intake and output, ECG, and dietary maintenance to

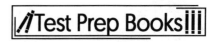

reduce risk for sodium and potassium imbalances. Depending on the etiology, the patient may require an adrenalectomy and/or pharmacological therapy, including spironolactone or eplerenone. Patient education should include the requirement for lifelong use of gluco- and mineralocorticosteroids for patients with bilateral adrenalectomy. Close monitoring of potassium is crucial, especially in patients with renal dysfunction.

Addison's disease, also known as **primary adrenal insufficiency**, involves adrenal hypofunction usually in response to autoimmune disease. Laboratory testing is used to determine whether the patient is suffering from a lack of glucocorticosteroids and mineralocorticosteroids, along with hypoglycemia and electrolyte imbalances. The progressive care nurse should assess the patient for signs and symptoms of weight loss, apathy, stress incontinence, and hyperpigmentation of skin folds. More hormone replacement is often needed during times of stress or illness. Lifelong replacement of gluco- and mineralocorticosteroids is typically necessary. An **Addisonian crisis**, also known as an **acute adrenal crisis**, can occur due to a lack of glucocorticoids (cortisol) and may be fatal. The nursing assessment includes watching for signs of acute hypotension, shock, tachycardia, and neurological dysfunction, including altered LOC and even loss of consciousness. To mitigate risk and improve patient outcomes, interventions include intravenous administration of sodium chloride (NaCl) and hydrocortisone; strict intake and output monitoring; and assessment of vital signs every fifteen minutes. The nurse should also closely monitor blood glucose levels.

Thyroid Disorders

Hypothyroidism, often seen in the autoimmune condition of **Hashimoto's thyroiditis**, leads to symptoms of fatigue, weight gain, loss of appetite, bradycardia, cold intolerance, puffy face, and dry skin. In the severe case of **myxedema coma**, the nurse should assess for hypotension, hypothermia, hypoglycemia, enlarged tongue, and slow, slurred speech. Laboratory testing may reveal elevated thyroid-stimulating hormone (TSH), along with either reduced or normal levels of triiodothyronine (T3) and thyroxine (T4). Thyroxine hormone replacement is typically delivered via natural or synthetic preparations. Close monitoring for signs and symptoms of hyperthyroidism during treatment should be maintained.

Hyperthyroidism, often seen in the autoimmune condition of **Grave's disease**, leads to symptoms of nervousness, weight loss, increased appetite, tachycardia, heat intolerance, hand tremor, protruding eyes, and warm, moist skin. In the severe case of **thyroid storm** or thyrotoxic crisis, the nurse should pay close attention to the presence of palpitations, fever, and delirium. Nursing care involves ensuring balanced nutrition with a high-caloric diet during this hyperbolic state and monitoring vital signs and cardiac output. Laboratory testing may reveal decreased thyroid-stimulating hormone (TSH) and elevated or normal levels of triiodothyronine (T3) and thyroxine (T4). Medication management involves propranolol, propylthiouracil, methimazole, and iodine. If **exophthalmos** is present, the nurse should ensure that conjunctivas remain moist and administer eye drops if necessary. Interventional therapies could include radioiodine ablation and thyroidectomy. In the event of a total **thyroidectomy**, the patient will then have hypothyroidism, requiring lifelong treatment with thyroid hormone replacement.

Hematology/Immunology/Oncology

Anemia

There are certain components in blood that can indicate the status of tissue oxygenation. These components are called the red blood cells (RBCs), hematocrit, and hemoglobin—all detected in a

117

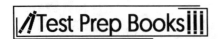

complete blood count (CBC). While hemoglobin is the protein within RBCs responsible for actually transporting oxygen cells, hematocrit and RBC count also play a vital role in detecting tissue oxygenation. Diagnosing **anemia** is typically done through a serum CBC by looking closely at the hemoglobin and hematocrit. For non-pregnant adult females, anemia is generally diagnosed when the hemoglobin is <11.9 g/dL and/or the hematocrit is <35%. For males, anemia is generally diagnosed when the hemoglobin is <13.6 g/dL and/or the hematocrit is <40%.

Often anemia is not a disease in and of itself but rather a symptom of an underlying disorder. The medical provider will investigate possible underlying causes of the anemia in order to determine and treat the etiological factors.

There are three broad categories of anemias, not including blood loss: microcytosis, normocytosis, and macrocytosis. In **microcytosis**, including iron-transport deficiency, lead toxicity, sickle cell disease, and thalassemia, the heme and globin synthesis is defective or deficient; this results in RBCs that are smaller in size than usual. In **normocytosis**, the RBC is normal in size but deficient in quantity. Examples of normocytic anemias include anemia of chronic disease and aplastic anemia acquired from primary bone marrow disorders. **Macrocytosis**, caused by abnormal DNA synthesis, leads to large RBCs that do not have sufficient oxygen-carrying ability. **Mean corpuscular volume** (MCV) is a vital serum measurement that can give insight to the average size of the patient's RBCs.

The symptoms commonly experienced by patients with anemia include fatigue, weakness, difficulty breathing during exercise, and a pale skin tone. **Pallor**, or paleness, can be assessed in a dark-skinned patient by looking at the bottoms of their feet, palms, lips, buccal mucosa, and conjunctiva of the eye. Dark-skinned patients will usually have a warm tone, but when anemic or cyanotic, they will have a more gray or ashen hue.

As mentioned, there are a variety of different types of anemias. **Thalassemia**, common in those of Mediterranean descent, is one type in which the amount of oxygen-carrying hemoglobin is decreased causing pallor, weakness, fatigue, and poor growth. **Folate deficiency anemia**, associated with alcoholism, is a result of poor absorption of nutrients and decreases the amount of folate available to RBCs, thus decreasing oxygen delivery to tissues. Infections, cancers, and many other illnesses may destroy RBCs, hemoglobin, and/or hematocrit, causing anemia.

The treatment of anemia will depend on the underlying cause and the severity of the patient's condition. If the patient is anemic because of massive blood loss, blood transfusions will be required. If the anemia is caused by deficient **erythropoiesis**, the process by which blood is formed, drugs like erythropoietin will be used to stimulate blood production.

In a patient requiring a **blood transfusion**, the progressive care nurse should first verify the order for a blood transfusion and confirm that a blood type and crossmatch or a type and screen have been obtained (type and crossmatch is typically used for emergency and type and screen is used for potential blood transfusions or nonemergent blood transfusions). The nurse should assess and record the patient's baseline status by examining vital signs and laboratory data. The blood product should be verified by **TWO** licensed nurses, with both licensed nurses verifying correctness of the following on both the patient's medical record and the blood product label: patient name, blood type, Rh factor, blood product order, serial number, expiration date/time noted on the bag. The same two licensed nurses should also verify the patient rights prior to administration.

Common types of blood products include whole blood, packed red blood cells (PRBC), fresh frozen plasma (FFP), platelets, and albumin. Complications of a blood transfusion include mild-moderate allergic reaction, anaphylactic reaction, acute hemolytic reaction, febrile non-hemolytic reaction (FNHTR), septic reaction, transfusion-associated circulatory overload (TACO), and transfusion-related acute lung injury (TRALI). If signs of a serious reaction are noted, the nurse should stop the transfusion, keep intravenous access while running the normal saline (through different tubing), and call the provider. Epinephrine should be available for administration if the patient shows signs of anaphylaxis.

Although blood transfusions may be the recommended lifesaving treatment for patients who are low on one, many, or all components of blood, not all patients will accept blood products for a variety of reasons. One of the most common reasons for refusal of blood products is religious beliefs, such as those of Jehovah's Witnesses. Others may refuse blood products due to risks of infection or previous adverse reactions to blood products. Regardless of the reason for refusal, it is important that the patient is fully educated on why the physician is recommending blood product transfusion and the risks of not accepting the transfusion. Ultimately, the patient's decision should be respected, and blood products should not be given to any patient who refuses them. The care team may look into alternative solutions, such as autotransfusion, pharmacologic erythropoiesis, iron supplementation, or other treatments for the cause of anemia. The nurse should advocate for the patient's autonomy and ensure that they are provided with the education needed to make an informed decision.

Medication-Induced Coagulopathies

Medication-induced coagulopathies occur when an individual's blood is unable to effectively form clots due to pharmacological therapy. Similar to most coagulopathies, medication-induced coagulopathies may increase the risk of nosebleeds, excessive bleeding wounds, or bruising, and women may experience longer menstruation periods.

Some diseases require the formation of clots to be slowed or decreased. For example, patients who are at high risk of heart attack or stroke are often required to take medications to reduce the formation of clots. These medications are anticoagulants and antiplatelets, but both work differently in the coagulation ("clotting") cascade.

Anticoagulants work by hindering the production of thrombin, a prominent clotting factor. The most common anticoagulants include the medications warfarin and heparin. **Antiplatelets** work by reducing the aggregation of platelets, essentially making the platelets less able to stick together and make a clot. Common antiplatelets include clopidogrel and aspirin. Most anticoagulants will require routine lab monitoring and have an associated reversal agent. Antiplatelets will not require routine lab monitoring, but there is no specific reversal agent. Blood transfusions will be administered in cases of severe hemorrhage for the patient with antiplatelet-induced coagulopathy, but it is not considered a reversal agent.

Heparin-induced thrombocytopenia (HIT) occurs when the anticoagulation caused by the administration of heparin leads to thrombosis and thus, thrombocytopenia. This condition results when the patient's body has an abnormal antibody response to the heparin that activates platelets.

Two forms of heparin-induced thrombocytopenia have been identified: HIT type I and HIT type II. **HIT type I**, also called **heparin-associated thrombocytopenia**, occurs at the beginning of therapy, is most often a benign condition that does not result in thrombotic events, is not the end-product of an immune response, and quickly resolves spontaneously. HIT I results in a transient decrease in the platelet count, which recovers rapidly when heparin is discontinued and rarely results in a thrombotic event.

HIT type II is defined as an immune-mediated reaction resulting in platelet activation and hypercoagulability that is caused by the presence of heparin. HIT type II can result in increased risk of a thrombotic event or life-threatening gangrene. Since it is an immune-mediated response, the onset is typically 5–14 days after receiving any type or amount of heparin product. The immediate medical intervention is to discontinue any heparin products and initiate a non-heparinized anticoagulant.

Autoimmune Disorders

An **immunocompromised** person refers to any individual who has a less than optimally functioning immune system. This could be the result of a genetic disorder, a viral or cancerous disease, medication, injury, surgery, age, or nutrition. An immunocompromised person is more susceptible to infection and illness than someone whose immune system is functioning optimally.

Systemic Lupus Erythematosus (SLE)

Systemic lupus erythematosus (SLE) is an autoimmune disease in which the immune system attacks tissues throughout the body, causing damage and widespread inflammation. This can affect any of the organs in the body, including the skin, heart, lungs, liver, kidneys, nervous system, and digestive system. Because of this, symptoms can be varied and systemic. For example, should the disease attack the nervous system, the patient may present with fatigue, headaches, seizures, and memory problems. Should it attack the heart, the patient may present with palpitations, murmurs, and arrythmias.

Diagnosis of SLE can be a lengthy process, as the patient may present with many seemingly unrelated symptoms. Depending on presentation, the patient may have basic laboratory work, imaging of various organs, ECG, EEG, or biopsies completed. SLE is more definitively diagnosed with a positive antinuclear antibody test along with clinical findings.

Treatment for SLE is much like that of other autoimmune disorders, in that it involves suppression of the overactive immune system along with treatment of the damage it has caused to the body. Patients with SLE may be given NSAIDs for pain management and to decrease inflammation. They may also be placed on steroids for inflammation and immunosuppressants to decrease immune response. Those at risk of blood clots may also be placed on anticoagulants. Treatment beyond this varies significantly depending on the organs affected. For example, if the disease is affecting the heart, the patient may require antihypertensives, antiarrhythmics, or even procedures like valve replacements. Those who have had kidney damage due to lupus may end up requiring hemodialysis or kidney transplantation.

Nursing management of the SLE patient is also multifaceted. The patient may be admitted to the progressive care unit for disruption of any number of their organ systems. This will require thorough head-to-toe assessment and continuous monitoring. Additionally, nurses should be aware that those on immunosuppressants are at greater risk of infection, and thus, nurses should be especially careful about infection prevention with SLE patients. Finally, nurses should provide thorough education to the SLE patient, informing them about infection prevention, the need to wear protective garments, when to seek emergency care, and how to decrease adverse outcomes by maintaining a healthy diet, exercising (when possible), and avoiding drugs, alcohol, and smoking.

This material is provided for exam preparation purposes only and does not indicate an endorsement of any specific scientific, political, or religious point of view. © TPB Publishing. You have been licensed one copy of this document for personal use only. Any other reproduction or redistribution is strictly prohibited. All rights reserved.

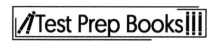

Guillain-Barre Syndrome

Guillain-Barré syndrome is an autoimmune disorder in which the immune system progressively attacks the peripheral nervous system. The exact cause of Guillain-Barré syndrome is currently unknown, but it has been correlated with recent viral infection, *Campylobacter* infection, trauma, surgery, and recent vaccinations. Symptoms of Guillain-Barré syndrome tend to start with neuropathy in the lower extremities, progress into weakness in the legs, and can eventually progress into paralysis, including the diaphragm.

Initially, diagnosis of Guillain-Barré syndrome involves a thorough clinical assessment and past medical history. The patient will likely have a CBC and CMP drawn to rule out other causes of neurological symptoms, but these tests will likely be normal and not definitive in diagnosing Guillain-Barré syndrome. **Lumbar puncture** may be performed during the acute phase, which may show elevated protein in the cerebral spinal fluid. The patient may also have **electromyography** to test motor nerve function, which will likely indicate demyelination of the nerves.

While there is no cure for Guillain-Barré syndrome, there are several treatments that can slow its progression; as a result, most patients are able to recover much of their motor nerve function within a year of diagnosis. One treatment is **plasmapheresis**, a procedure in which the plasma is filtered through a machine to remove particles, such as antibodies, that are causing negative symptoms in the patient. Prior to the procedure, the patient should drink plenty of fluids to maintain their fluid and electrolyte balance, and they should be encouraged to eat. The patient is at risk of electrolyte imbalances following plasmapheresis, including hypocalcemia and hypomagnesemia. Therefore, serum electrolytes should be monitored and potentially replaced, and the patient should be on continuous cardiac monitoring in case of arrythmia. The patient may also become hypotensive due to fluid loss, which may be treated with fluid resuscitation or blood products. Finally, the nurse should monitor for hypothermia, providing warming measures to reduce potential worsening outcomes.

Immunoglobulin therapy, in which healthy antibodies are infused into the blood, may also be helpful. Patients will also benefit from routine physical therapy to reduce muscle atrophy and regain function. In more severe cases (when the disease progresses to the diaphragm), treatment may become supportive, including respiratory support through mechanical ventilation.

The first priority of nursing management of the patient with Guillain-Barré syndrome is to monitor for progression of the disease. The nurse should monitor for difficulty breathing, aspiration risks, and urinary incontinence or retention. Analgesics may be administered as needed to improve the patient's comfort, especially in anticipation of physical therapy. Additionally, because of their immobility, these patients are at an increased risk of blood clots. Therefore, the nurse should administer prophylactic anticoagulation therapy as ordered, encourage mobility where possible, and provide sequential compression devices as needed.

Amyotrophic Lateral Sclerosis (ALS)

Amyotrophic lateral sclerosis (ALS) is a degenerative disease of the central nervous system, mainly affecting the body's motor nerve function. The most common initial symptoms involve the large muscle groups, resulting in difficulty walking, foot drop, and decreased muscle tone. In some cases, patients may also have difficulty talking and swallowing food. Other patients may develop symptoms similar to dementia, with changes in cognitive function and personality. As the disease progresses, the patient will increasingly lose muscle function, have clear atrophy to the limbs, more advanced changes to speech or

121

loss of speech, and drooling. Eventually, the patient will likely require mechanical ventilation. ALS is incurable and fatal; only in rare cases do patients live beyond five years after diagnosis.

Diagnosis of ALS can be difficult, requiring months of data collection to confirm the cause of the patient's symptoms. MRI and CT may be done to rule out structural neurological changes, but these results will appear normal in the ALS patient. Various laboratory tests may also be done but will likely only rule out other conditions. Electromyography can be assistive in testing neuromuscular function.

Since ALS has no cure and is a terminal illness, treatment is mostly supportive and dependent upon the patient's symptoms and needs for quality-of-life improvement. The medication riluzole may be given to extend the patient's life and delay the need for mechanical ventilation. Muscle relaxers may be given to decrease contractions and pain from muscle spasms, while anticholinergics can decrease drooling. Physical therapy and range of motion exercises can help with muscle atrophy. As the disease progresses, the patient will likely require mobility aids, tube feeding, and mechanical ventilation.

Nursing management of the ALS patient prioritizes maintenance of their airway and ventilation. Even in the earlier stages of the disease process, the nurse should be mindful of aspiration risks, ensuring the patient is eating upright as well as chewing and swallowing effectively. The nurse may need to modify the patient's diet for aspiration risks by providing softened foods or thickened liquids. Eventually, the nurse may also need to maintain the patient's gastric tube. Additional care responsibilities include monitoring for signs of difficulty breathing in the earlier stages, followed by eventual management of a chronic mechanical ventilator. Upon discharge, patients and their families should be provided education on what to expect with disease progression and ways to improve the patient's quality of life throughout the disease process.

Multiple Sclerosis (MS)

Multiple sclerosis (MS) is an autoimmune disease in which the immune system attacks and demyelinates the nerves of the central nervous system throughout the body. While symptoms vary, the most common early sign of MS is decreased sensation. Patients may also experience muscle cramping, vision changes, nystagmus, bladder or bowel dysfunction, neurological pain, dizziness, fatigue, and psychological changes. Symptoms may not always be present, as the patient may experience exacerbations as well as periods with minimal symptoms. Exacerbations can be caused by stress, illness, trauma, or noncompliance with medications.

Definitive diagnosis of MS generally involves of a correlation of symptoms with MRI findings. Blood tests may be done to rule out other disease processes but will likely be normal in the MS patient. The patient may also have an EEG completed, which may show abnormal findings but is not a definitive diagnostic tool.

Treatment of MS in both acute and long-term phases aims to decrease disease progression. During an MS exacerbation, the patient will likely be given corticosteroids to decrease inflammation and immune response. If corticosteroids are ineffective, plasmapheresis may also be conducted to decrease the number of antibodies in the patient's blood that may be attacking the nervous system. In the long term, the patient may receive infusions of monoclonal antibodies as well as oral immunosuppressants. In addition to pharmacological treatment, patients with MS can benefit from physical and occupational therapy to improve muscle strength and their ability to perform activities of daily living.

Nurses caring for patients with MS should be mindful of their risk of infection and maintain strict infection prevention measures. Nurses can also assist in decreasing MS exacerbation by supporting a therapeutic, cool, and calming environment of care. Nurses should promote a balanced diet and regular exercise to decrease muscle spasticity. Patients should also receive education on infection prevention, how to decrease the risk of MS exacerbation, and the importance of treatment compliance.

Oncology

While there are oncological nurses and certifications required to administer certain treatments, the progressive care nurse will need to be familiar with the pathological process, diagnosis, treatment, and nursing care practices for the oncology patient. **Oncology** includes the study, diagnosis, and treatment of cancers. **Cancer** is a large group of diseases that are commonly expressed as carcinomas, sarcomas, melanomas, lymphomas, and leukemia. The normal cells experience mutation due to one or multiple carcinogens, such as diesel exhaust, radiation, or viruses, which results in changes in the cell membrane that inhibit the tumor-suppressing action of the normal cell and alter the cell surface antigens. This, in turn, diminishes the immune response. The abnormal cell matures through the process already described and eventually manifests the following characteristics: abnormal cell structure; haphazard, uncontrolled cellular replication; and destructive invasiveness. Malignant cells cause harm not only by occupying space, but by invading adjacent and distant tissues; although benign tumors can also cause harm by occupying space, the tumors remain encapsulated and do not invade surrounding tissues.

Once the normal tissue has been invaded, the malignant cells are able to create an extracellular environment that supports the growth of the tumor and facilitates ongoing **metastasis** by making alterations in three processes that control normal cellular proliferation: density-dependent inhibition, cell-surface adhesion, and contact inhibition. The proliferation of normal cells depends on the level of growth hormones and the action of the cellular growth factors. When the cell density is sufficient for normal function, the levels of the hormones and growth factors decrease, which slows proliferation. Malignant cells continue to replicate because the cells are independently capable of producing sufficient growth factors even when hormone levels do not support growth. Normal cells create an orderly matrix that is supported by cell surface adhesion molecules; however, malignant cells can suppress these molecules, which allows the malignant cells to more easily invade normal tissue. During normal cellular growth, replication is stopped when cells come in contact with one another in accordance with the concept of cell contact inhibition; however, malignant cells do not respond to those signals. When a new tumor grows to a density of approximately one million cells, malignant cells are capable of initiating **angiogenesis**, which is the development of new blood vessels that support tumor growth and provide new pathways for metastasis.

Chemotherapy is a broad term referring to the use of drugs in cancer treatment. This type of therapy is intended to target and treat the entire body, especially in advanced stages of cancer where malignant cells may be widespread. However, it may also be used in earlier stages of cancer to eliminate many of the cancerous cells. This is done with the intention that the patient will go into remission and potentially not experience cancer again in the future. If this does not seem like a viable prognosis, chemotherapy can be used to control early stages of cancer from advancing. In advanced stages of cancer, chemotherapy can be used to manage pain and suffering from cancerous tumors, even if the patient's prognosis is poor.

The aggressiveness of chemotherapy (such as which drugs are used, dosing amount, and frequency) is contingent on many factors, such as the type and stage of cancer. Chemotherapy treatment plans also

123

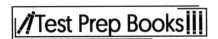

consider the patient's personal and medical history. Since this form of treatment is so aggressive, it is often effective in reducing or eliminating cancer cells. However, chemotherapy can also kill healthy cells in the process. The intensity of this side effect varies by person, but almost all patients experience some degree of immunocompromise. This is because chemotherapy almost always inadvertently targets bone marrow, where white blood cells are made. White blood cells, especially neutrophils, play an important role in fighting infection. When there are not enough white blood cells present in the patient's blood, the patient can become seriously ill from sickness or infection that would be mild in a healthy individual. Medical personnel usually monitor neutrophil counts during and between chemotherapy cycles to make sure these levels do not fall too low. Chemotherapy cycles can last up to six months, and patients are considered to have a compromised immune system for the entire time they are undergoing chemotherapy. Once a full cycle of chemotherapy ends, it takes approximately one month for the immune system to return to its normal state.

Patients undergoing chemotherapy should be especially mindful of personal hygiene habits such as handwashing and showering, as well as avoiding cuts, scrapes, insect bites, or other instances where the skin may break. They may also need help taking care of a pet and handling pet waste or other trash. Additionally, it is important to practice extra caution when handling foods, such as cooking meats well, avoiding unpasteurized foods, washing produce with produce cleaner, cooking many foods that typically could be eaten raw, and avoiding certain cheeses. They also need to be more cautious in public places; since these areas tend to be dirtier and more populated, there is an increased risk of contracting infections. Medical personnel and those visiting the patient should be aware of these practices as well.

Oncological Emergencies

Oncological emergencies can vary between patients depending on their specific form of cancer, the stage of cancer, and what form of treatment they are currently receiving.

One of the most common oncological emergencies is sepsis, as patients receiving chemotherapy are often immunocompromised. Effective treatment of sepsis requires early identification and intervention. Should a patient who is actively receiving oncological treatment present with signs of infection, the patient should have blood cultures drawn, antibiotics administered, and fluids given (if indicated). Nurses should also maintain **neutropenic precautions** for oncologic patients to prevent nosocomial infections while in the hospital.

Oncological patients are also at risk of alterations to their coagulopathy. As a result, patients may have an increased risk of deep vein thrombosis (DVT), **disseminated intravascular coagulation** (DIC), and hemorrhage. Patients at risk of DVT may require prophylactic anticoagulation. Nurses should also monitor for signs of shortness of breath, chest pain, and stroke, as these could be signs of a thrombus traveling from the peripheral veins into the heart, lungs, or brain. DIC is a systemic extreme coagulation response that overwhelms the body's clotting factors, causing clots and hemorrhage simultaneously. This is a true emergency, requiring strict cardiac monitoring, neurological assessments, and likely blood product transfusion.

Finally, depending on the patient, oncological patients may be at greater risk of cardiac emergencies, such as arrythmias from electrolyte imbalances or cardiac tamponade from compression by tumors. All oncological patients should be on continuous cardiac monitoring, with regular monitoring of serum electrolytes for potential supplementation as needed. Signs of cardiac tamponade include jugular vein

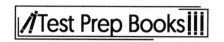

distension, muffled heart tones, and hypotension. This condition must be treated quickly through pericardiocentesis to prevent cardiac arrest.

Neurology

Encephalopathy

Any form of brain damage, disease, or dysfunction can fall under the umbrella term of **encephalopathy**. There are numerous different causes and forms of encephalopathy, including hypoxic-ischemic, metabolic, hepatic, and infectious. A patient with an altered mental state may be suffering from a form of encephalopathy and the cause should be investigated.

Infections, trauma, adverse drug effects, metabolic abnormalities, and states of oxygen deprivation to the brain tissue can all cause encephalopathic states. Encephalopathy may be diagnosed using blood and urine tests to determine the cause as well as imaging studies, such as a CT scan, MRI, and EEG. CSF fluid may be obtained via a lumbar puncture ("spinal tap") for diagnostic purposes if metabolic abnormalities or non-infectious causes are suspected.

Hypoxic Ischemic Encephalopathy

Hypoxic-ischemic encephalopathy (HIE) occurs as a result of the brain having inadequate blood and oxygen supply to meet metabolic needs. In the United States, the most common cause is due to cardiac arrest, although other causes include shock, near-drowning, strangulation, and carbon monoxide poisoning.

HIE often results in an impaired level of consciousness, with many patients unable to follow verbal commands. Since patients often present in a coma, healthcare providers must rely on family or witnesses to produce relevant medical histories. It is important to obtain the circumstances around the brain injury to assess for associated injuries, such as cervical spine involvement, as well as inquire about comorbidities, prescription medications, drug use, or toxin exposures.

Diagnostic workup includes laboratory and radiological testing consisting of basic blood work, arterial blood gas, drug screen, and CT scan of the head without contrast. The CT scan will reveal structural impairments of the brain, such as lesions, skull fractures, or hydrocephalus. CT angiography may be performed to evaluate vascular injuries, while EEG may be used to evaluate seizure activity.

Treatment and management focus on treating the underlying cause and preventing further brain injury. For patients who are in a coma after cardiac arrest, **therapeutic hypothermia** is recommended. Mild hypothermia, where the body temperature is maintained between 32°C and 36°C, protects the brain by inhibiting cell death, lowering the metabolic rate to reduce oxygen consumption, and stabilizing the blood-brain barrier to decrease edema. Therapeutic hypothermia should begin within 6 hours of the brain injury and is typically maintained for 24 hours. In a hypothermic state, there will be impacts to regulation of glucose and electrolyte levels, renal function, clotting activity, heart rate, blood pressure, and drug metabolism. Measures should be taken to prevent shivering, which can lead to increased intracranial pressure and metabolic needs of the body; additionally, by attempting to warm the body, it can slow cooling. The following methods should be used to prevent and treat shivering: adequate analgesia and sedation; antipyretics and alpha-2 blockers; and counter-warming the hands, face, and upper chest.

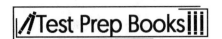
Metabolic Encephalopathy

Metabolic encephalopathy (ME) occurs when there is an alteration to the brain function as a result of conditions that alter electrolyte or vitamin balance in the body. Examples of these conditions include diabetes, liver disease, and renal failure. ME occurs acutely or sub-acutely and is usually reversible if the underlying condition is treated. However, if left untreated, ME can lead to secondary structural damage, resulting in permanent changes to neurologic function.

With ME, patients present with confusion, drowsiness, irritability, difficulty concentrating, fatigue, depression, anxiety, or loss of consciousness. Diagnostic tests include basic blood tests (e.g., CMP), arterial blood gas testing, urine testing, and spinal fluid testing to determine the root cause of symptoms. Radiological tests, such as CT or MRI, may rule out structural conditions, while an EEG is used to rule out subclinical seizures.

Interventions focus on treatment of the underlying cause. Electrolyte imbalances caused by renal impairment (e.g., hyponatremia, hypernatremia, hypercalcemia, hypocalcemia, hypomagnesemia, and hypophosphatemia) can be readily treated through the correction of electrolyte levels. Uncontrolled diabetes is a leading cause for hyperglycemia and can be addressed with appropriate use of insulin. Liver disease, as well as alcoholism, can lead to hypoglycemia-related encephalopathy, which can be treated through administration of glucose.

Haloperidol can be given to treat severe agitation. Medications that can worsen delirium caused by encephalopathy and should be avoided include diphenhydramine, lorazepam, zolpidem, metoclopramide, promethazine, prochlorperazine, famotidine, and fentanyl.

Nursing care involves keeping the environment as quiet as possible, such as by bundling care to allow for more periods of uninterrupted rest at night. Patients should also be encouraged to mobilize and spend time out of bed as appropriate. Nurses should perform neurological exams regularly to detect changes from baseline. Fall prevention is important, as confusion can result in unsafe ambulation. Education provided to caregivers should encourage safe practices and prevention of subsequent events once the patient is discharged. Many patients, especially alcoholics and newly diagnosed diabetics, can benefit from education on management of the condition at home and potential nutritional impacts. To provide support, nurses can arrange a nutrition consult and provide ongoing assistance during hospitalization.

Infectious Encephalopathy

Infectious encephalopathy is an inflammatory condition of the brain caused by a viral, bacterial, or protozoal infection. The damage may either be caused by the organism directly invading the central nervous system (neurotropism) or peripherally through a secondary inflammatory response of the brain (neuroinflammation). While the incidence is low (with approximately 20,000 new cases each year in the United States), immunocompromised patients are at higher risk of acquiring such infections. Often those with infectious encephalopathy have also had exposure to a mosquito or tick bite. Symptoms often begin similarly to the flu, presenting with fever, chills, headaches, body aches, and neck stiffness. As time progresses, however, patients will develop neurological symptoms, such as changes in balance, coordination, mood, cognition, sensitivity to light, and seizures. Although treatment of the underlying cause can prevent further damage, some of these symptoms may continue after treatment.

As with other types of encephalopathy, correct diagnosis is vital in resolving the condition. Blood and spinal fluid tests are used to determine the type of organism causing the infection. While the primary

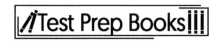

focus is on treating the underlying cause with antibiotics or antivirals, there is a significant role for nursing and supportive care services in rehabilitation.

Many patients will continue to have symptoms of fatigue, depression, memory loss, coordination, and balance issues after the infection has resolved. Therefore, a multidisciplinary approach is essential for managing the various effects. Physical and occupational therapy are utilized to assist patients in regaining strength and participation in activities of daily living. Speech therapy may be useful if the patient is experiencing difficulties with speaking, swallowing, and/or cognition (e.g., organizing thoughts, attention span, remembering, and planning). Caregiver education is essential to ensure they understand that the patient may need long-term assistance due to chronic impact of the disease.

Hepatic Encephalopathy

Hepatic encephalopathy (HE) occurs as a result of liver dysfunction, when neurotoxins are no longer being removed from the blood and thereby impact the function of the brain. Two forms are recognized: acute and chronic. Acute hepatic encephalopathy is seen in patients with acute onset hepatic failure, which is often caused by viral hepatitis, sepsis, or exposure to toxic substances, and is associated with pronounced cerebral edema. Chronic hepatic encephalopathy occurs in patients with chronic liver disease and those with a portosystemic shunt. While serious, HE may be reversible.

Patients often present with confusion, lethargy, personality changes, disorientation, altered levels of consciousness, and symptoms suggestive of liver failure (e.g., jaundice and pruritis). Disruptions in the sleep-wake cycle, where patients are awake during the night and asleep during the day, often occur in early stages. In advanced stages, coma can occur.

With impairment of liver function, ammonia accumulates in the bloodstream and disrupts normal neuronal function. Tests to confirm diagnosis should include blood tests (to identify abnormal liver function and ammonia levels); radiologic imaging (to rule out stroke, seizure, lesions, or masses); and ultrasound (to determine the presence of a portosystemic shunt).

Treatment of HE requires addressing the underlying cause and therapies to lower the ammonia levels in the blood. Other critical aspects include supporting nutrition, adequate hydration, management of electrolyte abnormalities, and ensuring a safe environment. Patients should meet caloric goals and avoid protein restriction. Additionally, they should consume small, frequent meals to prevent fasting, which can cause an increase in ammonia production. Sedative medications, such as benzodiazepines, can worsen encephalopathy and should be avoided. Lactulose is an ammonia-lowering therapy that is highly effective in 70 to 80 percent of patients with HE. It works by facilitating the conversion of NH3 ammonia to NH4+ ammonia in the gut, therefore reducing the amount of NH3 being diffused into the blood stream. Lactulose also has an osmotic effect in the colon and promotes the excretion of NH3 in the stool; ideally, the goal is to have two to three soft stools daily.

Patients who have chronic liver disease have a risk of HE recurrence. Patients and caregivers should be educated on the early signs of HE and when to seek medical attention. They should be made aware of potential triggers and hepatotoxins to avoid as well as counseled on the importance of adherence to prescription medications.

Seizure Disorders

A **seizure** is defined as a chaotic period of uncoordinated electrical activity in the brain, which results in one of several characteristic behaviors. Although the exact cause is unknown, several possible triggers

127

have been proposed. The recently revised classification system categorizes seizure activity according to the area of the brain where the seizure initiates, the patient's level of awareness during the seizure, and other descriptive features (e.g., the presence of an aura). The unclassified category includes seizure patterns that do not conform to the primary categories. Seizures that originate in a single area of the brain are designated as **focal seizures**, while seizures that originate in two or more different networks are designated as **generalized seizures**. The remaining seizures in the onset category include seizures without an identified point of onset and those that progress from focal seizures to generalized seizures.

Risk factors associated with seizures include genetic predisposition, illnesses with severe temperature elevation, head trauma, cerebral edema, inappropriate use or discontinuance of anti-epileptic drugs (AEDs), intracerebral infection, excess or deficiency of sodium and/or glucose, toxin exposure, hypoxia, and acute drug or alcohol withdrawal. Patients are encouraged to identify any conditions that may be triggers for their seizure activity. Although the triggers vary greatly from one patient to another, commonly identified events include increased physical activity, excessive stress, hyperventilation, fatigue, acute ETOH (ethyl alcohol) ingestion, exposure to flashing lights, and inhaled chemicals (including cocaine).

The **tonic phase** presents as stiffening of the limbs for a brief period, while the **clonic phase** is evidenced by jerking motions of the limbs. These manifestations may be accompanied by a decreased level of consciousness, respiratory alterations, cyanosis, incontinence, and biting of the tongue. **Absence seizures** are manifested by a decreased level of awareness without abnormal muscular activity. The manifestations of the **postictal phase** include alterations in consciousness and awareness as well as increased oral secretions.

Associated lab studies that aid in diagnosis of seizure disorders include those that identify excess alcohol and recreational drugs, metabolic alterations, and kidney and liver function. **Electroencephalography** (EEG) and enhanced **magnetoencephalography** (MEG) are used to identify the origin of the altered electrical activity in the brain. Additionally, MRI, skull films, and CSF analysis are used to rule out possible sources of the seizure disorder (such as tumor formation). For patients undergoing EEG, the nurse's primary function is to understand the rationale for testing, ensure electrodes remain in proper position, provide patient and family education, and initiate and maintain seizure precautions per institutional standards. During placement of electrodes, the nurse may assist with patient positioning and collaborate with neurological personnel to identify any monitoring devices, incisions, or other areas to avoid for placement. Throughout monitoring, the nurse should help to ensure quality waveforms and audiovisual clarity of recording devices. Careful assessment of the headwrap should be completed twice daily to ensure the electrodes do not become loose or dislodged. If able to visualize the scalp, the nurse should assess for signs of infection, breakdown, bleeding, or CSF leak. The patient should be monitored for headache or discomfort as well as changes in neurological assessment. The nurse should maintain accurate charting and note when there are clinical events for review, such as seizures or medication administration.

Seizure disorders are treated with AEDs that stabilize the neuron cell membrane by facilitating the inhibitory mechanisms or opposing the excitatory mechanisms. Patients with a chronic seizure disorder, or **epilepsy**, usually require a combination of medications to minimize seizure activity. Elderly patients respond differently to the AEDs and may require frequent assessment and revision of the treatment plan. The emergency care of the patient with seizures is focused on patient safety during and after the seizure and the cessation and prevention of the seizure activity. Prolonged seizure activity is defined as **status epilepticus**, which is the occurrence of multiple seizures, each lasting more than 5 minutes over a

30-minute period. This condition is life-threatening, as the brain does not have sufficient recovery time to reoxygenate. Causes of this condition include epilepsy, metabolic imbalances, stroke, uncontrolled infections, and acute drug/alcohol withdrawal. Care of this condition includes the immediate administration of the first-line pharmacological therapy, benzodiazepines. The second-line therapy is any compatible antiseizure medication, with the third-line therapy typically being general anesthesia and endotracheal intubation.

Stroke

A **cerebrovascular accident** (CVA), commonly referred to as a **stroke**, is defined as the death of brain tissue due to ischemic or hemorrhagic injury. Ischemic strokes are more common than hemorrhagic strokes; however, the differential diagnosis of these conditions requires careful attention to the patient's history and physical examination. In general, an acute onset of neurological symptoms and seizures is more common with hemorrhagic stroke, while ischemic stroke is more frequently associated with a history of trauma or prolonged disease process (e.g., hyperlipidemia, HTN, or CAD). The **National Institutes of Health Stroke Scale** (NIHSS) represents an international effort to standardize the assessment and treatment protocols for stroke. The scale includes detailed criteria and the protocol for assessment of the neurological system. The stroke scale items are to be administered in the official order listed, and there are directions that denote how to score each item. The NIH scale has the examiner test for the following:

- Level of consciousness (LOC)
    - General LOC or alertness (scores range from 0–3)
    - LOC in response to basic questions or orientation (scores range from 0–2)
    - LOC in following one-step commands (scores range from 0–2)
- Best gaze (scores range from 0–2)
    - Measuring horizontal eye movements to determine any gaze palsies or deviations
- Visual fields (scores range from 0–3)
    - Assessing peripheral vision by confrontation to determine any hemianopia
- Facial palsy (scores range from 0–3)
- Motor deficits of the arms (scores range from 0–4, or untestable)
- Motor deficits of the legs (scores range from 0–4, or untestable)
- Limb ataxia (scores range from 0–2, or untestable)
- Sensory loss (scores range from 0–2)
- Best language (scores range from 0–3)
- Dysarthria (scores range from 0–2, or "untestable")
- Extinction/Inattention (scores range from 0–2)

With a lower score (typically less than 5), the patient has a better general prognosis and milder residual effects from the stroke. Conversely, the higher scores (typically greater than 14) indicate severe residual effects from the stroke that will likely require skilled assistance for care.

Ischemic Stroke

Ischemic strokes result from occlusion of the cerebral vasculature as a result of a thrombotic or embolic event. At the cellular level, the ischemia leads to hypoxia that rapidly depletes the ATP stores. As a result, the cellular membrane pressure gradient is lost, and there is an influx of sodium, calcium, and water into the cell, which leads to cytotoxic edema. This process creates scattered regions of ischemia in the affected area, containing cells that are dead within minutes of the precipitating event. This core of

129

ischemic tissue is surrounded by an area with minimally adequate perfusion that may remain viable for several hours after the event. These necrotic areas are eventually liquefied and acted upon by macrophages, resulting in the loss of brain parenchyma. If the affected sites are sufficiently large, they may be prone to hemorrhage due to the formation of collateral vascular supply, with or without the use of medications such as tissue plasminogen activator (tPA). The ischemic process also compromises the **blood-brain barrier**, which leads to the movement of water and protein into the extracellular space within 4 to 6 hours after the onset of the stroke, resulting in **vasogenic edema**.

Nonmodifiable risk factors for ischemic stroke include age, gender, ethnicity, history of migraine headaches with aura, and a family history of stroke or transient ischemic attacks (TIAs). Modifiable risk factors include hypertension, diabetes, hypercholesterolemia, cardiac disease (e.g., atrial fibrillation, valvular disease, and heart failure), elevated homocysteine levels, obesity, illicit drug use, alcohol abuse, smoking, and sedentary lifestyle. The research related to the occurrence of stroke in women indicates the need to treat hypertension aggressively prior to and during pregnancy, as well as prior to the use of contraceptives, to prevent irreversible damage to the microvasculature. In addition, it is recommended that women with a history of migraine headaches with aura should improve any present modifiable risk factors to reduce their risk of stroke. Furthermore, all women over the age of 75 years old should be routinely assessed for the onset of atrial fibrillation.

Heredity is associated with identified gene mutations and the process of atherosclerosis and cholesterol metabolism. Hypercholesterolemia and the progression of atherosclerosis in genetically susceptible individuals are now both regarded as active inflammatory processes that contribute to endothelial damage of the cerebral vasculature, thereby increasing the risk for strokes.

The presenting manifestations of ischemic stroke must be differentiated from other common diseases, including brain tumor formation, hyponatremia, hypoglycemia, seizure disorders, and systemic infection. The sudden onset of hemisensory losses, visual alterations, hemiparesis, ataxia, nystagmus, and aphasia are commonly, although not exclusively, associated with ischemic strokes. Immediate diagnostic studies include a non-contrast brain CT or brain MRI. The nurse should also immediately obtain a point-of-care blood glucose reading and a pulse oximetry reading. Additional diagnostics include an ECG and laboratory studies, including a CBC, coagulation studies, chemistry panels, cardiac biomarkers, toxicology assays, and pregnancy testing as appropriate.

Care of the patient with symptoms of an ischemic stroke is focused on the stabilization of the patient's ABCs, completion of the physical examination and appropriate diagnostic studies, and initiation of reperfusion therapy as appropriate. The exact time of initial onset of stroke symptoms should be documented, as many reperfusion therapies must be started within 4.5 hours of onset of symptoms. Reperfusion therapies include the use of alteplase (the only fibrinolytic agent that is approved for the treatment of ischemic stroke), antiplatelet agents, and mechanical thrombectomy. A crucial vital sign to closely monitor in the acute period of an ischemic stroke is blood pressure. Rapid reduction in blood pressure can result in further cerebral hypoperfusion, making the 24-hour period after an ischemic stroke vital to regulate blood pressure within safe parameters. Healthcare providers must also be alert for hyperthermia, hypoxia, and signs of cardiac ischemia or cardiac arrhythmias.

Hemorrhagic Stroke
Hemorrhagic strokes are less common than ischemic strokes; however, hemorrhagic strokes have a higher mortality rate than ischemic strokes. A hemorrhagic stroke is the result of bleeding into the parenchymal tissue of the brain due to leakage of blood from damaged intracerebral arteries. These

hemorrhagic events occur more often in specific areas of the brain, including the thalamus, cerebellum, and brain stem. The tissue surrounding the hemorrhagic area is also subject to injury due to the mass effect of the accumulated blood volume. Understanding the diagnostics and medical interventions for a hemorrhagic stroke will require the knowledge of the two different types, intracerebral hemorrhage (ICH) and subarachnoid hemorrhage (SAH).

Intracerebral hemorrhage (ICH) is a type of stroke that occurs when there is bleeding within the brain tissue itself. It is often a morbid event, with a 50 percent mortality rate at 30 days, and most of those deaths occurring within the first 24 hours. There are two subsets of ICH: primary (or spontaneous) ICH and secondary ICH. Primary ICH is the more common type, comprising 85 percent of hemorrhagic strokes, and is caused by hypertension or amyloid angiopathy. Secondary ICH is due to an underlying structural issue, such as a malignancy or vascular abnormality.

ICH occurs in three phases: initial bleeding into the brain tissue, subsequent bleeding around the clot causing expansion, and resulting edema around the hematoma. The blood and resulting edema cause compression and disruption of the brain tissue. This impacts the signaling pathways of the nearby cells, resulting in neurological deficit.

High blood pressure and a significant smoking history are significant risk factors for ICH. These events occur suddenly and are often associated with exercise, heavy lifting, and cocaine or alcohol use. Patients most commonly present with a focal neurological deficit that is dependent on the location of the hemorrhage, including headache, decrease in consciousness, nausea/vomiting, seizures, and diastolic blood pressure over 110 mmHg.

A non-contrast head CT scan is most often used to diagnose ICH and can determine swelling, size of the hemorrhage, compression of surrounding tissues (mass effect), intraventricular clot extension, and raised intracranial pressure. MRI can also be useful but is not the first imaging resource for assessment.

After ensuring stability of airway, breathing, and circulation, aggressive medical management will be implemented to reduce long-term effects and morbidity. Intervention should occur as quickly as possible to minimize expansion of the hematoma in the first 24 to 72 hours. First, any abnormal coagulation needs to be addressed to stop bleeding. Management must also include controlling blood pressure to reduce hematoma expansion while maintaining adequate perfusion. If the patient presented with seizures, those should also be managed with an anticonvulsant. To preserve appropriate cerebral perfusion pressure (CPP), the nurse should place the head of the bed at 30 degrees and provide appropriate pain management, bowel management (to prevent straining), hyperventilation, and sedation when appropriate.

Patients who survive will often experience significant impacts in their ability to care for themselves and perform activities of daily living. Patients and families should be informed and counseled on supportive services, such as physical therapy, occupational therapy, and speech therapy. Nurses should provide education to those at high risk for a stroke, including signs and symptoms and ways to lower the risk (e.g., blood pressure control and smoking cessation).

When a hemorrhage occurs in the subarachnoid space between the pia and arachnoid membranes of the brain, it is called a **subarachnoid hemorrhage** (SAH). This type of brain bleed is traumatic or aneurysmal in nature, with the most common reason being a ruptured cerebral aneurysm. Risk factors for subarachnoid hemorrhage include older age, a history of hypertension, personal history or familial history, alcohol abuse, history of smoking, and illicit drug use. Coagulopathies and pharmacological treatments that alter the coagulation cascade are also risk factors that can exacerbate SAH.

A patient experiencing a subarachnoid brain bleed will present with a sudden and severe headache, orbital pain, dizziness, diplopia, and/or loss of vision. Some patients may experience **prodromal symptoms** that occur before the actual event, such as sensory or motor disturbances, seizures, ptosis, bruits, and/or dysphasia. Upon assessment, the nurse may find the patient tachycardic, feverish, hypertensive, and with swelling around the eyes or hemorrhage of the retinas.

If a subarachnoid hemorrhage is suspected, a CT is the most common diagnostic tool. Obtaining a point-of-care blood glucose reading and pulse oximetry reading is also a vital nursing task, as to gain quick insight without delaying the emergent CT scan. If diagnosed with a subarachnoid hemorrhage, the immediate medical assessments and interventions include maintaining ABCs; constant hemodynamic monitoring; neurologic monitoring (e.g., neuro checks and ICP monitoring if applicable); and surgical stabilization (through clipping or endovascular coiling as necessary). Nursing management for the patient with increased ICP typically requires osmotic diuretic therapy, close monitoring of intake/output and electrolytes, elevation of the head of the bed to 30 degrees, and reduction of external stimuli. Blood pressure is a crucial vital sign for the nurse, as normal hypertensive parameters are not the goal of hemodynamic stability. The general guidelines are to gradually bring the systolic blood pressure to below <160 mmHg, or MAP <110 mmHg, avoiding both a drastic drop in blood pressure and severe hypertension. The patient who has had a subarachnoid bleed must be monitored for the development of complications, such as re-bleed, vasospasm, seizures, hyponatremia, and hydrocephalus.

Lumbar drain

A **lumbar drain** is a thin, flexible catheter placed into the subarachnoid space of the lower spine to drain cerebrospinal fluid (CSF) and therefore reduce ICP. Because the brain and spinal cord share membranes and CSF, drainage of CSF from the spine results in reduced ICP. In the case of subarachnoid hemorrhage, a vascular drain helps remove blood, relieves pressure on the brain, and prevents arterial vasospasms and hydrocephalus.

Prior to insertion, the nurse should perform a baseline neurological exam. During the procedure, the nurse may help the patient into a side-lying position, or sitting up leaning over a bedside table, with a rounded back to widen the intravertebral space. The drain will be placed into the subarachnoid space of the lumbar spine. Since this is a sterile procedure with a closed system, patients and caregivers should be instructed not to touch or allow visitors to touch the catheter.

Nurses should document the volume, color, and clarity of the drainage as well as assess the system for patency and signs or symptoms of infection. Neurologic status should be regularly assessed to note any changes from baseline. Aside from infection, a lumbar drain can lead to intracranial venous thrombus, so nurses should assess the patient for new onset of headache, confusion, disorientation, and nausea/vomiting. Patients may experience numbness, tingling, radicular pain, and changes in deep tendon reflexes due to root nerve irritation. This is likely a temporary discomfort; however, if it persists, the drain will likely be removed.

In addition to strategies to avoid infections, patients should be advised to avoid coughing or sneezing, as the strain can increase intracranial pressure. Patients and caregivers should be instructed to ask for assistance with position changes and activity.

External ventricular drain (EVD)

An **external ventricular drain** (EVD) is a thin, flexible catheter inserted into the ventricle of the brain to directly drain CSF and therefore reduce ICP. EVD is indicated for hydrocephalus when there is excess CSF production in the ventricles, leading to increased pressure on the brain. **Hydrocephalus** is a common result of subarachnoid hemorrhage due to the blood in the subarachnoid space, which impairs circulation and absorption of CSF.

The EVD is surgically placed by tunneling a few centimeters under the scalp, entering through a burr hole into the skull, and then passing into the ventricle. The catheter is sutured to the skull, and the incision is sutured and dressed with a sterile occlusive dressing. This site and the drainage system should be monitored for signs of infection, damage, or disconnection.

The catheter is connected externally to a drainage system that flows to gravity. A collection chamber is attached to a pressure scale and drainage bag, which is typically hung on an IV pole near the patient. A stopcock system between the collection chamber and drainage bag is used to control the drainage of the CSF. The pressure scale hangs next to the collection chamber and includes both negative and positive measurements. It is very important for the zero on the scale to be level horizontally with the tragus of the patient's ear; therefore, nurses should carefully manage the positioning of the scale. The prescribed pressure indicates what the level of pressure inside the ventricle must be before drainage occurs. A pressure level that is too high would result in too much intracranial pressure, while a pressure level that is too low may result in over drainage. Nurses should monitor the patient for changes in neurologic status that indicate over or under drainage.

Dysphagia

A patient with either type of stroke is at increased risk of **dysphagia**. Bedside swallow screens are usually part of hospital protocol for any patient that presents with a stroke prior to receiving anything orally. These screens should be done per protocol and thoroughly documented. Some other conditions that may place a patient at higher risk for dysphagia or aspiration include Parkinson's disease, muscular dystrophies, and Sjogren's syndrome. While a speech therapist is often acutely involved in the detailed bedside **swallow screen** for dysphagia, the nurse may assist or be responsible for some or all aspects of the test, according to facility protocols.

Prior to performing the bedside screen, the nurse must ensure that the patient is consistently alert and tolerates being seated in an upright position. Certain circumstances that will typically prevent the nurse from performing a bedside screen and require a speech therapy consultation include:

- History of dysphagia prior to stroke
- Brainstem stroke
- Active enteral feeding
- Tracheostomy present

The next step is assessing the motor skills of swallowing. The patient should be able to clinch teeth and close lips, along with maintaining facial symmetry. Other indicators that would indicate a nursing bedside screen is appropriate would include voluntary coughing/gag reflex and articulation of words. If the patient is unable to adequately swallow oral secretions or slurs speech, they will need a speech therapy consultation.

133

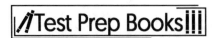

Once the patient has been determined medically appropriate to have a nursing bedside swallow screen, the nurse will need to ensure proper patient positioning. The patient will need to be in High Fowler's position (bed angle of 90 degrees is advised), with their head in a midline position. The nurse will give the patient plain water, in an amount to be determined by facility, and assess the patient's response. If the patient can swallow the liquid without coughing, choking, drooling, or gurgling, the patient will pass the screening. The nurse should continue to assess for delayed signs of aspiration that include slow feeding with noted tachypnea, fever of unknown origin, and productive cough.

Transient Ischemic Attack

A **transient ischemic attack** (TIA) is defined as a short-term episode of altered neurological function that lasts for less than one hour; in some cases, it may be imperceptible to the patient. The deficit may be related to speech, movement, behavior, or memory and may be caused by an ischemic event in the brain, spinal cord, or retina. The patient's history and neurological assessment according to the NIHSS establish the diagnosis. Additional diagnostic studies include CBC, glucose, sedimentation rate, electrolytes, lipid profile, toxicology screen, 12-lead ECG, and CSF analysis. Imaging studies include non-contrast MRI or CT, carotid Doppler exam, and angiography.

Initial care of the patient with a TIA is focused on the assessment of any neurological deficits and the identification of comorbid conditions that may be related to the attack. Hospital admission is required in the event that an attack lasts greater than one hour, the patient has experienced more than a single attack in a one-week period, or the attack is related to a cardiac source (e.g., atrial fibrillation or myocardial infarction). The **ABCD^2 stroke risk score** calculates the patient's risk for experiencing a true stroke within two days after the TIA based on five factors (see the table below). Interventions aimed at stroke prevention in relation to the risk stratification as calculated by the ABCD^2 score are specific to underlying comorbidities; however, treatment with aspirin and clopidogrel is commonly prescribed.

ABCD^2 Stroke Risk Score		
Risk Factor	Parameter	Score
Age	≥ 60 years	1
Blood Pressure	≥ 140/90 mmHg	1
Clinical Features	Speech impairment but no focal weakness	1
	Focal weakness	2
Duration of Symptoms	<10 minutes	0
	10-59 minutes	1
	>60 minutes	2
Diabetes	Active diagnosis	1
Total Score	Denotes risk for stroke (CVA) within 2 days after TIA	

Traumatic Brain Injury (TBI)

Traumatic brain injury (TBI) occurs where there is damage to the brain by a bump, blow, or jolt. Falls are a common cause of TBI, making up 81 percent of TBI-related ER visits in adults over 65-years-old. Males are typically impacted more than females, with mortality being highest in the elderly population.

Patients may present with nausea, vomiting, headaches, tinnitus, dizziness, visual changes, confusion, and may or may not have experienced loss of consciousness. Patients with TBI may also have ICH from the injury, which may present with numbness, weakness, incontinence of bladder or bowel, slurred speech, or changes in mental status. If these symptoms are identified, this should be treated as an emergency to evaluate for and treat ICH. Laboratory tests may be considered depending on the severity of the injury. A head CT scan is typically performed and preferred due to quickness and availability.

TBI can occur at various levels from mild to life threatening. Patients with mild symptoms, scoring 15 on the **Glasgow Coma Scale** (GCS) with no neurological defects, may be safely discharged home. Patients and caregivers should be counselled on post-concussive symptoms, such as headaches, mood changes, nausea, and difficulty concentrating. They should be instructed to seek emergency evaluation if persistent nausea/vomiting, seizures, changes in mental status, severe headache, drainage from ears or nose, or other neurological symptoms appear or worsen.

Patients with a GCS of less than 15 or concerning exam findings may require further evaluation, such as a CT angiography or MRI. In severe cases, patients may require intubation if they have a GCS of less than 8, as they are unlikely to maintain their own airway. Patients with a GCS of less than 10 are at risk for seizure and should be placed on seizure precautions according to organizational standards. Patients should be frequently assessed for changes in neurologic function and placed in a quiet space with low levels of stimulation.

Early collaboration with physical therapy, occupational therapy, and speech therapy can be beneficial for many patients with TBI to improve daily function. Assistive devices may be required if TBI has impacted the patient's ability to perform ADLs independently. Patients should be encouraged to continue these therapies on an outpatient basis. Many patients may experience ongoing psychological effects, including mood disorders, post-traumatic stress disorder, and schizophrenia, and may be referred to appropriate psychological services.

Space-Occupying Lesions

Space-occupying lesions (SOLs) are a damaged area of the brain tissue that disrupts the function of the brain. The mass of the lesion creates pressure, which cuts off metabolic pathways and neurological signaling of the brain in the affected area. While SOLs include malignant or benign tumors, they can also refer to hematoma or abscess. As space in the brain is limited, these lesions create pressure on the surrounding brain tissues, which results in damage. Specifically, SOLs may invade and damage important structures in the central nervous system. They may also impair the flow of cerebrospinal fluid, resulting in hydrocephalus. Malignancies can induce angiogenesis, which may result in vasogenic edema.

Patients will present with generalized neurologic symptoms, such as headache, nausea/vomiting, changes in mental status, and seizures. Other symptoms that may be present depending on the location of the lesion include:

- **Frontal lobe lesion**: may result in agitation; mood swings; changes in attention span, learning, or motor function; and loss of smell

135

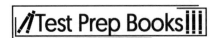

- **Temporal lobe lesion**: may lead to trouble understanding words, hallucinations, and difficulty processing sounds
- **Parietal lobe lesion**: may present with the inability to write, do math, recognize own hands and fingers, and confusion of left and right
- **Occipital lobe lesion**: may result in loss of vision, color blindness, or difficulties recognizing visual objects
- **Cerebellum lesion**: may result in loss of coordination, dizziness, shaking/tremors, paralysis, and difficulty controlling eye movement
- **Brainstem lesion**: may cause changes in heart rhythm, blood pressure, and breathing

Diagnostic work up includes standard blood tests, such as CBC and CMP, as well as radiologic studies including x-ray, CT scan, or MRI. Once a lesion is identified, a biopsy is typically completed to identify the etiology of the mass. An EEG may be indicated to evaluate seizure activity.

Treatment strategies should be implemented in a timely manner. Treatments may include reducing edema through pharmacological methods, therapies to reduce the intracranial pressure, use of an external ventricular drain, and surgery to remove the lesion or necrotic tissue.

Neurological surgery management

The nurse plays an important role for patients undergoing **neurological surgery**. Pre-operatively, they ensure the patient is well-equipped to have a successful surgery. Post-operatively, the nurse monitors the patient's healing and recovery, along with encouraging collaboration of the interdisciplinary team to ensure resources are available to be successful upon discharge.

Pre-operatively, the nurse should perform a thorough history and assessment, including allergies, current medications, vital signs, and laboratory results. They will assist in educating the patient and caregivers on the surgery, expected outcomes, and recovery process. While not responsible for obtaining informed consent, the nurse should provide education to ensure patient and caregiver understanding of the process, risks, and post-operative care. The nurse should also ensure administration of pre-operative antibiotics and anxiety medications as indicated.

Post-operatively, the nurse is responsible for monitoring the patient for complications, encouraging healing and activities for recovery, and preparing them for discharge. Regular assessments to monitor vital signs, changes in neurological status, and surgical sites should be completed for early detection of any complications, which leads to lessened risk of morbidity and mortality. Such complications include increased intracranial pressure and infection, but other risks may be present depending on the type of surgery.

Nurses should follow physician orders for timely medication administration and necessary laboratory tests. Once appropriate, mobilization should be encouraged to reduce risk of pneumonia, maintain skin integrity, and rebuild strength and stamina. Nurses should collaborate with supportive services, such as physical therapy, occupational therapy, and speech therapy, to assist in the transition to discharge. Referrals to social work or patient navigation may be necessary for nursing care facilities, depending on the patient's function and outcomes.

Pharmacologic methods to reduce cerebral edema include osmotherapy, diuretics, and corticosteroids. An external ventricular drain is a temporary measure to aid in the reduction of intracranial pressure by redirecting the CSF fluid from the ventricles of the brain. Surgical interventions aim to remove the lesion and necrotic tissue in order to reduce the pressure on surrounding tissues and prevent further damage to healthy brain tissue.

Nursing interventions should be implemented based on the type of lesion and therapy used to treat it. For medical management, nurses should administer medications as ordered and assess the patient for changes in neurological status at frequent intervals. Frequent monitoring of vital signs should include watching for **Cushing's triad**, a signal of high intracranial pressure that is characterized by three clinical symptoms: bradycardia, irregular respirations, and widened pulse pressure (large gap between systolic and diastolic blood pressures). It is considered a medical emergency if identified.

The clinical environment should remain calm and quiet to reduce agitation and, thereby, intracranial pressure. The head of the bed should be maintained between 30 and 45 degrees. If an external ventricular drain is placed, the color, clarity, and volume should be documented along with an assessment of the insertion site to ensure it is working properly and not infected. For patients receiving surgical intervention, the nurse should be sure to assess the surgical sites for signs of infection. Pain should be adequately controlled with adherence to a pain regimen in order to promote patient comfort and lower intracranial pressure.

Brain Tumor

A **brain tumor** is a growth of abnormal cells in the brain that can be malignant or benign. Tumors can be primary, meaning they originate in the brain, or they can be secondary, resulting as a metastasis from a separate location. In adults, secondary brain tumors are more common than primary tumors and are frequently from lung, breast, colon, and melanoma origins. Additionally, there are two types of brain tumors: gliomas and non-gliomas. **Gliomas** are the most common type of malignant brain tumor.

Brain tumors are a type of space-occupying lesion; as a result, symptoms are specific to the location and size of the tumor. Common symptoms include headache that is often worse in the morning, nausea/vomiting, vision changes, dizziness, confusion, and seizures. Diagnosis is made with radiologic imaging using a CT or MRI of the head. Sometimes, a biopsy is required to make the definitive diagnosis.

Treatment of both benign and malignant brain tumors involves surgery, radiation, and/or chemotherapy. The treatment regimen often involves a combination of multiple modalities, although it can be singular. Surgery is used to achieve a complete (or nearly complete) removal of the brain tumor without damaging healthy brain tissue or impacting neurological function. Radiation uses high energy x-rays to kill cancer cells and is often used when surgery is unable to fully resect the tumor. Chemotherapy uses cytotoxic medication to induce cell death during various stages of cell division; as the least specific option of the three, it will result in systemic side effects. Additionally, very few chemotherapy agents cross the blood-brain barrier, making it a relatively ineffective treatment for most adult brain tumors.

Subdural Hematoma

A **subdural hematoma** forms when blood accumulates under the protective layer of the brain known as the dura mater. The brain is covered by three protective layers (known as **meninges**): the **dura** being the outermost layer, the **arachnoid mater** being the middle layer, and the **pia mater** being the inner layer closest to the brain. In a subdural hematoma, blood accumulates between the dura and the arachnoid layer, where there is rupture of the veins that bridge these three layers. Most commonly, subdural hematomas are caused by trauma, such as falls or motor vehicle accidents. As blood presses against the brain, this leads to damage to the tissues. Patients on blood thinners or with conditions that impair coagulation are at high risk for subdural hematoma with even mild injury to the head.

137

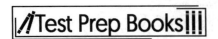
Symptoms include confusion, dizziness, nausea/vomiting, seizures, loss of consciousness, and changes to speech, vision, or balance. Diagnosis requires imaging, such as a CT scan of the head, to look for signs of bleeding. Blood tests to evaluate clotting factors and platelet levels may also be indicated. If patients are on blood thinners, have low platelets, or a high INR/PTT, reverse coagulopathy (e.g., platelet transfusion, fresh frozen plasma, or vitamin K) may be indicated.

The goal of treatment is to decrease pressure on the brain from the blood and stop the bleeding. To treat the bleeding, a **craniotomy** may be used to evacuate the blood. Alternatively, a **burr hole** may be drilled to allow the blood to drain. Nurses should monitor these sites to ensure there is no abnormal drainage or signs of infection.

Abscess

An **abscess** is a localized collection of pus in the brain that results from an infection elsewhere in the body. Paranasal sinus infections and dental infections are the most common causes of brain abscess, while pulmonary infections and endocarditis are the most common causes from distant sites. Brain abscesses are uncommon, making up 8 percent of SOL cases. Patients who are immunocompromised, such as those with AIDS, are at higher risk of developing a brain abscess.

Approximately 66 percent of patients will present with symptoms occurring for two weeks or less. Because of the nonspecific nature of symptoms, diagnosis is often delayed. Frequent symptoms include intense localized headache not relieved by over-the-counter medications, changes in mental status, fever, seizures, nausea/vomiting, focalized neurologic deficits, and neck stiffness. A sudden worsening headache followed by meningismus (stiff neck, sensitivity to light, and nausea/vomiting) is typically associated with rupture of the abscess, which is a fatal complication.

Diagnostic workup involves laboratory work, including CBC, ESR, CRP, and blood cultures. Preferred imaging modality is an MRI; however, a CT scan is often used in an emergency due to availability. Once an abscess is identified, a biopsy through aspiration or surgical drainage is often performed to identify the organism causing the infection.

Because a brain abscess can lead to increased intracranial pressure and therefore an increased risk of damage and death, large abscesses (typically larger than 2 cm) are treated with aspiration or excision. Multiple abscesses are treated with a 4–8 week course of high-dose antibiotics, sometimes in addition to aspiration. The antibiotic regimen is determined based on results of the biopsy.

In addition to typical nursing management of patients with SOL, nurses should provide education to patients and their caregivers emphasizing the importance of adherence to the antibiotic administration schedule. They should also be given strict return precautions if there is new onset of fever, worsening of symptoms, or development of symptoms indicating rising intracranial pressure.

Altered Mental Status

Altered mental status is a broad symptom that is common to many neurological defects. It can be described by changes of alertness or orientation and is categorized as delirium, depression, dementia, or coma. Additional forms of altered mental status include Alzheimer's disease and agitation.

Delirium is an acute confused state that develops in hours to days. This state often fluctuates between periods of lucidity and confusion and may be worse at night, also known as sundowning. **Depression** is a chronic change in alertness characterized by withdrawal, slow speech, or poor cognition. Patients with

138

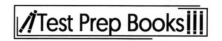

this condition are typically orientated, able to follow commands, and do not experience rapid fluctuation of symptoms. Dementia is a chronic, slow progressing loss of mental capacity that eventually results in poor cognition and changes in behavior. **Coma** occurs when there is an absent level of alertness and response to basic stimulus is impaired.

Since altered mental status may be acute or chronic, it is important to determine the cause of the condition in order to form a treatment plan. A history should be obtained to assess for possible supplement/medication use, trauma, or substance use. Routine lab work and vital signs can serve as indicators of infection, while a CT scan can be obtained to look for structural causes. If there are no infectious symptoms or trauma-related reason, toxic or metabolic causes should be considered.

When caring for patients with dementia or delirium, the nurse should consider the environment and work to keep it quiet and soothing. Lighting should be utilized to mimic day/night cycles and care should be clustered to avoid excessive interruptions overnight and reduce sundowning behavior.

Delirium

A patient with a sudden, severe change in level of consciousness and disturbed cognition may be experiencing **delirium**. Delirium is somewhat common in an acute care setting, as patients are critically ill, dealing with potential adverse side effects of medications, and outside of their normal environment. Delirium, unlike dementia, is reversible in most cases.

Medications increase a patient's risk for the development of delirium include opioids, psychoactive drugs, and anticholinergics. There are many conditions that may cause delirium, such as infections (especially UTIs and pneumonia in the geriatric population), dehydration, dementia, stroke, and traumatic brain injury. Rapid cessation of certain drugs and alcohol can also cause delirium.

Assessment tools can be utilized to identify delirium earlier in the course of its development. A commonly used screening tool is the **Confusion Assessment Method** (CAM). Early recognition of delirium is important to be able to reverse or reduce hospital stays and complications. CAM empowers providers who are not specialized in psychiatry to identify delirium quickly through four features: acute onset and fluctuating course, inattention, disorganized thinking, and altered levels of consciousness. Patients with delirium must exhibit the first two features (acute onset and fluctuating course as well as inattention) in addition to either disorganized thinking or altered levels of consciousness.

Treatment of delirium depends on the underlying cause. If it is the adverse side effect of a medication, adjustment of the dose or cessation of its administration may be in order. A dose of lorazepam, a type of benzodiazepine, may be helpful in relieving delirium when alcohol withdrawal is the primary cause. The main goal of nursing care for the patient experiencing delirium is to provide a safe environment by avoiding any further aggravating factors.

Dementia

Dementia is a general term used to describe a state of general cognitive decline. Although Alzheimer's disease accounts for up to 80 percent of all cases of dementia in the United States, the remaining 20 percent may result from any one of several additional causes. Less common causes of dementia include vascular dementia, Lewy body dementia (LBD), frontotemporal dementia, Parkinson's disease dementia (PDD), and conditions that are potentially reversible, such as vitamin B-12 deficiency, Korsakoff syndrome, and altered function of the thyroid gland. The destruction of cortical tissue resulting from a stroke, or more commonly from multiple small strokes, can lead to vascular dementia. Repetitive head injuries over an extended period can also potentially result in permanent damage, limiting normal brain activity. The onset and progression of the disease relate to the underlying cause and associated patient comorbidities.

Alzheimer's Disease

Alzheimer's disease is a chronic progressive form of dementia with an insidious onset that is caused by the abnormal accumulation of amyloid-β plaque in the brain. The accumulation of this plaque eventually interferes with neural functioning and is responsible for the progressive manifestations of the disease. Although the exact etiology is unknown, environmental toxins, vascular alterations due to hemorrhagic or embolic events, infections, advanced age, and genetic factors have all been proposed as the triggering mechanism for the plaque formation. The progression of the disease and the associated manifestations are specific to the individual; however, in all individuals, there is measurable decline over time in cognitive functioning, including short-term and long-term memory, behavior and mood, and the ability to perform activities of daily living (ADLs).

The diagnosis is based on the patient's presenting history and manifestations, imaging studies of the brain, protein analysis of the cerebrospinal fluid (CSF), and cognitive assessment with measures such as the **Mini-Mental State Exam**. An amyloid blood test can also be used in conjunction with other diagnostics, as new research indicates this diagnostic tool can accurately detect the amount of beta-amyloid plaques in the brain. Current treatments are only supportive, although cholinesterase inhibitors and N-Methyl-D-aspartate (NMDA) receptor antagonists may slow the progression of the manifestations for a limited period if administered early in the course of the disease. All patients will suffer an eventual decline in all aspects of cognitive functioning, with the average survival rate dependent on the presence of comorbidities and the level of care and support available to the patient.

Experiencing a fall (with or without a resulting fracture), somatic illnesses, and caregiver strain are the most common reasons for healthcare visits in this population. The nursing care of patients with Alzheimer's disease in progressive care facilities must focus on patient safety, as the usual chaotic environment of the department is disorienting to the already confused patient. Safeguards against increased confusion and wandering, which is a common behavior in this patient population, should be implemented. In addition, the entire family unit should be assessed by the interdisciplinary health team to identify any alterations of family processes or additional resources that are required for adequate patient care after discharge.

Agitation

Agitation is a heightened emotional state where an individual demonstrates distress through increased physical activity or verbal communication. Agitation can be brought on by a multitude of psychological and medical factors, whether pre-existing or not. Agitated patients are common in many working medical environments. Therefore, knowing how to identify and treat agitation is paramount. Nervousness and anxiety are common signs of agitation in patients. When a critically ill patient demonstrates unusually high agitation, it may indicate signs of mental disturbance.

Two commonly utilized agitation scales in the hospital setting include the **Behavioral Activity Rating Scale** (BARS) and the **Richmond Agitation-Sedation Scale** (RASS). The BARS gives the medical team a quick overview of patient agitation, with a scale of 1–7 (with 1 being difficult to arouse/unarousable and 7 being violent) based on overall patient presentation. Slightly more detailed, the RASS is commonly used in the critical care setting but can be used for any hospitalized patient. A scale of −5 to +4 is used

140

(with −5 being unarousable, 0 being alert and calm, and +4 being combative) to provide the medical team with an overview of patient agitation. Both scales are widely used and effective in determining a real-time agitation level.

Agitation can occur due to withdrawal from certain medications, alcohol intoxication, withdrawal from chronic alcohol consumption, endocrine dysfunction, psychological disorders, and a genetic predisposition. It's crucial to understand the cause of a patient's agitation, as the treatment plan will revolve around the etiology. For example, if a patient's agitation is caused by a disturbance in their mental health, their current treatment plan should be evaluated for possible adjustments in medication regimen.

If pharmacological agents are necessary for the treatment of agitation, one of the following three classes will likely be used. **First-generation antipsychotics**, such as haloperidol, work by inhibiting dopamine transmission to the brain, which has a calming effect on the patient. Second-generation antipsychotics, formally called **atypical antipsychotics**, are serotonin-dopamine antagonists and less likely than first-generation antipsychotics to cause extrapyramidal motor control issues. Benzodiazepines act on GABA receptors to reduce anxiety, relax muscles, produce a sedative effect, and can be used as an anticonvulsant. A last resort for a severely agitated patient that is threatening physical harm to self or others is the use of physical restraints, which require a physician order and must meet strict hospital protocols.

Gastrointestinal

GI Motility Disorders

Obstruction

There are three anatomical areas of the GI system that are prone to obstruction, including the gastric outlet at the pylorus, the small intestine, and the bowel. The small intestine is the most commonly affected site, and adhesions are responsible for more than 60 percent of all obstructions. These conditions may also be categorized as mechanical or nonmechanical depending on the cause. Mechanical obstructions are due to an extrinsic source (e.g., adhesions, tumor formation, intussusception, or hernias), while nonmechanical obstructions are due to decreased peristalsis (e.g., neurogenic disorders, vascular insufficiency, or electrolyte imbalance). Mechanical obstructions of the biliary tract can be due to the effects of cirrhosis and hepatitis.

The manifestations are specific to the anatomical site of obstruction. The gastric outlet obstruction occurs most commonly in the pylorus and is associated with upper abdominal distention, nausea, vomiting, weight loss, and anorexia. Diagnostic tests include endoscopy and assessment of nutritional deficits, in addition to testing to eliminate *H. pylori* or diabetic gastric paresis as the cause. Obstruction of the small bowel is associated with severe fluid and electrolyte losses, metabolic acidosis, nausea and vomiting, fever, and tachycardia, and may lead to strangulation of the affected bowel segment. Bowel obstruction, most frequently due to tumor formation or stricture resulting from diverticular disease, is manifested by lower abdominal distention, possible metabolic acidosis, cramping abdominal pain, and minimal fluid and electrolyte losses. Common diagnostic studies include endoscopy, common lab studies, flat plate of the abdomen to assess for free air, and CT imaging. Esophageal obstructions may be caused by a foreign object, tumor, or secondary to GERD (resulting in obstructive scar tissue).

Treatments are specific to the cause and may include tumor excision, antibiotic therapy for *H. pylori*, colectomy to remove the affected bowel segment, and/or colostomy placement. Although some obstructions may be treated with gastric or enteric decompression, bowel rest, and fluids, emergency intervention is usually necessary to prevent complications, such as peritonitis, hemorrhage, and foreign body obstruction in the esophagus.

Ileus

An **ileus** refers to a segment of the large intestine that has lost forward propulsive movement, allowing the accumulation of gas and fluid. This pathology is most likely due to the interplay between the autonomic nervous system and the central nervous system, which is necessary to maintain bowel motility under normal circumstances. An ileus is most commonly seen following abdominal surgery and its development is related to the type of surgery and anesthetic. Spinal anesthesia and sympathectomy target the long reflex arcs that can contribute to the ileus, thereby reducing the incidence of the condition. The stress response related to the surgical intervention also contributes to the development of the altered motility by secreting inflammatory mediators that are capable of altering the function of the bowel wall.

A partial list of the most common causes includes sepsis, head injuries, heart failure, adrenal disease, spinal trauma, hypokalemia, and post-operative opioid pain management. An ileus is most often a temporary event; however, if the condition is not resolved after successful treatment of the underlying cause and symptom management, imaging studies are done to identify a possible mechanical bowel obstruction. Symptomatic interventions include nasogastric suctioning, fluid volume maintenance, and electrolyte homeostasis.

Diabetic Gastroparesis

Diabetic gastroparesis is defined as delayed gastric emptying that can be objectively measured and is not associated with mechanical intestinal obstruction. The most common manifestations include nausea, vomiting, early satiety, and upper abdominal pain. The condition is associated with several possible alterations in the function of the autonomic nervous system, which result in general nervous impairment of gastric function.

In type I diabetics with any degree of autonomic neuropathy, there is a bi-directional relationship between gastric emptying and blood glucose levels. Acute hyperglycemia delays gastric emptying under fasting or postprandial conditions. The opposite reaction occurs in the state of hypoglycemia, and the rate of gastric emptying is increased. The degree of gastroparesis also affects carbohydrate absorption and the absorption of some medications, including oral hypoglycemic medications. Common manifestations include nausea, vomiting, satiety, abdominal pain, fullness, bloating after meals, and possible weight loss. Diagnostic studies, including scintigraphy, endoscopy, CT, and MRI, are aimed at confirming the presence of gastroparesis and eliminating any additional causes that may be responsible for the patient's symptoms. Treatment is aimed at glycemic control, diet changes, and prokinetic and antiemetic medications.

GI Bleed

Gastrointestinal (GI) bleeding is defined according to the area of the defect. Upper GI bleeding occurs superiorly to the junction of the duodenum and jejunum. Lower GI bleeding occurs in the large and small intestine.

Conditions associated with an **upper GI bleed** include esophageal varices, gastric and duodenal ulcers, cancer, and Mallory-Weiss tears. Risk factors include age, history of gastroesophageal reflux disorder (GERD), use of nonsteroidal anti-inflammatory drugs (NSAIDs) and steroids, and alcoholism. Acute

142

presenting manifestations include hematemesis, melena, hematochezia, and lightheadedness or fainting. The diagnosis is made by the patient's history and physical examination, routine lab studies including complete blood count (CBC) and coagulation tests, endoscopy, and chest films. Treatment is specific to the cause; for example, peptic ulcer disease will be treated with the appropriate antibiotic and a proton-pump inhibitor (PPI).

Causative factors for a **lower GI bleed** include anatomical defects such as diverticulosis, ischemic events of the vasculature related to radiation therapy or other embolic events, cancer, and infectious or noninfectious inflammatory conditions. Manifestations that are specific to the cause and location of the hemorrhage include melena, maroon stools or bright red blood, fever, dehydration, possible abdominal pain or distention, and hematochezia. Common diagnostic studies include routine lab studies, endoscopy, radionucleotide studies, and angiography. Treatment is focused on the identification and resolution of the source of the bleeding and correction of any hematologic deficits that resulted from the hemorrhage.

Orthostatic hypotension, defined as a decrease in diastolic blood pressure of at least 10 mmHg, is associated with a blood loss of approximately 1000 mL. Therefore, care of massive GI bleeding requires aggressive fluid volume replacement with isotonic crystalloids while the exact source of the bleeding is being confirmed.

In order to target the source of the bleed, a tool called an endoscope will often be used. Depending on the suspected region of the GI tract, an upper or lower endoscopy may be used. **Colonoscopy** refers to a scope of the colon, part of the lower GI tract, while **esophagogastroduodenoscopy** (EGD) looks at the esophagus, stomach, and duodenum, or the upper GI tract. In endoscopy, a thin tube with a camera affixed to the end of it is threaded into the body and images are produced. During endoscopy, areas that are bleeding may be cauterized to stop bleeding. **Cauterization** is the application of heat to the lesion to bring about hemostasis. Once a patient has an endoscopy of either type scheduled, they will usually be NPO for at least 4–8 hours prior to the procedure.

While many providers will allow patients to take their oral medications with a sip of water on the day of the procedure, some medications may need to be specifically clarified, such as diabetic medications (as the patient will be NPO for an extended time) and anticoagulants (for which risk and benefit for each patient will need to be considered by the provider). For patients undergoing a colonoscopy, thorough education and assistance must be provided regarding the colon preparation. Patients should understand that prepping the bowels appropriately will lead to watery amber to yellow diarrhea, if the prep has been effective. Patients should provide informed consent before the procedure or receiving any medications for anesthesia. When patients return to their room following either an EGD or colonoscopy, they should be immediately assessed for level of consciousness, vital signs, and signs of any unexpected bleeding. Patients should be educated that feeling bloated, belching, and even cramping after these procedures is generally considered normal because of air used during the procedure.

Ulcers

Ulcers of the GI tract are categorized as to the anatomical site of injury. **Gastric ulcers** are located in the body of the stomach, and **peptic ulcers** are located in the duodenum. The presenting symptom is abdominal pain 2 to 4 hours after eating for **duodenal ulcers**, in addition to hematemesis and melena. The defect is due to erosion of the mucosal lining by infectious agents, most commonly *H. pylori;* extreme systemic stress such as burns or head trauma; ETOH abuse; chronic kidney and respiratory

143

disease; and psychological stress. If left untreated, the mucosal erosion can progress to perforation, hemorrhage, and peritonitis.

Laboratory studies include examination of endoscopic tissue samples for the presence of the *H. pylori* organism, urea breath test, CBC, stool samples, and metabolic panel. Endoscopy, which is used to obtain tissue samples and achieve hemostasis, and double barium imaging studies made be obtained. The treatment depends on the extent of the erosion and will be focused on healing the ulcerated tissue and preventing additional damage. The treatment protocol for *H. pylori* infection includes the use of a PPI, amoxicillin, and clarithromycin for a minimum of 7 to 14 days. Subsequent testing will be necessary to ensure that the organism has been eradicated. Patients infected with *H. pylori* also must discontinue the use of NSAIDs or continue the long-term use of PPIs. Surgery may be indicated for significant areas of hemorrhage that were not successfully treated by ultrasound, and the procedure will be specific to the anatomical area of ulceration.

GI Infections

Most commonly, the identification of the causative agent for self-limiting foodborne illness of the gastrointestinal tract requires additional information beyond the presenting symptoms; however, there are some characteristic manifestations that indicate the exact nature of the agent. Diarrhea that is "watery" is known to be specific to organisms of the small bowel, while infection by pathogens native to the large intestine produce inflammatory manifestations, such as mucoid or bloody diarrhea with fever. Additional clues to the causative agent are provided by the exposure history, especially when the infection is the result of an outbreak that is associated with a known source. Other exposure sources include animal contact, travel to high-risk areas, occupational exposure, water-borne outbreaks, and recent antibiotic use.

Additional manifestations include vomiting (which may or may not be present), abdominal cramping and bloating, systemic manifestations, neurological manifestations due to the ingestion of toxins, and hepatitis. Diagnostic studies include stool cultures, fecal occult analysis, CBC, and other organism-specific studies. In general, the onset of symptoms is 24 to 48 after the initial exposure to the pathogen, and recovery occurs within an additional 48 to 72 hours. The plan of care focuses on treatment of the underlying cause, fluid volume maintenance, and symptom management.

Clostridium Difficile

Clostridium difficile (*C. diff*) is a bacterium known for causing infectious diarrhea and a more serious condition called *C. diff* colitis. The symptoms of infection can range from minor (frequent watery diarrhea, abdominal pain and tenderness) to lethal (as many as fifteen watery stools/day, severe abdominal pain, anorexia, fever, weight loss, and blood or pus in stool).

If an individual suspects that he or she may be infected, that person may want to consult a physician before self-administering an antidiarrheal medication, as stopping the diarrhea will almost certainly make the *C. diff* infection worse, thus leading to other complications.

In the healthcare setting, *C. diff* is spread mainly by hand-to-hand contact. Healthy people can occasionally fall prey to *C. diff* infection; however, individuals at greatest risk for contracting *C. diff* are mainly those who are hospitalized or in long-term care (LTC) facilities. Patients who are under a multiple-antibiotic regimen also have an increased chance to be infected, as the wide range of broad-spectrum antibiotics administered will eradicate the "good" intestinal bacteria that can prevent overgrowth of *C. diff*. Other risk factors include (but are not limited to) GI tract surgery, certain diseases

144

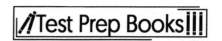

of the colon (e.g., inflammatory bowel disease and colorectal cancer), use of chemotherapy drugs, previous infection with *C. diff*, age 65 years or older, and kidney disease.

Nursing considerations when caring for a patient presenting for *C. diff* will focus on immediate hydration and pain management. Stabilization of vital signs is required if the patient presents with fever and **hematochezia** (bright red blood in stool). A CBC, as well as a basic metabolic panel (BMP) or comprehensive metabolic panel (CMP), will be collected to determine any metabolic disturbances as a result of frequent diarrhea; in addition, a stool sample may be necessary. A physician will typically prescribe a 10-to-14-day course of antibiotic therapy consisting of one of the following: metronidazole (Flagyl), fidaxomicin (Dificid), or vancomycin (Vancocin). An improvement of symptoms will usually occur about 72 hours after starting antibiotics, but diarrhea may still reappear briefly. In addition to prescribed medications, probiotics may also be considered as an alternative treatment.

Due to medications, enteral feedings, and disease process, acutely ill patients are at high risk for fecal incontinence, which can lead to skin breakdown and increased risk of infection. A **fecal containment device** (FCD) may reduce these complications and pressure injuries in critically ill patients. Nurses should continue to provide meticulous skin care, including cleansing the skin after all periods of incontinence, application of moisturizer with a skin protectant, and use of absorbent pads to wick moisture from the skin. The FCD adheres directly to the skin and can remain in place for 1 to 2 days without leaking. The nurse should assess the system frequently to ensure it is in the correct position, draining properly, not leaking, and that there are no changes to the stool amount, consistency, or presence of blood.

Upon discharge from the healthcare facility, the patient will need to be encouraged to increase fluid intake to prevent dehydration from recurrent diarrhea (if and when it persists).

Prevention of the illness focuses on excellent hygiene; examples of prevention techniques include frequent handwashing after coming into contact with an infected individual, using chlorine bleach-based cleaning agents for home use, and washing soiled clothing with detergent and bleach.

GI Surgeries
There are many conditions of the various organs of the abdomen that may need surgical intervention to fix.

Gastrectomy
A **gastrectomy** is a surgery performed to remove all or a portion of the stomach. It is typically performed to treat stomach cancer; however, it is also used to treat ulcers, obesity, and polyps. It can be a total gastrectomy, partial gastrectomy, or sleeve gastrectomy. In the event of a **partial gastrectomy**, only a portion is removed, typically the lower part of the stomach, and the intestine will be reconnected to the portion of the stomach that remains. In a **total gastrectomy**, the entirety of the stomach is removed, and the esophagus will be connected to the intestine instead. In a **sleeve gastrectomy**, the left side of the stomach is removed.

The surgery can be performed as either an open surgery, where a large incision is made into the abdomen or chest, or laparoscopically, where several smaller incisions are made for surgical tools and insertion of a camera.

With the removal of all or a portion of the stomach, patients need counseling on nutritional changes and considerations. Patients will receive parenteral nutrition for several days until some healing has

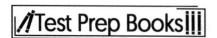

occurred, followed by a slow progression from a liquid diet to a soft diet, and then to light meals. Consulting with a nutrition specialist is vital in order to maximize nutrition and avoid complications, such as **dumping syndrome**.

Esophagectomy

An **esophagectomy** is a surgical removal of the esophagus. It is typically performed to treat esophageal cancer or Barrett's esophagus if precancerous cells are present. In an esophagectomy, an incision is made in the neck, chest, or abdomen to remove the affected parts of the esophagus and reconstruct it with a portion of stomach or intestine. Enteral nutrition is used after surgery until the patient can tolerate a regular diet without losing weight or requiring supplementation. Since the esophagus is often rebuilt with a portion of the stomach, the remaining smaller stomach size results in the need for frequent, smaller meals afterwards.

Post-surgically, patients may be given an epidural or a patient-controlled analgesic (PCA) pump to manage pain. Early mobility is encouraged to minimize complications associated with sedentary behavior, such as pneumonia and pressure ulcers. Patients and caregivers will need education on proper nutrition strategies, including care of the feeding tube. Consults from physical and occupational therapy are helpful to assist with strategies for ADLs upon discharge. Patients should be reminded it may be months until their functional status returns to near baseline.

Esophagogastrostomy

An **esophagogastrostomy** is a surgical procedure to remove the upper portion of the stomach and the portion of the esophagus that connects to the stomach. The connection is replaced by either moving the remaining portion of the stomach up and connecting it to the remaining portion of the esophagus, or by using a portion of intestine to make the connection. This is performed to treat malignancies that are present in that area.

Similar to an esophagectomy, enteral feedings through a jejunostomy tube (J-tube) will be used for the first one to two weeks after surgery to allow the site to heal. The patient's diet will be slowly advanced until they are eating regular meals, at which time the J-tube will be removed. Patients will need nutrition consults to optimize healing and accommodate the shorter digestive system. High-fat and high-sugar meals may be more difficult to tolerate after surgery, and patients may experience early satiety. Patients should be counselled to eat small, frequent meals and remain upright for 30 minutes afterwards to reduce reflux and encourage digestion.

Cholecystectomy

A **cholecystectomy** is a procedure in which the entire gallbladder is removed. The gallbladder is a pear-shaped organ that is positioned below the liver and adjacent to the stomach. The decision to take out the gallbladder is based on patient condition and, specifically, if gallstone formation is causing pain.

Cholecystectomy begins with the physician inflating the abdomen for a clear view with which to work. After this, the physician makes small incisions and insets a thin tube with a camera at the end into the abdomen. The physician visualizes the gallbladder and then removes it.

This type of surgical procedure, in which there is minimal invasion, a camera or scope is used, and smaller incisions are made, is called a laparoscopic procedure.

A **JP drain** is placed after a cholecystectomy to remove excess bile and blood that may drain and collect in the abdomen. Removing these fluids is thought to allow for better healing and prevent infection, although results of its efficacy are mixed.

Nurses should assess the drain site for patency and any signs or symptoms of infection, including redness, pain, or purulent discharge from the site. This involves double checking that the bulb is properly compressed to allow suction to pull fluid from the abdominal space. Additionally, the drain should be emptied when it becomes full to encourage proper drainage, and the output should be recorded at least once each shift. This measurement provides a trend of how much fluid is being pulled out of the space and is often used to determine how long a drain will remain in place.

Colectomy

A **colectomy** is the surgical removal of the large bowel. It can include the removal of a portion of the colon, or the totality of it, and may or may not include the rectum. A colectomy is performed to treat colon cancer, a blockage, or diseased areas of the colon from conditions such as ulcerative colitis. The surgery can be open or laparoscopic in nature.

An **anastomosis** (to connect the ends of the portions of healthy large intestine) will be created if there is enough left after surgery. If there is not enough healthy bowel, a colostomy will be created by making a **stoma**, or opening, in the abdominal wall, and attaching the colon to the stoma. This allows for the body to continue to excrete waste through the large intestine. The colostomy may only be temporary if there is enough viable bowel left that needs time to heal, and the reconnection will happen later.

After surgery, nurses should encourage early mobilization as tolerated. The patient should be assessed for return of bowel function, and their diet should be progressed as bowel function returns. Patients will require education and encouragement to participate with ostomy care if a colostomy was created, as it is often an emotionally distressing event. Collaboration with a nurse specialized in wound and ostomy care (WORN nurse) can be helpful in troubleshooting, providing correct supplies, and ensuring proper fit of the ostomy bag. The nurse should frequently assess and document the surgical sites and stoma appearance. The stoma should appear moist, pink or red, and above the skin level. If the stoma takes on a dusky appearance or retracts, the surgical team should promptly be made aware.

Ileostomy and Colostomy

Ileostomy and colostomy are surgical procedures in which a portion of the bowel is rerouted up through a hole in the abdomen. **Ileostomy** involves the small intestine or ileum, while **colostomy** involves the large intestine or colon. These two procedures are performed in the cases of severe bowel disease, such as bowel cancer, diverticulitis, and inflammatory bowel disease.

The patient with a stoma as a result of an ileostomy or colostomy will need to be educated on how to care for it. A bag is attached to the stoma for the purpose of collecting fecal matter. This bag can be taken off and replaced as needed. The stoma needs to be assessed regularly to make sure it has not become infected. The stoma should be pink, and the area surrounding it should be kept clean and dry.

Healthy stoma site postcolostomy

Stoma is pink; area surrounding is clean and dry

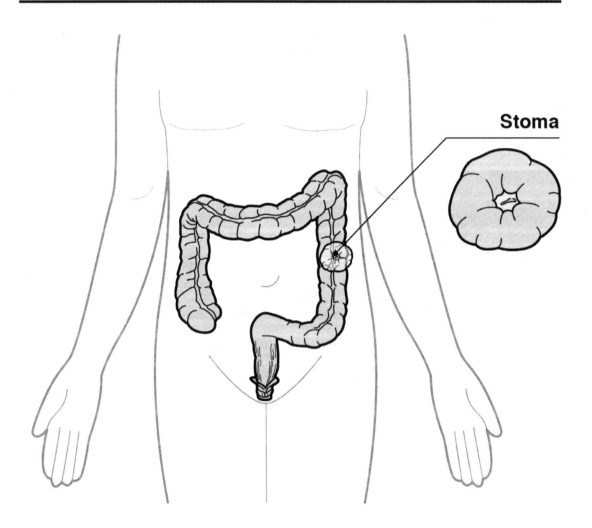

Stoma

Bariatric Surgeries

Bariatric surgeries pose risk for complications both acutely and long-term that require early recognition and management. Priority management of the post-operative patient is focused on management of nausea, vomiting, and pain; pulmonary hygiene (e.g., incentive spirometer, cough, deep breathing); and early ambulation. With bariatric surgery, nurses need to watch for additional complications specific to the procedure, such as leaks and stenosis. As patients move beyond the first 24 hours from surgery, they should be monitored for hypertension, diabetes, dumping syndrome, and other gastrointestinal disorders.

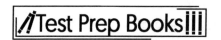

An anastomotic leak can lead to an increase in the following: morbidity to 61 percent and mortality to 15 percent; prolonged hospital stays; and the risk for gastroenteric or gastrobronchial fistula, which take an extended period to heal. Nurses should be assessing patients for tachycardia, dyspnea, fever, and abdominal pain; upon discharge, patients will need to continue to monitor for these symptoms. Management requires explorative operation to determine site of the leak, removal of contamination, and use of drains to control the leak. An attempt to close the leak may also be performed.

Stenosis, or narrowing, can result in blockage of food from passing beyond this area. Patients may report the sensation of "stuck food" or vomiting. This can result in malnutrition and nutrient deficiencies. Some forms of stenosis can be treated with **endoscopic balloon dilation** if kinking is not present. If the stenosis is caused by a kink, further surgical intervention may be required.

As patients move through their recovery, their diet will be gradually progressed from a full-liquid diet to a soft diet. As patients make this progression, they will often experience abdominal pain and nausea/vomiting. This can be prevented (to some extent) by eating slowly, stopping when full, and not consuming liquids at the same time as eating solids. Antiemetics should also be utilized at this time to prevent nausea/vomiting. Due to reduced intake, patients will have lower glycemic load and are at risk of hypoglycemia. In patients with diabetes, they should be counseled on watching their blood sugar, as their medication dosage will likely need to be adjusted. In the post-operative period, nurses can expect to monitor blood sugar frequently and provide management with sliding scale insulin as needed. Most oral medications will be discontinued until the blood sugar stabilizes and the patient is eating more regularly.

Dumping syndrome occurs when contents of the stomach move too quickly from the stomach to the small intestine, which does not allow for proper digestion. The patient may experience rapid heart rate, abdominal pain, sweating, nausea, vomiting, diarrhea, and hypoglycemia within an hour of eating. The risk is higher when high levels of simple carbohydrates are ingested. Therefore, patients should avoid foods high in simple sugar and instead eat foods high in fiber and protein.

Hepatic Disorders

Hepatitis is an inflammatory condition of the liver, which is further categorized as infectious or noninfectious. Causative infectious agents for hepatitis may be viral, fungal, or bacterial, while noninfectious causes include autoimmune disease, prescription and recreational drugs, alcohol abuse, and metabolic disorders. More than 50 percent of the cases of acute hepatitis in the United States are caused by a virus. Transmission routes include fecal-oral, parenteral, sexual contact, and perinatal transmission. There are four phases of the course of viral hepatitis. During phase one, which is asymptomatic, the host is infected, and the virus replicates. The onset of mild symptoms occurs in phase two, while progressive symptoms of liver dysfunction appear in phase three. Finally, recovery from the infection occurs in phase four. These phases are specific to the causative agent and the individual.

The most common viral agents are hepatitis A (HAV), hepatitis B (HBV), and hepatitis C (HCV). Less commonly, hepatitis D (HDV), hepatitis E (HEV), CMV, Epstein-Barr virus, and adenovirus may cause hepatitis. HAV and HBV often present with nausea, jaundice, anorexia, right upper quadrant pain, fatigue, and malaise. HCV may be asymptomatic or, alternatively, may present with similar symptoms. Approximately 20 percent of acute infections with HBV and HCV result in chronic hepatitis, which is a risk factor for the development of cirrhosis and liver failure. The care of the patient with acute hepatitis due to HAV and HCV is focused on symptom relief, while the antiviral treatment for HBV is effective in decreasing the incidence of adenocarcinoma.

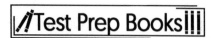

Chronic hepatitis is a complication of acute hepatitis and frequently progresses to hepatic failure, which is associated with deteriorating coagulation status and the onset of hepatic encephalopathy due to alterations in the blood-brain barrier that result in brain cell edema. Care of the patient with hepatic failure is focused on fluid volume and coagulation homeostasis and reduction of encephalopathy.

Acute hepatic failure is a condition in which the liver is no longer performing at its normal level of metabolic function, often caused by drug toxicity or viral infection. For instance, acetaminophen is known to cause liver damage and failure in toxic overdoses. The common viral culprit of liver failure is hepatitis B, with hepatitis C being less common.

A patient experiencing liver failure will exhibit signs of encephalopathy, including confusion, as well as jaundice and ascites. **Jaundice** is a yellowing of the skin, and **ascites** is a bloating of the abdomen resulting from an accumulation of free fluid. In severe cases, this fluid will be drained off the abdomen to relieve pressure.

Portal hypertension is a condition most often caused by cirrhosis or scarring of the liver in which the pressure of the portal vein is elevated. The portal vein drains blood from the organs of the upper GI tract, such as the spleen, intestines, and pancreas into the liver. When the liver cannot receive the normal amount of blood due to scarring or disease, the resistance to the incoming blood rises, resulting in the higher pressure. Complications of portal hypertension include ascites, splenomegaly, and acute variceal bleeding. Variceal bleeding has a high mortality rate as it is difficult to control.

Treatment of portal hypertension includes monitoring, banding via endoscopy, and pharmacologic therapy, such as beta-blockers.

Cirrhosis is a scarring of the liver tissue over time and is an associated condition of acute liver failure. Chronic alcoholism is a leading cause of cirrhosis. The scarring of the liver can be slowed with treatment and alcohol abuse cessation, but ultimately is irreversible.

Esophageal varices are dilated veins located in the esophagus and are a result of portal hypertension. These varices are highly vulnerable to massive bleeding, but are otherwise asymptomatic. Esophageal varices may be treated with banding procedures as well as intravenous administration of octreotide.

Fulminant hepatitis is a type of acute liver failure that occurs without the presence of pre-existing, chronic disease states. This type of liver failure is usually preceded by hepatic viruses, exposure to toxins, or drug injury. Fulminant hepatitis causes a large amount of necrosis or tissue death in the liver. As a result, liver transplantation may be needed in order for the patient to fully recover.

Biliary atresia is a condition of the bile duct in which it is blocked or possibly even absent. This condition occurs in newborns because of abnormal fetal development. Newborns with biliary atresia are jaundiced because of the bile-duct atresia. A procedure called the **Kasai procedure** is often used to repair biliary atresia. In this procedure, the small intestine is attached to the liver to create a new pathway for bile to drain. The intestine is then reattached to a lower portion of the small intestine to reconnect it with the GI tract. Many infants with biliary atresia will develop liver failure later in life and will likely need liver transplants.

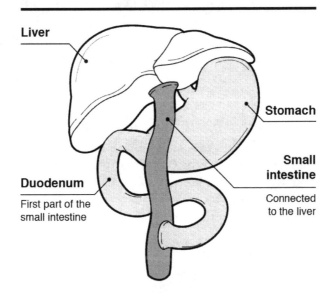

Illustration of the Kasai procedure performed for biliary atresia

Liver

Stomach

Small intestine
Connected to the liver

Duodenum
First part of the small intestine

Ischemic Bowel

Ischemic bowel disease is a potentially serious condition in which an artery that should be perfusing the intestines is narrowed or blocked, causing inadequate blood flow. A blockage in the arteries can be due to a blood clot or tumor, while narrowing is usually due to atherosclerosis. Inadequate blood flow to the intestines can also be due to an obstruction in the colon, hypotension, or certain medications, such as non-steroidal anti-inflammatories, diuretics, and some chemotherapy agents.

Symptoms of ischemic bowel disease include abdominal pain and cramping, diarrhea and a frequent urge to defecate, bloody stools, abdominal distension, and nausea and vomiting.

Malnutrition

Malnutrition is a disorder that includes overnutrition and undernutrition. **Overnutrition** is a form of malnutrition that is associated with obesity and metabolic syndrome, in which a person is consuming far more calories from food than needed for healthy body function. **Undernutrition** is a result of deficient consumption of necessary nutrients for the body's function. Nutrients can be lost as a result of diarrhea or vomiting, leading to an undernourished state. **Anorexia**, a psychological condition in which a person refrains from eating in order to lose weight to achieve an unrealistic body image, is another form of undernutrition.

Progression of malnutrition may be slow or rapid, depending on the case. Anorexia is a slow decline in nourishment, while the body wasting, or **cachexia**, associated with cancers may result in rapid undernourishment.

Undernutrition often manifests as weakness, muscle wasting, weight loss, and irritability. The patient may become pale and fatigued.

Treatment of undernutrition includes diet control, correction of fluid and electrolyte irregularities, and correction of complications that may have developed.

Malabsorption is a disorder of the small intestine in which nutrients are not properly absorbed into the bloodstream, resulting in a malnourished state of the body. Chronic diarrhea is the most common manifestation of malabsorption. **Steatorrhea**, or fatty stools, is a common sign of malabsorption, reflecting the fat loss of the body. Treatment of malabsorption will be aimed at correcting the cause. Common causes of malabsorption include bacterial overgrowth syndrome, celiac disease, Whipple disease, and short-bowel syndrome.

Methods of Nutrition Supplementation

Enteral nutrition is provided through the GI tract and therefore does not require ingestion by the patient. This is often used in situations in which the GI tract is functional, but the patient cannot maintain adequate nutrition on their own. This includes patients who are comatose or have one of the following conditions: a neuromuscular disorder affecting swallowing (e.g., Parkinson's, multiple sclerosis, or cerebrovascular accident); severe anorexia; upper GI obstruction; dementia; or increased metabolic demands (e.g., sepsis, cystic fibrosis, or burns). Enteral feedings should be avoided in patients with bowel ischemia, small or large bowel obstruction, active GI bleeding, malabsorption, or paralytic ileus.

Complications can occur from the placement of the tube or infection risk. Mechanical issues can occur if the tube is misplaced, obstructed, dislodged, broken, leaking, or eroding the tissue. When a tube is inserted nasally at the bedside, there is risk of the tube being placed into the trachea, bronchi, or lungs. If the tube feeding is inadvertently administered while placed in the respiratory system, it can lead to pneumonia, abscess, or pneumothorax. As a result, all bedside placements should be confirmed with imaging prior to use.

Infection can occur due to contamination of the tube feeding insertion site or through aspiration of the feedings. Other complications include nausea, vomiting, diarrhea, constipation, cramps, and bloating. Nausea and vomiting are common after the initiation of tube feeding, while diarrhea is the most common complication of tube feeding, which is often due to concomitant use of antibiotics, antacids, and magnesium.

Tube feedings may also contain sorbitol, which can trigger diarrhea. While diarrhea is common for many patients, those on chronic tube feeds may also experience constipation. Patients who are receiving tube feedings due to anorexia nervosa, alcoholism, or malabsorption syndromes are prone to **refeeding syndrome**. This occurs when rapid reversal of malnutrition causes fluid and electrolyte shifts within the cell, leading to hypophosphatemia and damage to the muscles, and ultimately resulting in cardiac failure, arrhythmia, seizure, and death.

Parenteral nutrition is administered intravenously and is utilized when a patient is unable to receive adequate nutrition due to an impairment in the GI tract that does not allow for enteral nutrition. This can be due to chronic obstruction, complete bowel rest, post-operative bowel leak, or severe diarrhea or vomiting.

Parenteral nutrition should be administered through a central line, thus creating a risk for infection, thrombus, or vascular injury. As with enteral feedings, the introduction of nutrients can result in refeeding syndrome in patients who have been in a prolonged state of starvation. Other metabolic impacts include hyperglycemia and, when discontinued suddenly, hypoglycemia, electrolyte abnormalities, Wernicke's encephalopathy, and cholestasis.

Pancreatitis

Pancreatitis has a rapid onset and progression to a critical illness, which is manifested by characteristic abdominal pain, nausea, vomiting, and diarrhea. In addition, fever, tachycardia, hypotension, and abdominal distention and rebound tenderness may be present. The exocrine function of the pancreas is the production and secretion of digestive enzymes. Pancreatitis exists when one of the causative agents inhibits the homeostatic suppression of the enzyme secretion, resulting in excessive amounts of the enzymes in the pancreas. This excess of enzymes precipitates the inflammatory response, which results in increased pancreatic vascular permeability, leading to edema, hemorrhage, and eventual necrosis of the pancreas. The inflammatory mediators can result in systemic complications that may include sepsis, respiratory distress syndrome, renal failure, and GI hemorrhage. Chronic alcoholism and biliary tract obstruction are the most common causes of pancreatitis; however, as many as 35 percent of the cases of pancreatitis are idiopathic. Pancreatitis can also occur after endoscopic retrograde cholangiopancreatography (ERCP) due to defects in the sphincter of Oddi. Aggressive pre-procedure hydration and rectal indomethacin post-procedure are employed to prevent this complication. Less common causes include some antibiotics and chemotherapy agents.

Diagnosis is based on the patient's presenting history and routine lab studies that include amylase P, lipase, metabolic panel, liver panel, C-reactive protein, CBC, and arterial blood gases (ABGs). Imaging studies may be used if the diagnosis is unclear to rule out gallbladder disease. Nonsurgical treatment includes bowel rest with nasogastric decompression, analgesics, and IV fluid administration. Surgical procedures may be open or minimally invasive and are aimed at removing diseased tissue to limit the progression to systemic complications, to repair the pancreatic duct, or to repair defects in the biliary tree. The initial care of pancreatitis focuses on prompt diagnosis, aggressive fluid management, and treatment of the cause because the disease is associated with the rapid onset of systemic complications.

Renal

Acute Kidney Injury (AKI)

Acute kidney injury is a sudden decrease in performance by the kidneys, which leads to build-up of wastes in the body. The kidneys are a pair of organs located in the posterior portion of the abdomen. They filter the blood for waste that later leaves the body in urine. The kidneys are also influenced by **antidiuretic hormone**, which signals when the kidneys should retain water. Consequently, the kidneys play an important role in electrolyte balance and hydration.

Kidney (or renal) failure is usually a gradual process; often, it is the last stage of chronic, progressive renal disease. However, renal failure can also be sudden. This is referred to as acute kidney injury and usually results from sudden trauma to the kidneys. Acute kidney injury is often caused by drug overdose, lengthy surgeries, heart attack, or crush syndrome. Additional causes include conditions such as hypovolemia, hypotension, renal vasoconstriction, renal or ureteral calculi, manual obstruction of the ureter, or urethral obstructions.

In many cases, medications are the primary cause and include agents such as NSAIDs, iodinated contrast, ACE inhibitors, and antibiotics such as vancomycin. The primary intervention to prevent and treat the progression of AKI is to provide the patient with a fluid bolus and maintain adequate hydration, which enhances blood flow through the kidney to reduce drug concentration. If the AKI is related to a

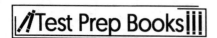
medication toxicity, the suspected medication should be stopped. Many medications require adjusted doses in patients with impaired renal function to prevent drug accumulation and reduce risk of toxicities. As many older adults are on multiple medications, the pharmacy team should be consulted to check for nephrotoxic combinations of drugs on patient's medication list. When possible, the use of non-nephrotoxic drugs should be used. Blood pressure should be closely followed and managed to promote adequate perfusion of the kidneys. Patients who are septic will likely be hypotensive, which reduces the blood flow through the kidneys; likewise, hypertension results in narrowed vessels of the kidneys and also restricts functioning.

Renal failure results in the body's inability to filter waste and balance fluids and electrolytes. Symptoms include nausea, swelling of the extremities and abdomen, cramping, decreased urine output, blood or excess protein in the urine, excess waste products in the blood, acidic blood pH levels, and elevated or low electrolyte levels. Testing includes checking blood creatinine and urea levels and may also include comprehensive metabolic panels.

Renal failure that results from chronic kidney disease is not curable but managed based on the progression of disease. Stage 1 kidney disease shows few symptoms, while stage 5 kidney disease requires dialysis and may result in the need for a kidney transplant. During the progression of these five stages, lifestyle changes are usually incorporated alongside medical interventions to manage symptoms and hinder disease progression. These changes usually include dietary modifications, such as decreasing red meat and sugar intake, along with smoking cessation and increasing exercise frequency and duration. These changes decrease the strain on the body's cardiovascular system, and therefore ease the process of blood filtration for the kidneys.

Chronic Kidney Disease (CKD)

While acute injury and failure of the kidney can often be corrected, **chronic kidney disease** is a slow, progressive, and irreversible decline in function of the kidney. The most common causes of CKD are diabetes, hypertension, and diseases of the glomerulus. **Metabolic syndrome**, in which the patient has both diabetes and hypertension, is a major factor in CKD development.

Over time, these causative factors slowly destroy vital cells in the renal tissue. Renal function first becomes insufficient and then fails altogether, which is called end-stage renal disease (ESRD).

As the kidney fails, waste products build up in the body. Creatinine and urea are markers for kidney decline, though they are not the only waste products that cause the symptoms of **uremia**, or "urine in the blood." Sodium, water, potassium, and other fluid and electrolyte imbalances will occur as a result of CKD.

The kidney is responsible for releasing **erythropoietin**, a hormone that stimulates the production of red blood cells. When kidneys fail, as is the case in CKD, erythropoietin release is decreased as well, resulting in decreased erythropoiesis, or RBC production. Thus, anemia results. Patients with CKD often must be treated for anemia along with many other conditions.

A patient with CKD will present with weight loss, anorexia, nausea, vomiting, and stomatitis. They may have a yellow-brown tint to their skin, as well as itchiness and crystallization of their sweat called uremic frost.

Treating a patient with CKD is a complicated matter, as so many other systems are involved as a result of the kidneys failing. Management of diabetes and hypertension is crucial, as these are often the

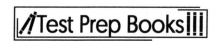

underlying causes. Heart failure and anemia must be addressed. Patients should quit smoking; keep cholesterol levels, glucose levels, and blood pressure within normal limits; and eat a reduced-salt diet to protect the kidneys. Patients with CKD should have a pharmacist carefully consider all medications to look for drugs that are **nephrotoxic**, such as many antibiotics (vancomycin) and analgesics (NSAIDs). A CT scan with contrast is a common procedure that can be nephrotoxic, so it is important to evaluate renal labs prior to the procedure. Dialysis will likely be an option in the future of the CKD patient to replace the function of the kidney.

Electrolyte Imbalance

Electrolytes are minerals that, when dissolved, break down into ions. They can be acids, bases, or salts. In the body, different electrolytes are responsible for specific cellular functions. These functions make up larger, critical system-wide processes, such as hydration, homeostasis, pH balance, and muscle contraction. Electrolytes typically enter the body through food and drink consumption, but in severe cases of imbalance, they may be medically-administered. They are found in the fluids of the body, such as blood.

Key electrolytes found in the body include the following:

Sodium and Chloride

Sodium (Na^+) is mainly responsible for managing hydration, blood pressure, and blood volume in the body. It is found in blood, plasma, and lymph. It is important to note that sodium is primarily found outside of cells and is accessed by a number of different systems and organs to tightly regulate water and blood levels. For example, in cases of severe dehydration, the circulatory and endocrine systems will transmit signals to the kidneys to retain sodium and, consequently, water.

Sodium also affects muscle and nerve function. It is a positively-charged ion and contributes to **membrane potential**—an electrochemical balance between sodium and potassium (another electrolyte) that is responsible for up to 40 percent of resting energy expenditure in a healthy adult. This balance strongly influences the functioning of nerve impulses and the ability of muscles to contract. Healthy heart functioning and contraction is dependent on membrane potential.

Sodium is available in large quantities in the standard diets of developed countries, especially in processed foods, as it is found in table salt. Consequently, sodium deficiencies (**hyponatremia**) are possible, but rare, in the average person. Hyponatremia can result from endocrine or nervous system disorders where sodium regulation is affected. It can also result from excessive sweating, vomiting, or diarrhea, such as in endurance sporting events, improper use of diuretics, or gastrointestinal illness. Hyponatremia may be treated with an IV **hypertonic solution**.

Hypertonic solutions are fluids that have a higher concentrate of solutes than surrounding fluids. To achieve equilibrium of solute concentration, fluid moves from the cell into the vascular space due to the principles of diffusion. This leads to shrinking of the cell and can impact function on a cellular level. Hypertonic solutions are often used to address hyponatremia, so nurses caring for patients on a hypertonic solution should monitor sodium levels to prevent hypernatremia. Due to the influx of fluid into the intravascular space, patients receiving hypertonic solutions are at a high risk of hypervolemia. To reduce the risk, the fluids should be infused at a low rate and nurses should monitor the patient for swelling, shortness of breath, high blood pressure, headache, or muscle cramps. Patients who are dehydrated should not be given hypertonic solutions, as they can worsen symptoms of kidney and heart disease. Hypertonic solutions should be avoided in patients with a history of these conditions.

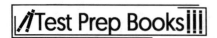

Too much sodium (**hypernatremia**) is usually a result of dehydration. Hypernatremia may be treated by introducing water quantities appropriate for normalizing the sodium level that is present in the patient's blood and urine.

Chloride (Cl^-) is a negatively-charged ion found outside of the cells that works closely with sodium. It shares many of the same physiologic responsibilities as sodium. Any imbalances (**hypochloremia** and **hyperchloremia**) are rare but may affect overall pH levels of the body. Chloride imbalances usually occur in response to an imbalance in other electrolytes, so treating a chloride imbalance directly is uncommon.

Potassium

Potassium (K^+) is mainly responsible for regulating muscular function and is especially important in cardiac and digestive functions. In women, it is believed to promote bone density. Potassium works in tandem with sodium to create membrane potential, as potassium is a positively-charged ion and is usually found inside cells.

As a result, it plays a role in maintaining homeostasis between the intracellular and extracellular environments.

1.

The sodium-potassium pump binds three sodium ions and a molecule of ATP.

2.

The splitting of ATP provides energy to change the shape of the channel. The sodium ions are driven through the channel.

3.

The sodium ions are released to the outside of the membrane, and the new shape of the channel allows two potassium ions to bind.

4.

Release of the phosphate allows the channel to revert to its original form, releasing the potassium ions on the inside of the membrane.

Potassium is found in all animal protein and animal dairy products and in most fruits and vegetables. Low potassium levels (**hypokalemia**) may be caused by dehydration due to excessive vomiting, urination, or diarrhea. In severe or acute cases, hypokalemia may be a result of renal dysfunction and may cause lethargy, muscle cramps, or heart dysrhythmia. It may be treated by stopping the cause of potassium loss (e.g., diuretics), followed by oral or IV potassium replenishment.

High potassium levels (**hyperkalemia**) can quickly become fatal. Hyperkalemia is often the result of a serious condition, such as sudden kidney or adrenal failure, and may cause nausea, vomiting, chest pain, and muscle dysfunction. It is treated based on its severity, with treatment options ranging from diuretic use to IV insulin or glucose. IV calcium may be administered if potentially dangerous heart arrhythmias are present.

157

Calcium and Phosphorus

Calcium (Ca^{2+}) is plentiful in the body, with most calcium stored throughout the skeletal system. However, if there is not enough calcium in the blood (usually available through proper diet), the body will take calcium from the bones. This can become detrimental over time. If enough calcium becomes present in the blood, the body will return extra calcium stores to the bones. Besides contributing to the skeletal structure, this electrolyte is important in nerve signaling, muscle function, and blood coagulation. It is found in dairy products, leafy greens, and fatty fishes. Many other consumables, such as fruit juices and cereals, are often fortified with calcium.

Low calcium levels (**hypocalcemia**) can be caused by poor diet, thyroid or kidney disorders, and some medications. Symptoms can include lethargy, poor memory, inability to concentrate, muscle cramps, and general stiffness and achiness in the body. Supplementation can rapidly restore blood calcium levels. In cases where symptoms are present, IV calcium administration in conjunction with an oral or IV vitamin D supplement may be utilized.

High calcium levels (**hypercalcemia**) are usually caused by thyroid dysfunction but can also be the result of diet, limited mobility (such as in paralyzed individuals), some cancers, or the use of some diuretics. Symptoms can include thirst, excess urination, gastrointestinal issues, and unexplained pain in the abdominal area or bones. Severe or untreated hypercalcemia can result in kidney stones, kidney failure, confusion, depression, lethargy, irregular heartbeat, or bone problems.

There is an intricate balance between calcium levels and the levels of phosphorus, another electrolyte. Phosphorus, like calcium, is stored in the bones and found in many of the same foods as calcium. These electrolytes work together to maintain bone integrity. When too much calcium exists in the blood, the bones release more phosphorus to balance the two levels. When there is too much phosphorus in the blood, the bones release calcium. Therefore, the presence or absence of one directly impacts the presence or absence of the other. Indicators of hypocalcemia and hypercalcemia usually also indicate low levels of phosphorus (**hypophosphatemia**) and high levels of phosphorus (**hyperphosphatemia**), respectively.

Magnesium

Magnesium (Mg^{2+}) is another electrolyte that is usually plentiful in the body. It is responsible for an array of life-sustaining functions, including hundreds of biochemical reactions such as oxidative phosphorylation and glycolysis. It is also an important factor in DNA and RNA synthesis, bone development, nerve signaling, and muscle function. Magnesium is stored inside cells or within the structure of the bones. It can be consumed through leafy greens, nuts, seeds, beans, unrefined grains, and most foods that contain fiber. Some water sources may also contain high levels of magnesium.

Low levels of magnesium (**hypomagnesemia**) are primarily the result of chronic alcohol or drug abuse, some prescription medications, or gastrointestinal diseases (e.g., celiac or Crohn's disease). Symptoms of hypomagnesemia include nausea, vomiting, depression, personality and mood disorders, and muscle dysfunction. Chronically depleted patients may have an increased risk of cardiovascular and metabolic disorders.

High levels of magnesium (**hypermagnesemia**) are rare and usually result in conjunction with kidney disorders when medications are used improperly. Symptoms include low blood pressure that may result in heart failure. Hypermagnesemia is usually treated by removing any magnesium sources (such as salts or laxatives) and may also require the IV administration of calcium gluconate.

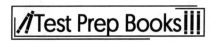

Magnesium imbalance can lead to calcium or potassium imbalance over time, as these electrolytes work together to achieve homeostasis in the body.

Hydration is critical to fluid presence in the body, as water is a critical component of blood, plasma, and lymph. When fluid levels are too high or too low, electrolytes cannot move freely or carry out their intended functions. Therefore, treating an electrolyte imbalance almost always involves managing a fluid imbalance as well. Typically, as fluid levels rise, electrolyte levels decrease. As fluid levels decrease, electrolyte levels rise. Common tests to determine electrolyte fluid imbalances include basic and comprehensive metabolic panels, which test levels of sodium, potassium, chloride, and any other electrolyte in question.

End-Stage Renal Disease (ESRD)

Chronic renal failure is defined by specific parameters for glomerular filtration rate, serum creatinine, and other clinical markers of kidney function; however, there is no generally accepted definition for the point at which chronic renal failure becomes **end-stage renal failure**. The initiation of dialysis, or a **glomerular filtration rate** (GFR) less than 15 mL per minute per $1.73m^2$, are cited as plausible definitions of ESRD; however, survival rates confirm that patients often survive months or years beyond the onset of these alterations.

The most common causes of the original damage to the kidneys include hypertension, diabetes, nephrotoxic medications, radiocontrast dyes, severe dehydration and shock, altered calcium and phosphate metabolism, genetics, and smoking (as shown in the figure below).

When **nephrons** are injured, the remaining nephrons are capable of increasing the filtration rate to maintain normal kidney function until fewer than 50 percent of functional nephrons remain. However, this adaptive response of hyperfiltration also damages the functioning nephrons due to the effects of capillary hypertension and hypertrophy of the nephrons, resulting in glomerular sclerosis. Indications for renal replacement therapies (e.g., peritoneal dialysis, hemodialysis, and renal transplantation) include hyperkalemia, metabolic acidosis, encephalopathy, peripheral neuropathy, and severe fluid overload. Asymptomatic patients with a GFR of 5 to 9 mL per minute per $1.73m^2$ will also require acute intervention. Prevention of the original injury is the focus of patient education.

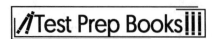
Dialysis

Dialysis is used to maintain homeostasis in patients whose kidneys are not functioning properly by removing waste product and extra fluid from the blood. For patients with acute kidney injury, dialysis is a temporary intervention to support bodily function while allowing the kidneys time to recover. For many patients, it is a chronic need and can only be resolved through a kidney transplant. If they are not transplant candidates, patients will remain on dialysis for life. The end goal of dialysis is to increase the time of progression to end-stage renal disease, which has increased in incidence over the past several years due to rising rates of diabetes mellitus and hypertension.

Dialysis uses a solution called dialysate, which consists of highly purified water mixed with bicarbonate, potassium, sodium, magnesium, calcium, chloride, and dextrose. The dialysate mixture has a lower molecular weight than the waste that is present in the blood. A semipermeable membrane separates the blood from the dialysate and, due to the concentration gradient, the concentration of permeable waste products will equalize between the two sides of the membrane. During dialysis, equalization is prevented through continuously refilling dialysate solution and replacing dialyzed blood with undialyzed blood.

Two types of dialysis include hemodialysis and peritoneal dialysis. The type of dialysis used is typically decided through a shared decision model between the patient and provider by considering convenience, comfort, and proximity to the clinic. The decision to start or maintain dialysis is not decided by one factor, such as a specific lab value, but rather by considering the patient's health status. This includes assessment of signs and symptoms of renal failure, volume dysregulation, blood pressure dysregulation, and deterioration in nutrition.

Hemodialysis removes waste and fluid from the blood via a dialysis machine and filter for patients with renal failure. The clean blood is then infused back into the body. This process typically occurs several times per week and lasts about four hours. Potassium, calcium, and sodium are regulated through hemodialysis to promote homeostasis, and sedating medication is held prior to avoid complications with reduced blood pressure. To gain venous access, the patient undergoes a minor surgical procedure to establish a catheter, graft, or fistula. The nurse should maintain patency of the site and monitor for complications related to occlusion, infection, or cannula separation. Documentation should include the status and location of the shunt, graft, or fistula, along with vital signs and pulses distal to the site. Nursing care involves maintaining comfort and assessing color, temperature, and pain level of the affected extremity (site). Dressing changes should be performed and documented as well. Cannula separation can lead to hemorrhage; therefore, if this occurs, the nurse must clamp off the shunt until a new cannula is inserted. Patient education involves care of the access site and dressing management.

Peritoneal dialysis utilizes the peritoneum of the abdomen to act as a filter for the blood. A catheter is used to administer dialysis fluid into the abdomen. The fluid absorbs waste product and extra water from the patient, who then drains the fluid after four to six hours. Patients undergoing peritoneal dialysis typically do so at home, with exchanges occurring four to six times per day. Nurses will have an important role in providing education to set the patient up for success at home. Patients should be instructed to keep the access site clean and dry, wash their hands prior to handling the catheter, and to monitor for signs of infection, such as drainage, redness, swelling, or pain. When not in use, the catheter should be taped to the body and kept away from sharp objects to prevent accidental pulling, cutting, or piercing of the tubing. Patients should be instructed to call their care team promptly if they develop fever, chills, abdominal pain, or any changes to the catheter or access site. Nursing assessments should be completed to monitor for changes in the patient's condition or response to dialysis that need to be

160

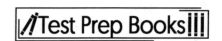

escalated to the provider. The nurse should also reinforce dietary recommendations and arrange for referrals to supportive care services as needed.

Prior to undergoing dialysis, patients should be carefully assessed to determine appropriateness of the procedure. The patient's weight should be obtained to determine the amount of fluid to be removed. Vital signs should be monitored to prevent blood pressure instability and screen for infections. Labs should be reviewed, paying close attention to the potassium level to determine the amount to be included in the dialysate. Medications that pass through the dialysis membrane should be held prior to dialysis along with antihypertensives, especially if the systolic blood pressure is less than 100 mmHg. The nurse should assess the vascular access (e.g., fistula or graft) to ensure there are no signs or symptoms of infection, listen for bruit, and palpate for thrill (vibration).

After dialysis, a weight should be obtained and compared to the pre-dialysis weight, with the goal being a change equal to the amount of fluid removed. The nurse should reassess vital signs, watch for bleeding at the vascular access site, and document any changes or abnormal findings. If any medications were held prior, they should be administered afterwards. Hemodialysis can result in removal of drugs that are small enough to move through the semipermeable membrane. The specific amount of drug removed is dependent on factors such as the patient's condition, length of dialysis, type of dialysate used, rate of flow or dwell time, the purpose of the dialysis, and the drug properties. Drugs that will be cleared by dialysis pose a challenge, as they may be rapidly cleared on an intermittent schedule. If medications are given once daily, it is best practice to administer the medications after dialysis, especially in the case of antibiotics. Medications dosed more than once daily typically see timing unchanged to increase adherence to therapy. Consultation of a reference guide is often necessary to correctly dose drugs that may be impacted by poor renal function or dialysis. Peritoneal dialysis, on the other hand, clears small molecules slowly and does not typically require changes to dose timing.

Dialysis is not without side effects. In peritoneal dialysis, the primary complication is infection of the peritoneal cavity. The incidence can be reduced with education on the importance of aseptic technique to the patient and caregiver. With hemodialysis, the main complications are intradialytic hypotension and muscle cramps. Both can be managed with a bolus of normal saline. Nurses should also watch for signs and symptoms of emergent conditions, such as dialysis disequilibrium syndrome, dialyzer reactions, hemolysis, air embolism, and electrolyte imbalances. **Dialysis disequilibrium syndrome** occurs when rapid changes in waste products (normally found in the blood) cause water movement into the CNS and increased intracranial pressure. This complication is most common during or soon after the first treatment. Patients may exhibit neurological changes, such as headache, restlessness, changes in mental status, and muscle twitching. **Dialyzer reaction** is an anaphylactic reaction characterized by dyspnea, chest tightness, itching, increased temperature, abdominal cramping, and diarrhea. Symptoms typically appear within the first 30 minutes of dialysis and management includes antihistamines, steroids, and epinephrine. **Hemolysis** is the destruction of red blood cells, often indicated by changes to the coloring of the blood in the venous line (e.g., becoming pale red and less opaque). Blood work will be ordered and will show a decrease in the hematocrit levels. Additional risks to be aware of include cardiac arrest, which is twice as likely in patients undergoing hemodialysis than peritoneal dialysis and usually occurs during the first two months after initiation.

Patients receiving dialysis should be managed by an interdisciplinary team consisting of a nephrologist, advanced provider (nurse practitioner or physician's assistant), nurse, social work, dietician, and patient care technician. A nephrology nurse will oversee the dialysis process, from assessment to administering medications and treatment, as well as provide education for patients who receive dialysis at home.

Nurses will often need to reinforce the information provided by the other specialties, such as dietary recommendations made by the dietician. Social workers can provide access to resources and help with patient and caregiver coping mechanisms.

Practice Quiz

1. Which of the following statements correctly identifies the relationship between hypokalemia and the development and duration of an ileus?
   a. K level of 6.0 mEq/L causes metabolic alkalosis, which affects the bowel wall motility.
   b. K level of 2.6 mEq/L causes muscle weakness that can progress to paralysis of the intestinal musculature.
   c. K level of 4.5 mEq/L decreases the capillary permeability of the bowel wall, which decreases the amount of gastric fluid in the bowel.
   d. K level of 3.7 mEq/L increases the incidence of vomiting, which further decreases the bowel contents.

2. The nurse is caring for a patient with diabetic nephropathy. Which of the following statements correctly identifies the relationship between diabetes and kidney injury?
   a. Chronically elevated glucose levels damage the renal basement membrane.
   b. Oral hypoglycemic agents are nephrotoxic in the elderly population.
   c. Insulin administration decreases the glomerular capillary permeability, resulting in fluid overload.
   d. Only type I diabetes is associated with renal injury.

3. What is the specific pathology responsible for brain damage in Alzheimer's disease?
   a. Invasion of the cortex by infectious prions
   b. Multiple hemorrhagic strokes
   c. Deposition of amyloid-β plaques
   d. Formation of Lewy bodies

4. Which of the following statements correctly identifies the difference between the forgetfulness that is common to the normal aging process and the memory alterations associated with Alzheimer's disease?
   a. The processes are the same; however, memory alterations associated with Alzheimer's disease include only short-term memory loss.
   b. Forgetfulness is progressive and eventually results in the individual's inability to perform ADLs independently.
   c. Memory lapses associated with Alzheimer's disease improve with frequent cueing.
   d. The end stage of memory impairment in Alzheimer's disease is the inability to recognize family members.

5. Which of the following complications of dialysis results in increased intracranial pressure and presents with neurological changes, headache, and muscle twitching?
   a. Dialyzer disequilibrium syndrome
   b. Dialyzer reaction
   c. Infection
   d. Hemolysis

See answers on the next page.

163

Answer Explanations

1. B: Serum potassium levels less than 3 mEq/L are associated with generalized muscle weakness, which includes the intestinal musculature. If hypokalemia is present in post-operative patients, the potential for the development of an ileus increases, and the duration of an existing ileus also increases. A potassium level of 6.0 mEq/L (Choice *A*) is associated with metabolic acidosis, rather than alkalosis, and there is no relationship between this potassium level and the motility of the bowel wall. The remaining potassium levels (Choices *C* and *D*) are normal and not associated with any alteration of the intestine.

2. A: Diabetic nephropathy is associated with alterations in the basement membrane that result in thickening and decreased filtration efficiency. Diabetes is also commonly associated with systemic hypertension which further damages the glomeruli. Pre-diabetes conditions such as obesity and metabolic syndrome are also associated with structural changes in the glomeruli that may be evidenced by microalbuminuria. Insulin protects the capillary permeability by controlling the serum glucose concentration, making Choice *B* incorrect. Oral hypoglycemic agents are not nephrotoxic at therapeutic doses, making Choice *C* incorrect; however, the hypoglycemic effect of the medications is greatly increased in the presence of renal insufficiency. Either form of diabetes can affect kidney function because those effects are the result of an elevated serum glucose level, and both are commonly associated with systemic hypertension, making Choice *D* incorrect.

3. C: The destruction of brain tissue in Alzheimer's disease is the result of amyloid-β plaque formation in the cerebral cortex. Creutzfeldt-Jakob disease is a rare form of dementia that results from tissue damage caused by infectious prions; therefore, Choice *A* is incorrect. Multiple hemorrhagic strokes may be a trigger for the deposition of amyloid-β plaque formation; however, this form of damage can exist without causing Alzheimer's disease. It is not the specific causative process for the disease; therefore, Choice *B* is incorrect. The formation of Lewy bodies is responsible for the damage associated with Parkinson's disease, not Alzheimer's disease; therefore, Choice *D* is incorrect.

4. D: Early manifestations of memory impairment in Alzheimer's disease are associated with short-term memory loss and the inability to assimilate new knowledge, with progressive impairment that affects long-term memory, mood, and independent functioning. The end stage of this process is the inability to recognize family members. The processes are not the same. Memory lapses associated with Alzheimer's disease improve with cueing, and forgetfulness do not progress to the inability to recognize family members or perform ADLs independently. Therefore, Choices *A*, *B*, and *C* are incorrect.

5. A: Dialyzer equilibrium syndrome is an emergent complication of dialysis that occurs when rapid changes in waste products cause water movement into the CNS. This results in increased intracranial pressure and presents with neurological changes, headache, and muscle twitching. Dialyzer reaction, infection, and hemolysis (Choices *B*, *C*, and *D*), while complications of dialysis, are not represented by these symptoms.

Musculoskeletal/Multisystem/Psychosocial

Musculoskeletal

Functional Issues

Walking is a complex motor function that is often taken for granted. Those with an able body don't have to actively account for dexterity and fine motor control. Unfortunately, unassisted walking becomes much harder as a person grows older. Let's not forget individuals with physical and mental alignments that impair their ability to walk. Once one reaches 70 years of age, locomotion becomes more strenuous as muscles shrink and reactions slow.

With age, the body becomes more fragile, affecting walking ability and form. Elderly adults are often stereotyped with shorter gaits, hobbling from one point to another. This is due to the fact an elderly adult's calf muscles have become weaker. They must place more force into their hips and extensor muscles. They also develop a more pronounced pelvic and spinal tilt. Some factors include weakened abdominal muscles, abdominal fat, and tighter flexor muscles. Many subtle changes in the body force gradual changes in locomotion.

An individual may have trouble walking or consistently moving. They may struggle to shift their weight and can only stand in place. Many diseases and disorders can cause gait issues. A common disease that causes locomotion issues is **Parkinson's disease**. Individuals with Parkinson's often suffer from **festination**, meaning they have to take small, rapid steps to stay upright; otherwise, they may fall and injure themselves. They will often freeze in place out of caution or even fear. Parkinson's disease can even cause foot drop or dragging.

It's important to discuss any movement-related issues with elderly patients alongside their medical history. Primary care practitioners and physical therapists can conduct gait and mobility assessments if needed. MRI and CT scans help identify underlying neurological issues causing locomotion difficulties.

Prolonged bed rest and a sedentary lifestyle can result in physiological changes known as **deconditioning**, or a decline in an individual's physical and mental health. A loss in physical activity will cause muscle atrophy, which can inhibit essential motor functions. Individuals must receive frequent mental stimulation and communication to prevent a decline in mental health. Limited socialization can cause depression, anxiety, loneliness, and more. Clinical studies have shown that the bedbound patient suffers a 20 percent decrease in muscle strength per week and a 50 percent decrease in muscle strength after a month in bed. Within seven days, there is a 3 percent loss of thigh muscle mass, and the muscle fibers and connective tissues are maintained in a shortened position; furthermore, contractures begin within three weeks.

Elderly patients, those with cognitive dysfunction, and patients whose illnesses have left them debilitated and weak are at a considerable risk of falling. Falls are a leading cause of injury and accidental deaths in the elderly. Gait and balance disorders, functional impairments, visual defects, cognitive impairments, and use of psychotropic medications are the most important risk factors for falls. Primary prevention of falls includes high levels of physical activity, even in patients with disease. Secondary prevention includes improving gait along with resistance and balance training. The effects of an active lifestyle on mood and confidence are probably as important as their effect on physiology.

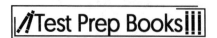

All acutely ill patients should be considered fall risks. Environmental factors such as the lighting of the room, objects on the floor, and proximity to the call light must all be factored in to help prevent a fall. Most hospitals have a fall risk policy and a method to identify the high-risk patients. Indicators such as yellow fall risk armbands, signs on doors, or yellow slippers can all alert the staff that the patient is a fall risk. The progressive care nurse should work closely with the family and caregivers so that patients at risk can have the monitoring they need to prevent a fall. Bed alarms and sitters may be indicated.

Compartment Syndrome

Compartment syndrome occurs when there is bleeding or swelling within a muscle that creates increased pressure. Because there is limited space for expansion due to the fascia (fibrous covering around the muscle), increased pressure can impair circulation to the tissue and result in tissue damage or necrosis. Compartment syndrome is typically associated with both open and closed fractures; however, it can occur with other conditions that cause swelling or constrict space in the muscle. This includes burns, infections, clots, and strains and bruises of the soft tissue. Compartment syndrome is considered an emergency and should be identified and treated as quickly as possible, ideally in less than six hours.

Patients will complain of a tense or rigid feeling of the extremity and extreme pain, often out of proportion with the injury. The patient may report alterations in sensation (e.g., numbness, tingling, or paresthesia), and there may be some impairment to function. Upon examination, the limb will be pale, and a pulse may not be present. However, in some cases, there may be a pulse even in severely compromised extremities.

An ultrasound may be used to determine if a thrombus or occlusion is responsible for the symptoms. If compartment syndrome is suspected, it should be treated as an emergency, and significant time should not be spent confirming diagnosis. A surgical consult should be obtained, any casts or restrictive dressings should be removed, and the limb should be kept at the level of the heart to optimize perfusion. Supplemental oxygen may be applied to increase availability to the extremity. The patient will then undergo a **fasciotomy** to relieve the pressure and prevent further damage. However, if the injury is over 36 hours old, a fasciotomy may not be beneficial. In this scenario, infection is likely, and patients may require amputation or debridement to prevent systemic spread of the infection.

Multisystem

End-of-Life

Patients should be encouraged to discuss end-of-life wishes with their family members early on in the process when possible. The decision-making process can be complex, intense, and stressful for those left to make the decision for the patient. Having a plan in place that makes the patient's wishes clear can reduce the level of stress for both the family and the patient.

It is helpful for the patient to establish a plan that outlines specifically what their wishes are as it relates to end-of-life care. A **healthcare proxy** can assist with ensuring such wishes are honored. Core topics and/or decisions a healthcare proxy can assist with include the location of healthcare (e.g., at home or in a facility) and resuscitation expectations.

Nurses may need to provide some guidance in pointing their patients in the right direction to complete an advanced directive and/or living will. Advanced directives and living wills are two additional resources that should be kept on file to assist with the documentation and communication of a patient's wishes.

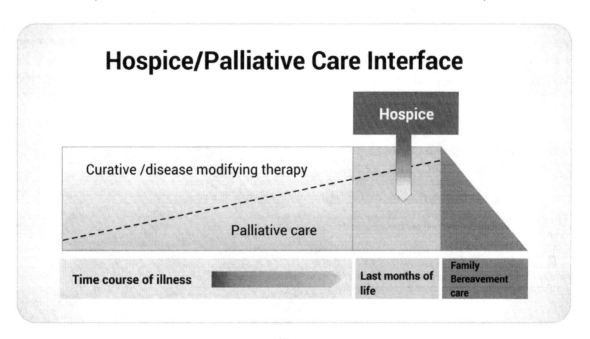

End-of-life issues can be complicated from both a logistical and an emotional perspective. For many patients, end-of-life issues may not have been discussed or resolved with family members. A nurse or other healthcare professional may have to step into the role of facilitating this sensitive subject. Even when the situation has been planned for, it can come unexpectedly for both the patient and family members. Most end-of-life situations will require managing the physical and emotional pain of the patient and family members, helping the patient transition in a dignified manner, and dealing with legal paperwork. Many healthcare providers report not feeling emotionally equipped to handle these aspects, do not feel they have time on the job to adequately do so, or feel there is no financial compensation to provide these services. Being aware that job duties may require these uncomfortable tasks can be the first step in being able to provide some level of effective end-of-life support for the patient and family. Understanding common end-of-life issues can also help.

Organ and tissue donation refers to the process of removing healthy, functional organs and tissues from the patient's body after death and transplanting them to another patient in need. This may be a topic that the patient has already considered; for example, many people make this decision when applying for a driver's license and have it notated on their card. Common organs that can be donated include the heart, lungs, liver, and kidneys. Common tissues that can be donated include heart, skin, components of the eyeball, and bone.

Advanced directives are legal documents that note how a patient would like to receive or guide medical treatments in the case of terminal diagnosis, cases where the patient is in a vegetative state, or in other end-of-life contexts. Having this document prepared in advance is extremely helpful for healthcare providers and the patient's family, as the patient's personal decisions are known and can be accounted for. However, many people do not take the time to develop these. Advance directives may only be utilized when a physician has declared the patient to be in an end-of-life state. Other rules may vary by state, so it is useful to be informed of the specific guidelines set forth by the state in which providers are practicing. In emergency cases, support staff do not usually have the legal right to follow instructions written in an advanced directive until a physician confirms that the patient will not recover. Therefore, support staff must continue to provide comprehensive, life-sustaining care unless otherwise instructed (i.e. a DNR order must be written by the physician).

More healthcare organizations are beginning to allow family members to be present during end-of-life procedures, including intense procedures that can be harrowing to watch. New research shows this can be beneficial for family members as they cope in the long term. While remaining present with the patient is often the wish of family members, they may be unaware of the emotional upheaval they may feel when watching a loved one go through resuscitative procedures. Nursing staff should be equipped to be able to continue working in the presence of distraught family members and be able to provide compassionate and honest support if needed.

Withholding and withdrawing treatments are components of palliative care, most often seen in tragic, traumatic events or in hospice care. These procedures occur when a patient is believed to be terminal, and interventions that were previously being utilized to sustain the patient are gradually ceased to let the patient pass comfortably. Withholding and withdrawing treatments are often requested by patients who are aware of their situation and are ready to move on but may also be done at the request of family members or medical proxy if the patient is in a vegetative state.

Healthcare-Acquired Infections

Hospital-acquired and healthcare-associated infections may occur in patients receiving healthcare. Common **healthcare-acquired infections** include surgical site infections, pneumonias, catheter-associated infections, and central-line associated infections. Surgical site infections are infections that occur following surgery in the region of the procedure; they can vary from superficial infections that require minimal treatment to systemic infections that can be life-threatening. Healthcare-acquired pneumonias occur in patients in medical settings and is especially common in patients who require intubation. These patients are likely to have been infected with gram-negative bacilli, such as *Pseudomonas aeruginosa*, and antibiotic-resistant strains, such as *methicillin-resistant Staphylococcus aureus* (MRSA). Like the other pneumonias, diagnosis is based on clinical presentation and chest x-ray. Treatment is usually a regimen of broad-spectrum antibiotics. Prevention includes keeping the head of the bed greater than 30 degrees, assisting patients to keep good oral hygiene (suctioning subglottic secretions as needed), and general aspiration precautions.

Catheter-Associated Urinary Tract Infections

Catheter-associated urinary tract infections (CAUTIs) are the most common hospital-acquired infections. The duration of indwelling urinary catheter use is directly associated with the incidence of infection, especially in at-risk populations such as women, diabetics, and immobile patients. The most common causative agents are enteric pathogens; however, yeast infections are also common while the catheter is in place and after removal. The indwelling catheter is the source of the infection, and if left in place for two weeks, the biofilm formed on the surface of the catheter is totally "immune" to antibiotic therapy. Due to infection risk, current efforts focused on reducing the incidence of CAUTI even include limitations on short-term or intermittent use of catheters.

Complications of CAUTI include extended hospital stays, increased cost, and morbidity and mortality. The most effective method of prevention is through appropriate use of indwelling catheters and aseptic technique with placement. Patients with catheters should be evaluated daily to ensure they still require a catheter. If the nurse does not think a catheter is still required, they should discuss with the provider or follow the nurse-driven protocol, if applicable per organizational policies. Patients being considered for catheter placement should be carefully evaluated to determine if a catheter is truly needed. Catheters should be cleaned daily and secured to the patient to prevent irritation of the urethra. The drainage bag should be monitored for kinks, kept below the bladder, and off the floor in order to maintain drainage and prevent backflow into the bladder. Patients being treated for CAUTI should receive antibiotics and be monitored for worsening signs of infection, such as fever, chills, tachycardia, hypotension, and decreased urine output.

Central-Line Associated Bloodstream Infections

Central-line associated bloodstream infection (CLABSI) is a significant hospital-acquired infection with mortality rates varying from 10–15 percent. The most common organisms are *Staphylococcus aureus*, gram negative bacilli, and candida, which gain entry to the bloodstream because of manipulation of the intravenous catheter. To qualify as a CLABSI, the patient must have a positive blood culture and the presence of a central line within at least 48 hours of the culture. As one of the most frequent causes of healthcare-associated bloodstream infections, the rate of infection is associated with the duration of the therapy and the patient's baseline health status. As with the CAUTIs discussed previously, there are nationwide efforts to decrease the incidence of the CLABSIs with meticulous care because the use of central lines is an essential therapy. Aseptic technique upon insertion, prompt removal when medically appropriate, and routine hand hygiene when handling a central venous catheter (CVC) are all protocols for the prevention of a CLABSI.

The most important methods of prevention include meticulous hand hygiene, scrubbing access sites with antiseptic immediately prior to use, and maintaining sterility during dressing changes and line access. The site should be assessed at least once daily for redness, pain, swelling, or drainage to look for signs of infection, along with monitoring for changes in patients' vital signs.

If CLABSI is suspected, the nurse can expect orders for blood cultures from both the central line and a peripheral site. Broad-spectrum antibiotics will be ordered while the results of the cultures are obtained, and the nurse should administer these as scheduled. Depending on the type of line, the catheter may be removed once an infection is suspected or confirmed. If the line is not removed, the nurse should monitor the patient for persistent symptoms and positive blood cultures despite antibiotics. If present, this may prompt the provider to remove the line.

Surgical Site Infections

Surgical site infections occur in the area that a surgery was performed in the hours or days following its completion. They can occur superficially, only impacting the skin, or can affect deeper tissues, organs, or an implanted device.

The primary goal of care is to prevent SSI by ensuring best practices in the operation. This includes ensuring prophylactic antibiotics are administered prior to surgery as ordered, avoiding use of razors to remove hair, controlling blood glucose, using alcohol-based skin prep, and educating patients and caregivers on their role in preventing SSI. When possible, patients should be counseled on smoking cessation and blood sugar control prior to the surgery. In the perioperative period, the body temperature should be maintained at 35.5°C or higher since hypothermia can increase the risk for infection by causing vasoconstriction.

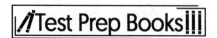

Timely identification of SSI is an important role of the nurse caring for a patient after surgery. The sterile dressing should remain on the incision for 24–48 hours after surgery. Once removed, the patient should be assessed frequently for fever, chills, redness at the incision, and any drainage (especially purulent) from the surgical site.

If an SSI is suspected, the patient will be started on antibiotics and timely administration of all doses should be prioritized. The nurse should monitor the patient for side effects, such as diarrhea and renal impairment, and follow vital signs and lab values closely for signs of sepsis. The patient and caregiver should be provided education on care of the incision, including hand hygiene, dressing change technique and frequency, and recognition of abnormal healing or infection.

Hospital-acquired pneumonia

Hospital-acquired pneumonia (HAP) occurs when there is a diagnosis of pneumonia more than 48 hours after admission to the hospital when the patient did not have symptoms upon admit. Patients on a ventilator are at high-risk of developing a subset of HAP known as ventilator-associated pneumonia (VAP). Nurses should assess and monitor all patients who are hospitalized for signs and symptoms of pneumonia. Patients will often develop fever, chills, pleuritic chest pain, dyspnea, tachycardia, changes in mental status, and consolidations or crackles upon lung auscultation. An elevated white blood cell count may be seen; however, this can also be normal in immunocompromised patients. Nurses may be asked to assist the patient in obtaining a sputum sample for analysis and culture if HAP is suspected.

Initial therapy for HAP involves treatment with a broad-spectrum antibiotic that is effective against the most common organisms, such as *Staphylococcus aureus* (a gram-positive bacteria) as well as *Pseudomonas aeruginosa* and other gram-negative bacteria. Gram-negative bacteria tend to be the most resistant to antibiotics, and patients infected with them are at a high risk of morbidity and mortality. If cultures were obtained, the antibiotic agent may change to target the causative organism. Antibiotics should be administered on time and as ordered to ensure consistent drug levels throughout the treatment course. Upon discharge, patients should be instructed to continue the full course of antibiotics, even if they are feeling better.

In addition to antibiotics, the nurse can expect orders for IV hydration, antipyretics, pain and cough management, strict I&Os, and supplemental oxygen as needed. Semi-fowlers position should be utilized to help the patient clear secretions. The nurse should encourage adequate nutrition, such as protein shakes and fluids, to meet increased metabolic demands. While rest is needed for recovery, the patient should be encouraged to ambulate as able and spend time out of bed as tolerated. The patient should continue to be monitored for fever, worsening of symptoms, changes in oxygen requirements, or mental status alterations once started on antibiotics.

Infectious Diseases
Influenza
Influenza is a type of virus that causes an upper respiratory infection. True influenza comes in three varieties: A, B, and C. Some infections are mistakenly called the "flu," but are not actually caused by the influenza virus, resulting in a bit of confusion. A nasal swab can differentiate between influenza and other upper respiratory infection-causing organisms.

Symptoms of the flu include cough, rhinitis, fever, headache, and a generalized malaise. **Rhinitis** (also known as coryza or "stuffy nose") is the term for inflammation and mucus production in the airways.

There is a time of year in which flu commonly occurs, called flu season. Flu season differs around the world, occurring in the coldest months of the year when the flu virus thrives.

The number of influenza infections in a geographic region sometimes escalates rapidly, turning into an **epidemic**. The term pandemic refers to when the infection rate of the flu affects populations worldwide, not contained to one region.

Everyone over six months of age should be vaccinated against the flu annually, at the beginning of their respective flu season. Vaccination greatly decreases the prevalence of infections. Patients at high risk of developing a severe case of influenza infection may be given antivirals; others at lower risk may be treated for symptoms alone, allowing the virus to run its course naturally.

Influenza, when it occurs at the epidemic or pandemic level, may even be severe enough to become life-threatening for young, healthy patients. For this reason, vaccination of the population is vital. Progressive care nurses may do their part in educating and encouraging the public to get their vaccination to prevent large-scale flu infections.

Multidrug-Resistant Organisms

Multidrug-resistant organisms (MDROs) are defined as bacteria that have become impervious to certain antibiotics, rendering the antibiotic incapable of killing the bacteria. MDROs commonly develop when antibiotics are self-administered longer than necessary or when they are not needed at all but still taken.

Staphylococcus aureus (*S. aureus*) is a bacterium that is generally located on the skin or in the nasal passages of healthy people. When present without symptoms, it is known as colonization, and when symptoms are present, it is an infection. **Methicillin-resistant Staphylococcus aureus** (MRSA) is a strain of *S. aureus* that is resistant to methicillin and most often occurs in individuals who have been hospitalized for an extended period or frequently visit a healthcare facility (hospital-acquired) for treatment of an illness (e.g., dialysis).

Infection can also ensue as community-associated MRSA, which occurs in healthy individuals who have not recently been hospitalized or treated for an illness in a facility. People at risk for this type of MRSA consist of athletes, prisoners, daycare attendees, military recruits, IV drug abusers, and those who live in crowded settings, have poor hygiene practices, and/or are immunocompromised. Community-associated MRSA is communicated through human-to-human contact, contact with MRSA-contaminated items, or infection of a preexisting abrasion or wound that has not been properly dressed. MRSA enters the bloodstream via this kind of abrasion and can result in sepsis, cellulitis, **endocarditis** (inflammation of the inner lining of the heart), osteomyelitis, septic arthritis, toxic shock syndrome, organ failure, and death. Prevention of infection focuses on strict handwashing, practicing good personal hygiene, avoiding sharing personal items (e.g., toothbrushes, mouth guards, clothing, bedclothes), and thoroughly cleansing an abrasion or wound.

The individual infected with MRSA will present with a fever and the appearance of an erythematous, edematous skin area, which is warm to the touch, painful, and draining pus. A more severe infection will manifest as the previously described rash, chest pain, cough, fatigue, chills, fever, malaise, headache, muscle aches, and shortness of breath.

Interventions to be implemented upon initiating care for the individual infected with MRSA consist of a detailed assessment of skin lesions; anticipation of drainage of an infected skin site and culturing of

171

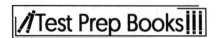

secretions; preparation of blood, sputum, and urine culture; administration of antibiotics; and in-depth education to the patient and caregivers with regard to causes and modes of transmission, signs and symptoms, and the importance of adherence to recommended treatment measures.

Vancomycin-resistant enterococci (VRE) are enterococci that have developed a resistance to many antibiotics, particularly vancomycin. Enterococci live in the intestines and on the skin and normally do not cause any issues until they become unaffected by certain antibiotic therapies. Common sites of infection include the intestines, the urinary tract, and wounds. VRE, like many other bacteria, can be spread by casual contact or contact with contaminated objects. Similar to MRSA, VRE are most oftem communicated from a healthcare worker to those who are hospitalized or in a nursing home. Additionally, those who are immunocompromised, have long-term illnesses, have had major surgery, or have been treated with multiple antibiotics have a greater chance of becoming infected. Understandably, VRE prevail most heavily in individuals who have used vancomycin often.

Signs and symptoms of a VRE infection depend largely on where the infection is located. If VRE is present in a wound, the affected area will be erythematous and painful to the touch. One who is suffering from a urinary tract infection caused by VRE will exhibit flank pain as well as burning and pain upon urination. Some people have general symptoms such as fever, diarrhea, and generalized weakness.

Diagnosis of VRE starts with a blood culture, wound culture, urine sample, or stool sample to determine the cause of the illness. Severe VRE infections are treated with caution, and the hospitalized individual is placed in contact isolation to prevent the spread of infection to others. VRE infections, by nature, are difficult to manage due to the antibiotic resistance of the strain. Antibiotic treatment may consist of oral and/or IV agents; furthermore, blood, urine, and stool samples will be sent to the lab for testing after initiation of antibiotic therapy to determine if VRE bacteria are still present in the body.

Extended-spectrum beta-lactamases (ESBLs), found predominantly in gram-negative bacteria, make these bacteria more resistant to many commonly used antibiotics. Patients are more at risk for ESBLs if they have catheters, have prolonged hospital stays, and have already received antibiotics during the hospital stay. ESBL infections are usually treated with a carbapenem, like meropenem.

Carbapenem-resistant enterobacteriaceae (CRE) are on the rise, especially in critical care areas. CREs are more common in patients with long hospitalizations, prior antibiotic use, and patients with multiple comorbidities. Strict contact precautions must be used to prevent the spread of these drug resistant organisms to another immunocompromised patient.

Pain

Pain has been called the fifth vital sign. This is because along with heart rate, blood pressure, temperature, and rate of breathing, pain as reported by the patient is an important clue as to how well the patient is doing.

Pain is almost completely subjective data. Pain is as the patient reports it and is very difficult to measure otherwise. Whereas the heart rate can easily and accurately be counted in beats per minute, assessing pain requires the nurse to use clinical judgement by applying a patient-by-patient assessment.

The most common measure of pain is the **Numerical Rating Pain Scale**, rated zero to ten, with zero being no pain at all and ten being the worst pain imaginable to the patient.

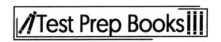

The progressive care nurse will assess pain by asking the patient what exacerbates the pain and what alleviates the pain. The nurse should ask about the location of the pain, the quality, and the onset. The nurse should ask about when exacerbations occur and what signs and symptoms accompany an exacerbation. Finally, the nurse should assess how the pain affects the patient's overall functioning ability, how intense it becomes, and its temporal characteristics.

Grimacing, sweating, clutching, and guarding are all examples of non-verbal signs that pain is being experienced. Additional pain scales for the progressive care nurse include the **Wong-Baker Faces Pain Scale**, FLACC Pain Scale, and COMFORT Pain Scale. These pain scales are used predominantly for pediatric patients or those who cannot adequately communicate their pain level.

Pain can also be acute or chronic. **Acute pain** is pain that is generally related to an injury and slowly gets better over time as the injury heals. Acute pain usually lasts for less than three months. **Chronic pain** continues for at least three months and is often caused by underlying disease. Patients who come to the hospital setting may be experiencing acute on top of chronic pain, and their pain may be more difficult to manage, as they may have developed a tolerance to pain medications.

Pain Management and Procedural Sedation

Pain is one of the most encountered symptoms in the progressive care setting, as many situations necessitating progressive care involve a high level of pain. However, since cases in healthcare settings often vary widely in scope and every patient will have a different personal threshold for pain tolerance, best practices are difficult to develop when it comes to pain management. It is often done on a case-by-case basis. However, when a patient's pain is not managed in a way that seems appropriate to that individual, it can cause patient and family dissatisfaction with the healthcare organization. As a result, medical staff must try to provide effective and safe pain management options that can make the patient comfortable at the present time, but that also do not cause harm over time. In some cases, like a sprained muscle, ice therapy and rest can provide adequate pain management. More serious cases, defined as pain that does not subside after an objectively reasonable period for the injury, may require topical, intramuscular, or oral pain medication. These can include stronger doses of common over-the-counter pain medications or prescription pain medications.

Prescription pain medications, especially opioids and muscle relaxers, are known for causing debilitating addiction; therefore, when prescribing them to a patient, the lowest dose and dosing frequency necessary should be utilized. Additionally, patients should be closely monitored for their reactions to their pain medications. Finally, some individuals who are addicted to prescription painkillers and muscle relaxers may feign injuries to receive another prescription. Therefore, all patients' medical histories should be thoroughly evaluated to note their history of pain medication usage. As a large majority of those addicted are still experiencing pain, the medical team must evaluate each situation, being a patient advocate for safe, effective pain management.

Procedural sedation and analgesia (PSA) allows patients to remain somewhat alert during medical procedures that may be uncomfortable but not unbearably painful, such as resetting bones. Unlike general anesthesia, where patients are completely sedated and do not feel any sensations, PSA allows patients to be somewhat conscious and aware of bodily functions. It can be utilized with or without pain-relieving medications. Practitioner awareness is crucial when administering procedural sedation, especially when pain relief is also utilized. Progressive care nurses who will assist with PSA must be well trained, ACLS certified, and know their related facility policies. Prior to a patient having procedural sedation, the nurse should confirm that the patient has informed consent on the chart and that pre-

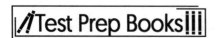

procedure vital signs and rhythm strips have been obtained. If procedural sedation is to be done at the bedside, the nurse should ensure that airway management devices are within reach and that the patient is being appropriately monitored with continuous oxygen saturation, heart rate and rhythm, respiratory rate, and end tidal carbon dioxide monitoring. During the procedure, frequent blood pressure readings should be obtained. Any abnormalities should be immediately reported to the practitioner. The nurse should make sure all ACLS medications as well as reversal medications, such as naloxone and flumazenil, are available if needed and that the patient has patent IV access. Most hospital policies require 1:1 nursing care for the patient during procedural sedation and for 30 minutes after, provided the patient has returned to pre-procedure baseline.

Palliative Care

Palliative care is comprehensive care provided for symptoms and illness exacerbated by a chronic condition, including cancer, liver failure, end-stage renal disease (ESRD), dementia, and chronic obstructive pulmonary disease (COPD). Palliative care is delivered by a multidisciplinary team of physicians, nurses, nutritionists, pharmacists, social workers, case managers, and several specialists in a collaborative manner.

The characteristics that distinguish palliative care from hospice care are the timing of services and the continuation of curative care in palliative care. Progressive care nurses may advocate for palliative care to be administered at any stage of an illness or at any age. Ideally, palliative care should be initiated upon diagnosis for conditions like cancer and continue for the duration of therapy, follow-up care, and end-of-life care, as indicated. **Hospice care** is typically administered as a component of end-of-life care to those who are suffering from terminal illness with less than six months to live.

Palliative care can improve one's quality of life, addressing physical, behavioral, spiritual, and practical needs. Palliative care delivers a variety of options to patients that go far beyond pain assessments and management.

Palliative care may be delivered in the patient's home if they are under the supervision of a physician, or it may be a component of hospice or provided in a facility. It is typically covered by health insurance and in some instances may be covered by Medicare and Medicaid, while hospice care is always a covered benefit for Original Medicare recipients. Those who do not qualify for palliative care by any of the identified entities may need further assistance from their progressive care nurse and/or social worker to identify potential resources that can provide the necessary support.

Pandemic Management

A **pandemic** refers to a widespread outbreak of disease across several countries or continents that is disruptive to society. The primary goals for hospital staff during a pandemic are containment and mitigation. While the purpose of containment is to reduce the spread of disease, mitigation aims to continue to provide healthcare services while managing the influx of patients experiencing the infection.

In the hospital, nurses should follow the appropriate guidelines for use of personal protective equipment (PPE) and isolation requirements of suspected and confirmed cases. Since the pandemic may result in disrupted supply chain, PPE requirements may change as time passes and more is learned about the disease. In the beginning stages of an outbreak, little is often understood about the pathogen and the highest level of precautions maybe used. This can include placing infected patients on airborne precautions and requiring the use of respirators. As time goes on and more is understood, the isolation level will likely be downgraded to be more appropriate for the specific transmission type.

One of the challenging aspects of a pandemic is caring for the influx of patients, along with patients who are already commonly cared for on a unit. Nurses can expect to see patients on services outside of their normal areas and procedures that they may not be as familiar with. To maximize space and free up hospital beds, patients may be discharged earlier and have their care managed outpatient or with home-care services. Nurses should ensure patients understand discharge instructions as well as concerning signs and symptoms that would need to be reevaluated. Reinforcing these emergent symptoms is important, since patients may be fearful to be seen in an emergency room during a pandemic due to fear of acquiring the infection.

During a pandemic, nurses will be regarded as leaders on the healthcare team. Physicians and mid-level providers may be overwhelmed and will rely on the nursing team to be carefully assessing patients, reviewing lab results, monitoring orders, and serving as patient advocates to provide high quality care. Use of a multidisciplinary team is of highest importance to ensure patients are receiving proper care.

Rhabdomyolysis

Rhabdomyolysis occurs in the presence of a muscle injury that causes the release of myoglobin and creatine kinase into the plasma, resulting in tubular toxicity and decreases in the glomerular filtration rate. Statins, recreational drugs, ketamine, methadone, and methamphetamines are associated with rhabdomyolysis.

Sepsis

Sepsis is a serious condition in which the body has a destructive immune and inflammatory response to a wound, infection, or illness. It can progress through stages of severity, with septic shock being the most life-threatening stage. It always accompanies the presence of an underlying condition, including pneumonia, kidney infections, and blood infections. The frequency of cases has been rising in the United States; this increase is attributed to aging populations, antibiotic resistance, increased chronic illness rates, and increased reporting of sepsis cases.

Sepsis Screening Tools

The inflammatory response of the body was defined in 25 CE by the Roman encyclopedist Celsius as rubor, calor, dolor, and tumor. These Latin terms mean redness, heat, pain, and swelling, comprising the classic signs of inflammation that the progressive care nurse is familiar with today.

In the case of **systemic inflammatory response syndrome (SIRS)**, two or more criteria must be met: a temperature of greater than 38°C (100.4°F) or less than 36°C (96.8°F), a pulse of greater than 90 beats/min, a respiratory rate of greater than 20 breaths/min, or a white blood cell count of greater than 12,000. Two or more of these criteria being met in a critically ill patient would suggest that a systemic inflammatory response is afoot and potential complications may be up ahead for the patient.

SIRS criteria remain a vital tool in detecting worsening illness but has been controversial in its accuracy in detecting sepsis. SIRS may also be present in the burn victim, trauma patient, or occurring as an adverse reaction to certain medications. While SIRS criteria remain prevalent in the progressive care and critical care settings, it should not be the sole indicator of sepsis.

Another more recently accepted screening tool for sepsis is the **quick Sepsis-Related Organ Failure Assessment (qSOFA)**. This tool isn't used for a sepsis diagnosis, but rather a bedside screening tool and generalized prediction of mortality. The qSOFA assesses the patient's mental status, respiratory rate, and systolic blood pressure.

175

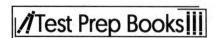

Sepsis Management

The first stage of this continuum is sepsis, in which clinical assessment criteria, laboratory results, and radiology reports indicate the patient has noted organ dysfunction resulting from an inappropriate immune response from an infection. In 2016, the Sepsis-3 Committee revised both the definition and the categorization of sepsis. While there were previously three stages in the sepsis continuum, now there are only two—sepsis and septic shock; severe sepsis is no longer a categorization of the sepsis continuum. While sepsis was previously defined by a patient meeting two or more SIRS criteria with a known infection, the current definition is focused on the severity of the disease process—noting it is a life-threatening condition.

Sepsis can present with a myriad of symptoms, especially considering the patient population and infectious process, but can be generally characterized by a high fever, extreme pain, confusion, lethargy, tachycardia, tachypnea, anxiety, and low urine output.

It is important to administer treatment as soon as possible to keep a sepsis diagnosis from progressing to septic shock. The first line of intervention usually includes antibiotics and IV fluid administration. In more severe cases, surgery to remove affected tissues may be necessary to prevent septic shock.

Septic Shock

Septic shock occurs when there is substantial dysfunction at the cellular and metabolic level. The patient with septic shock will have hypotension that is typically unresponsive to fluid resuscitation, and hypoperfusion abnormalities will be present. Lactic acidosis, oliguria, and altered mental status are examples of hypoperfusion abnormalities.

Once a patient goes into septic shock, the main concern shifts from organ dysfunction to organ failure. Half of all septic shock cases are fatal, while prognosis after treatment for mild and severe sepsis can vary. With early and adequate treatment, most people who experience mild sepsis return to their normal quality of life. However, immunocompromised patients or patients who have other health problems may quickly progress on the sepsis continuum. They may require surgical amputation related to gangrene, experience irreparable organ damage, or suffer from other long-term complications. Even in the event of a full recovery, most of these patients remain with an increased risk of another sepsis episode in the future.

Shock States

Shock refers to any context where the body is unable to circulate an adequate amount of blood to carry out essential physiological functions. It commonly occurs in emergencies of the cardiovascular system. In addition to the previously discussed septic shock, the progressive care nurse should recognize the following states of shock: cardiogenic shock, hypovolemic shock, and anaphylactic shock.

Cardiogenic

Cardiogenic shock occurs because of direct cardiac muscle damage. It often presents due to heart attack or heart failure. Any condition that results in poor heart contractility can result in cardiogenic shock related to severe hypoperfusion.

Hypovolemic

Hypovolemic shock occurs because of overall low blood volume, preventing adequate systemic circulation. Hypovolemic shock typically occurs from severe hemorrhage but can also be a result of anything causing a severe fluid/electrolyte imbalance. Shock patients will always exhibit low blood

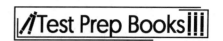

pressure. They may also present with cold, clammy, bluish skin; dehydration; shallow breathing; chest pain; and abnormal pulses. Patients in a state of severe shock may be unconscious. Shock patients will likely progress to asystole, requiring chest compressions, suctioning and mechanical ventilation, and/or defibrillation.

Anaphylactic

An allergic reaction occurs when an individual's immune system responds negatively to a substance within the immediate environment, either through touch, consumption, or inhalation. The substance that causes an allergic reaction is referred to as an **allergen**, and the reaction occurs as a result of the individual's immune system treating the allergen as a threat. Since immune systems between individuals vary widely, the presence and severity of an allergic reaction—even to the same allergen—varies also. A potential allergen (e.g., a plant pollen or a peanut) may cause no response in one individual, cause a mild uncomfortable response in a second individual, and be life-threatening to a third individual. Usually, allergic reactions happen relatively soon (immediately to within a few hours) after exposure to an allergen. Repeated exposure can eventually result in **hypersensitivity** to the allergen and produce more intense allergic reactions. Family history typically influences the presence and severity of allergies. Symptoms of a mild allergic reaction include rashes, itching, congestion, watery eyes, and other cold-like symptoms. Many mild allergic reactions can be treated by eliminating the presence of the allergen or taking anti-allergy medications.

More severe allergic reactions can include symptoms such as physical pain in the chest or stomach, diarrhea, skin swelling or redness, fainting, and trouble breathing deeply. The most severe allergic reactions occur almost instantly and can intensify to result in **anaphylaxis**, which is a medical emergency requiring immediate attention. Anaphylaxis comprises severe swelling of the tongue or throat (which can result in suffocation), vomiting, dizziness, or hives. If anaphylaxis goes untreated, it can result in death. The most common treatment of anaphylaxis is an epinephrine injection, and many individuals who know they have a severe allergy carry an epinephrine injection pen with them.

Common allergens include nuts, shellfish, some fruits, eggs, dairy, gluten, a variety of pollen types, latex, animal dander and hair, and insect or reptilian venom. Some of these allergens, like food allergens, can be present from birth onward; others will develop later in life. Allergens such as bee venom or snake venom may remain unknown unless there is an incident causing exposure.

Toxic Ingestions, Inhalations, and Drug Overdose

Any chemical that can cause harm to the body when ingested or inhaled is considered **toxic**. Exhaust fumes from cars, lead in drinking water, asbestos in old buildings, and pesticides on plants can all cause harm to the body if ingested or inhaled. Ingestion occurs through eating or swallowing the substance, which then travels through the body's GI tract and is absorbed into the circulatory system from the small intestine. A short-term effect would be headache and vomiting, while long-term effects could include cancer and autoimmune disorders. Substances that are inhaled travel through the airways, into the lungs, and are absorbed into the circulation through the pulmonary capillary beds.

Treatment of toxic ingestions depends on the toxic substance ingested as well as the amount ingested. Patient monitoring usually includes level of consciousness, cardiac monitoring, pulse oximetry, vital signs, and blood glucose measurements. Many patients can be managed with supportive care, or activated charcoal may be necessary to rid the body of the toxin. Activated charcoal works by absorbing the toxin before the body gets a chance to, decreasing the systemic toxic effects. If activated charcoal is not effective, hemodialysis, hemoperfusion, or urinary alkalization may be considered on a patient-by-

177

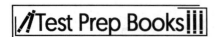

patient basis. For certain poisonings, there are specific treatments that may decrease hepatotoxicity, for example giving N-acetylcysteine for patients with acetaminophen poisoning. When poisoning is confirmed, progressive care nurses should follow institution protocols for reporting to poison control centers and, when appropriate, obtain psychiatric consultation if the poisoning may be related to a suicide-attempt.

Wounds

Knowing how to care for each wound type is crucial in restoring the skin barrier. As a nurse serving a vast patient demographic with varying disease processes, the progressive care nurse should be prepared to encounter the following types of wounds: skin tears, venous ulcers, arterial ulcers, diabetic ulcers, pressure injuries, and surgical wounds.

Types of Wounds

Skin tears are commonly seen in the hospital setting from mechanical force or friction. A skin tear can commonly occur from positional changes, falls, and trauma. Patient-specific factors that predispose the patient to a skin tear include older age, history of skin damage, long-term corticosteroid therapy, and being bedbound.

Venous ulcers are a result of blood pooling from chronic venous insufficiency, meaning blood return to the heart is inadequate. Blood pooling then leads to an alteration in the skin's hydrostatic pressure, leading to maceration and potentially a venous ulcer. Risk factors for venous ulcers include a history of venous disease or dysfunction (e.g., DVT, varicose veins, and genetic predispositions), older age, obesity, and sedentary lifestyle.

Causing similar symptoms in a different manner, **arterial ulcers** develop from poor perfusion resulting in tissue ischemia. Arterial ulcers typically occur in the lower extremities, with heels, toes, and ankles being the most common sites. Risk factors for arterial ulcers include diabetes mellitus, obesity, sedentary lifestyle, and limited range of motion or trauma to the affected area.

Diabetic ulcers can be seen in patients with uncontrolled diabetes mellitus, typically on the foot and related to the peripheral neuropathy that hinders the sensation of pain. The patient with a diabetic ulcer may complain of paresthesia. Education is vital for the diabetic patient, as prevention is the best form of treatment for a diabetic ulcer. Once the ulceration is present, delayed healing and increased risk of infection related to diabetes mellitus can increase the likelihood of necrosis and limb amputation.

Pressure injuries are most commonly seen in immobile, bedridden patients. Because of immobility, pressure against vulnerable parts of the body results in tissue necrosis and resulting injury. Bony prominences are especially susceptible to injury due to less adipose tissue and reduced perfusion upon pressure. Risk factors for developing pressure injuries include increased age, immobility, malnutrition, and urinary and/or fecal incontinence. Factors that contribute to pressure injuries include shear, friction, pressure, and moisture. Increased exposure in compromised patients results in ulceration.

Pressure injuries can be staged into several categories, including stages I, II, III, and IV, unstageable, and suspected deep tissue injury (DTI). Each category looks at depth of wound and tissues affected. Wounds do not necessarily progress from one stage to the next; they can sometimes develop very quickly, skipping stages. Prevention is the best intervention when addressing pressure injuries. The progressive care nurse can help prevent pressure injuries by turning the patient every two hours, reducing pressure where possible with facility-approved support, encouraging early mobilization and proper nutrition, and meticulously caring for wounds that do develop to prevent infection and loss of tissue.

A **surgical wound** is a byproduct of any surgery. Whether a small or large incision is needed, the surgeon will open the body cavity in some form to access the specific internal tissue or organ. Surgical wounds will usually be dressed by the operating room (OR) team, but the progressive care nurse will be responsible for monitoring the wound and changing the dressing while the patient is in the unit. A surgical wound will often have sutures in place. Sometimes these sutures will dissolve and be absorbed by the patient, and sometimes they will need to be removed after a certain amount of time, depending on the procedure, the surgeon, and the facility policy. Signs of an infected surgical wound include redness, swelling, discharge of pus, odor, pain, and lack of healing.

Wound Drains

Multiple types of wound drains exist, including Penrose, Hemovac, Jackson-Pratt (JP drain), and T-tube. The progressive care nurse should carefully remove dressings to not dislodge the drain and then dispose in a biohazard bag according to facility policy. Wound assessment should include the amount, color, and consistency of drainage along with general wound appearance and signs of infection. After cleaning the wound from the drain tubing outward in a circular motion, a clean dressing should be applied around the insertion site and timed and dated. The nurse should then check that the tubing is not kinked or dislodged. Drain tubes should be emptied to prevent overfill and tension on the suture site. Documentation should include the status and condition of the wound, incision site, drain, and dressing, along with the solution used to clean and medications applied to the wound. The nurse should note the patient's tolerance to the procedure and address knowledge deficits, while providing emotional support.

Alcohol Withdrawal Syndrome

Alcohol withdrawal syndrome (AWS) is defined as the occurrence of an alcohol-specific condition that follows the termination of, or decline in, the habitual consumption of alcohol. A mild presentation of AWS commonly presents as anxiety, irritability, insomnia, GI dysfunction, diaphoresis, and decreased attention span. Moderate to severe AWS can result in seizures, hallucinations, and **delirium tremens** (DTs). An interesting facet of the delirium tremens presentation is the interruption of normal vestibular function. The patient may think the floor is moving, the room is rotating, and the walls are falling. A classic symptom of any stage of AWS is tremoring of the hands. Patients in withdrawal are also prone to ataxia, increasing the need for a safe environment and preventing accidental injuries.

The progressive care nurse must collect a comprehensive history and physical to determine the time of last consumption, duration of alcohol usage, reason for the current cessation, alternative therapies used to manage withdrawal symptoms, and baseline vital signs. The nurse must also remove unnecessary items from the environment; provide a quiet and calm atmosphere with minimal stimuli; maintain patient orientation (to person, place, and time); ensure patient safety by implementing seizure precautions; initiate security devices if necessary and as prescribed to prevent the individual from harming self and others; and administer prescribed medications to lessen withdrawal symptoms.

Patients presenting with mild alcohol withdrawal may be treated on an outpatient basis, provided that no comorbidities require the individual to be admitted as an inpatient. Moderate or severe alcohol withdrawal, along with the presence of DTs, requires hospitalization and likely ICU admission. This is because of the high mortality rate from severe alcohol withdrawal with DTs. To evaluate the severity of a patient's withdrawal symptoms, the **Clinical Institute Withdrawal Assessment Alcohol Scale Revised** (CIWA-AR) tool may be utilized. This scale measures ten symptoms of withdrawal, including agitation,

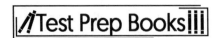

anxiety, auditory disturbances, clouding of sensorium, headache, nausea/vomiting, paroxysmal sweats, tactile disturbances, tremor, and visual disturbances. By totaling the patient's severity score in each category, they can be categorized into mild, moderate, or severe withdrawal.

Sedatives are the chief medications for treatment of alcohol withdrawal syndrome because they are cross-tolerant drugs that modulate GABA (Gamma-Aminobutyric Acid) function. GABA receptors are the major inhibitory neurotransmitter receptors in the brain. These drugs commonly consist of benzodiazepines and barbiturates. Other medications used to treat withdrawal may include phenytoin to treat and prevent seizure activity and IV thiamine to prevent Wernicke-Korsakoff syndrome, which includes Wernicke's encephalopathy and Korsakoff's psychosis.

Substance Withdrawal

The **clinical opioid withdrawal scale (COWS)** is a tool that can be used in any care setting to evaluate and monitor the severity of symptoms associated with **opioid withdrawal**. The clinician observes the patient and assigns a score to each of the eleven items on the scale. The total score is then calculated, with a higher score indicating a higher severity of withdrawal. The following symptoms are evaluated:

- Resting heart rate: From normal resting pulse to tachycardia
- GI upset: From stomach cramps to multiple episodes of diarrhea or vomiting
- Sweating: From reports of flushing to visible running of sweat
- Tremor: From no tremor to gross twitching
- Restlessness: From able to sit still to unable to for more than a few seconds
- Yawning: From no yawning present to multiple times in a minute
- Pupil size: From normal for light conditions to greatly dilated
- Anxiety or irritability: From none to impacting the assessment
- Bone or joint aches: From none to impacting ability to sit still
- Piloerection of skin: From none to visible goosebumps on skin
- Runny nose or tearing: From none to constant tearing or running nose

Often, withdrawal symptoms can be missed because they mimic overdose symptoms, and patients are not always truthful about drug use. When used correctly, the COWS assessment guides providers on managing side effects of withdrawal.

COWS is frequently used when initiating patients on buprenorphine/naloxone combinations, which cause a rapid drug withdrawal by displacing the drug molecule from the receptor. In addition to buprenorphine/naloxone dosing, the nurse can expect to see orders for supportive care medications to help manage symptoms of withdrawal. This can include the following: ondansetron or promethazine for nausea; acetaminophen for headache and mild pain; clonidine for cramping; hydroxyzine and ropinirole for restless legs; loperamide for diarrhea; and trazadone for insomnia. If there is not a protocol in place already at the organization, the nurse can use this tool to request additional orders that will lessen the effects of withdrawal for the patient.

Behavioral/Psychosocial

Disruptive Behaviors, Aggression, Violence

Progressive care nurses may encounter patients who exhibit disruptive behaviors, aggression, and violence. Patients may be situationally upset or may have an underlying behavioral or mood disorder.

180

For example, people with **antisocial personality disorders** (ASPD) show no signs of empathy. They have no awareness of how others perceive them, how to interact with others, or how to anticipate their feelings or reactions. To people without empathy, the feelings and emotions of others are not a factor in decision-making, which can lead to a spectrum of behaviors that range from social awkwardness to acts of cruelty and negligence. Antisocial actions are what cause many people with antisocial behaviors to break the law or hurt others. There may be a disregard for the truth in pursuit of entertainment or personal gain, usually as a kind of manipulation. Lack of empathy makes it difficult for those with ASPD to contemplate why moral standards constructed for other people are applicable to them. Those with ASPD often lie repeatedly and consistently for personal satisfaction alone.

ASPD involves aggression that stems from poor impulse control, also known as **reactive aggression**. People diagnosed with ASPD have a predisposition to hostile intention bias. Individuals are more likely to anticipate and expect the worst from others, making them more prone to reactive outbreaks of aggression. Unlike reactive aggression, **instrumental aggression** involves an individual leveraging their aggression as a tool.

A study in 2009 found that people with ASPD have very strong rapid-response impulsivity but the same level of impulse control as non-sufferers when it came to future planning. There is a strong need to be independent and resist being controlled by others, who are usually held in contempt. There is a willingness to use untamed aggression to back up the need for control or independence. The antisocial personality usually presents in a friendly, sociable manner, but that friendliness is always accompanied by a baseline position of detachment. There is a total lack of investment in the comfort of others, a complete focus on their own feelings, and complete lack of remorse. It is very common that the person with ASPD is not the one who seeks help; often friends, families, or intimate partners attempt to get a diagnosis.

If the patient is officially diagnosed, they may be prescribed cognitive-behavioral therapy, mood stabilizers, and antidepressants. ASPD often comes with accompanying diagnoses of substance abuse disorder, borderline personality disorder, narcissistic personality disorder, and conduct disorder.

When patients are acting violently or aggressively (whether due to ASPD or otherwise), they may require the use of restraints. **Restraints** can be defined as anything that is used, done, or said to intentionally limit a person's ability to move freely. Restraints, when applied properly, cannot be easily removed or controlled by the person. In addition to physical form, restraints can also be emotional, chemical, or environmental. Use of restraints is very controversial due to the ethical issue of personal freedom. These are a temporary solution to a problem and must always be used as a last resort. Restraints are used to limit a patient's movement to prevent injury to themselves or others and always require a physician's order.

Types of restraints include:

- Physical: vests, wrist restraints, straps, or anything that confines the body
- Emotional: verbal cues or emotions used to coerce the patient to act a certain way
- Environmental: side rails, locked doors, closed windows, or locked beds
- Chemical: any medication used to restrict a patient's movement

The medical doctor or practitioner is responsible for ordering the use of restraints. Nurses and caregivers are responsible for applying restraints safely and for the management of a patient with a

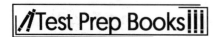

restraint. After an order is given, the physician must visit the patient within 24 hours of placing the order to assess its further necessity.

Other methods must be tried before restraints. They include:

- Talking with the patient about being cooperative
- Using distractions such as television, music, knitting, and folding towels or cloths
- Placing the patient within view of a caregiver (i.e., near the main desk)
- Having someone sit with the patient
- Ensuring the patient's area is calming
- Ensuring that the patient's bathroom needs are being met
- Ensuring personal items are within reach

Each facility will have a specific protocol that must be followed for restraint use. Circumstances under which restraints could be used include:

- Signs of patient aggression toward self, staff, or other patients
- Interference with important medical devices, such as an IV or a catheter
- Patient movements that are potentially harmful to their health or may cause further injury
- Potential for a patient to interfere with a procedure

The following guidelines should be used whenever applying restraints:

- Always follow the facility's restraint policy.
- Obtain an order from a physician or medical practitioner.
- Obtain consent from the patient or their legal representative if the patient is not capable of understanding.
- Explain to the patient what is going to happen, even if the patient is unable to understand due to confusion or dementia.
- Always monitor the patient per facility policy, such as checking the positioning of the restraint every thirty minutes and removing every two hours for range of motion. Remember to reposition the patient and offer toileting every two hours.
- Explain the need for restraints and how long the restraints will be used.

Vest restraints have holes for the arms and the opening crosses in the back. The straps will be secured on either side of the bed or chair, depending on the patient's location. Tie it in a quick-release knot to a lower part of the bed that does not move. Make sure that two fingers fit underneath the vest on the patient's chest so that it is not too tight.

Wrist or ankle restraints are cloths that wrap around each wrist or ankle. They have a strap that is tied to a lower, immovable part of the bed or chair. Tie it in a quick-release knot. Ensure the restraints aren't too tight and that the patient's arms or legs aren't in an awkward position.

If restraints aren't used correctly or are used for the wrong reasons, the patient's family can take legal action against the facility. A patient in restraints becomes completely vulnerable and may feel helpless. They are at a greater risk of sexual abuse, elder abuse, psychological abuse, or violence from other patients.

Possible injuries from restraints can include:

- Broken bones
- Bruises
- Falls
- Skin tears or pressure sores
- Depression or fear due to lack of freedom
- Death from strangulation

Psychological Disorders

Anxiety Disorders

Anxiety and panic attacks are characterized by extreme, sudden, and often unpredictable feelings of paralyzing fear, nervousness, and discomfort. These situations are often debilitating for the individual experiencing them, with some reporting symptoms such as chest pain, the inability to breathe, and feeling a sense of impending death. Other common symptoms include overwhelming dizziness, nausea, sweating, trembling, accelerated heart rate, and feelings of "checking out" from reality. For a true medical diagnosis, four or more of these symptoms must be present. Typically, these episodes can last anywhere from 10 minutes to over an hour. Individuals who experience an anxiety or panic attack for the first time may be unfamiliar with the event, and it can warrant a trip to the healthcare facility. Consequently, it is important for nurses to know how to address these situations to help the patient to receive proper, adequate, and cost-efficient treatment in the future. It is important to show support and compassion toward the patient's feelings, even if the patient's fears seem irrational.

For recurrent anxiety and panic attacks, medication and/or psychotherapy is often needed to support the patient's quality of life. Selective serotonin reuptake inhibitors (SSRIs) are often prescribed to help manage anxiety symptoms. Common SSRIs used for anxiety include names include fluoxetine, sertraline, paroxetine, and escitalopram.

Depression

Depression is characterized by feelings of lethargy; hopelessness; an inability to derive pleasure from once pleasurable activities; problems with sleep, eating, and substances; and/or sexual dysfunction that lasts longer than two weeks. It can be caused by genetics, an imbalance of neurochemicals, or situational contexts. Depression often presents differently in men, women, children, and older adults. Men tend to exhibit increased anger and irritability, while women tend to feel sad, worthless, and guilty. Women tend to internalize symptoms and experience depression at a higher rate and frequency than men due to unique societal issues, hormonal changes, and other factors. Children present symptoms of depression through isolation, anxiety, or acting out. Older adults are more prone to hide symptoms of depression, attribute the feelings to another health problem, or be taken less seriously than other age demographics. It should be noted that these are generalizations and not hard rules, as depression can have a different clinical presentation depending on the specific patient.

Depression is usually managed through psychotherapy and sometimes medication. Common medications to treat depression include SSRIs, like those used to treat anxiety. Depression can also be treated with serotonin and norepinephrine reuptake inhibitors, such as duloxetine and venlafaxine. When these options don't work, tricyclic antidepressants may be prescribed. Because they tend to have more intense side effects, tricyclic antidepressants are not usually prescribed unless other options have been exhausted. Even with medication, some periods of depression can become so intense and unmanageable that the patient enters a major depressive episode or has suicidal ideation. In this context, emergency services are usually needed. It is important to show the depressed patient reassurance, comfort, and support, including directly asking the patient what would help comfort and support him or her during this time. Noting verbal and nonverbal communication will help determine if the patient is at risk for suicide and how severe that risk might be. A critical factor of assessing a potentially suicidal patient is inquiring if there is a suicide plan in place.

The nurse should assess patients for **suicidal ideation** using nonjudgmental, therapeutic methods that support the patient in being honest with the healthcare staff. This should include clear, direct questions related to plan, intent, and history of attempts. Euphemisms should not be used. If the patient is determined to be high risk, this should be communicated with the healthcare team and the patient should not be left alone until further assessment by a social worker or psychiatry specialist can take place. Patient safety attendants are often utilized in hospitals for this purpose.

High-risk patients must be continually monitored, and their environment should be adapted for safety. In the hospital, this can mean removing cords, tubing, sharp items, and anything that could be used to cause harm. A patient's belongings should be checked for weapons and hoarded medications, which need to be removed if found. The nurse should work with the patient to create a safety plan and explain the precautions to the patient and the family. When administering medications, the nurse should ensure the medicine is taken promptly by the patient and not being stored for a future attempt. Social work should be involved, and discharge planning should include family and caregivers.

Bipolar Disorder

Bipolar disorder is characterized by extremes in mood, energy, and functioning. The individual tends to experience manic periods, marked by highly energetic, almost frenzied behaviors and excitable moods, as well as depressive periods, marked by lethargy, sadness, and isolation. Clinically, manic periods must last at least a week and depressive periods at least two weeks for an individual to be diagnosed with bipolar disorder. Bipolar is a brain disorder that may be caused by physiological distinctions in the brain or genetics. It is often treated with mood-stabilizing medications in conjunction with psychotherapy. Common medications to manage symptoms of bipolar disorder include lithium and valproate.

Due to the nature of the disorder, the extremes experienced by an individual with bipolar disorder can result in a trip to the emergency department or other acute care facility. Individuals experiencing a manic period are at risk of engaging in impulsive behaviors, such as drug abuse, violence, unsafe sexual encounters, and following through with suicidal thoughts. Individuals experiencing a depressive period are also at risk of having suicidal thoughts or tendencies due to a marked increase in feelings of hopelessness. Individuals with bipolar disorder can also experience periods of psychosis and have delusions or hallucinations. Nurses should be prepared to show sympathy and compassion while still being firm and direct with the patient. Patient behavior will likely be unpredictable, especially if he or she is in a manic phase.

Substance Use Disorder

Substance abuse is defined, most simply, as extreme use of a drug. Abuse occurs for many reasons, such as mental health instability, inability to cope with everyday life stressors, the loss of a loved one, or enjoyment of the euphoric state that the overindulgence in a substance causes. Abused substances create some type of intoxication that alters decision-making, awareness, attentiveness, or physical impulses.

Substance abuse results in tolerance, withdrawal, and compulsive drug-taking behavior. **Tolerance** occurs when increased amounts of the substance are needed to achieve the desired effects. **Withdrawal** manifests as physiological and substance-specific cognitive symptoms (e.g., cold sweats, shivering, nausea, vomiting, paranoia, hallucinations). Withdrawal not only happens when an individual stops abusing the substance, but also occurs when he or she attempts to reduce the amount taken to stop using altogether.

Chronic Alcohol Abuse

Considering alcohol is a central nervous system (CNS) depressant, effects of alcohol ingestion tend to include relaxation and lowered inhibitions. However, it also slurs speech and impairs muscle control, coordination, and reflex time. **Alcohol abuse** can cause cirrhosis of the liver; liver, esophagus, and stomach cancers; heart enlargement; chronic inflammation of the pancreas; vitamin deficiencies; certain anemias; and brain damage. Withdrawal from chronic alcohol abuse must be done with caution and in an appropriate timeframe to avoid alcohol withdrawal syndrome.

Chronic Tobacco Abuse

People abuse **tobacco** either in cigarette, cigar, pipe, or snuff form. People report many reasons for tobacco use, including a calming effect, suppression of appetite, and relief of depression. The primary addictive component in tobacco is nicotine, but tobacco smoke also contains about 700 carcinogens (cancer-causing agents) that may result in lung and throat cancers as well as heart disease, emphysema, peptic ulcer disease, and stroke. Withdrawal indicators include insomnia, irritability, overwhelming nicotine craving, anxiety, and depression.

Marijuana

Marijuana is considered the most frequently abused illicit drug in the United States. General effects of marijuana use include pleasure, relaxation, and weakened dexterity and memory. The active addictive ingredient in marijuana is tetrahydrocannabinol (THC). It is normally smoked (but can be eaten), and its smoke has more carcinogens than that of tobacco. The individual withdrawing from marijuana will experience increased irritability and anxiety.

Cocaine

Cocaine is a stimulant that can be smoked, injected, snorted, or swallowed. Reported effects include pleasure, enhanced alertness, and increased energy. Both temporary and prolonged use have been known to contribute to damage to the brain, heart, lungs, and kidneys. Withdrawal symptoms include severe depression and reduced energy.

Heroin

Heroin is rapid-acting opioid that is highly addictive. Effects of heroin abuse include pleasure, slower respirations, and drowsiness. Overdose and/or overuse of heroin can cause respiratory depression, resulting in death. Use of heroin as an injectable substance can lead to other complications, such as heart valve damage, tetanus, botulism, hepatitis B, or human immunodeficiency virus (HIV)/AIDS infection from sharing dirty needles. Withdrawal is usually intense and presents as vomiting, abdominal cramps, diarrhea, confusion, body aches, and diaphoresis.

Methamphetamines

Methamphetamine is categorized as a stimulant that produces such effects as pleasure, increased alertness, and decreased appetite. Similar to cocaine, it can be snorted, smoked, or injected, and it can

185

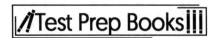

be taken orally as well. Like cocaine, it shares many of the same detrimental effects, such as myocardial infarction, hypertension, and stroke. Other prolonged usage effects include paranoia, hallucinations, damage to and loss of dentition, and heart damage. Withdrawal symptoms involve depression, abdominal cramps, and increased appetite.

Nursing interventions for the individual addicted to tobacco, alcohol, and other drugs centers around the prevention of relapse, and treatment depends on the individual and the substance that is abused. Behavioral treatment assists with recognition of abuse triggers, habits, and drug cravings, as well as providing the tactics to help one cope with these issues. A physician may prescribe nicotine patches for the tobacco abuser and methadone or Suboxone to manage withdrawal symptoms and certain drug yearnings.

Substance Dependence Disorder
When a patient becomes dependent on a substance that causes a disruption in their relationships and physical health, it is called a **substance dependence disorder**. There are several different substances that may cause addiction, including alcohol, tobacco, opioids, hallucinogens, stimulants (e.g., cocaine and amphetamines), and sedatives/hypnotics/anxiolytics (e.g., lorazepam). The patient begins to seek these drugs obsessively, always chasing after the next high. These drug-dependent behaviors, including manipulation, lying, and doing whatever it takes to get the substance, destroy relationships and the patient's ability to function normally.

Practice Quiz

1. A progressive care nurse is educating a patient regarding a flu shot before his discharge. He states that he had one two years ago. While educating a patient on the importance of the flu vaccine, the nurse advises that the patient get the flu vaccine administered how often?
    a. Once per lifetime
    b. Every three months
    c. Annually
    d. Every two years

2. The nurse is admitting a postoperative patient following repair of multiple tears and lacerations after being stabbed several times. The nurse knows that which of the following signs indicates an improvement in the patient's condition?
    a. Rise in heart rate
    b. Stabilization of blood pressure
    c. Development of fever
    d. Low urine output

3. A patient tells the nurse that his pain is in his abdomen, just below the rib cage and to the right of his stomach. The nurse knows that the patient has reported which component of pain assessment?
    a. Location
    b. Exacerbation
    c. Alleviation
    d. Aggravation

4. What amount of total body blood loss is considered life-threatening and will throw a patient into hypovolemic shock?
    a. 1/8
    b. 1/7
    c. 1/5
    d. 1/10

5. Which of the following interventions will NOT help prevent a pressure injury from occurring in a bedridden patient?
    a. Turning the patient every two hours
    b. Encouraging early mobility
    c. Removing the pillows from the bed
    d. Ensuring proper nutrition

See answers on the next page.

Answer Explanations

1. C: The flu vaccine should be administered every year at the beginning of the flu season. Each year, a specific strain of the virus is identified as being the likely culprit for cases of the flu and is used in the vaccines; thus, everyone 6 months of age and older should get their flu shot every year. Choices *A*, *B*, and *D* are incorrect timelines for administration of the flu vaccine.

2. B: Stabilizing the patient's blood pressure is an excellent sign that their condition is improving. Fever, oliguria, and tachycardia (Choices *A*, *C*, and *D*) are all signs of deterioration and may point toward complications such as shock, bleeding, and/or infection, which need further investigation.

3. A: The patient has reported the location of his pain. Alleviation (Choice *B*) refers to an action that makes the pain better. Aggravation (Choice *C*) refers to an action that makes the pain worse. Exacerbation (Choice *D*) is a particularly intense flare-up of a chronic pain issue.

4. C: Losing 1/5 (or 20 percent) of one's blood volume will throw a person into hypovolemic shock and is considered life threatening. Organ failure with profound hypotension will likely follow; fluid resuscitation and blood transfusions will be needed as soon as possible. Choices *A*, *B*, and *D* represent values less than 15–20 percent, or the amount of blood volume loss required to cause hypovolemic shock.

5. C: Removing the pillows from the bed is not the best option, as these are used to support the patient's limbs and reduce pressure to bony prominences. The interventions listed in Choices *A*, *B*, and *D* (encouraging early mobility, proper nutrition, and turning and repositioning the patient every two hours) will help prevent the development of pressure injuries.

Professional Caring and Ethical Practice

Advocacy/Moral Agency

Advocacy

Advocacy is the promotion of the common good, especially as it applies to at-risk populations. It involves speaking out in support of policies and decisions that affect the lives of individuals who do not otherwise have a voice. Nurses meet this standard of practice by actively participating in the politics of healthcare accessibility and delivery. They are educationally and professionally prepared to evaluate and comment on the needs of patients at the local, state, and national level. This participation requires an understanding of the legislative process, the ability to negotiate with public officials, and a willingness to provide expert testimony in support of policy decisions. The advocacy role of nurses has the potential to address the needs of the individual patient, society, and members of the nursing profession.

In clinical practice, nurses represent the patient's interests through active participation in the development of the plan of care and subsequent care decisions. Advocacy, in this sense, is related to patient autonomy and the patient's right to informed consent and self-determination. Nurses provide the appropriate information, assess the patient's comprehension of the implications of the care decisions, and act as patient advocates by supporting the patient's decisions. Patient advocacy for acutely ill patients requires the nurse to represent the patient's decisions even though those decisions may be opposed to those of the healthcare providers and family members.

Nurses understand the complex care requirements of patients with multiple comorbidities. Therefore, they are often called upon to intercede on a patient's behalf to facilitate the delivery of adequate and appropriate care in both the acute care setting and the primary care environment. In addition, nurses understand the care needs of the greater community and serve as advocates for the provision of preventative interventions and policies that affect public health. Nurses advocate for increased resources to address the needs of specific community populations, including school-age children. In this way, nurses practice **beneficence**, defined as doing good for another individual, including acting as an advocate, supporting the individual's autonomy, and working to ensure justice. Related to beneficence is the concept of **nonmaleficence**, which means non-harming, or inflicting the least harm possible to reach a beneficial outcome.

Professionally, nurses advocate for policies that support and promote the practice of all nurses regarding access to education, role identity, workplace conditions, and compensation. The responsibility for professional advocacy requires nurses to provide leadership in the development of the professional nursing role in all practice settings that may include acute care facilities, colleges and universities, or community agencies. Leadership roles in acute care settings involve participation in professional practice and shared governance committees, providing support for basic nursing education by facilitating clinical and preceptorship experiences, and mentoring novice graduate nurses to the professional nursing role. In the academic setting, nurses work to ensure the diversity of the student population by participating in the governance structure of the institution, conducting and publishing research that supports the positive impact of professional nursing care on patient outcomes, and serving as an advocate to individual nursing students to promote their academic success. In the community, nurses may collaborate with government officials to meet the needs that are specific to that location.

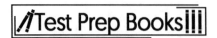

The role requirements for advocacy require nurses to maintain clinical expertise through continuing education (formal and informal), to actively follow and comment on legislative initiatives that affect at-risk populations, and to model the professional nursing role in practice.

Moral Agency

The nurse must function as a moral agent. This means that the nurse must be morally accountable and responsible for personal judgment and actions. Moral integrity is doing what is true to your values without compromising them. Nurses often act and conduct their responsibilities as they feel morally correct. **Moral agency** is defined as the ability to identify right and wrong actions based on widely accepted moral criteria. The performance of nurses as moral agents is dependent on life experiences, advanced education, and clinical experience in healthcare agencies. Moral agency can often cause cognitive dissonance in nurses as some decisions go against their training and beliefs. However, as nurses undertake more responsibilities, they need to be able to address ethical dilemmas without deemphasizing care.

The role of moral agent requires nurses to have a strong sense of self and a clear understanding of the definition of right and wrong; however, nurses must also be aware that these perceptions of right and wrong will be challenged every day. The nurse can expect to encounter difficult situations where the moral action related to the patient's right to self-determination is opposed to the moral action with respect to competent patient care.

Caring Practices

Models of Caring

There are several models that were created to define the art and science of nursing. This is different from the practice of medicine, although nurses also expertly use assessment, diagnosing, planning, intervention, and evaluation to provide holistic care for all patients. Caring is the most commonly identified characteristic of nursing care, and it is the central concept of most nursing models. One such framework is the **6 C's of Caring** model that was proposed to define the unique characteristics of nursing practice that distinguish nursing from the remaining patient care disciplines. These personal attributes shape the skilled nursing practice of nurses.

In the 6 C's of Caring model, **compassion** is defined as being in a state of empathy with another individual, especially with regard to pain and suffering. **Competence** requires the active pursuit of knowledge, and it is demonstrated by nurses' performance in each domain of learning, including the psychomotor, cognitive, and affective domains. The **conscience** directs nurses' moral and ethical decisions and prompts a response to instances of injustice. **Confidence** is a direct reflection of nurses' trust in their own ability to provide appropriate care for all assigned patients. Confidence is gained through formal and informal education, clinical experience, and life experience. It is evident in all aspects of the nurses' professional practice, including the clinical environment and the community. **Commitment** is the pursuit of excellence in all areas of professional nursing practice, including direct patient care, promotion of the profession, personal enrichment through education, mentoring of novice nurses, and support of public health initiatives at all levels of government. **Comportment** refers to all aspects of nurses' professional behavior in the clinical setting and the community.

While the 6 C's model is used to define nursing as a caring profession, the **Synergy Model** proposes a novel paradigm for nursing that considers patients' specific needs as the driving force in healthcare. Nursing is viewed as a coordinated, competence-based response to such needs rather than as a series of tasks that may or may not satisfy them. The model is based on the following assumptions: the patient is viewed holistically with attention to the mind, body, and spirit dimensions; the patient, the family, and the community all contribute context to the nurse-patient relationship; characteristics of either the patient or the nurse cannot be viewed in isolation because they are interrelated; and the goal of nursing is the return of the patient to the optimal level of wellness as defined by the patient. Death is considered an acceptable outcome of care to all nurses, but to different degrees according to their experience level. Novice, or level 1 nurses, understand that the patient's death is a possibility, yet they do not comprehend that the death is inevitable or acceptable. Experienced, or level 2 nurses, know from interacting with the patient and family, and from expert assessment of the patient's progress, that death may be an acceptable outcome. Expert, or level 3 nurses, recognize death as an acceptable outcome, and demonstrate skills in managing end-of-life care. They create care plans to manage patient death in the best way possible, to the benefit of the patient and the family.

The Synergy Model

Patients' characteristics

Low   Medium   High

Health ◄——————————————► Illness

Continuum of characteristics

Intrinsic

1 Resiliency
2 Vulnerability
3 Stability
4 Complexity
5 Predictability

Extrinsic

Resource 6
availability
Participation in 7
decision-making
Participation in care 8

Nurses' competencies

Measured on a continuum and provides a basis for differentiating levels of nursing practice

Level 1   Level 2   Level 3
Competent **Proficient** **Expert**

Clinical judgment   System thinking
Advocacy/   Response
moral agency   to diversity

Nurses' competencies

Caring   Clinical
practices   inquiry

                                      Facilitator
Collaboration   of learning

Synergy model - outcomes

1	2	3
Patient-driven outcomes	**Nurse-driven outcomes**	**System-driven outcomes**
Functional changes, behavioral changes, trust, comfort, QOL, satisfaction	Physiological changes, complications, goal achievements	Readmissions, LOS, cost effectiveness, resource utilization

Caring practices are identified as one of the eight nursing competencies in the Synergy Model. Nurses establish and maintain a therapeutic patient-care environment, based on consideration of the needs of

191

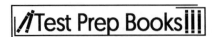

the patient and the family, that promotes healing and minimizes discomfort and stress. The model identifies vigilance and engagement as essential elements of the caring practices. **Vigilance** as a caring skill is viewed on a continuum according to the ability of nurses to recognize and respond to patient needs. Novice nurses are capable of responding to usual and predictable changes in the patient's condition; however, responding to more subtle cues requires an increased level of clinical competence, and preventing any potential hazards requires even greater nursing skill. **Engagement** refers to the degree to which nurses commit to the nurse-patient relationship. Researchers note that favorable patient outcomes are associated with the degree of caregiver engagement; however, there is also evidence that the incidence of burnout in experienced nurses is related to the degree of their engagement in patient care. The third attribute of the caring practices is **responsiveness**, which means that the reaction of the patient's family, the healthcare institution, and the nursing staff will all have an effect on the patient's progress.

Ethical Dilemmas

Healthcare providers routinely face situations with patients where they must analyze various moral and ethical considerations. In acute settings, where quick judgment and action is necessary to care and where patients are often not fully sound in body or mind, ethical dilemmas can arise without much time to process resolutions.

The AACN Certification Corporation adheres to an established **Code of Ethics**, which outlines moral and ethical guidelines for nursing practice. Above all else, nurses have the responsibility to do no harm while serving as advocates, minimizing injury, and protecting the overall health and functioning of their patients. It is important to consider the patient holistically when applying these values, such as considering what the patient may view as a good quality of life, what family values the patient holds, other family members that may be affected (such as a spouse or children), legal considerations, and logistical considerations (such as how much time and medical resources are available). When patients are unable to make decisions autonomously or provide consent to treatment (as can be common in emergency cases), nurses should act from these responsibilities to make wise and compassionate decisions on the patients' behalf.

Dilemmas that can arise for nursing staff include situations where the patient may have cultural or personal beliefs that prevent lifesaving treatment. For example, a female patient may not want to be treated by any male staff, or a patient that needs a blood transfusion may not accept this procedure due to religious beliefs. In cases where the patient is able to directly communicate their wishes, the nurse may need to defer to the patient's wishes in order to preserve the patient's autonomy. This may mean providing alternative means of care (such as finding available female medical providers to assist with the female patient that does not want to be treated by male staff). It may mean withholding treatment that the patient refuses. If the patient's life is in question and rapid medical action is necessary to save the patient's life, nursing staff interventions will need to consider the patient's wishes. Ethical considerations like these will vary by case and patient, and will depend on the severity of the case, the medical and personal history of the patient, and the judgment of the medical team. In all cases, it is ideal if the nurse and patient are able to communicate openly with each other about the case and potential medical options, with the goal that the resolution will allow for the greatest good.

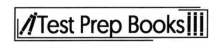

Response to Diversity

Characteristics of **diversity** include, but are not limited to, ethnicity, race, gender, religious preference, age, lifestyle, and values. According to the Synergy Model, patient needs and characteristics must be "linked" to nursing competencies to achieve maximum health. Nurses are aware that unmet cultural or diversity needs and preferences can adversely affect patient outcomes in much the same way that somatic illness affects outcomes; therefore, **cultural sensitivity** is an essential nurse competency. The development of cultural sensitivity and demonstrated appreciation of diversity by nurses is also viewed as a continuum in the Synergy Model. Novice nurses, who are learning to negotiate the institutional environment, may assess the patient's preferences but often continue to provide care that is consistent with their own belief system. As competent nurses gain life and clinical experience, they actively question patients to learn about and accommodate the traditions and customs of a diverse population, while helping the patient and family to understand the culture of the institution. Expert nurses are able to anticipate the needs of the patient and family by integrating cultural differences into the plan of care whenever possible. All of these nursing interventions work to alleviate the stress related to the acute care environment.

Research indicates that diversity in the workplace strengthens the workgroup by allowing consideration of multiple worldviews and a better understanding of the patient population served by the institution. Multiple viewpoints can also be an advantage in **conflict resolution**, especially when the conflict is related to diversity issues. The Synergy Model suggests that nurses become more sensitive to diversity issues with experience and that this sensitivity is applicable to the work environment as well as direct patient care. Attention to diversity issues also, however, requires institutional support for resource allocation and management. Depending on the specific needs of the patient population, services such as foreign language interpreters, appropriate food service, counseling services, and accommodation for religious observances must be considered. To optimize patient care, expert nurses assess the needs of the patient and family and provide access to the appropriate institutional resources.

The most significant threat to success in this process is **ethnocentrism**, which means that group members are unable to consider views that are contrary to their own beliefs. Alternative definitions in the literature view ethnocentrism as possessing false assumptions about another culture, which assumes that ethnocentric behavior is based on incorrect or incomplete information about other traditions and practices. Attention to diversity issues requires that providers proceed on the assumption that ethnocentrism is a universal human characteristic that must be addressed by the provision of appropriate information and instruction. In addition to understanding their own cultural views, nurses must be aware that many patients have preconceived views of "westerners" and their cultural norms, which may or may not be accurate, but can potentially affect the nurse-patient relationship. The resolution of ethnocentrism in a caring relationship requires acknowledgment of its existence and education as to the meaning of the traditions and practices.

Cultural Considerations

Patients will come from all backgrounds and cultures, and medical providers should be aware of the different cultural needs that may present themselves in a healthcare setting. **Culture** can encompass anything from a person's geographical location, race, ethnicity, age, socioeconomic status, and religious beliefs that influence the behaviors, traditions, and rituals that he or she chooses to engage in each day. It is important to note that cultural considerations will present themselves daily. Some patients may be unable to speak English and will need interpretive services. Some patients may request that only same-sex providers treat them. Some patients may need to keep culturally valuable adornments in place that could interfere with treatment (i.e., a metal symbol on a patient that needs magnetic resonance imaging, a procedure where metal poses an extreme danger). Respecting and attending to different cultural needs will provide the patient with a better healthcare experience, lead to increased patient satisfaction, and impact overall health outcomes (as patients will be more likely to seek out care if they feel comfortable doing so).

Medical providers can show that they consider cultural differences by kindly and compassionately asking patients to share cultural viewpoints, to share aspects of the medical system and services that make them comfortable or uncomfortable, and to continuously create rapport that allows the patient to feel comfortable in voicing their concerns. Medical providers should be mindful of any preconceived notions that they hold of certain cultures and, if possible, actively work to dispel these. Medical providers should also be mindful to not make presumptions, even if those presumptions come from an intention to be empathetic. For example, a patient who looks to be of Asian descent may have been born and raised in the United States and not identify well with any part of Asian culture. Finally, many healthcare organizations offer internal trainings that cover cultural considerations and cultural diversity. For staff that feel their knowledge and experience is limited in this aspect, these trainings can provide an avenue for personal and professional growth.

Having a diverse staff can be extremely beneficial when servicing a patient demographic that encompasses many cultures. Having a medical provider who is able to relate directly with a patient's culture can make the patient feel more comfortable and open. Additionally, a diverse staff can overcome common obstacles such as language barriers or lack of patient education. In this regard, healthcare organizations and nursing leadership should work to actively recruit a diverse workforce.

Multicultural, Spiritual, and Religious Factors That May Affect the Client's Health Status

Multiculturalism is an integral aspect of culture in the United States, which comprises people from many countries and cultures, often speaking different languages. When it comes to nursing care, each client will come from a different cultural and religious background. This can lead to many challenges, such as language barriers, or more subtle but complex differences. Both the client and the nurse will have their own cultural and religious biases and beliefs that will influence the way they look at treatment.

One aspect of multiculturalism is that cultures can be individualistic or collectivist, which will play a part in how the client views health and healthcare. In **individualistic** societies, decisions are made by the individual and values include privacy and independence. On the other hand, in a **collectivist** society, decisions related to health may be a community responsibility, and the assumption will be that the whole family will be involved in a client's treatment. This may not only involve the family but also the spiritual or religious community as well. While upholding ethical guidelines around confidentiality and privacy, a progressive care nurse must also respect the culture that the client comes from and involve the community as much or as little as the client desires.

There are many things that are affected by spiritual, religious, and cultural beliefs. First, it is beneficial to describe the difference between spirituality and religion. **Spirituality** is a client's belief in the operation of a higher self and/or higher components of the universe. A spiritual client may not profess a certain religion but may engage in practices such as yoga or meditation. On the other hand, **religion** is a profession of belief in a God(s) or divine being and a belief in a higher order that controls the universe. Religious clients often identify by the title of the doctrine they subscribe to.

Consequently, it is important for the progressive care nurse to be aware of differing practices, such as cupping, candling, acupuncture, refusal to accept blood transfusions, and dietary restrictions, that could be confused with abuse or neglect when compared against traditional Western American culture. Traditional medicines of the client's culture or medical practices of that culture may be preferred over what doctors recommend. Moreover, there are gender roles that may affect the nature of the relationship with the client and the services provided. For example, there may be a gender preference with a doctor or the client may opt out of medical care altogether when in the presence of an opposite-sex provider. Different cultures also have different views of doctors: some are held in such high esteem that they will never be questioned, even if a client is confused or in disagreement. In addition, the client's view of death and what happens after death may play a large role in decisions that are made and will be particularly significant in palliative and hospice care.

Being culturally competent is a necessity for every nurse. **Cultural competency** refers to the ability to understand, accept, and respect a client's culture and religion, while recognizing one's own cultural and religious biases. Nurses cannot assume that every client will share the same cultural and ideological beliefs but must view every single client as different and coming from a unique cultural background. One obvious aspect of cultural competence is to ensure that there are no language or communication barriers and that a translator is available if needed. It is also important for the nurse ask questions that help to understand, recognize, and support the client's specific cultural and religious beliefs. Diversity should not be feared or avoided but embraced and affirmed by the progressive care nurse. Patient education can serve to inform the client about treatment options while still acknowledging and respecting their beliefs.

Facilitation of Learning

Facilitation of learning refers to the process of assessing the learning needs of the patient and family, the nursing staff, and caregivers in the community, and creating, implementing, and evaluating formal and informal educational programs to address those needs. Novice nurses often view patient care and patient education as separate entities; however, experienced nurses can integrate the patient's educational needs into the plan of care. Nurses are aware that the patient often requires continued reinforcement of the educational plan after discharge, which necessitates coordination with home care services.

As facilitators of learning, nurses may be involved in a large-scale effort to educate all patients over 65 years of age about the need for both Prevnar 13 and Pneumovax 23 vaccinations to prevent pneumonia. In contrast, nurses may provide one-on-one instruction for a patient recently diagnosed with diabetes. The first step of any teaching-learning initiative is the assessment of the learning needs of the participants. Specific needs that will influence the design and content of the educational offering include the language preference and reading level of the participants. In addition, nurses must consider the effect of certain patient characteristics identified in the Synergy Model on the patient's capacity to process information. Diminished resiliency or stability, as well as extreme complexity, are examples of characteristics that must be considered in the development of the educational plan. Nurses are also responsible for creating a bridge between teaching-learning in the acute care setting and the home

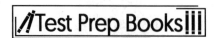

environment. A detailed discharge plan, close coordination with outpatient providers, and follow-up phone calls to the patient may be used to reinforce the patient's knowledge of the plan of care.

Successful learning plans for staff members and colleagues also consider the motivation of the participants to engage in the process. Successful facilitators include a variety of teaching strategies to develop the content and evaluate learning in order to address adult learning needs and preferences, such as preferred language and reading level. Research indicates that when adults do not have a vested interest in the outcomes of the teaching/learning process, they may not participate as active learners.

The remaining element of successful facilitation of learning to be considered is the availability and quality of learning resources. There is evidence that individuals with different learning styles respond differently to various learning devices. For instance, visual learners may be attracted to digital tools such as the iPad that can create interactive educational plans, which include self-study options for the patient. The minimum requirements for successful facilitation of learning include the skilled staff to develop the educational materials, paper, a copy machine, and staff to interact with the patient in the learning session.

Barriers to the facilitation of learning must be anticipated and accommodated. Changes in the patient's condition commonly require reduction in the time spent in each learning session due to fatigue. Cognitive impairment can impede comprehension and retention of the information and will require appropriate teaching aids. The learning abilities of the patient's family members must also be assessed. Adequate instruction time might be the greatest barrier. Learning needs are assessed and discharge planning is begun on the day of admission; however, shortened inpatient stays require evaluation of the patient's comprehension of the plan of care.

Lifelong Learning

Since the medical and healthcare fields are always rapidly changing due to technological advances, new research, organizational and governmental regulations, and through continuous process improvements in healthcare delivery, nurses can expect to continue their education throughout the course of their careers. Consequently, the ability to learn new topics will be a necessary skill in order to remain a competent practitioner. Lifelong learning and **continuing education** are associated with improved patient outcomes, job satisfaction, personal validation and achievement, and obtaining skills that were not taught or available at the time that the nurse was enrolled in a formal education program. The most crucial association with lifelong learning activities is the improvement in quality of care. Incompetent or unaware nursing staff means a great deal of risk for the patient. By constantly striving to improve their knowledge and practical skills, nurses decrease the chance that they will be held liable for negligence or malpractice, and they are taking tangible actions to adhere to the ethical tenets of the healthcare profession.

While avenues to continue professional development in the nursing field may be formal (e.g., obtaining extra relevant degrees or certifications, publishing research, or enrolling in trainings offered by the nurse's workplace), many opportunities require intrinsic motivation (e.g., taking personal initiative to keep abreast of current relevant literature, consulting with mentors, or experiencing different responsibilities within the field). However, even with these varied opportunities and the multitude of personal and professional benefits associated with lifelong learning activities, there are still some barriers for nurses. These include obstacles like disinterest, lack of time on the job or outside of the job to participate in activities, an inability to balance work and life needs with job demands, and lack of financial resources (to pay for educational activities and/or to take the time off to participate in them). In this regard, it is helpful for leadership and subordinate employees to work together to overcome these barriers.

Nurses who are in positions of leadership can promote a culture of lifelong learning by pushing for organizational support for development activities. In the event that development activities are free or hosted by the nurse's workplace, the nurse should recognize the valuable opportunity and take the time to attend and fully engage in the experience. This shows that such activities are in demand and valued and is likely to make affordable and accessible professional development activities part of the workplace culture.

Research

Nursing research is a crucial component of evidence-based practice (EBP), high quality healthcare delivery, and positive patient outcomes. Effective nursing research creates and compiles bodies of knowledge relating to all clinical and non-clinical aspects of nursing. Nurses who play a role in nursing research are typically advanced-level, senior practitioners who have the necessary experience to contribute further to existing bodies of nursing knowledge through personal expertise, the ability to run or be involved in conducting research trials, and in accurately collecting and analyzing data. **Nurse researchers** typically have advanced educational degrees, such as a master's or doctorate degree, and may work in specialized fields as a nurse practitioner. However, as entry-level nurses spend more time and gain more exposure to different aspects of the field, they should keep in mind that a nurse researcher is a highly skilled and rewarding career path that is critical to the development and advancement of the nursing field. High quality nursing research shapes the scope of clinical education for entry-level and experienced nurses; influences healthcare policy at the local, state, and federal levels; and enhances standard operating procedures within a healthcare organization. Together, these allow for organizations to deliver the highest level of care to patients who need them at the lowest costs.

Nurses who choose to pursue research as a career can expect to become involved in different aspects of research design and the research process. Nurse researchers will need to pass training modules that review the legalities and ethics of working with human populations in research, which is a different avenue than treating patients for disease or injury. Nurse researchers can expect to learn how to write research proposals, which serves as a large component of applying for funding, in addition to becoming familiar with seeking out viable funding sources. Depending on the end goal of the study, nurse researchers may learn how to design objective study trials, collect data through laboratory work or through sample surveys, conduct and interpret statistical data analysis, and write conclusive discussions about their findings.

Upon completion, nurse researchers can expect to be involved in the publication process, where a formal manuscript detailing the design and findings of the research study are submitted to scholarly journals. Journals often require extensive revisions and editing, so nurses should be prepared to follow up with their manuscripts. Most research projects include collaboration with doctorate-level researchers from other disciplines who share a vested interest in the topic or have skills to contribute to the project. For example, health research teams often include a biostatistician whose primary contribution is to compile, analyze, and interpret collected data. Entry-level nurses, interns, or students may choose to assist with simpler, but necessary, tasks such as survey administration or data entry. Recruiting individuals to help with these sorts of tasks can provide a great support to the research team.

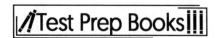
The National League for Nursing (NLN) is an organization in the United States that promotes research activities through networking, support, guidelines, and funding. The NLN publishes research priorities every four years. Current priorities include further investigating evidence-based practices, promoting research exposure to student learners in order to set the foundation for health promotion and disease prevention, and evaluating best practices relating to end-of-life and other life transitional care for both patients and their families. The NLN's website, www.nln.org, is an excellent resource for current nurses to find continuing education opportunities and explore research tools to support and enhance their career paths.

Evidence-Based Practice and Dissemination of Findings

Evidence-based practice (EBP) is a research-driven and facts-based methodology that allows healthcare providers to make scientifically supported, reliable, and validated decisions in delivering care. EBP considers rigorously tested, peer-reviewed, and published research relating to the case; the knowledge and experience of the healthcare provider; and clinical guidelines established by reputable governing bodies. This framework allows healthcare providers to reach case resolutions that result in positive patient outcomes in the most efficient manner, therefore allowing the organization to provide the best care using the least resources.

There are seven steps to successfully utilizing EBP as a methodology in the nursing field. First, the work culture should be one of a "spirit of inquiry." This culture allows staff to ask questions to promote continuous improvement and positive process change to workflow, clinical routines, and non-clinical duties. Second, the **PICOT framework** should be utilized when searching for an effective intervention, or working with a specific interest, in a case. The PICOT framework encourages nurses to develop a specific, measurable, goal-oriented research question that accounts for the patient population and demographics (P) involved in the case, the proposed intervention or issue of interest (I), a relevant comparison (C) group in which a defined outcome (O) has been positive, and the amount of time (T) needed to implement the intervention or address the issue. Once this question has been developed, staff can move onto the third step, which is to research. In this step, staff will explore reputable sources of literature (such as peer-reviewed scholarly journals, interviews with subject matter experts, or widely accepted textbooks) to find studies and narratives with evidence that supports a resolution for their question.

Once all research has been compiled, it must be thoroughly analyzed as part of the fourth step in the process. Analysis of data ensures that the staff is using unbiased research (stringent methodology, statistically significant outcomes, and reliable and valid research designs) and that all information collected is actually applicable to their patient. For example, if a certain treatment worked with statistical significance in a longitudinal study of pediatric patients with a large sample size, and all other influencing variables were controlled for, this treatment may not necessarily work in a middle-aged adult. Therefore, though the research collected is scientifically backed and evidence-based for a pediatric population, it does not support EBP for an older population. The fifth step is to integrate the evidence to create a treatment or intervention plan for the patient. The sixth step is to monitor the implementation of the treatment or intervention and evaluate whether it was associated with positive health outcomes in the patient. Finally, practitioners have a moral obligation to share the results with colleagues at the organization and across the field, so that it may be best utilized (or not) for other patients.

Evidence-Based Practice Flowchart

Specify Research Question

↓

Locate Potentially-Relevant Evidence

↓

Discard Poor Evidence ← Evaluate Evidence ↔ Update Evidence

↓

Assemble Relevant Evidence

↓

Use Evidence to Inform Decisions

Collaboration

Collaboration occurs when interested parties work together to achieve a mutual goal. According to the Synergy Model, nurses collaborate with the patient, family, and other providers to satisfy the patient's healthcare needs. Several attributes of the process have been identified, including goal setting, problem-solving, communicating, and decision-making, which serve as an indication of the skills required of the individuals involved in the collaborative process. Some of the benefits of collaboration include improved patient outcomes, decreased healthcare costs, decreased length of stay, improved patient and nurse satisfaction, and improved teamwork. Collaboration related to patient care has been widely studied and is considered as both a process and an outcome, which occurs when no single individual is able to solve a stakeholder (patient) problem. Collaboration as a process is defined as a synthesis of diverse opinions and skills that is employed to solve complex problems. As an outcome, collaboration is defined as a complex solution to a problem that requires the expertise of more than one individual. This view of collaboration characterizes the process as a series of actions by more than one individual, which creates a solution to a complex problem.

Initially, all members of the collaborative team must identify their own biases and acknowledge the effect of these mental models on the decision-making process. In addition, members must also be aware that the complexity of the problem will be matched by the complexity of the mental models of the collaborative team members, which will influence the decision-making process. It is also essential for team members to recognize the elements of diversity in the group. For instance, while stereotyping is obviously to be avoided, there are gender differences that should be considered. Research indicates that men tend to be more task-oriented, and women tend to be more relationship-oriented in the problem-solving process; this means that consideration of both points of view is necessary for genuine collaboration.

Another requisite skill of the collaborative team is the development and usage of conflict resolution skills, which are required to counteract this common barrier to effective collaboration. Team members are required to separate the task from the emotions that are inherent in the discussion. Effective collaboration also requires that members of the team display a cooperative effort that works to create a win-win situation, while recognizing that collaboration is a series of activities that require time and patience for satisfactory completion.

Common barriers to effective collaboration include conflicting professional opinions, ineffective communication related to the conflict, and incomplete assessment of the required elements of the care plan. Research indicates that physicians tend to stress "cure" related activities while nurses tend to encourage "care" related activities, which means that some resolution of these differences is required for effective communication. Although the Synergy Model defines collaboration as a necessary part of the process that matches the patient's needs with the appropriate nursing competencies, it is also possible that the end product of the collaborative process may be the best possible solution for the patient and at the same time be totally unacceptable to the patient. Collaborative team members should also be aware that while successful collaboration improves patient outcomes, research indicates that genuine collaborative efforts are rarely noted in patient care, often because the group is unable to integrate the diverse mental models of the group members. This means the initial first steps of the process mentioned previously are essential to the success of the collaborative process.

Systems Thinking

Systems thinking is defined as a link between individuals and their environment. For nurses, this refers to their ability to understand the influence of the healthcare environment on patient outcomes. Systems thinking is identified as the goal of all of the **Quality and Safety Education for Nurses** (QSEN) competencies, which are acquired by nurses on a continuum that ranges from the care of the individual patient to the care of the entire patient population. The QSEN competencies were originally identified to improve patient outcomes in response to extensive research that identified a significant difference between the care of patients and the improvement in patient outcomes resulting from that care. The nursing competencies include patient-centered care, evidence-based practice, teamwork and collaboration, safety, quality and improvement, and informatics. Successful interventions associated with each of these criteria for professional nursing practice require the ability to apply the systems thinking approach to care.

Competency related to systems thinking requires appropriate education and clinical experience and is also identified as one of the nursing competencies in the Synergy Model. In that model, novice nurses view the patient and family as isolated in the nursing unit rather than being influenced by the healthcare

200

system, while experienced nurses are able to integrate all of the resources in the healthcare system to improve patient outcomes. Several of the learning activities designed to improve nurses' ability to acquire systems thinking include creation of a grid that identifies the nursing competencies across the continuum from isolated, individual care to the level of care associated with systems thinking. There are assessment models that apply this exercise to specialty care units, such as emergency care, long-term care, and outpatient care, which identify specific systems needed for these areas.

Other exercises include tracking unit statistics for the QSEN competencies, followed by the creation, implementation, and evaluation of a plan that applies systems thinking to address that competency. All of these activities assist nurses to integrate patients' needs with all available resources in order to improve outcomes. **Root cause analysis** can also be used as a learning exercise for systems theory because this process, which is commonly used to investigate errors, looks at all elements of an institution's relationship with the error. Case studies and reflection are also recommended as useful learning aids for systems thinking. In addition, there are valid assessment instruments that can be used to assess systems thinking skills acquired through these learning activities.

The influence of systems thinking on patient outcomes is widely recognized, and most acute care institutions and nursing programs report that educational opportunities to provide nurses with the appropriate skills are offered; however, research indicates that there has been little progress toward the goal of systems thinking by all professional nurses since the initiation of the QSEN competencies more than 15 years ago. This lack of progress applies to both physicians and nurses, according to the available research related to physician education. Professional nurses are responsible for accessing all available resources to support their ability to employ systems thinking in the care of patients and in their role as preceptors for novice nurses. The ultimate benefit of systems thinking, related to the QSEN competencies, is improved patient safety, while the ultimate benefit of systems thinking in professional nursing practice is improved patient outcomes.

Clinical Inquiry

Clinical inquiry is an ongoing process that evaluates and challenges clinical practice in order to propose the needed change. Clinical inquiry has several components or attributes, including critical thinking, clinical reasoning, clinical judgment, critical reasoning and judgment, and creative thinking. The process is viewed as the critical structure for the establishment of evidence-based practice and quality improvement efforts. In the Synergy Model, professional nurses employ clinical inquiry to innovate and facilitate interventions that are appropriate to patient care needs. Clinical inquiry is a rigorous process that requires attention to the rules of nursing research, such as attention to sample size, and a correct match among the data, the study design, and the statistical measures. When used to implement evidence-based practice, clinical inquiry can result in replacing an outdated, even counterproductive nursing intervention with an intervention that effectively addresses the needs of the patient. Nurses who are involved in this form of clinical inquiry are viewed as evaluators and innovators in the Synergy Model. Matching patient needs with nursing competencies means that professional nurses are responsible for challenging all nursing interventions to be sure that they represent current best practice standards. As innovators, nurses are in the best position to research, implement, and evaluate alternative care practices.

Nurses acquire clinical inquiry skills on a continuum that is based on education and clinical experience. As is the case with the other nursing competencies included in the Synergy Model, this progressive development is consistent with **Benner's Novice to Expert model** that views the development of nursing expertise as a progressive process that requires ongoing education and clinical experience. Novice nurses are able to implement clinical innovations developed by others, identify their own learning needs, and enlist the aid of other nurses to identify critical needs of the patient. Experienced nurses are able to question the adequacy of interventions and challenge the "we have always done it this way" philosophy that is the most common rationale for many nursing interventions. They are also able to assess the utility of alternative interventions. The Synergy Model views the practice of expert nurses as the point at which clinical inquiry and clinical reasoning become inseparable elements of clinical practice. Expert nurses are able to predict changes in the patient's condition that require revision of the plan of care and are also able to develop and implement alternative approaches to address those changes.

Public funds are the most common source of research funding, which means that researchers are obligated to design studies that provide valid results that are applicable to some form of patient care and to disseminate the results appropriately. Common barriers to nursing research efforts include inadequate funding, limited access to appropriate patient populations, and lack of institutional support for research initiatives. The rapid expansion of new knowledge from multiple sources can also inhibit the assimilation and application of new care interventions by expert nurses. In addition, the final step of the clinical inquiry process, knowledge translation or dissemination, may be the most important step. **Knowledge translation** refers to the complex process of synthesizing the research findings, disseminating those findings to others, and integrating the findings into clinical practice. Barriers to this process include lack of rigor in the original research design with respect to sample size, data interpretation, and the applicability of the research findings. The failure of nursing researchers to access all possible modes of the dissemination of study results has also been identified as a significant barrier to the application of new interventions. All of these system-wide and individual barriers potentially limit the use of innovative patient care interventions.

Practice Quiz

1. Which of the following is cited as the MOST common source of funding for nursing research?
   a. Pharmaceutical companies
   b. Public funds
   c. Non-profit organizations
   d. Private institutions

2. The clinical practice of expert nurses reflects all of the nursing competencies identified in the Synergy Model. Which of the following ethical principles is the overall principle guiding nurses' actions?
   a. Beneficence
   b. Advocacy
   c. Autonomy
   d. Justice

3. Which of the following statements is consistent with the concept of moral agency?
   a. The patient's decisions will always be honored.
   b. Nurses assume accountability for their decisions.
   c. Institutions rarely act as moral agents.
   d. Advocacy and moral agency are interchangeable concepts.

4. Which of the following choices represents the learning sequence of a nurse, in the correct order from novice to expert, with regard to caring practices?
   a. The nurse anticipates the needs of the patient in the community; then, acknowledges death as a potential outcome; and finally, learns to respond to subtle changes in the patient's condition.
   b. The nurse facilitates solutions to patient and family concerns related to death and dying; then, modifies caring practices to the individual patient; and finally, learns to maintain a safe physical environment.
   c. The nurse bases care on standards and protocols; then, views death as an acceptable outcome; and finally, learns to anticipate and avoid patient problems.
   d. The nurse recognizes the patient as a unique being; then, facilitates the care of the patient across the caring continuum; and finally, learns to focus on the patient's customary needs.

5. Which of the following choices is most consistent with nursing responsibilities associated with advocacy?
   a. Notifying the nursing supervisor of any conflict to assure resolution of the patient issue
   b. Considering the patient's point of view and being prepared to support and explain the point of view as needed
   c. Providing comprehensive documentation of the patient's care in the EHR
   d. Understanding all relevant laws associated with the nursing care of the patient

See answers on the next page.

Answer Explanations

1. B: Research indicates that public funds are the most common source of funding, which means that researchers are obligated to design studies that provide valid results that are applicable to some form of patient care and to disseminate the results appropriately. The remaining sources listed in Choices *A*, *C*, and *D* also provide funding; however, public funds are noted to be the common source.

2. A: Beneficence is defined as doing good for another individual, which would include acting as an advocate, supporting the individual's autonomy, and working to ensure justice. While advocacy, autonomy, and justice (Choices *B*, *C*, and *D*) are relevant considerations in nursing practice, they are not the overall principle guiding nursing actions.

3. B: When nurses act as moral agents, they are required to also assume responsibility for their decisions. The patient's opinions will be identified and accommodated whenever possible; however, there may be conflict between the patient's opinions and the recommended plan of care, making Choice *A* incorrect. The institution may act as the moral agent for patients without any social support, making Choice *C* incorrect. The difference between moral agency and advocacy is the element of accountability. Moral agents are required to take responsibility for their decisions, making Choice *D* incorrect.

4. C: Novice nurses base their care on standards and protocols, experienced nurses view death as an acceptable outcome, and expert nurses anticipate and avoid patient problems. Choices *A*, *B*, and *D* identify the progression of novice to expert caring practices in random order. Choice *A*: Expert nurses anticipate the needs of the patient in the community, novice nurses acknowledge death as a potential outcome, and experienced nurses respond to subtle changes in the patient's condition. Choice *B*: Expert nurses facilitate solutions to patient and family concerns related to death and dying, experienced nurses modify caring practices for the individual patient, and novice nurses maintain a safe physical environment. Choice *D*: Experienced nurses recognize the patient as a unique being, expert nurses facilitate the care of the patient across the caring continuum, and novice nurses focus on the patient's customary needs.

5. B: Sharing, supporting, and explaining the patient's point of view are activities that are consistent with advocacy. Choices *A*, *C*, and *D* contribute to good professional practice but are not specifically related to the concept of advocacy.

PCCN Practice Test #1

1. A patient with worsening confusion is brought to the emergency department by their family. The patient is visibly jaundiced and has a history of liver failure. The patient is diagnosed with hepatic encephalopathy. What medication does the nurse anticipate administering to the patient?
   a. Haloperidol
   b. Lactulose
   c. Kayexalate
   d. Zyprexa

2. The nurse has noticed what appears to be an increase in patient falls on the unit in the last several months. What would be the most effective way to address this observation?
   a. Speak up in huddle, encouraging colleagues to be more vigilant about preventing patient falls.
   b. Submit a quality report if there is a patient fall. The hospital fall champion will follow the data.
   c. Observe the practice of interdisciplinary colleagues to see who is responsible for most of the falls.
   d. Talk to the unit manager and hospital falls champion to determine if there is an upward trend in falls and develop ideas for improvement.

3. A 55-year-old male presents with a cough producing rust-colored sputum, a fever (102° F), and shortness of breath. A complete blood count (CBC) reveals an elevated white blood cell count with predominant neutrophils. A chest x-ray reveals consolidation of the left, lower lobe of the lung. Blood cultures reveal gram-positive diplococci. What is the most likely cause of this patient's pneumonia?
   a. *Haemophilus influenzae*
   b. *Moraxella catarrhalis*
   c. *Streptococcus pneumoniae*
   d. *Staphylococcus aureus*

4. The nurse is caring for a patient with COPD who is prescribed tiotropium bromide. Which of the following statements by the patient indicates an understanding of the medication's action?
   a. "This medication will relax the muscles in my airways and help me breathe easier."
   b. "This medication will decrease the inflammation in my lungs and prevent exacerbations."
   c. "This medication will thin the mucus in my airways and make it easier to cough up."
   d. "This medication will stimulate the production of natural surfactant in my lungs."

5. The nurse is providing education to a patient with a history of PE who is prescribed Warfarin and asks about consuming foods high in vitamin K. Which of the following statements by the nurse is the most appropriate response?
   a. "It is important to avoid foods high in vitamin K because they can interfere with the effectiveness of Warfarin."
   b. "You should consume foods with vitamin K consistently to maintain a balanced diet while on Warfarin."
   c. "It is important to maintain a consistent intake of vitamin K to avoid sudden changes in Warfarin's effectiveness."
   d. "You should completely eliminate foods high in vitamin K from your diet to ensure the optimal effects of Warfarin."

6. A progressive care nurse is preparing a discharge plan for a patient with risk factors for acute pancreatitis. Which of the following information should be included in this plan?
   a. Endoscopic retrograde cholangiopancreatography (ERCP) imaging is required to confirm the diagnosis.
   b. Ultrasonography is the most useful imaging study when significant abdominal distention is present.
   c. Current research confirms the efficacy of rectal administration of indomethacin to reduce the incidence of pancreatitis due to the ERCP procedure.
   d. There is no scientific rationale to explain why some individuals with chronic ETOH abuse develop acute pancreatitis while others do not develop pancreatitis.

7. Which of the following words describes delirium and differentiates it from dementia?
   a. Slow onset
   b. Irreversible
   c. Chronic
   d. Transient

8. Which of the following correctly identifies a critical distinction between the two concepts of advocacy and moral agency?
   a. Advocacy is legally binding.
   b. Moral agency requires accountability for right and wrong decisions.
   c. Advocacy is implied in the paternalistic view of patient care.
   d. Moral agency only refers to support for at-risk populations.

9. What myocardial conduction defect is hereditary, may result in syncope or sudden death, and often occurs in healthy adults or children?
   a. Third-degree heart block
   b. First-degree heart block
   c. Bundle branch block
   d. Long QT syndrome

10. While assessing a patient who takes amitriptyline, which symptom supports the nurse's concern that the patient may be developing tardive dyskinesia?
   a. Tongue thrusting
   b. Headache
   c. Blurred vision
   d. Fever

11. Which of the following is a commonly used blood thinner that works by blocking the body's ability to adhere platelets together?
   a. Paroxetine
   b. Coumadin
   c. Heparin
   d. Aspirin

PCCN Practice Test #1

12. What is one evidence-based reason that some microbial bacteria have become resistant to antibiotics?
    a. Patients who are prescribed antibiotics and fail to finish the dosage
    b. Improper hand hygiene technique
    c. The presence of genetically modified organisms in the food system
    d. Overly sterile hospital environments

13. A hospice patient who is actively dying is experiencing Cheyne-Stokes respirations. What should the nurse explain to the family about this finding?
    a. The patient is unable to clear her airway and will need to be suctioned to make her more comfortable.
    b. The patient may be near death and may experience longer and longer pauses between breaths.
    c. The patient is in a comfortable deep sleep state.
    d. The patient is overly sedated from morphine.

14. The nurse is caring for a patient with manifestations of peptic ulcer disease (PUD). Which of the following statements is correct?
    a. Stomach pain begins 20 to 30 minutes after eating.
    b. The condition is associated with an increased risk of malignancy.
    c. An endoscopy is used to establish hemostasis.
    d. Chronic NSAID use is the most common etiology.

15. Which of the following nursing interventions is most consistent with the competencies of caring practices, advocacy, and moral agency?
    a. Developing cultural awareness of care team members
    b. Mentoring novice nurses in the use of research findings
    c. Facilitating the patient's transition from one level of care to another on the health continuum
    d. Refining educational programs for patients and families

16. All EXCEPT which of the following are components of Virchow's triad?
    a. Heart disease
    b. Hypercoagulability
    c. Endothelial injury/dysfunction
    d. Hemodynamic changes such as stasis or turbulence

17. A 49-year-old patient experiencing severe alcohol withdrawal exhibits vestibular disturbance by reporting which of the following symptoms?
    a. "I have a terrible headache."
    b. "The room seems like it's spinning!"
    c. "My hands won't stop shaking!"
    d. "I feel like I'm going to throw up."

207

18. A 77-year-old patient is admitted with pneumonia. The patient is on three different antibiotics to treat the pneumonia. The patient begins to produce a foul-smelling diarrhea. Which intervention should the nurse anticipate?
   a. Place a contact sign on the door and collect a stool sample for testing.
   b. Place a bedside commode next to the patient's bed and provide wipes.
   c. Start the patient on intravenous fluids and monitor intake and output.
   d. Place the patient on nothing by mouth status and provide only ice chips.

19. The nurse is caring for a long-term steroid user with an extensive trauma wound. As part of the shift assessment, the nurse changes the wound dressing and notes that the area around the wound is red and warm and there is pus in the wound bed. The patient's vital signs are BP 108/70, pulse 110, respiration 20, and temperature 101.2 °F. What is the best INITIAL action for the nurse to take?
   a. Complete the assessment and recheck the wound site in one hour.
   b. Administer medication for pain.
   c. Notify the physician and prepare to draw blood cultures.
   d. Call the medical emergency team.

20. Which of the following statements is true?
   a. As fluid levels decrease, electrolyte levels increase.
   b. As fluid levels increase, electrolyte levels increase.
   c. As fluid levels osmose, electrolyte levels diffuse.
   d. As fluid levels homogenize, electrolyte levels dissipate.

21. A progressive care nurse is caring for a patient with the following entries in the EHR: 1) patient admitted with fever of unknown origin and atypical abdominal pain for three days; 2) patient has requested DNR status; however, the patient's son has voiced objections to that order; and 3) patient demonstrates lab evidence of chronic renal failure. According to the Synergy Model, which of the following statements is consistent with this information?
   a. The patient demonstrates high stability.
   b. The patient's history is consistent with multiple resources.
   c. The patient's condition indicates low vulnerability.
   d. The patient's status is highly complex.

22. A patient with elevated liver enzymes, ascites, jaundice, weight loss, and anemia is admitted to the hospital. The patient is diagnosed with uncompensated cirrhosis. What modifiable risk factor likely contributed to this patient's condition?
   a. History of intravenous drug abuse
   b. History of controlled diabetes with an A1c of 5.9
   c. History of uncontrolled hypertension
   d. History of alcohol abuse

23. High blood sugar stimulates the kidneys to do which of the following?
   a. Produce less urine
   b. Concentrate the urine
   c. Retain more sodium
   d. Produce more urine

24. When attempting to diagnose a PE in a patient with renal failure, which type of scan will likely be performed?
    a. Transesophageal echocardiography
    b. CT scan with contrast
    c. MRI of the thoracic cage
    d. V/Q scan

25. Which of the following statements is consistent with the basic assumption of the QSEN competencies?
    a. The use of systems thinking by all providers will narrow the differences between the care that is delivered and the rate of positive outcomes.
    b. Systems thinking is the goal of all nursing competencies.
    c. Successful application of all QSEN nursing competencies will improve patient safety.
    d. The ability to use systems thinking is dictated by the nurse's level of basic nursing education.

26. Which of the following statements made by the patient would cause the nurse to suspect an abdominal aortic aneurysm (AAA)?
    a. "I have indigestion when I lie down."
    b. "I often have a pulsating sensation in my abdomen."
    c. "I get fatigued and short of breath on exertion."
    d. "I have extreme pain radiating down my left arm."

27. The nurse is caring for a patient who presents with a pneumothorax. Upon assessment, the nurse notes that the patient has no evidence of a rib fracture or associated lung disease. Which type of pneumothorax should the nurse suspect in this patient?
    a. Tension pneumothorax
    b. Spontaneous pneumothorax
    c. Traumatic pneumothorax
    d. Iatrogenic pneumothorax

28. While working with a patient who is three days post-op from an open coronary artery bypass graft (CABG), the progressive care nurse notices that the patient looks pale and feels cold while ambulating in their room. What action does the nurse take first to prevent a fall?
    a. Assist the patient back to bed.
    b. Encourage the patient to eat a snack.
    c. Increase the flow rate on the patient's nasal cannula.
    d. Assess the patient's vital signs.

29. A diabetic patient presents to the emergency department with vision changes and weakness in the left arm starting three hours ago. An NIHSS is completed with a score of 6. The VAN stroke assessment is negative. A CT scan shows no hemorrhage. What intervention should be the nurse's priority?
    a. Echocardiogram with bubble study
    b. Cerebral angiogram
    c. Administration of thrombolytic medication
    d. Preparing patient for thrombectomy

209

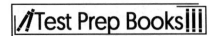

30. Diabetic ketoacidosis is an acute complication that occurs primarily in patients who have which of the following?
    a. Type 1 diabetes
    b. Type 2 diabetes
    c. Gestational diabetes
    d. A primarily ketogenic diet

31. What serological marker indicates that cardiac muscle tissue has been damaged and cell contents are being released into the bloodstream?
    a. Creatinine
    b. BUN
    c. CK-MB
    d. Troponin

32. The progressive care nurse is caring for a patient with an emerging ischemic stroke. The nurse should prepare to administer which of the following fibrinolytic agents?
    a. Urokinase
    b. Streptokinase
    c. Alteplase
    d. Tenecteplase

33. Which of the following is a contraindication for thrombolytic therapy?
    a. Current anticoagulant therapy
    b. Over age 75
    c. Severe hepatic disease
    d. INR of 3.5

34. The progressive care nurse is caring for a patient recovering from an ischemic stroke. The patient has been cleared for a bedside swallow screening. Which of the following patient responses would require prompt cessation of the screening and a further evaluation from a speech-language pathologist?
    a. Excessive chewing
    b. Pocketing food
    c. Frequently requesting water
    d. Eating slowly

35. A patient is admitted due to altered mental status and presents with a distended abdomen, bilateral lower extremity edema, and yellow conjunctiva. The patient's laboratory results reveal elevated liver enzymes and elevated serum ammonia. Which of the following medications does the nurse anticipate administering to treat this patient?
    a. Lactulose
    b. Thiamine
    c. Furosemide
    d. Hydrochlorothiazide

Test Prep Books

36. Which of the following nursing interventions would be an example of systems thinking?
    a. Ensuring that the patients who are being discharged have all of their prescriptions
    b. Organizing a teaching/learning session for patients and families on the nursing unit related to the importance of handwashing
    c. Soliciting performance evaluations from colleagues
    d. Participating in the agency implementation of the electronic health record

37. A patient with a known femur fracture begins to complain of severe pain to the affected leg. The leg is unrelieved with pain medication. The nurse notes that the patient's foot is pale and pedal pulse is not palpable. What should be the nurse's initial intervention?
    a. Call for an x-ray.
    b. Loosen the patient's splint.
    c. Elevate the limb above the level of the heart.
    d. Prepare for heparin infusion.

38. A patient has been admitted to the progressive care unit for intercranial hemorrhage following a fall while on apixaban. The patient presents with left-sided facial droop, slurred speech, severe headache, and weakness on the left. Which of the following orders would the nurse question?
    a. Pupillometry monitoring every 2 hours
    b. IV administration of prothrombin complex concentrate
    c. Oral levetiracetam
    d. IV esmolol

39. Which of the following is a common symptom of COPD?
    a. Dry cough
    b. Morning headache
    c. Narrow chest
    d. Weight gain

40. Which item in the family history assessment performed by the progressive care nurse is a red flag for hypertrophic cardiomyopathy and should be investigated further?
    a. Heart disease of the father
    b. Diabetes mellitus of the mother
    c. Sudden death of a grandmother
    d. Stroke of a grandfather

41. According to the Synergy Model, at what level of nursing competence do the nursing competencies of clinical inquiry and clinical reasoning become inseparable in the research process?
    a. The experienced nurse
    b. The novice nurse
    c. The expert nurse
    d. All levels of competency

42. Immunocompromised patients should do which of the following?

      I. Always practice extraordinary personal hygiene and handwashing habits.
      II. Avoid eating moldy cheeses, such as blue cheese.
      III. Only drink bottled water.
      IV. Ask for help with caring for pets and taking out trash.

    a. I and IV only
    b. I, II, and III
    c. I, II, and IV
    d. All of the above

43. The primary cause of catheter-associated urinary tract infection (CAUTI) is which of the following?
    a. Urinary retention when the catheter becomes blocked
    b. Immune system compromise in acutely ill, hospitalized patients
    c. Trauma to the urethra from catheter insertion
    d. Bacteria that ascend either on the surface or in the lumen of the catheter

44. A patient who has been NPO all morning for a cardiac catheterization complains of nausea and "just not feeling right." The nurse notices that he is sweating. What condition should the nurse suspect and investigate right away?
    a. Hypochondria
    b. Hypoglycemia
    c. Hypotension
    d. Hypothyroidism

45. A patient with uncontrolled diabetes is admitted due to intractable nausea and vomiting. Diabetic gastroparesis is their diagnosis. What medication is likely to be ordered for the patient to help with gastric emptying?
    a. Ondansetron
    b. Long-acting Insulin
    c. Dicyclomine
    d. Metoclopramide

46. Which of the following would NOT indicate arterial insufficiency?
    a. Cyanosis of lower extremities
    b. Loss of hair in legs
    c. Sores that will not heal
    d. Pooling of blood and edema

47. Which of the following surgeries performed by a cardiothoracic surgeon removes a section of an airway leading to the lung, sewing together the top and bottom of the section removed?
    a. Pneumonectomy
    b. Lobectomy
    c. Sleeve resection
    d. Wedge resection

48. Which type of drug class is often used to reduce preload in cardiogenic pulmonary edema?
    a. Beta-blockers such as metoprolol
    b. Calcium channel blockers such as verapamil
    c. Narcotics such as morphine
    d. Diuretics such as furosemide

49. Which of the following patients is NOT at increased risk for the development of an embolism?
    a. A 24-year-old with a broken femur
    b. An 85-year-old female with a history of a stroke
    c. A 62-year-old male with first-degree heart block
    d. A 19-year-old female two weeks postpartum

50. What differentiating factor would let a nurse know that a lower extremity ulcer is arterial rather than venous?
    a. Color of wound
    b. Culture taken from wound
    c. Depth of wound
    d. Measurement of wound

51. How long should a patient have a central line?
    a. The shortest possible time, as decided by the patient's care team
    b. Until the patient is discharged from the hospital
    c. Until the patient requests its removal
    d. Until the care team anticipates that the patient no longer needs intravenous medication

52. Which of the following medications administered during status asthmaticus targets the systemic inflammation being experienced by the patient?
    a. Inhaled bronchodilators
    b. Subcutaneous epinephrine
    c. Nebulized albuterol
    d. Oral corticosteroids

53. A progressive care nurse is caring for a patient who had a colectomy two days ago. While assisting the patient back to bed, the nurse notes that the patient's heart rate and respiratory rate are slightly elevated, and the patient states, "I can feel my pulse." The nurse assesses the patient for additional signs of heart failure. This intervention is an example of which of the following caring practices according to the Synergy Model?
    a. Engagement by a novice nurse
    b. Vigilance by an experienced nurse
    c. An expected response to predictable changes by the novice nurse
    d. Collaboration by an experienced nurse

213

54. An 18-year-old female on the unit is complaining of worsening wheezing, shortness of breath, and a cough over the past twelve hours. She has a history of asthma and has been using her albuterol metered-dose inhaler (MDI) frequently for the last two hours. She was given supplemental oxygen, both albuterol and ipratropium via nebulizer, and methylprednisolone IV in quick succession. Shortly afterwards, she began complaining of anxiety, hand tremors, and her pulse rate increased from 80 to 120 beats per minute (bpm). Which treatment is most likely responsible for her anxiety, tremors, and tachycardia?

    a. Supplemental oxygen
    b. Albuterol
    c. Ipratropium
    d. Methylprednisolone

55. Which of the following options correctly names the type of common medication used to treat anxiety and depression?

    a. Antipsychotics
    b. Selective serotonin reuptake inhibitors (SSRIs)
    c. Dopamine reuptake inhibitors
    d. Homeopathic options

56. The nurse is providing discharge teaching to a patient on how to de-access a portacath after delivery of a three-day infusion. Which technique will best prepare the patient to perform the de-access successfully and safely?

    a. Providing and reviewing detailed written instructions from the hospital's patient education library
    b. Explaining the process to the patient and then asking the patient questions to assess whether they have understood
    c. Referring the patient to a hospital-approved video on the process
    d. Using a model portacath and port needle to teach the patient and then having the patient teach the process back to the nurse

57. There is a sentinel event on the acute care floor involving a medication error made by a nurse. Which is the most appropriate group of people to participate in a root cause analysis?

    a. The nurse who gave the drug, the nurse manager, the chief nursing officer, and hospital risk management
    b. The nurse who gave the drug, the physician who wrote the order, the attorney for the hospital, and a representative from the community
    c. All members of the nursing staff on the unit
    d. The nurse who gave the drug, the physician who wrote the order, and representatives from pharmacy, nursing, and medical leadership

58. A patient with an acute kidney injury has the following medications ordered. Which order should the nurse question?

    a. Bumetanide
    b. Vancomycin
    c. Acetaminophen
    d. Senna glycoside

59. Which category of pneumonia is more likely to occur in a patient who is undergoing chemotherapy for metastatic lung cancer?
    a. Community-acquired
    b. Hospital-acquired
    c. Immunocompromised
    d. Healthcare-associated

60. Which of the following is NOT an example of a drug that may cause respiratory failure in higher doses or in sensitive patients?
    a. Morphine
    b. Hydrocodone
    c. Naloxone
    d. Alprazolam

61. A patient with a diagnosis of seasonal influenza is being admitted to the acute care floor after surgery that followed a motor vehicle crash. The patient has been on antiviral medication for three days. Their temperature has been normal, but they are still showing symptoms of cough and fatigue. How should the nurse prepare to admit this patient?
    a. The patient should be placed on droplet precautions in a private room.
    b. The patient should be placed on airborne precautions in a negative pressure room.
    c. The patient can be admitted on standard precautions since they have started their antiviral treatment for influenza.
    d. The patient should be placed on droplet precautions in a shared room.

62. According to the literature, which of the following interventions would most likely be chosen by a physician in a collaborative group?
    a. Initiating a Social Service referral to address caregiver strain
    b. Fitting the patient with a brace to treat the effects of foot drop
    c. Providing the patient's wife with the names of local Parkinson's support groups
    d. Facilitating the family's request for spiritual care

63. A nurse is about to enter the room of an acutely ill patient in droplet isolation. Which personal protective equipment (PPE) should the nurse don FIRST?
    a. Gloves
    b. Mask
    c. Gown
    d. Goggles

64. During a level of consciousness assessment, the nurse finds no articulated verbal response with limited moaning, accompanied by arousal only after vigorous stimulation. How should the nurse document these findings?
    a. "The patient is lethargic."
    b. "The patient is obtunded."
    c. "The patient is stuporous."
    d. "The patient is comatose."

65. The nurse is forming a question using the PICOT (population, intervention, control, outcome, time) format to examine methods of urinary catheterization in the clinical setting. Which formulation meets the PICOT criteria?
   a. Does intermittent catheterization result in fewer cases of CAUTI than indwelling catheterization?
   b. For post surgical patients, does intermittent catheterization result in fewer cases of CAUTI over seven days as compared to indwelling catheterization?
   c. For post-surgical patients, does intermittent catheterization result in fewer cases of CAUTI over seven days?
   d. Over seven days, does intermittent catheterization result in fewer cases of CAUTI than indwelling catheterization?

66. Which of the following metabolic components involved in diabetic ketoacidosis is responsible for the "fruity" smell that a person with DKA gives off when they breathe?
   a. Alanine
   b. Triglycerides
   c. Acetone
   d. Glycerol

67. The nurse is caring for a patient with an acute exacerbation of congestive heart failure (CHF). Which clinical manifestation should be most concerning to the nurse?
   a. An oxygenation level of 92%
   b. Dyspnea on exertion
   c. New onset of peripheral edema
   d. Elevated BNP levels

68. A patient who is 3 days postoperative following a burr hole surgery becomes confused, febrile, and diaphoretic, with a severe headache and nuchal rigidity. The care team suspects meningitis. Which of the following would confirm this diagnosis?
   a. Blood cultures
   b. Nasopharyngeal swab
   c. Head CT
   d. Lumbar puncture

69. Patients on the cusp of respiratory failure may exhibit which of the following symptoms?
   a. Decreased respiratory rate
   b. Unconsciousness
   c. Cyanosis
   d. Agitation

216

70. The nurse is caring for a patient with influenza during a widespread, national outbreak of a new strain. A vaccine for the strain has been developed, but the patient's son says, "I don't need to get vaccinated. Eventually enough people will get sick that we'll have herd immunity to protect us." What is the best response by the nurse?
   a. "You're right. Getting vaccinated is a personal choice, and your choice to not get vaccinated won't hurt anyone."
   b. "It might be true that getting the vaccine is as dangerous as getting sick with influenza, but vaccination is still a good idea."
   c. "If you don't get vaccinated, you'll have blood on your hands."
   d. "There is overwhelming scientific evidence indicating that vaccination is safer than getting the disease. To protect vulnerable people during an outbreak, all healthy people should get vaccinated."

71. A 65-year-old ex-smoker presents with a complaint of increasing shortness of breath over the past 24 hours. He has a medical history of chronic obstructive pulmonary disease (COPD). The following therapeutic agents were administered to this patient: supplemental oxygen, albuterol via nebulizer, methylprednisolone IV, and a dose of azithromycin IV. Which of these therapies has been clinically proven to decrease the risk of treatment failure and death?
   a. Supplemental oxygen
   b. Albuterol
   c. Methylprednisolone
   d. Azithromycin

72. A 44-year-old male patient calls the progressive care nurse to the room, complaining of chest pain and shortness of breath. Examination by the nurse reveals distended neck veins and muffled heart sounds. The patient's blood pressure is 80/55 mmHg. The nurse should suspect which of the following?
   a. Cardiac tamponade
   b. Abdominal aortic aneurysm (AAA)
   c. Cardiopulmonary arrest
   d. Cardiogenic shock

73. The PCCN who is employed in the Cardiac Care Unit is reassigned to the Neonatal Intensive Care Unit for the evening. The PCCN refuses the assignment based on a lack of experience caring for newborn infants. This action is based on which of the following ethical principles?
   a. Advocacy
   b. Nonmaleficence
   c. Autonomy
   d. Fidelity

74. Stage 5 of chronic kidney disease usually requires which of the following to manage the condition?
   a. Steroid and antidiuretic hormone injections
   b. Dialysis or a kidney transplant
   c. A full-time home health aide
   d. Hospice services

75. What is one way a woman may present differently than a man when experiencing a myocardial infarction (MI)?
    a. Symptoms beginning days to weeks before actual attack
    b. Profuse sweating
    c. Crushing chest pain
    d. Elevated serological markers

76. PCCN practice is based on the principles of ethical behavior. Which of the following correctly identifies the moral principle that may require knowledge of the legislative process?
    a. Fidelity
    b. Autonomy
    c. Advocacy
    d. Beneficence

77. The nurse is caring for an 80-year-old patient who has been confined to bed on the acute care floor for three days. The nurse notes an area of redness on the patient's elbows. The patient says, "I probably bumped them on the bed rail." Upon assessment, the nurse notes that the skin is unbroken, the redness does not blanch, and the area feels warm to the touch. The nurse knows that this most likely reflects which finding?
    a. Abrasion from the bed linens
    b. Bruising from the bed rails
    c. A stage two pressure injury
    d. A stage one pressure injury

78. What is the most common bacterial cause of pneumonias in patients?
    a. *Streptococcus pneumoniae*
    b. *Klebsiella pneumoniae*
    c. *Chlamydophila pneumoniae*
    d. *Mycoplasma pneumoniae*

79. Which of the following is an indication for the placement of a vena cava filter to prevent pulmonary embolism (PE)?
    a. Pregnancy
    b. Documented recurrent PE
    c. Active smoking history
    d. Age > 65 years

80. Which of the following is the best antibiotic treatment for pneumonia caused by community-associated methicillin-resistant Staphylococcus aureus (CA-MRSA)?
    a. Azithromycin
    b. Doxycycline
    c. Vancomycin
    d. Levofloxacin

81. Which pH imbalance is the patient experiencing with the following ABG results: pH 7.51, PaCO2 72 mm/Hg, HCO3 41 mEq/L.
    a. Metabolic acidosis
    b. Fully compensated metabolic alkalosis
    c. Respiratory alkalosis
    d. Partially compensated metabolic alkalosis

82. The nurse is caring for a patient with OSA who has been prescribed CPAP therapy. Which of the following statements by the patient indicates an understanding of the purpose of CPAP therapy?
    a. "The CPAP machine will help me fall asleep faster."
    b. "CPAP therapy will cure my sleep apnea completely."
    c. "The CPAP machine will keep my airway open while I sleep."
    d. "CPAP therapy will help me breathe in more oxygen during the night."

83. Which of the following learning exercises related to systems thinking potentially provides the most comprehensive view of the institution?
    a. Root cause analysis
    b. Competency grids
    c. Process diagrams
    d. Case studies

84. Which patient would have an absolute contraindication to being placed in the prone position as a treatment plan for ARDS?
    a. The 22-year-old female patient following abdominal surgery for a hysterectomy
    b. The 68-year-old male patient following a hemorrhagic stroke with marginally increased ICP
    c. The 35-year-old male patient with an unstable vertebral fracture following an MVC
    d. The 83-year-old female patient following a minimally invasive CABG

85. Which of the following anemia categories, in which heme and globin do not synthesize appropriately, does thalassemia fall into?
    a. Thrombocytopenic
    b. Macrocytic
    c. Normocytic
    d. Microcytic

86. The nurse is caring for a patient with acute kidney injury who is prescribed erythropoietin. The nurse understands that this medication is used for what purpose?
    a. To stimulate red blood cell production
    b. To increase urine output
    c. To combat infection
    d. To suppress the immune system

87. An acutely ill patient with broken ribs after trauma is being given IV and PO pain medications. What additional medication does the nurse expect to see ordered at this time to combat a common side effect of this drug class?
    a. Methadone
    b. Clarithromycin
    c. Carbamazepine
    d. Docusate sodium

88. The nurse is teaching a student how to draw blood cultures to assess a patient with neutropenic fever for a central line-associated blood stream infection (CLABSI). Which statement by the student would show that they require further teaching?
    a. "I will draw samples from two sites: the central line and a venipuncture on the other arm."
    b. "Samples from both sites will go in both an aerobic container and an anaerobic container."
    c. "I will flush the central line and waste 5 mL of blood before drawing my sample."
    d. "I will draw blood cultures before the initiation of antibiotics, if possible."

89. A progressive care nurse is providing discharge education for a 66-year-old patient with type 2 diabetes who has had a TIA. Which of the following patient statements indicates that the teaching has been effective?
    a. "There is nothing I can do to change my risk for another episode."
    b. "The best thing I can do is to keep my A1C level below 6.5 like my doctor said."
    c. "I only have type 2 diabetes, so that doesn't affect my blood vessels."
    d. "I'm glad I don't have to take insulin to fix this."

90. A nurse is preparing a teaching plan for a patient with the following characteristics: moderately impaired resiliency, stability, and complexity. Which of the following teaching-learning approaches is most appropriate for this patient?
    a. Provide a one-hour teaching-learning session twice a day for the next two days.
    b. Provide the patient with written information from a nursing journal.
    c. Leave the instructions for the outpatient care provider.
    d. Meet with the patient for 15–20 minutes to assess their ability to participate.

91. A patient is admitted to the progressive care unit for a stroke. The patient is alert and interactive with staff. The patient is able to tell the nurse their age but cannot remember the month. The patient follows commands when asked to close their eyes and make a fist. The patient has no visual deficits; however, they have a facial droop when they smile. The patient is unable to move their right arm or leg, but the left limbs move smoothly with no drift or ataxia. The patient's sensation is intact. The patient's speech is slightly slurred. While they struggle to identify some objects, they are able to express themselves with some time. The patient appears to have no extinction. What is this patient's score on the NIH Stroke Scale?
    a. 9
    b. 12
    c. 13
    d. 10

92. A decreased amount of vasopressin in the body will likely produce which of the following conditions?
    a. SIADH
    b. Diabetes type I
    c. Diabetes insipidus
    d. Diabetes type II

93. A patient with end-stage renal disease has been admitted after missing two scheduled dialysis appointments due to being ill. Upon admission, which ECG finding does the nurse initially expect?
    a. Peaked T waves
    b. Depressed T waves
    c. Widened QRS
    d. Shortened QRS

94. Which of the following has NOT been identified as a barrier to the application of nursing research findings to clinical practice?
    a. Inadequate funding
    b. Insufficient translation
    c. Lack of qualified nursing staff
    d. Limited patient populations

95. A patient with primary hypertension is being treated with medications to reduce blood volume and lower systemic vascular resistance (SVR). Which of the following medication combinations should the progressive care nurse anticipate for the patient?
    a. A diuretic and a calcium channel blocker (CCB)
    b. A diuretic and an angiotensin-converting enzyme (ACE) inhibitor
    c. An angiotensin II receptor blocker (ARB) and morphine
    d. A diuretic and a beta-blocker

96. Which of the following statements about diabetes is correct?
    a. Type 2 diabetes mellitus is diagnosed based on the pancreas's inability to produce insulin.
    b. Gestational diabetes mellitus is diagnosed based on the mother's inability to produce glucose.
    c. Type 3 diabetes mellitus is diagnosed based on the pancreas's inability to produce insulin.
    d. Type 1 diabetes mellitus is diagnosed based on the pancreas's inability to produce insulin.

97. Which of the following is NOT a congenital heart defect found in the tetralogy of Fallot?
    a. Pulmonary valve stenosis
    b. Ventricular septal defect
    c. Atrial septal defect
    d. Hypertrophic right ventricle

98. The nurse is doing a pain assessment on a patient who had hip replacement surgery two years ago. The patient describes their pain as a dull ache deep in the affected hip. It is improved with movement but gets worse with cold. It does not radiate, burn, or sting. The patient has been experiencing this pain daily for six months despite medical assessment and various pain relief modalities. The patient is most likely experiencing which type of pain?
   a. Acute pain
   b. Neuropathic pain
   c. Visceral pain
   d. Chronic pain

99. What other condition may mimic the symptoms of a heart attack?
   a. Cirrhosis of the liver
   b. Kidney failure
   c. Acid reflux
   d. Pneumonia

100. What type of drug therapy coupled with antithrombotic therapy is often used post-endarterectomy?
   a. Antiplatelet
   b. Beta-blocker
   c. Angiotensin-converting enzyme
   d. Angiotensin II receptor blockers

101. Which of the following is an appropriate protocol in attempts to prevent hospital-acquired pneumonia?
   a. Administer broad-spectrum antibiotics to all high-risk patients.
   b. Limit patient visitors to prevent excessive exposure to pathogens.
   c. Provide routine oral hygiene for all high-risk patients.
   d. Encourage sufficient fluid intake.

102. Which of the following solutions is used to correct the hyponatremia associated with syndrome of inappropriate antidiuretic hormone (SIADH)?
   a. Normal saline
   b. Hypertonic saline
   c. Hypotonic saline
   d. Lactated ringer's solution

103. Which of the following lifestyle modifications would address the major cause of most aortic aneurysms?
   a. Low-fat diet
   b. Smoking cessation
   c. Exercise program
   d. Meditation

104. Which of the following actions by a patient with COPD creates their own positive end-expiratory pressure?
    a. Tripod posing
    b. Wide open-mouth breathing
    c. Pursed-lip breathing
    d. Frequent coughing

105. What is the purpose of assessing a post-void residual on a stroke patient?
    a. To monitor for neurogenic bladder
    b. To monitor for urinary tract infection
    c. To ensure catheter is placed correctly
    d. To monitor for diabetes insipidus

106. All EXCEPT which of the following help define acute respiratory distress syndrome (ARDS)?
    a. Timing
    b. Origin of edema
    c. Pulmonary artery wedge pressure
    d. Severity of hypoxemia

107. The progressive care nurse is caring for a patient with congestive heart failure and is reviewing their medications with them during medication teaching. The patient expresses concern about their potassium level after recalling an issue with low potassium when prescribed a diuretic in the past. Which medication does the nurse explain is a potassium-sparing diuretic during this teaching?
    a. Furosemide
    b. Torsemide
    c. Spironolactone
    d. Hydrochlorothiazide

108. Which of the following ethical principles is most closely related to advocacy?
    a. Distributive justice
    b. Beneficence
    c. Nonmaleficence
    d. Fidelity

109. A patient with a bowel obstruction is admitted to the progressive care unit. The patient is nauseated and feels the need to vomit. The patient's orders include intravenous fluids for dehydration as well as pain medication. What is the nurse's priority intervention?
    a. Give nausea medication.
    b. Place a nasogastric tube to low intermittent suction.
    c. Start intravenous fluids for dehydration.
    d. Administer pain medication.

110. The Synergy Model proposes a novel paradigm of nursing. Which of the following statements correctly identifies a characteristic of nursing practice in this model?
    a. Resiliency
    b. Creativity
    c. Collaboration
    d. Complexity

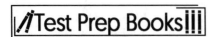

111. A patient with a bowel obstruction begins to have increasing abdominal pain and distention. The patient is found to have a fever and increased heart rate. Morning labs showed an increased white blood cell count. Ischemic bowel is suspected. What noninvasive diagnostic study will help with identification of this disease?
    a. Abdominal x-ray
    b. Mesenteric angiography
    c. Abdominal computed tomography (CT) scan
    d. CT angiography

112. A progressive care nurse is caring for a patient who had a seizure today for the first time. The patient said that she noticed a strange odor just prior to "not feeling well." Vital signs: BP 120/74, HR 76, and an oral temperature 97.8°F. The patient has no complaints of pain and no recent history of viral or bacterial illness. A friend witnessed that seizure and stated that the muscular movement lasted about 30 seconds. The patient was incontinent during the seizure but did not suffer any injuries. The patient recovered without any further manifestations of seizure activity. Which of the following interventions is most appropriate for this patient?
    a. Obtain laboratory analysis of recreational drug use.
    b. Institute oral therapy of AEDs.
    c. Prepare the patient for an immediate lumbar puncture for CSF analysis.
    d. Obtain an EEG and an MRI.

113. The progressive care nurse understands that which of the following is the most concerning symptom associated with peripheral vascular disease (PVD)?
    a. Faint peripheral pulses
    b. Restricted mobility
    c. Critical limb ischemia
    d. Pale feet when elevated

114. What test is often used to determine if a patient has peripheral arterial disease?
    a. Echocardiography
    b. CT scan of the leg
    c. Electrocardiogram
    d. Ankle-brachial BP index

115. Which of the following word pairs identifies the six Cs of caring practices that are most closely associated with caring for acutely ill patients?
    a. Compassion and curiosity
    b. Confidence and collaboration
    c. Conscience and creativity
    d. Commitment and competence

116. A progressive care nurse is caring for a patient who is being evaluated for a small-bowel obstruction. Which of the following assessment findings is consistent with this condition?
    a. pH 7.32, PCO_2 38, HCO_3 20
    b. Serum osmolality 285 mOsm/kg
    c. Serum sodium 128 mmol/L
    d. Lower abdominal distention

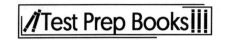

117. A STEMI, in which the full thickness of the heart wall has been damaged, results in which of the following ECG changes?
    a. T-wave inversion
    b. ST-segment elevation
    c. QT prolongation
    d. U-wave elevation

118. The hospital pharmacy is going through a critical system update. As a result, the nurse experiences a temporary delay in availability of certain non-urgent medications. Which action represents systems thinking on the nurse's part?
    a. Submit a quality report to the hospital's reporting system because medications should be available immediately and the delay is unacceptable.
    b. Tell the patient, "I know it's frustrating how slow the pharmacy is today."
    c. Explain to the patient the reason for the delay and work with the charge nurse to manage the delays.
    d. Call the pharmacy to request that the medications be sent immediately.

119. A patient is admitted with a diagnosis of heart failure. Which assessment finding supports the diagnosis of left-sided heart failure?
    a. Pitting edema
    b. Ascites
    c. Fatigue
    d. Tachycardia

120. What is the most common cause of edema caused by venous insufficiency?
    a. Deep vein thrombosis (DVT)
    b. Obesity
    c. Pregnancy
    d. Old age

121. The progressive care nurse is admitting a new 72-year-old male patient to the unit. As she works through her assessment, the nurse recognizes that which of the following is NOT a risk factor for falls for this patient in this environment?
    a. Using a cane to walk
    b. Inadequate lighting in a room
    c. Muscle weakness
    d. Slower reflexes

122. The geriatric care unit has started using linens from a new vendor. Over the course of a few months, the nurse notices that it seems like there are more patients with pressure injuries than before the change. Which step by the nurse best reflects the spirit of clinical inquiry?
    a. Getting permission to examine data on pressure injuries before and after the vendor change
    b. Going to hospital administration and advocating for a return to the old vendor
    c. Telling the manager and letting leadership handle it
    d. Asking hospital leadership why the vendor change was made

123. Which of the following is NOT a usual sign that a patient is in shock?
   a. Increased urine output
   b. Distant heart sounds
   c. Bluish tinted skin
   d. Faint and rapid pulse

124. Which of the following statements is correct?
   a. The sodium-potassium pump is responsible for membrane potential.
   b. The calcium-phosphorus balance is responsible for membrane potential.
   c. The sodium chloride molecule is responsible for hormone production.
   d. The magnesium channel is responsible for regular waste excretion.

125. Which of the following is a commonly used anticoagulant that works by preventing the activation of thrombin?
   a. Paxil
   b. Warfarin
   c. Heparin
   d. Aspirin

126. The nurse is caring for a patient being assessed for hospital-acquired pneumonia (HAP). The nurse knows that which organism(s) is/are the most likely source of HAP?
   a. Gram-negative bacilli and gram-positive cocci
   b. Helicobacter pylori
   c. Gram-positive bacilli and spiral bacteria
   d. Viruses

127. Which of the following statements about the cardiac catheterization procedure is true?
   a. The brachial artery is a common access site.
   b. The thin tube threaded into the patient's heart has a camera called a scope on the end for visualization of heart structures.
   c. Angioplasty and stent placement are commonly performed to open occluded coronary vessels.
   d. The patient is put under general anesthesia for the procedure.

128. The hospital has a non-punitive quality report (QR) system for reporting undesirable deviations in care. The nurse understands that which is the primary goal of the QR system?
   a. Enhancing patient safety by providing leadership with data that is critical to solving local and system-level problems
   b. Enhancing patient safety by identifying underperforming staff members so they can be disciplined
   c. Alerting leadership to data that may look bad on hospital safety reports
   d. Allowing nurses to make anonymous complaints about physicians

226

PCCN Practice Test #1

129. The nurse is administering medications and makes an error, giving the patient 20 mg of PO labetalol instead of 10 mg. What action should the nurse take?
    a. No action is necessary. The difference of 10 mg will not affect the patient.
    b. Tell the physician about the error. If the physician says it's okay, then no further steps are needed.
    c. Tell the patient and physician, reassess the patient and take vitals in one hour, and submit a quality report.
    d. Go immediately to the nurse manager's office, apologize, and admit the error.

130. The nurse is educating a patient regarding assistive devices and answers a question regarding the proper length of a cane. Which response by the nurse correctly answers this question?
    a. "Canes should be the length that feels most comfortable for each individual."
    b. "The length of the cane should support the elbow to be only slightly flexed."
    c. "It is best for the cane to be the length that encourages full flexion of the elbow."
    d. "A properly fitted cane allows you to lean forward with full extension of the elbow during ambulation."

131. A patient with a terminal cancer diagnosis is placed in hospice care. Which of the following is the title of the person who will make his healthcare decisions when he becomes incapacitated?
    a. Hospice nurse
    b. Healthcare power of attorney
    c. Caregiver
    d. Legal guardian

132. According to the Synergy Model, which of the following choices is associated with the patient's vulnerability?
    a. The patient is financially stable.
    b. The patient smoked cigarettes for thirty years prior to quitting five years ago.
    c. The patient is married.
    d. The patient actively participates in decisions related to the plan of care.

133. A nurse is developing a plan of care for a patient population that is culturally diverse. Which of the following statements correctly identifies the appropriate nursing actions?
    a. The nurse follows the standard protocol for the predominant culture of the community.
    b. The nurse focuses on the cultural needs of the largest group in the population.
    c. The nurse Identifies and acknowledges their own biases and addresses the needs of the patient.
    d. The nurse meets the needs of the group according to their own values and beliefs.

134. A patient is admitted to the hospital for a gastrointestinal (GI) bleed. After the nurse's morning assessment, the patient reports a large amount of reddish black stool. Upon assessment, the nurse identifies the stool as being blood. What is the most important intervention for the nurse to perform first?
    a. Start intravenous fluids.
    b. Fill out a consent form for the anticipated esophagogastroduodenoscopy (EGD).
    c. Draw a complete blood count and type and crossmatch for blood administration.
    d. Monitor compete blood count every 6 hours.

135. A patient with dementia has become increasingly confused, is agitated with staff after dinner, and is wandering around the unit, asking to leave. Which of the following interventions should the nurse try first for this patient?
   a. Remind the patient that they are in the hospital.
   b. Request an order for lorazepam.
   c. Request an order for restraints.
   d. Provide the patient with a distracting task to perform.

136. A patient has had three separate blood pressure readings of 138/88, 132/80, and 135/89, respectively. The progressive care nurse anticipates the patient to be categorized by the physician as which of the following?
   a. Prehypertensive
   b. Normal
   c. Stage 1 hypertensive
   d. Stage 2 hypertensive

137. Which of the following statements is consistent with the description of clinical inquiry in the Synergy Model?
   a. Novice nurses begin to compare and contrast alternative solutions to patient problems.
   b. Changes in clinical practice result from clinical experience and the application of research findings.
   c. Clinical inquiry is critical to the care of the vulnerable patient.
   d. The model identifies clinical inquiry as identical to clinical reasoning.

138. A patient recently admitted to the floor as a direct admit from her cardiologist office begins complaining of new onset chest pain, 10/10 to left chest and shoulder. The patient is diaphoretic, and vital signs reveal patient's heart rate is 64 bpm, BP is 132/78 mmHg, respiratory rate is 20, and oxygen saturation is 98% on room air. Which of the following actions should the nurse anticipate as part of the patient's care?

   I. IV administration of magnesium sulfate
   II. IV administration of morphine sulfate
   III. IV administration of nitroglycerin
   IV. IV administration of acetaminophen

   a. I and II only
   b. I, III, and IV only
   c. II and III only
   d. II, III, and IV only

139. If dopamine does not do an adequate job of maintaining blood pressure in a patient experiencing cardiogenic shock, which potent vasoconstrictor will be considered to raise the blood pressure?
   a. Dobutamine
   b. Norepinephrine
   c. Milrinone
   d. Nitroglycerin

140. The nurse has just admitted a patient to her unit with signs and symptoms of septic shock. The patient was discharged from the medical-surgical floor last week after being treated for pneumonia. What findings support a septic shock diagnosis?

> I. Metabolic acidosis
> II. Respiratory alkalosis
> III. Narrowing pulse pressure
> IV. Increased cardiac output

a. I only
b. I and II
c. I and III
d. I, II, III, and IV

141. The nurse is caring for several post-surgical patients. The nurse knows that which patient is likely to be at highest risk for surgical site infection (SSI)?
a. A 40-year-old vegetarian in good health with a BMI of 20, post-op day two from cholecystectomy
b. A 65-year-old with hypertension and hypercholesterolemia and a BMI of 26, post-op day one from ovarian cyst removal
c. An 85-year-old smoker with diabetes, malnutrition, and a BMI of 15, post-op day three from a lung lobectomy
d. A 25-year-old with a BMI of 30, post-op day three after a cesarean section

142. What is the main concern faced when using an artificial graft to bypass an occluded artery in the fem-pop bypass procedure?
a. Localized infection
b. Narrowing leading to reocclusion
c. Lower extremity edema
d. Tissue rejection

143. The nurse is caring for a patient whose wound assessment and dressing change is much more time-consuming and complex than expected. The nurse is concerned about falling behind on important tasks for other patients. What is the best approach to take when managing this situation?
a. Collaborate with unlicensed assistive personnel (UAPs), nurse colleagues, and the charge nurse to delegate tasks until the dressing change is complete.
b. Do the dressing change as quickly as possible, and then skip other tasks to get medication administration done for other patients.
c. Delegate the assessment and dressing change to a nurse colleague.
d. Complete the dressing change, and then get caught up on other tasks as soon as possible. It's okay if some are done late.

144. A nurse checks a patient's status post bariatric bypass procedure. The patient begins to experience dumping syndrome. Which is the most important to prevent this complication?
a. Eat larger meals so there is more absorption.
b. Avoid drinking anything with meals or for 2 hours after meals.
c. Drink fluids before meals and with meals.
d. Take multivitamins to avoid malnutrition.

229

145. A novice nurse is caring for a patient who requires a blood transfusion. The patient, however, has refused the transfusion due to a religious objection to the therapy. The nurse says, "I don't understand why the patient's sister can't donate the blood. No one should object to receiving blood from a family member when you need it." Which of the following statements correctly identifies the critical issue in this situation?
    a.   The nurse is displaying an ethnocentric attitude that dismisses the patient's religious practices as irrelevant to the need for the therapy.
    b.   The nurse thinks that the patient is concerned about contracting an infectious disease from the donated blood.
    c.   The nurse thinks that the patient doesn't understand the necessity of the blood transfusion.
    d.   The nurse believes that blood donation from family members is safe.

146. Which of the following are true regarding encephalopathy?

      I. It is complication of a primary problem.
      II. It is brain damage.
      III. It is an altered mental state.
      IV. It is caused by a lack of oxygen to the brain.

    a.   I, II, and III
    b.   I, II, and IV
    c.   II, III, and IV
    d.   All the above

147. What risk does high blood pressure pose in the postoperative period of an endarterectomy?
    a.   Bleeding
    b.   Infection
    c.   Pulmonary edema
    d.   Stroke

148. Patients with type 2 diabetes can manage their symptoms with which of the following?
    a.   An insulin pump and finger prick testing strips
    b.   Steroid injections and stevia sugar substitutes
    c.   A regular yoga practice
    d.   Lifestyle changes and metformin

149. The nurse taking care of a patient with an MRSA infection knows that multidrug-resistant organisms arise from which of the following causes?
    a.   Improper use of antivirals
    b.   Underuse of antivirals
    c.   Underuse of antibiotics
    d.   Overuse of antibiotics

150. The nurse is researching the evidence for a proposed change in patient positioning for lumbar puncture. Which type of evidence gives the strongest support for the proposed change?
    a. A randomized controlled trial
    b. A case-control study
    c. A meta-analysis of randomized controlled trials
    d. The position statement of a major medical professional organization

Answer Key and Explanations

1. B: The correct choice is Choice *B*, lactulose. Lactulose reduces ammonia production and absorption. Elevated ammonia levels can cause confusion and disorientation. Choices *A* and *D* are incorrect. These medications can be used to treat psychosis or to reduce agitation. These medications may help calm the patient but are not a treatment for hepatic encephalopathy. Choice *C* is also incorrect. Kayexalate is used to reduce high levels of potassium in the blood, not ammonia. Kayexalate can cause a patient to produce more stool but does not reduce ammonia.

2. D: The nurse should first determine whether what they are seeing anecdotally is a true trend before addressing options for improvement. Working with the nurse manager and hospital falls champion to examine the data would be the most effective step. Choice *A* is incorrect because, while speaking up in huddle is useful, it does not address whether what the nurse is seeing is a real trend, nor does it address potential solutions beyond increased vigilance. Choice *B* is incorrect because, while submitting quality reports on falls is important, this action alone is not the most effective way to address the nurse's observation. Choice *C* is incorrect because it does not confirm whether the nurse's observation is actually a documented trend, and it approaches the problem in an individually punitive manner.

3. C: This scenario depicts a case of community-acquired pneumonia (CAP), specifically pneumococcal pneumonia. The most common cause of CAP is *Streptococcus pneumoniae*, or pneumococcus. It's a gram-positive bacterium, usually occurring in pairs (diplococci). The other bacteria (*Haemophilus influenzae, Moraxella catarrhalis*, and *Staphylococcus aureus*) are less common causes of CAP.

4. A: Tiotropium bromide is an anticholinergic bronchodilator that helps to relax the smooth muscles in the airways, resulting in bronchodilation and improved airflow. It does not directly decrease inflammation, Choice *B*; thin mucus, Choice *C*; or stimulate surfactant production, Choice *D*.

5. C: Vitamin K plays a role in the body's natural clotting process, and Warfarin works by inhibiting the synthesis of certain clotting factors dependent on vitamin K. Maintaining a consistent intake of vitamin K helps maintain the desired therapeutic effect of Warfarin without unnecessary restrictions. Choice *A* is incorrect because it suggests avoiding vitamin K–rich foods altogether, which is not necessary for most patients on Warfarin. Although Choice *B* recognizes the importance of a balanced diet, it does not highlight the important fact that vitamin K may alter Warfarin's effectiveness; therefore, it is incorrect. Choice *D* is not necessary and may lead to nutritional imbalances.

6. D: Chronic alcohol abuse and biliary tract dysfunction are the most frequent causes of acute pancreatitis; however, there are no identified criteria that explain why some individuals will experience pancreatitis while others do not. Acute pancreatitis is most often diagnosed by the presenting history and physical examination. ECRP is only indicated in patients with acute pancreatitis and concomitant biliary disease; therefore, Choice *A* is incorrect. Ultrasonography is generally less useful than CT imaging for pancreatitis, and its efficacy is significantly decreased in the presence of abdominal distention, which distorts the images; therefore, Choice *B* is incorrect. Although rectal indomethacin is used commonly to treat acute pancreatitis resulting from ERCP imaging, controversy remains regarding the efficacy of the therapy; therefore, Choice *C* is incorrect.

7. D: Delirium is transient, reversible, and usually has an acute onset with an illness. Dementia, on the other hand, is a slow-developing, irreversible, and chronic condition often accompanied by another

232

chronic diagnosis such as Parkinson's or Alzheimer's. Dementia may be slowed, but never fully reversed. Delirium usually can be treated and reversed by treating the underlying cause.

8. B: Moral agency refers to decision-making that includes accountability for right and wrong decisions by the moral agent. Advocacy is an ethical principle that is not legally enforced. However, many argue that paternalism is contrary to advocacy because of the assumption that the "system" knows what is best for the patient without concern for the patient's wishes. Moral agency is not restricted to a specific population; however, the PCCN will assess the ability of all patients to make informed decisions.

9. D: Long QT syndrome is a rare, hereditary condition found many times in healthy children and adults that may be asymptomatic until a syncopal episode or even sudden death occurs. First- and third-degree heart block occurs when there are conduction problems between the atria and ventricles, resulting in "missed" heartbeats. Bundle branch block occurs when there is an interruption in the electrical impulse across the ventricles of the heart.

10. A: Tardive dyskinesia, a serious side effect of antipsychotic medication, produces many involuntary movements including tongue thrusting. Tardive dyskinesia is an involuntary neurologic movement disorder with persistent effect. Headache, Choice *B*; blurred vision, Choice *C*; and fever, Choice *D*, are not symptoms of tardive dyskinesia.

11. D: Aspirin works by inhibiting platelet aggregation to prevent clot formation. Paroxetine is used to treat anxiety and depression. Coumadin® (warfarin) works by blocking vitamin K-dependent clotting factors. Heparin enhances the effect of antithrombin III to inhibit thrombin activation.

12. A: There is a documented tendency for patients who are prescribed antibiotics to stop taking the dosage once their symptoms subside. However, stopping a prescription antibiotic before the dose is completed does not kill all the harmful bacteria. The bacteria that remain evolve to become resistant to the antibiotic, and the medicine is no longer effective. Other reasons for resistance include over-prescription for medical cases that do not necessarily require antibiotics.

13. B: Cheyne-Stokes breathing is an irregular breathing pattern characterized by several breaths followed by a long pause before breathing resumes. It is a specific pattern seen when death is approaching. Choice *A* is incorrect because Cheyne-Stokes breathing does not indicate a blocked airway. Choice *C* is incorrect because a patient in a normal deep sleep state will not exhibit Cheyne-Stokes breathing. Choice *D* is incorrect because oversedation by narcotic medication affects the respiratory rate by slowing it down; it does not cause this specific breathing pattern.

14. C: An endoscopy is used to diagnose the condition and to cauterize hemorrhagic sites. The treatment algorithm for peptic ulcer disease recommends surgical intervention if two endoscopic attempts at hemostasis are unsuccessful. The pain related to peptic ulcer disease does not begin until the ingested food has reached the duodenum; therefore, the pain does not begin for 2 to 3 hours after a meal, while the onset of pain with gastric ulcers is 20 to 30 minutes after a meal. Choice *A* is incorrect. Gastric ulcers are associated with an increased incidence of malignancy, not peptic ulcers; therefore, Choice *B* is incorrect. NSAID use is a commonly associated cause of peptic ulcer disease. However, even excluding patients who use NSAIDs, more than 60% of the cases of peptic ulcer disease are related to *H. pylori* infection; therefore, Choice *D* is incorrect.

15. C: Facilitating a patient's transition from one point on the health continuum to another requires caring practices in addition to advocacy and moral agency. Moral agency may be employed to ensure

233

that the patient's wishes are considered, especially those wishes associated with end-of-life concerns. Developing cultural awareness is an example of a response to diversity, and the remaining two choices refer to the facilitation of learning.

16. A: Virchow's triad identifies factors that contribute to the thrombotic process associated with deep venous thrombosis (DVT) and pulmonary embolism (PE). The triad consists of hypercoagulability, endothelial injury/dysfunction, and hemodynamic changes such as stasis and turbulence. Heart disease is a risk factor for DVT and PE, but it is not part of Virchow's triad.

17. B: All the symptoms reported by the patient are part of severe alcohol withdrawal; however, reporting that the room is spinning points towards vestibular disturbance. Patients experiencing vestibular disturbance will feel that the room is rotating, the walls are falling, and the floor is moving. The GI symptoms, headache, and tremors relate to different systems affected by the alcohol withdrawal.

18. A: The correct answer is Choice A. The nurse should suspect that the patient has developed *Clostridioides* (formerly *Clostridium*) *difficile* colitis (*C.diff*). The patient should be placed on contact isolation and a stool sample collected to test for the infection. Choice B is incorrect. While these interventions will likely make the patient more comfortable, they are not the priority actions. Choice C is incorrect. The patient may need hydration due to extensive diarrhea, but it is not the priority. Intake and output should already be monitored per progressive care unit protocol. Choice D is incorrect. The patient's diet should not be limited due to diarrhea, as this can lead to dehydration.

19. C: The wound is showing signs of infection, and the patient has a fever. The nurse should initiate assessment for bloodstream infection. The patient's long-term use of steroids puts them at higher risk of systemic infection. Choice A is incorrect because it does not take immediate action to address potential complications. Choice B is incorrect because pain medication will not address the risk of infection. Choice D is incorrect because, while the patient is at risk, they are still stable. However, the patient should be watched closely, and the emergency team should be called if there is rapid change in the patient's condition.

20. A: Since electrolytes need to be suspended in a certain amount of liquid to move optimally and carry out their intended function, fluid level in the body is important. As fluid levels increase beyond a state of fluid-electrolyte balance, electrolyte levels will decrease since there is too much fluid present. If fluid levels are too low, such as in a state of dehydration, there will be too many electrolytes per unit of fluid, which also prevents the electrolytes from carrying out their intended function.

21. D: The patient has evidence of high complexity due to the unknown nature of their diagnosis, altered family dynamics, and evidence of chronic renal failure. Complexity is related to the number of systems that are affected by the patient's health issues. This demonstrates alterations in at least three systems; therefore, the complexity is rated as high. The remaining choices are positive indicators. Stability refers to the patient's response to therapy; high stability is associated with a low risk of death, which is not consistent with this patient's chronic renal failure and other unknown conditions. Resources refers to family support and financial resources, and this patient's family is at odds with the care decisions; therefore, the patient is lacking strong social support. Vulnerability refers to the patient's potential of being affected by various stressors. The patient is vulnerable due to chronic illness and alterations in the family dynamic.

22. D: The correct answer is Choice *D*, a history of alcohol abuse. Choice *A* is incorrect. A history of prescription drug abuse is not a risk factor for cirrhosis. Choice *B* is incorrect. Diabetes well-controlled with an A1c is not a risk factor for cirrhosis; however, uncontrolled diabetes can be a risk factor. Choice *C* is also incorrect. Hypertension is not a risk factor for cirrhosis.

23. D: Massive urine production, or polyuria, is the result of a hyperglycemic state in the body and a hallmark sign of any diabetic condition. Urine is not concentrated, but rather diluted. Sodium, potassium, and other electrolyte imbalances may occur because of polyuria but are not a direct effect of hyperglycemia.

24. D: A patient with a suspected PE that is in renal failure will likely undergo V/Q scanning, in which ventilation and perfusion of the lungs are visualized. Transesophageal echocardiography is used for visualizing the back of the heart and is not appropriate in this scenario. CT scanning with contrast is contraindicated, as the patient with renal failure cannot tolerate the dye, which is primarily metabolized by the kidneys. MRI is not a usual scan for a PE.

25. C: The QSEN competencies were originally identified to improve patient safety in response to research that indicated that nearly 100,000 people died each year because of provider errors. The QSEN competencies refer to nursing activities and are often used as the basis for undergraduate nursing curricula. Systems thinking is the process by which nurses meet the competencies, and attainment of this ability is an incremental process based on nurses' continuing education and clinical experiences. Although systems thinking is associated with the QSEN competencies, and the use of systems thinking has improved patient outcomes, the basic assumption of the QSEN competencies was improved patient safety because of expert nursing care.

26. B: An abdominal aneurysm may present or be found on examination as a pulsating mass in the abdomen. Indigestion when lying down is associated with gastrointestinal reflux disease (GERD) and is not indicative of an AAA. Fatigue and shortness of breath on exertion may be indicative of coronary artery or pulmonary disease. It is not directly associated with an AAA. Pain radiating down the left arm is a classic sign of a myocardial infarction (MI).

27. B: Spontaneous pneumothorax occurs without any obvious cause or traumatic event. It is more common in individuals without any underlying lung disease and is frequently seen in tall, thin individuals. Choice *A* occurs when air enters the pleural space and cannot escape, leading to increasing pressure and compression of the heart and lungs. Choice *C* occurs because of trauma or injury to the chest, such as a rib fracture. Choice *D* is caused by a medical intervention or procedure, such as a lung biopsy or insertion of a central venous catheter.

28. A: The most immediate action the nurse should take after noticing that the patient looks pale and feels cold is to assist the patient back to bed to prevent a fall. Afterward, the nurse can assess the patient's nutrition and hemodynamic status, Choices *B*, *C*, and *D*.

29. C: The correct choice is Choice *C*. Based on the patient's results, they are experiencing an ischemic stroke. The patient is within the treatment guidelines for administration of thrombolytic medication to limit damage and disability caused by the stroke. This is the priority intervention. Choice *A* is incorrect. While an echocardiogram may be useful in determining the etiology of the stroke, it is not a priority. Choice *B* is also incorrect. Again, a cerebral angiogram may be useful for stroke etiology, but it is not the

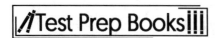

priority intervention. Choice *D* is incorrect. A thrombectomy is not indicated because the patient's VAN stroke assessment was negative, indicating the stroke was not embolic.

30. A: Patients with type 1 diabetes are prone to diabetic ketoacidosis due to the absence of adequate insulin in their blood. This absence makes it more likely for the body to use fatty acids for energy rather than carbohydrates, and without insulin, this can lead to excessive ketones in the blood. Excessive ketones lead to an acidic blood environment.

31. D: Troponin is a muscle cell protein that is released when cardiac tissue is broken down during an ischemic event. Elevated levels of troponin in the bloodstream indicate cardiac muscle damage. Creatinine and BUN are waste products of the body, and higher levels of these in the bloodstream indicate kidney failure or damage, not heart damage. CK-MB is a cardiac enzyme, not muscle cell content. Therefore, it is slightly different, but could also indicate cardiac damage.

32. C: Alteplase is the single fibrinolytic agent approved for the treatment of ischemic stroke because it is associated with fewer adverse effects than the remaining agents. Streptokinase and tenecteplase have been used effectively to treat patients with acute myocardial infarction; however, in patients with ischemic stroke, streptokinase has been associated with an increased risk of intracranial hemorrhage and death. Current evidence for the efficacy and safety of urokinase and tenecteplase does not support their use for the treatment of ischemic stroke. Therefore, Choices *A*, *B*, and *D* are incorrect.

33. D: An INR of 3.5 is elevated and will cause bleeding complications if thrombolytic therapy is initiated before the INR returns to the normal level of less than or equal to 1.1.

34. B: A patient that would not pass a nursing bedside swallow screen would be the patient pocketing food. Pocketing food can indicate that the patient is avoiding swallowing, either due to the pain or the discomfort. Pocketing food would indicate that the patient needs specialized care from a speech-language pathologist. Excessive chewing, frequently requesting water, and eating slowly would not require the immediate cessation of the screening alone.

35. A: The patient is showing signs and symptoms of hepatic encephalopathy, which is caused by an elevation in ammonia levels. Lactulose, Choice *A*, is administered in order to excrete excess ammonia through the GI tract. Choice *B* is incorrect; while thiamine insufficiency could be causing the altered mental status and often accompanies hepatic encephalopathy due to alcoholic cirrhosis, this supplementation will not lower the patient's ammonia levels. Further assessment is required to determine if its administration is indicated. Choices *C* and *D* are incorrect; while these diuretics may help control the patient's edema, they will not improve the patient's altered mental status caused by hepatic encephalopathy.

36. D: Participating in an agency-wide project is an example of systems thinking because it extends the focus of nurses beyond the care of an individual patient. The remaining interventions are examples of progressive systems thinking. The novice nurse is concerned with the meds for the individual patient; the nurse with more experience will be providing teaching-learning sessions in the nursing unit, rather than the entire institution, and soliciting performance evaluations from colleagues as well as supervisors.

37. B: The patient is showing signs of compartment syndrome. The nurse's initial intervention should be to loosen the patient's splint to decrease pressure on the limb, Choice *B*. While at bedside and monitoring the patient, the nurse should then notify the physician and prepare the patient for possible

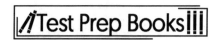

surgical intervention. Choice *A*, calling for an x-ray, is incorrect; while the doctor may order an x-ray to rule out causes of the patient's symptoms, this will not help to improve the patient's circulation, which appears to be impaired. Choice *C*, elevating the limb above the level of the heart, is incorrect; the patient's limb should not be elevated above the heart because this will decrease its perfusion. Rather, the limb should be at or below the level of the heart. Choice *D*, preparing for heparin infusion, is incorrect; while a heparin infusion may be indicated if the patient's symptoms are caused by deep vein thrombosis, this would more likely be an intervention started after further diagnostics and would not be an immediate, priority intervention to restore limb perfusion.

38. C: While the doctor may order anticonvulsants such as levetiracetam for the intercranial hemorrhage patient, this patient should not be given anything orally until cleared by a licensed speech and language pathologist. Patients with facial droop and slurred speech are considered at risk of aspiration and should not be given anything orally. Choice *A* is appropriate; changes in pupillometry could indicate worsening of the intercranial hemorrhage and need for further intervention. Choice *B* may be indicated in order to reverse the effects of the apixaban and slow the patient's intercranial bleeding. Choice *D* may be indicated to assist in lowering the patient's blood pressure and lowering intercranial pressure to reduce adverse outcomes.

39. B: A morning headache is a common symptom of COPD. The cough associated with COPD is usually productive. A barrel chest, not a narrowed chest, is common due to hyperinflation of the lungs. Patients with COPD will often experience weight loss and muscle wasting because of the disease.

40. C: The sudden death of a grandmother needs to be probed for if a cause was determined. If she passed away suddenly because of hypertrophic cardiomyopathy that had been previously undiagnosed before autopsy, the patient should be screened for this condition as well, as it often may be asymptomatic until syncope or sudden death occurs. The other three conditions listed are of value, but do not point toward hypertrophic cardiomyopathy specifically.

41. C: The Synergy Model identifies expert nursing practice as the level of nursing competency in which clinical reasoning becomes an integrated element in the process of clinical inquiry. According to the model, prior to that point, nurses are capable of performing at some level of clinical inquiry and may be able to use clinical reasoning in patient care, but the total integration of the two does not occur until the expert level of nursing practice.

42. C: Immunocompromised patients need to minimize their contact with potentially infectious or illness-causing agents as much as possible, since even mild illnesses can be life-threatening to them. All the practices listed are recommended for patients who have a compromised immune system except for only drinking bottled water. While clean water and clean drinking vessels should always be used, water does not need to necessarily be bottled.

43. D: Bacteria ascension into the urinary tract from poor insertion technique, backflow of urine, or inadequate catheter hygiene is the most common cause of CAUTI. Choice *A* is incorrect because urinary retention can exacerbate the risk of CAUTI but is not a primary cause. Choice *B* is incorrect because, while many hospitalized patients do have compromised immune systems that make them more vulnerable to a CAUTI, the bacterial infection itself is the cause of CAUTI. Choice *C* is incorrect because trauma to the urethra from catheter insertion is not itself infectious.

44. B: The nurse should suspect hypoglycemia based on the circumstances and symptoms being experienced by the patient. Hypoglycemia may occur when a patient receiving insulin therapy, as may be the case here if the patient is diabetic, has been NPO for a procedure. Fasting in addition to insulin therapy if not carefully monitored and tweaked will likely cause hypoglycemia. Sweating, nausea, and malaise are all hypoglycemic symptoms. A blood sugar reading should be immediately obtained to determine if hypoglycemia is the cause and, if so, treated with oral glucagon. Hypochondria is always possible but should be a diagnosis made by a psychiatrist. Hypotension is a less likely option given the circumstances, though not completely improbable. Hypothyroidism is unlikely and not a condition that the nurse would be able to independently diagnose without proper lab work and a clinical workup.

45. D: The correct choice is Choice *D*, metoclopramide. This medication helps in gastroparesis by reducing gastric emptying time and improving motility. Choice *A* is incorrect. Ondansetron helps with nausea but will not help with gastroparesis. Choice *B* is also incorrect. Long-acting insulin would be important for the patient's uncontrolled diabetes but not gastroparesis. Choice *C*, dicyclomine, is incorrect. Dicyclomine reduces stomach cramps but does not treat gastroparesis.

46. D: The pooling of blood and edematous swelling are signs of a venous insufficiency rather than an arterial one. Remember, arteries bring oxygen, so when there is a lack of oxygen, tissues cannot get oxygen, thus causing cyanosis and hair loss, and sores or wounds cannot heal. When venous blood is not returning to the heart, pooling and edema occur.

47. C: Sleeve resection is the correct answer, referring to a thoracic surgery in which an affected part of the airway is removed with the top and bottom sections being sewn together. This action is like cutting a stain off a sleeve and reattaching the top and bottom sections of the sleeve back together—hence, the name "sleeve resection." Pneumonectomy is the removal of an entire lung. Lobectomy is the removal of a lobe. Wedge resection refers to removing a part of an affected lobe.

48. D: Diuretics such as furosemide will help reduce preload in the patient experiencing cardiogenic pulmonary edema. Metoprolol and other beta-blockers are used in heart failure to slow the beating of the heart. Calcium channel blockers, such as verapamil, are used for heart dysrhythmias such as atrial fibrillation and in some cases of heart failure, improving the heart's ability to pump. Narcotics such as morphine are sometimes used to reduce anxiety and oxygen hunger in acute cases of pulmonary edema.

49. C: A first-degree heart block is NOT a direct risk factor for the development of an embolus. Women during pregnancy and in the postpartum period, individuals with a history of a previous stroke, and patients with fractures that involve long bones are all at risk for the development of an embolus.

50. C: The depth of the wound is the biggest clue as to whether the ulcer arose out of an arterial insufficiency or a venous insufficiency. Arterial ulcers are usually nonhealing and deep, eventually exposing tendons and bones if left untreated. The color of the ulcer may vary across a spectrum, regardless of the type. Cultures from the wound only tell what types of infectious agents have entered the ulcerative tissue. The size of the wound is irrelevant.

51. A: The longer a patient has a central line, the higher their risk of developing a CLABSI. The care team should regularly assess the necessity of the line and remove it as early as it is safe to do so. Choice *B* is incorrect because the central line should be removed when it is no longer needed, which may occur before discharge. Choice *C* is incorrect because, while the patient's preference should be considered,

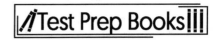

the choice of whether to maintain or remove the central line must be primarily guided by evidence and medical necessity. Choice *D* is incorrect because most intravenous medication can be administered through a peripheral intravenous catheter, which carries a much lower risk to the patient than maintaining a central line.

52. D: The big hint here is the route of administration: Oral corticosteroids will pass through the gastrointestinal tract, where they will be absorbed into the systemic circulation in the small intestine, affecting the body system as a whole. Inhaled and nebulized drugs such as bronchodilators and albuterol will directly affect the inflamed airways of status asthmaticus, thus not affecting systemic inflammation. The same goes for epinephrine administered subcutaneously. Its action will primarily be targeting the airways, with bronchodilation being the desired effect.

53. B: Vigilance refers to the ability of the nurse to recognize and respond to changes in the patient's condition. According to the Synergy Model, vigilance as a caring practice is a learned behavior that evolves with clinical experience, which means that the novice nurse will identify predictable alterations in the patient's condition, while the experienced nurse will identify and respond to more subtle changes. The most experienced nurse is capable of intervening to prevent some adverse events. Engagement refers to committing to the patient care relationship, rather than responding to changes in the patient's condition. The changes noted in the patient's condition are early, subtle indications of heart failure. The novice nurse would initially associate the changes with the surgical procedure, while the experienced nurse would assess the patient for heart failure. Although collaboration with other providers may have been an outcome of the nurse's assessment, the initial care was an independent action.

54. B: The scenario depicts an episode of status asthmaticus. Common pharmacological agents used to treat this condition include albuterol (short-acting Beta-2 agonist), ipratropium (anticholinergic), and methylprednisolone (corticosteroid). Her new symptoms (anxiety, tremors, and tachycardia) are all common side effects which can be attributed to albuterol. Anticholinergics can induce side effects such as dry mouth, blurred vision, and constipation. Corticosteroids (if used for longer than two weeks) can have side effects such as weight gain, osteoporosis, thinning of skin, cataracts, easy bruising, and diabetes. She should be switched to the short-acting Beta-2 agonist levalbuterol because it's as effective as albuterol but without the alarming side effects.

55. B: Selective serotonin reuptake inhibitors (SSRIs) are a class of drugs that can treat both anxiety and depression symptoms. SSRIs such as fluoxetine, sertraline, and escitalopram may be prescribed to individuals who are suffering from anxiety, depression, or a combination of both.

56. D: The hands-on, teach-back method is the most effective of the four methods for teaching the patient this multi-step process. Choice *A* is incorrect because, while the patient should have written instructions to refer to, giving written instructions alone does not allow the nurse to observe or assess if the teaching was effective. Choice *B* is incorrect because, while a verbal teach-back method is helpful, it is not as good as the hands-on practice in Choice *D*. Choice *C* is incorrect because referring the patient to a video does not allow the nurse to assess whether the education has been effective.

57. D: A root cause analysis is a multidisciplinary, collaborative process to determine the root cause(s) of an event. It should involve participants from all disciplines that may have contributed to the event. Choices *A* and *C* are incorrect because they include only nursing staff. Choice *B* is incorrect because it does not include pharmacy. The hospital attorney and risk manager should be kept informed regarding the progress of a root cause analysis, but they are not integral to the process.

58. B: Vancomycin, Choice *B*, is an antibiotic that is known for its nephrotoxic effects. An alternative antibiotic should be considered for this patient. Choice *A*, bumetanide, is a diuretic that may be administered when other diuretics are contraindicated due to their effect on renal function, as bumetanide has minimal effect on the kidneys. Choice *C*, acetaminophen, and Choice *D*, senna glycoside, should not affect kidney function.

59. C: Immunocompromised pneumonia occurs in patients whose immune systems have been weakened. It may occur in patients who have an HIV infection or are undergoing chemotherapy or radiation regimens. Community-acquired pneumonia occurs in persons who had little to no contact with medical facilities prior to the infection. Hospital-acquired pneumonias occur in patients who have been hospitalized and because of immobilization. Healthcare–associated pneumonias occur in patients in long-term facilities or some other healthcare facility besides a hospital.

60. C: Naloxone is the antidote for respiratory depression caused by an opioid overdose. Morphine and hydrocodone are examples of opioids that might cause respiratory failure if overdose occurs. Alprazolam is an example of a benzodiazepine, a known cause of respiratory failure if overdosed.

61. A: According to the CDC, "Droplet precautions should be implemented for patients with suspected or confirmed influenza for 7 days after illness onset or until 24 hours after the resolution of fever and respiratory symptoms, whichever is longer." This patient is still showing respiratory symptoms (cough), so they should remain on droplet precautions. Choice *B* is incorrect because it goes further than the CDC recommendations and thus wastes resources that may be necessary for other patients. Choice *C* is incorrect because the patient is still showing respiratory symptoms and could still be infectious to others. Choice *D* is incorrect because a patient on droplet precautions should be placed in a private room.

62. B: The literature indicates that physicians are most likely to opt for the "cure" rather than the "care," which means that they choose interventions that provide an action or treatment that will address the patient's problems. In contrast, nurses intervene to address relationship issues. According to this view, the physician would choose to apply a brace to treat the patient's condition, while the nurse would be more likely to address affective domain issues such as stress, social support, and spiritual needs.

63. C: The first piece of personal protective equipment the nurse should don is a gown, Choice *C*, per guidelines from the CDC. Gloves, Choice *A*, are donned next, followed by a mask, Choice *B*, and ultimately, goggles, Choice *D*, are donned last. The nurse must follow this sequence to ensure protection against infection transmission.

64. C: Choice *C* identifies a stuporous patient exhibiting no articulated verbal response with limited moaning, accompanied by arousal only after vigorous stimulation. Lethargic, Choice *A*, describes a patient who appears drowsy and arouses with gentle stimulation. Obtunded, Choice *B*, describes a patient who responds to repeated external stimulation to maintain attention. A patient that is comatose, Choice *D*, indicates they have no discernible response to stimulation. The levels of consciousness proceed with increasing severity from confused, to lethargic, to obtunded, to stuporous, and finally to comatose.

65. B: The PICOT elements in this scenario are post-surgical patients (population), intermittent catheterization (intervention), indwelling catheterization (control), fewer cases of CAUTI (outcome), and seven days (time). Choice *B* contains all five elements. Choice *A* is incorrect because it only contains

intervention, outcome, and control. Choice *C* is incorrect because it only includes population, intervention, outcome, and time. Choice *D* is incorrect because it only includes time, intervention, and control.

66. C: Acetone, a ketoacid produced during the breakdown of fatty acids during diabetic ketoacidosis, is expelled through respiration, thus giving a person in DKA a "fruity" smell to the breath. Glycerol and alanine are byproducts of fat and muscle breakdown as alternative energy sources convert to glucose. Triglycerides are broken down into free fatty acids as another alternative to glucose as energy for metabolism in the body.

67. C: New onset of peripheral edema may be signaling decompensation by the right side of the heart and progressive heart failure. Oxygenation levels for CHF patients are generally lower but tolerated well. An oxygen saturation level of 92% is acceptable for this patient. Dyspnea upon exertion is not an unusual finding during a CHF exacerbation. Elevated BNP levels, although abnormal, are anticipated with CHF.

68. D: The definitive diagnostic tool to confirm meningitis is lumbar puncture, Choice *D*. Choice *A*, blood cultures, may be performed to rule out other infections and sepsis, but meningeal infections are more likely to be found in the cerebral spinal fluid than the blood stream. Choice *B*, nasopharyngeal swab, may be indicated to test for viruses but will not definitively confirm that the infection is in the cerebral spinal fluid. Choice *C*, head CT, may show bleeding or inflammation in the brain but will not confirm the cause.

69. D: An early sign of respiratory distress is agitation, along with confusion and oxygen hunger. Later signs of respiratory distress occur when the patient has become fatigued because of the respiratory effort they have put forth. These signs include decreased respiratory rate, unconsciousness, and cyanosis.

70. D: The safety and efficacy of influenza vaccination is supported by copious amounts of medical and epidemiological research; the dangers of contracting influenza are also well-documented. While it is correct that "herd immunity" is protective, achieving herd immunity without vaccination would cause far more death and disability than if the healthy population were to get vaccinated. Choice *A* is incorrect because a healthy person's choice not to get vaccinated may contribute to the spread of disease and hurt people who are less likely to withstand the disease. Choice *B* is incorrect because contracting influenza presents a far greater risk than receiving the influenza vaccine. Choice *C* is incorrect because it is antagonistic and does not provide the patient with any rationale that might influence him to get vaccinated.

71. D: This scenario depicts a moderate to severe acute exacerbation of COPD. Azithromycin is a macrolide antibiotic. In clinical trials, the use of antibiotics in individuals with a moderate to severe exacerbation of COPD diminishes the risk of treatment failure and death. Oxygen and albuterol target dyspnea. In clinical trials, the administration of oral corticosteroids early during a COPD exacerbation decreased the need for hospitalization.

72. A: Beck's triad of muffled heart sounds, distended neck veins, and hypotension are cardinal signs of cardiac tamponade. Chest pain and back pain are the most common presenting symptoms with the AAA. Heart function, breathing, and consciousness are not evident in cardiopulmonary arrest. Cardiogenic shock includes ashen, cyanotic, or mottled extremities; distant heart sounds; and rapid and faint peripheral pulses.

73. B: The nurse is attempting to prevent possible harm that may occur because of lack of preparation for this specialty care assignment. The issue in this example is accepting or rejecting an assignment in the absence of adequate educational preparation. Although the infants in the NICU are an at-risk population, the nurse's actions are focused on unsafe care for the next eight hours as opposed to long-term solutions for staffing problems. The nurse is not promoting individual free will or the free will of the infants. As previously stated, the issue in this example is unsafe staffing, and while trust or fidelity might be an element of the PCCN's refusal to float to NICU, the most significant reason for the refusal is nonmaleficence.

74. B: Stage 5 chronic kidney disease is the last stage of progression for this condition. By this time, it is serious enough to require constant dialysis (a process that filters the blood for the kidneys) or a kidney transplant because the kidneys have failed.

75. A: A woman may have flulike symptoms, anxiety, or jaw or back pain days to weeks before the actual cardiac event. These symptoms may be overlooked, and the correct diagnosis may be missed if the clinician is unaware of gender differences. The other three symptoms listed are classic, well-known symptoms of a myocardial infarction.

76. C: Advocacy involves supporting appropriate programs and actions for marginalized or at-risk populations. At the community level, the role of advocate for the PCCN may require knowledge of the legislative process to bring about change. In direct patient care, the PCCN will be the advocate for the patient by providing the information necessary for informed choices and supporting those choices in the development of the plan of care. Fidelity refers to trust. Autonomy refers to the right to self-determination. Beneficence refers to acting in the best interest of other individuals in society.

77. D: Stage one pressure injuries have not yet broken through the skin. They do not blanch, and they feel warm to the touch. They often occur around bony prominences such as elbows, heels, and the sacrum. Choice *A* is incorrect because abrasions would appear as broken areas of skin. Choice *B* is incorrect because bruising would appear as blue, green, or yellowish in color and would not feel warm to the touch. Choice *C* is incorrect because stage two pressure injuries involve broken skin.

78. A: *Streptococcus pneumoniae* is the most common cause of bacterial pneumonia. The other three organisms listed are also bacterial and may cause pneumonia but are not as common as *S. pneumoniae*.

79. B: Vena cava filters are also known as inferior vena cava (IVC) filters or Greenfield filters. They are used to prevent a pulmonary embolism (PE). Indications for the placement of a vena cava filter include:

- An absolute contraindication to anticoagulants
- Survival after a massive PE and a high probability that a recurrent PE will be fatal
- Documented recurrent PE

80. C: Community-associated, methicillin-resistant Staphylococcus aureus (CA-MRSA) is notoriously resistant to most antibiotics, except vancomycin and linezolid, with linezolid quickly becoming the agent of choice for the treatment of CA-MRSA pneumonia.

81. A: An ABG result of pH 7.51, PaCO2 72 mmHg, and HCO3 41 mEq/L would indicate that the patient is in partially compensated metabolic alkalosis, making Choice *D* the correct answer. The patient is not in an acidotic state, making Choice *A* incorrect. A fully compensated metabolic alkalosis would have the pH returned to a normal level of 7.35-7.45, making Choice *B* incorrect. Lastly, the patient's PaCO2 is in the acidotic, not alkalotic, state to compensate for the metabolic alkalosis.

82. C: CPAP therapy is used in the management of OSA to provide constant positive pressure in the airway, preventing collapse and maintaining patency during sleep. It does not directly affect falling asleep, Choice *A*, or cure sleep apnea completely, Choice *B*. CPAP therapy does not increase the oxygen content of the air breathed in, Choice *D*, but it helps to maintain the airway and prevent interruptions in breathing.

83. A: Root cause analysis is a structured examination of an incident or procedure that is focused on identifying the point at which an error occurred. The process is based on a comprehensive review of all parts of the organizational structure, which would support nurses' understanding of the systems thinking. Competency grids, process diagrams, and case studies are strategies that measure nursing competence related to the QSEN patient safety criteria.

84. C: The only absolute contraindication to the prone position is an unstable spinal fracture, making Choice *C* the correct answer. An abdominal hysterectomy and a minimally invasive CABG are both not contraindicated for the prone position. While the patient with increased ICP should be monitored closely in a prone position, a marginally elevated ICP should not interfere with the oxygenation improvement that can be achieved with proning the ARDS patient.

85. D: Thalassemia is considered a microcytic anemia, in which heme and globin do not synthesize appropriately and oxygen-carrying capacity is compromised. Normocytic anemias are those that include normally sized red blood cells that are deficient in number. Aplastic anemia is an example of a normocytic anemia. Macrocytic anemias are defined as red blood cells that are quite large in shape, leading to abnormalities in oxygen-carrying ability and oxygen delivery. Thrombocytopenic refers to a low platelet count, a different component of the blood, and is thus irrelevant in this scenario.

86. A: Patients with acute kidney injury may experience anemia as the kidneys are unable to produce enough erythropoietin, a hormone that stimulates red blood cell production. To help with the anemia, erythropoietin can be given to help produce more red blood cells. Choices *B, C,* and *D* are all incorrect. Diuretics are used to increase urine output, antibiotics are used to treat infection, and immunosuppressants are used to suppress the immune system.

87. D: Docusate sodium, Choice *D*, can be prescribed alongside opiates to ease constipation, a common side effect of this drug class. Choice *A* represents a medication that is prescribed for opioid addiction and would not be prescribed at the time of opioid prescription for symptom management. Choice *B* and Choice *C* are both contraindicated for use while taking opiates and should be avoided at this time.

88. C: The nurse should correct the student if they attempt to flush and waste blood from the central line. Blood should be drawn directly from the line without flush or waste in order to capture any bacteria that may have colonized the catheter. Choice *A* is incorrect because drawing from the line and a peripheral venipuncture is correct procedure for assessing CLABSI. Choice *B* is incorrect because it is proper procedure to collect anaerobic and aerobic samples from both sites. Choice *D* is incorrect because it is proper procedure to draw blood cultures before the initiation of antibiotics in order to capture bacteria in the bloodstream.

89. B: The elevated glucose levels associated with both type 1 and type 2 diabetes result in atherosclerosis, or wall thickening of the small arterioles and capillaries, which alters the circulation in the brain, retina, peripheral nerves, and kidneys. These changes are cumulative and irreversible; however, long-term control of the serum glucose level as measured by the A1C can limit the progression of this process. Current research indicates that the optimum A1C level is patient specific. In this discussion, the patient knows his personal A1C target and understands the association between the elevated glucose levels and the occurrence of the TIA; therefore, Choice *B* is correct. Two of the ABCD^2 score categories are modifiable risk factors. Maintaining the systolic and diastolic blood pressure and blood glucose level as defined by the A1C within normal limits may lower the risk of a repeated attack. The patient should be encouraged to make the necessary lifestyle changes, including smoking cessation, dietary modifications, exercise participation, and compliance with the medication regimen that may include antihypertensive and glucose-lowering agents. Choice *A* is incorrect. There are differences in the pathophysiology between type 1 and type 2 diabetes; however, the complications are similar. In type 2 diabetes, hyperglycemia and insulin resistance contribute to increased low-density lipoproteins and triglycerides and decreased levels of high-density lipoproteins and alterations in microvasculature; therefore, Choice *C* is incorrect. To prevent further damage to the vascular system and reduce the risk of recurrent TIAs, the use of insulin may be necessary to control hyperglycemia as evidenced by the A1C level; therefore, Choice *D* is incorrect.

90. D: The information indicates that the patient may be relatively stable, yet it is necessary to assess their ability to participate in the lesson for more than 15–20 minutes due to fatigue. Teaching-learning sessions of one hour or more will most likely be unproductive for this patient because of the limitations from fatigue. Teaching-learning sessions of one hour or more will most likely be unproductive for the patient with the identified Synergy Model score due to the limitations imposed by their multiple morbidities and moderately impaired resiliency. Literature from a nursing journal may or may not be appropriate to the patient's learning needs, however, simply providing printed information without additional instruction or discussion does not allow for assessment of the patient's comprehension of the information. The nurse caring for a patient in the acute care environment is responsible for assessing the patient's learning and initiating the necessary instruction. The teaching plan and the patient's progress will be reported to the community provider; however, the process should be started by the inpatient nursing staff.

91. B: This patient scores a 12 on the NIH Stroke Scale. The patient's assessment reveals the following scores:

- Level of consciousness: 0
- Asking age and month: 1
- Following commands: 0
- Ocular movements: 0
- Visual fields: 0
- Facial palsy: 1
- Left arm motor: 0
- Right arm motor: 4
- Left leg motor: 0

- Right leg motor: 4
- Limb ataxia: 0
- Sensation: 0
- Language/aphasia: 1
- Dysarthria: 1
- Extinction: 0

92. C: Diabetes insipidus is caused by a decreased amount of vasopressin secreted by the pituitary gland in the body. This decrease will cause massive diuresis, leading to dehydration and hypovolemia. SIADH is the opposite situation in which vasopressin is overly released, also called antidiuretic hormone, and fluid is retained, leading to hyponatremia. Diabetes type I and diabetes type II, the two types of diabetes mellitus, share the name diabetes but are slightly different. Diabetes describes a condition in which polyuria occurs, and in the case of diabetes mellitus (mellitus is Latin for "sweetened with honey," describing the sweetness of urine in diabetes mellitus), it is because of hyperglycemia that the polyuria occurs.

93. A: When a person misses dialysis, their most likely electrolyte imbalance is hyperkalemia. Because of this, the nurse initially may see peaked T waves on the patient's ECG, Choice *A*. Choice *B*, depressed T waves, is incorrect; this is more an indication of hypokalemia. Choice *C*, widened QRS, is incorrect; this is more an indication of hypocalcemia. Choice *D*, shortened QRS, is incorrect; this is an indication of hypercalcemia.

94. B: Insufficient translation is not a common barrier to the application of nursing research in clinical practice. Common barriers include inadequate funding, limited access to appropriate patient populations, lack of institutional support for research initiatives, and the rapid expansion of new knowledge from multiple sources.

95. B: The diuretic reduces blood volume, while the ACE inhibitor reduces SVR by interfering with the RAAS. An ARB reduces systemic vascular resistance, but morphine is used to treat pain. The diuretic reduces blood volume, but a beta-blocker increases myocardial contractility. The diuretic reduces blood volume, but A CCB works by decreasing myocardial contractility.

96. D: Patients with type 1 diabetes cannot produce enough or any insulin and are required to manually administer it into their system. This answer option is the only one that has an appropriate, logical pairing; therefore, it is the correct statement.

97. C: An atrial septal defect is not part of the tetralogy of Fallot. The tetralogy of Fallot includes a ventricular septal defect, an aorta arising from both ventricles (an atrial septal defect), and hypertrophy of the overworked right ventricle due to pulmonary valve stenosis.

98. D: Pain that continues or recurs longer than three months is considered chronic pain. Choice *A* is incorrect because the patient's pain has lasted longer than three months, but acute pain lasts less than three months. Choice *B* is incorrect because, while neuropathic pain can also be chronic, the patient's description of the pain does not have any hallmark features of neuropathic pain such as shooting, tingling, sharpness, or a pins-and-needles sensation. Based on their description, the patient's pain is unlikely to have a neuropathic origin. Choice *C* is incorrect because again, while visceral pain can also become chronic, the patient's pain clearly exists in the hip joint, while visceral pain can originate from

245

the affected organ or be diffuse or referred. Based on the patient's description, the pain is unlikely to be visceral in origin.

99. C: Acid reflux, along with anxiety or panic attacks, may mimic the chest pain experienced during a heart attack. The proximity of the upper sphincters of the stomach involved in acid reflux to the heart muscle are the cause of the confusion. The patient's presentation, history, and physical along with lab testing and assessment will aid in correct diagnosis. While liver cirrhosis, kidney failure, and pneumonia all involve organs close to the heart, they do not mimic the symptoms of a heart attack.

100. A: Antiplatelet therapy, commonly aspirin, is coupled with antithrombotic therapy in the postoperative period following an endarterectomy to prevent blood clotting caused by platelet aggregation, thus reoccluding the blood vessels just operated on. Beta-blockers, ACE inhibitors, and ARBs are not commonly paired with antithrombotics; rather, they target blood pressure issues and heart failure.

101. C: An appropriate prevention protocol for hospital-acquired pneumonia includes routine oral hygiene, making Choice C correct. Choice A is incorrect, as overuse and inappropriate use of antibiotics is leading to antibiotic resistance. Choice B is incorrect, as limiting patient visitors is not always appropriate for all patients. Choice D is incorrect, as increased fluid intake is not appropriate for all patients and would not make a vast difference in the presence of hospital-acquired pneumonia.

102. B: Hypertonic saline, in which the sodium is more concentrated, is often used to correct the dilutional hyponatremia of SIADH. Normal saline has a 0.9% concentration of sodium, which is the same as circulating blood and thus will not be helpful in correcting hyponatremia. Hypotonic saline, in which there is less than 0.9% concentration of sodium, will also not be helpful in restoring normal sodium levels to the blood. Lactated ringer's solution is not a fluid used for the purpose of restoring normal sodium levels.

103. B: Cigarette smoking is a major cause of atherosclerosis, the most common cause of aortic aneurysms. Following a low-fat diet would help with dyslipidemia, which may be a contributor to atherosclerosis, but it is not as important as stopping smoking, which causes the inflammatory, toxic effects that produce atherosclerosis. Exercise is helpful in coping with stress effectively, as is meditation, but not specific to atherosclerosis that causes aortic aneurysms.

104. C: Pursed-lip breathing, breathing through a small, straw-like opening of the mouth, creates positive end-expiratory pressure (PEEP) for the patient with compromised lung function, as is the case with COPD patients. Tripod breathing is common in COPD patients but does not increase PEEP; rather, it creates more space for lung volume when they are having trouble breathing. Wide open-mouth breathing is not helpful for increasing PEEP. Frequent coughing is caused by the body's constant mucociliary response to try and clear mucus from inflamed airways.

105. A: Neurogenic bladder, Choice A, is one of the possible adverse effects of stroke in some patients. While the patient's kidneys continue to produce urine, the patient may be unable to control bladder function due to neuron damage, which can lead to retention requiring catheterization. Post-void residual allows the nurse to measure the patient's ability to empty their bladder with a bladder scanner. Choices B and D are incorrect; post-void residual will not indicate if a patient has an infection and diabetes insipidus. Choice C is incorrect; post-void residual is meant to test a patient's ability to empty their bladder without a catheter placed.

246

106. C: Acute respiratory distress syndrome (ARDS) is defined by the timing, a chest x-ray, the origin of the edema, and the severity of hypoxemia. In terms of timing, the onset of symptoms in ARDS is within one week of the inciting incident. A chest x-ray should reveal bilateral lung infiltrates not explained by consolidation, atelectasis, or effusions. The edema origin is not explained by heart failure or fluid overload, and the severity of hypoxemia is based on the PaO_2/FiO_2 ratio while on 5 cm of continuous positive airway pressure (CPAP).

107. C: Spironolactone, Choice *C,* is a potassium-sparing diuretic and supports the patient's concern regarding their potassium level currently. This medication does not encourage the excretion of potassium via urine. Furosemide and torsemide are loop diuretics and Microzide® (hydrochlorothiazide) is a thiazide diuretic. These medications do not specifically target conserving potassium in the body to address the patient's concern arising from their history. Therefore, Choices *A, B,* and *D* are incorrect.

108. A: Distributive justice refers to the allocation of scarce resources while advocacy is support for policies that protect at-risk populations. The PCCN understands that scarce resource allocation may be sub-standard in certain populations. In nursing, nonmaleficence means non-harming or inflicting the least harm possible to reach a beneficial outcome. Fidelity refers to faithfulness but does not specifically address resources or the patient population.

109. B: The correct choice is Choice *B.* A nasogastric tube should be placed as soon as possible to decompress the stomach and bowels and prevent further complications. Choice *A* is incorrect. While nausea medication should be given, the priority is decompression. Choice *C* is incorrect. While preventing and treating dehydration is important, it is not the top priority. Choice *D* is also incorrect. Pain medication is not the priority intervention.

110. C: In the Synergy Model, optimum patient care is achieved when the nurse facilitates communication and collaboration with the interdisciplinary team. The nurse possesses the clinical competence to anticipate the needs of the patient and respond appropriately by accessing the required system resources. Resiliency refers to the patient's potential for improved functional status. Creativity is not a characteristic of nursing care identified in the Synergy Model. The complexity of the patient's care needs is assessed according to the number of body systems that are involved.

111. C: The correct choice is Choice *C,* an abdominal CT scan. This is a noninvasive test that can identify ischemic changes related to ischemia. Choice *A* is incorrect. An x-ray would not be able to identify an ischemic bowel. Choices *B* and *D* are incorrect. These tests are both invasive procedures.

112. D: An infected wound will become reddened, inflamed, and discharge pus. A surgical wound should be clean with approximated boundaries. A trauma wound may be irregularly shaped and large. A healing wound develops scabbing and possibly scar tissue but should not appear as the wound described.

113. C: Critical limb ischemia (CLI) is the most concerning symptom of PVD. It is indicative of decreased circulation even at rest. Faint peripheral pulses may be a finding associated with PVD but are not the most concerning symptom. Restricted mobility may be a sequela to PVD, but it is also not the most concerning. Feet that become pale when elevated are a symptom of PVD, but this is not the most concerning symptom.

114. D: An ankle-brachial BP index is commonly used to diagnose peripheral arterial disease by comparing the blood pressures of the two sites, thus assessing blood flow. An echocardiogram is a sonographic test used to visualize the structures of the heart, such as in heart failure. A computed

247

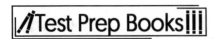

tomography (CT) scan would not be useful for visualizing arterial structures of the extremities, or at least it is not commonly used. An electrocardiogram is used to measure and track electrical activity of heart muscle.

115. D: The PCCN demonstrates professional competence because of a commitment to lifelong learning that is required for expert care of acutely ill patients. The remaining pairs each contain only a single element of the six elements of caring, compassion, confidence, and conscience.

116. C: Small-bowel obstruction is associated with severe fluid and electrolyte losses. The normal serum sodium level is 135 to 145 mEq/L; therefore, Choice *C* is indicative of deficient serum sodium and severe alterations in fluid balance. Small-bowel obstruction is manifested by metabolic alkalosis due to the loss of acids with vomiting. Choice *A* is consistent with metabolic acidosis, not alkalosis, and is therefore incorrect. As noted, small-bowel obstruction is associated with fluid volume deficits; however, the reported serum osmolality of 285 mOsm/kg is within the normal range for serum osmolality (275–295 mOsm/kg); therefore, Choice *B* is incorrect. Abdominal distention in large-bowel obstruction most commonly occurs in the lower abdomen, while abdominal distention in the small bowel most commonly occurs in the epigastric or upper abdominal area; therefore, Choice *D* is incorrect.

117. B: An ST-segment elevation is the classic ECG reading that indicates a STEMI, in which the full thickness of the heart wall has been damaged, leading to the significant ECG changes. T-wave inversion can be linked to several cardiac disorders, both benign and life-threatening, but in the case of heart attacks, it is linked to NSTEMIs. The QT-segment prolongation is part of a condition in which the patient experiences irregular, chaotic heart rhythms from time to time and is not associated with an active myocardial infarction. The U-wave is sometimes too small to be observed on a normal ECG. It follows the T-wave and is not significant in showing heart wall damage, although it can become elevated in hypokalemia.

118. C: Working with the delay and supporting colleagues in the pharmacy through a challenging process best represents systems thinking. Choice *A* is incorrect because the delay does not affect patient safety and potentially reflects poorly on the pharmacy during an unavoidable process. Choice *B* is incorrect because the nurse is disparaging her pharmacy colleagues for being "slow," which does not reflect systems thinking. Choice *D* is incorrect because it places unnecessary pressure on pharmacy colleagues.

119. D: Symptoms of left-sided heart failure are tachycardia, shortness of breath, and the expectoration of frothy pink sputum. Pitting edema is symptomatic of right-sided heart failure and increased venous pressure that backs up into the tissues, causing edema. Ascites is a result of diffuse congestion in the liver caused by the increased venous pressure that characterizes right-sided heart failure. Fatigue is a generalized symptom not associated with the diagnosis of either right- or left-sided heart failure.

120. A: DVT is the most common cause of edema caused by venous insufficiency. The other three factors are also causes, but not as common as DVT.

121. A: Use of a cane is not a risk factor for falls in the elderly. A cane would actually benefit a person by giving them extra stability when walking. Poor lighting is a risk factor because it could cause someone to stumble over items on the floor or cause an imbalance by bumping into unseen furniture. Muscle weakness and slower reflexes are also risk factors for falls in the elderly.

122. A: Clinical inquiry is the process of thinking critically about factors that affect patient care outcomes. It involves gathering and examining data, researching evidence, and applying the information gathered to improve patient care. Examining data before and after the change of linen vendor is a necessary first step to determine if there truly is a correlation between the vendor change and the increase in pressure injuries. Choices *B* and *D* are incorrect because they assume that there is an actual increase in pressure injuries and the new linen is the cause. Choice *C* is incorrect because it hands off responsibility for inquiry to the manager.

123. A: A patient in shock will usually exhibit oliguria, in which urine output has dramatically decreased or stopped altogether, signaling a shutting down of the kidneys due to lack of perfusion from the heart. Other signs of decreased perfusion as seen in a shock state are distant heart sounds, cyanosis, and faint and rapid pulse.

124. A: The sodium-potassium pump is a balance maintained between sodium on the inside of a cell and potassium in the blood outside of the cell. Maintaining this balance creates membrane potential across the cell. The other pairings listed in the statements do not make sense.

125. C: Heparin works by enhancing the effect of antithrombin III which prevents the activation of thrombin and thus prevents fibrinogen from being converted to fibrin. It is important to note that heparin does not get rid of preexisting clots, but it helps prevent clot expansion and formation of new clots. Paroxetine is used to treat anxiety and depression**Error! Bookmark not defined.**. Coumadin® (warfarin) works by blocking vitamin K-dependent clotting factors. Aspirin works on platelet aggregation.

126. A: Gram-negative bacilli (such as *Pseudomonas* and *Klebsiella*) and gram-positive cocci (such as *Streptococcus* and *Staphylococcus*) are the most common sources of HAP. Choice *B* is incorrect because *Helicobacter pylori* is a common pathogen for stomach ulcers and gastritis. Choice *C* is incorrect because gram-positive bacilli and spiral bacteria are not common causes of HAP. Choice *D* is incorrect because, while about a third of pneumonia cases are thought to be viral, it is not the most likely pathogen underlying HAP.

127. C: Angioplasty and stent placement often occur during routine cardiac catheterization to open up occluded blood vessels. There is no camera or scope; instead, dye is shot through the catheter and x-ray images are obtained to visualize structures. The femoral artery is the most commonly accessed blood vessel for left heart catheterization versus the brachial artery, which can be used but is not as common. The patient is not put to sleep, but rather given medicine to help them relax while keeping them awake.

128. A: A *non-punitive* quality reporting system allows for hospital leaders to identify potential risks to patient safety by providing data that can be investigated by multidisciplinary teams. It also incentivizes reporting because frontline staff can use the system without fear of penalty. Choice *B* is incorrect because it would represent using the quality reporting system in a punitive manner, which would disincentivize others from submitting QRs. Choice *C* is incorrect because QR systems are primarily intended to reveal systemic risks so that those risks can be remediated. Choice *D* is incorrect because the primary goal of a QR system is to enhance patient safety; while they may have an anonymous reporting option, they are not primarily intended to address complaints between staff members.

129. C: The nurse should tell the patient about the mistake and explain what the consequences may be, if any. Since the extra labetalol might affect the patient's blood pressure, the nurse should reassess the patient in an hour. The nurse should notify the physician in case any changes in subsequent doses may be warranted. The nurse should also submit a quality report, which will go to the nurse manager. Choice A is incorrect because the nurse cannot know what will and will not affect the patient, and all medication errors should be reported as part of an effort to improve care. Choice B is incorrect because even if the physician says that the error is unimportant, the nurse should still explain what happened to the patient and submit a quality report. Choice D is incorrect because unless the nurse needs the manager to act, going directly to their office is not necessary and takes the focus away from the patient. The nurse manager will see the error in the quality reporting and can decide what to do with the information.

130. B: Choice B represents the correct way to measure and use a cane. The length of the cane should ensure that the patient is able to slightly flex the elbow to allow for proper body mechanics and safety. Choice A is subjective and should be avoided. Choice C should be avoided, as full flexion does not represent properly supported posture or ambulation. Choice D must be avoided because full extension of the arm with a forward lean is unsafe and does not support a steady gait.

131. B: Healthcare power of attorney is the legal term for the person appointed by the patient to make their healthcare decisions should they become incapacitated. This may be a caregiver, but not necessarily. The hospice nurse does not make the decisions but rather follows the doctor's orders and gives counsel to the patient and their family. A legal guardian may also be appointed to be the healthcare power of attorney, but not necessarily.

132. B: According to the model, vulnerability refers to the presence of any stressor, actual or potential, that could adversely affect the patient's health. A history of smoking increases the patient's vulnerability to additional health alterations. Socioeconomic status and being married are related to resource availability, which refers to the availability of financial and emotional resources that are necessary to support the patient's recovery. The patient's active participation in the plan of care (Choice D) is considered to have a positive effect on care outcomes.

133. C: Nurses must acknowledge their own biases and recognize that those biases will affect their ability to provide culturally sensitive care. Standard protocols related to cultural beliefs and practices are an imperfect solution to the problem of culturally sensitive care because they are not individualized to the specific patient. Meeting the needs of the largest group in a population generally means that the cultural needs of the minority groups within the population are not met. As previously stated, culturally competent care results when caregivers first consider their own biases and the possible effect of those beliefs on patient care. If nurses base their care only on their own beliefs, the patient's beliefs and practices will be ignored.

134. C: The correct choice is Choice C. The priority is to draw labs. This will inform the nurse as to the severity of the bleed and start the process of identifying compatible blood if needed. Choice A is incorrect. Starting intravenous fluids is not the priority. Choice B is also incorrect. While an EGD will likely be scheduled, this is not the priority action. Choice D is incorrect. Labs will likely be ordered to monitor blood levels at least every six hours, but this choice does not include a type and crossmatch.

135. D: This patient is showing signs of sundowning, which is common among patients with dementia. They may become increasingly confused at certain times of day, especially in the afternoon and evening. Once the nurse has determined basic needs are met, such as meals and toileting, the nurse should attempt to provide the patient with a safe activity to keep them occupied. Choice A is incorrect;

reorienting the patient with dementia will often cause them to become more confused and agitated. It is typically best to meet the dementia patient within their own thought process and ensure safety. Choices *B* and *C* should only be implemented if all other options are ineffective and the patient is at risk of harming themselves or others.

136. A: Prehypertension is defined as systolic pressures ranging between 120 and 139 mmHg or diastolic pressures between 80 and 89 mmHg. Normal blood pressure is less than 120/80 mmHg. Stage 1 hypertension ranges from 140 to 159 mmHg systolic or 90 to 99 mmHg diastolic. Stage 2 hypertension is greater than or equal to 160 mmHg systolic or greater than or equal to 100 mmHg diastolic.

137. C: The Synergy model identifies clinical inquiry as a nursing competency that develops because of clinical experience and enables nurses to apply research findings to clinical practice. Novice nurses in the model can identify changes in the patient's condition, but do not have the skill to identify alternative interventions. Nursing competencies that are identified as critical to the care of vulnerable patients include advocacy, moral agency, collaboration, and systems thinking. Clinical reasoning is not discussed in the Synergy Model; however, clinical judgment is identified as an essential element of the clinical inquiry competency of expert nurses.

138. C: Morphine is part of most cardiac protocols given for cardiac pain relief when patients have an unacceptable pain level, while nitroglycerine is a vasodilator that reduces preload in the presence of chest pain. Magnesium sulfate is administered for the Torsade de pointes dysrhythmia and is not part of general chest pain protocol. With a pain level of 10/10 and diaphoresis, acetaminophen would not be an appropriate pain management choice.

139. B: Norepinephrine is a potent vasoconstrictor that may be used if dopamine is inadequate in maintaining normal blood pressure in a patient experiencing cardiogenic shock. Dobutamine is an option but is used for systemic vasodilation with stronger beta effects than the others mentioned here. Milrinone causes vasodilation and positive inotropic effects. Nitroglycerin is a potent vasodilator that would lower blood pressure rather than raise it.

140. B: During septic shock, metabolic acidosis and respiratory alkalosis are expected findings, along with a symptom presentation of shortness of breath, temperature changes, confusion, and diaphoresis. Thus, *I* and *II* are correct. *III* is incorrect, as the patient would likely experience a widening pulse pressure, not one that is narrowing. *IV* is incorrect, as the patient would display a decreased cardiac output.

141. C: Of the four patients, the one described in Choice *C* has the greatest number of risk factors for SSI: advanced age, smoking, diabetes, and malnutrition. The patient in Choice *A* has the lowest risk of the four patients. Choice *B* is incorrect because, while their BMI is a risk factor, they are at lower risk than the patient described in Choice *C*. Choice *D* is incorrect because, while their BMI is also a risk factor, they too have fewer risk factors than the patient described in Choice *C*.

142. B: When using an artificial graft, rather than a patient's own vessel, to graft in between the femoral and popliteal arteries in the leg, narrowing and reocclusion are a concern. This is a known complication of these types of grafts. Infection is always a risk but nonspecific to this instance. Edema is associated with venous occlusion and insufficiency. Tissue graft rejection is another nonspecific possibility.

143. A: The nurse should be proactive in using collaboration and delegation as much as possible to manage this temporary disruption in workflow. Choice *B* is incorrect because the nurse should not hurry

PCCN Practice Test #2

1. The nurse is preparing to remove a patient's indwelling urinary catheter after abdominal surgery. The patient asks the nurse to leave the catheter in because he is afraid it will hurt too much to get up to void. What is the best response to the patient's request?
   a. "You can keep the catheter. It will be much less painful for you than getting up to void, and it's important that we control your pain."
   b. "I will send a request to the physician to keep the catheter in and see what he says."
   c. "I need to remove the catheter. I'm sorry if it hurts, but you will need to use the bedside commode to void."
   d. "Leaving the catheter in puts you at greater risk for a UTI. It's also very important to get up and void on your own after surgery. But I will make sure to manage your pain."

2. Which patient is most likely to be developing sepsis?
   a. A 45-year-old post-orthopedic surgery with BP 100/50, temperature 37 °C, pulse 100, respiratory rate 22, normal mentation, and pain level 8/10
   b. An 85-year-old with community-acquired pneumonia, BP 88/45, temperature 35.6 °C, pulse 100, respiratory rate 20, and confusion
   c. A 55-year-old post-gastric surgery with signs of a surgical site infection (SSI), BP 145/90, temperature 39 °C, pulse 70, respiratory rate 18, pain level 7/10, irritability, and localized redness and swelling at the incision site
   d. A 25-year-old on immunosuppressive medication with BP 110/55, temperature 36.5 °C, pulse 85, respiratory rate 18, drowsiness, anorexia, and nausea

3. Who should the nurse collaborate with for a patient that has complex wounds that require specialized care?
   a. Wound-ostomy nurse
   b. Patient care assistant
   c. Primary care provider
   d. Dietician

4. A patient who was previously alert and oriented appears to be lethargic and disoriented. The nurse checks their blood glucose and finds that it is 25. Which of the following is the best initial intervention for this patient?
   a. Provide the patient with orange juice.
   b. Administer IM glucagon.
   c. Administer IV D5W drip.
   d. Administer IV D50 push.

5. Which of the following interventions should the nurse implement when caring for a patient with acute kidney injury?
   a. Obtain daily weights.
   b. Administer intravenous spironolactone.
   c. Encourage increased fluids.
   d. Administer cyclosporine by mouth.

6. The nurse is caring for a 79-year-old patient who presents with severe shortness of breath, hypotension, and crackles in the lower lobes bilaterally. The patient's cardiac index is low, and the physician suspects cardiogenic shock. Which of the following conditions in the patient's medical history might have contributed to this diagnosis?
   a. Chronic obstructive pulmonary disease (COPD)
   b. Acute myocardial infarction (AMI)
   c. Pneumonia
   d. Asthma

7. The nurse is caring for a diabetic patient on insulin therapy. She notes that the patient's blood glucose levels have been elevated despite receiving scheduled insulin. The nurse should collaborate with which healthcare professional?
   a. Endocrinologist
   b. Gastroenterologist
   c. Dietician
   d. Urologist

8. The nurse is assessing a patient for risk factors associated with PE. Which of the following factors should the nurse consider as a potential risk factor for PE in this patient?
   a. Older than 65 years of age
   b. History of DVT
   c. COPD
   d. Body mass index (BMI) of 22 kg/m²

9. A patient has developed an unexpected complication after having a surgical procedure. Which action should the nurse take to best help the patient?
   a. Discuss the complication with the surgeon.
   b. Conduct a literature review to gather evidence-based information on the surgery and its complications.
   c. Document the complication in the patient's medical records.
   d. Notify the charge nurse of the complication.

10. The nurse is caring for a 65-year-old patient who has been diagnosed with pneumonia. Which of the following is an appropriate nursing intervention to promote effective airway clearance in this patient?
    a. Administering nebulized bronchodilators
    b. Assisting with incentive spirometry
    c. Providing chest physiotherapy
    d. Performing endotracheal suctioning

11. A 45-year-old patient is diagnosed with pulmonary hypertension. Which of the following best describes the underlying pathophysiology of this condition?
    a. Dilated and weakened pulmonary arteries, leading to decreased blood flow
    b. Inflammation and infection of the pulmonary vasculature, causing narrowing and occlusion
    c. Impaired gas exchange in the alveoli, leading to reduced oxygen uptake
    d. Increased pulmonary vascular resistance due to vasoconstriction and remodeling of pulmonary arterioles

12. A 75-year-old male patient has a history of aortic stenosis and is in the progressive care unit following a transcatheter aortic valve replacement (TAVR) procedure. Which of the following postoperative complications should the nurse be vigilant for in this patient?
 a. Acute kidney injury
 b. Pericardial effusion
 c. Aortic dissection
 d. Stroke

13. The nurse is providing an educational session on asthma triggers and management for individuals with asthma. Which of the following actions by the nurses will help facilitate learning the best?
 a. Present a PowerPoint lecture.
 b. Show a video on asthma management.
 c. Encourage people in the group to share their personal asthma triggers and experiences.
 d. Hand out pamphlets on asthma triggers and management.

14. The nurse is caring for a patient who presents with dizziness, tachycardia, and diaphoresis. The patient's blood sugar is 50 mg/dL. What action should the nurse take?
 a. Have the patient sit down and take deep breaths.
 b. Have the patient eat a fast-acting carbohydrate.
 c. Administer insulin.
 d. Do not administer anything per mouth.

15. All of the following are precursors to ischemic stroke EXCEPT:
 a. Diabetes
 b. Hypolipidemia
 c. Smoking
 d. Hypertension

16. A 55-year-old patient is admitted to the progressive care unit with a diagnosis of severe ARDS. Which of the following interventions is a key component in the management of ARDS?
 a. Administering corticosteroids
 b. Implementing lung-protective ventilation strategies
 c. Providing high-flow oxygen therapy
 d. Administering diuretic medications

17. The nurse is caring for a patient who is postoperative day one following an abdominal aortic aneurysm (AAA) repair. Which of the following assessment findings would be of most concern to the nurse?
 a. Absent bowel sounds
 b. Mild incisional pain
 c. Decreased sensation and movement in the legs
 d. Urine output of 50 mL/hr

18. The nurse is caring for a patient diagnosed with pericarditis. Which of the following symptoms is a typical clinical manifestation of this condition?
   a. Pulsus paradoxus
   b. Chest pain that improves when leaning forward
   c. Peripheral edema
   d. Wheezing

19. A patient who has been admitted for pneumonia begins having a seizure. The patient's seizure lasts for four minutes and then recurs a few minutes later. What is this condition called?
   a. Grand mal seizure
   b. Serial epilepsy
   c. Tonic-clonic seizure
   d. Status epilepticus

20. A 68-year-old patient is admitted to the progressive care unit with a large pleural effusion. The nurse recognizes that which of the following interventions is a priority in managing this condition?
   a. Administering diuretic medications
   b. Performing thoracentesis
   c. Providing supplemental oxygen therapy
   d. Initiating antibiotic therapy

21. The progressive care nurse is caring for patient that has recently been diagnosed with pulmonary fibrosis and prescribed pirfenidone. What labs should the healthcare team routinely monitor while taking this anti-fibrotic drug?
   a. ALT, AST, and bilirubin
   b. GFT, serum creatinine, and BUN
   c. Glucose, sodium, and potassium
   d. PT and INR

22. A 68-year-old patient with a history of hypertension, hyperlipidemia, and smoking is admitted to the progressive care unit after presenting to the emergency department with chest pain and shortness of breath. The patient's ECG on arrival showed no significant ST-segment changes. Which of the following pathophysiological differences is most helpful in differentiating between NSTEMI and unstable angina?
   a. Degree of coronary artery blockage
   b. Presence of myocardial cell death
   c. Location of the affected coronary artery
   d. Severity of chest pain

23. The hospital where the nurse works has been experiencing an increase in patient readmissions. How can the nurse become involved in addressing this issue?
   a. Provide detailed written discharge instructions for patients.
   b. Create an improved, standardized discharge education process with the interdisciplinary team.
   c. Conduct a root cause analysis on reasons for readmission.
   d. Reiterate the importance of medication adherence to the patients.

24. A 50-year-old patient with known obstructive sleep apnea (OSA) is admitted to the progressive care unit for overnight monitoring. The nurse understands that the primary goal of treatment for OSA is which of the following?
   a. To promote weight loss
   b. To maintain a regular sleep schedule
   c. To provide CPAP therapy
   d. To administer sedative medications at bedtime

25. The nurse is reviewing recent blood work drawn on a patient. She sees that the patient's potassium level is 7.0 mEq/L. Which of the following clinical manifestations would the nurse expect her patient to present with?
   a. Cardiac arrhythmia
   b. Hyperreflexia
   c. Nausea and vomiting
   d. Mental status changes

26. The nurse is caring for a patient with pre-existing hypertension and regular use of antihypertensives who presents with unexplained hypokalemia. The patient denies diarrhea. What steps should the nurse take to assess the possible cause of this patient's hypokalemia?
   a. Ask the patient if they use any illicit drugs and search their belongings.
   b. Review the patient's home medication list for diuretics and ask the patient to describe how they take them.
   c. Review the patient's home medication list for magnesium supplements and ask the patient to describe their use.
   d. Examine the patient's CBC for indications of leukemia.

27. The nurse is caring for a patient with a history of heavy alcohol use who is suspected of developing Wernicke Encephalopathy. To prevent the condition from quickly progressing to coma and death, what should the nurse anticipate doing first?
   a. Drawing a comprehensive metabolic panel and thyroid level and treating based on results
   b. Hydrating aggressively with continuous IV 5% dextrose
   c. Administering IV magnesium
   d. Administering IV thiamine

28. A nurse in the neurology unit is caring for a patient with a history of seizures. While taking the patient's vital signs, she notices that the patient is having a focal aware seizure. What manifestations would the nurse see for this type of seizure?
   a. Muscle jerking and rigidity
   b. Loss of consciousness
   c. Automatisms
   d. Sphincter relaxation

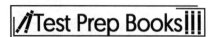

29. A 62-year-old patient is admitted with fever, fatigue, and new-onset heart murmur. After further diagnostic tests, the patient is diagnosed with infective endocarditis. Which of the following pathogens should the nurse recognize as the most common culprit of infective endocarditis?
   a. *Staphylococcus aureus*
   b. *Clostridium difficile*
   c. *Pseudomonas aeruginosa*
   d. *Streptococcus pneumoniae*

30. Which of the following clinical manifestations are indicative of iron-deficiency anemia?
   a. An inflamed and sore tongue
   b. Hyperactivity
   c. Bradycardia
   d. Fingernail clubbing

31. What laboratory test is used to monitor the effectiveness of a patient receiving Coumadin (warfarin) therapy?
   a. Platelet count
   b. Hemoglobin count
   c. Prothrombin time (PT)
   d. Activated partial thromboplastin time (aPTT)

32. Which of the following urinalysis findings would indicate that a patient may be experiencing diabetic ketoacidosis?
   a. Positive nitrites
   b. Positive leukocytes
   c. Positive bilirubin
   d. Positive ketones

33. The nurse in the orthopedic unit is caring for an elderly patient with a hip fracture who is currently bedridden. Which of the following interventions should the nurse implement for this patient?
   a. Assist the patient in performing range of motion exercises.
   b. Apply compression stockings to the patient's lower extremities.
   c. Administer pain medication as needed.
   d. Turn and reposition the patient every two hours.

34. The nurse is providing education to a patient with asthma who has been prescribed corticosteroids in the form of an inhaler. Which of the following statements by the patient indicates understanding of the importance of rinsing the mouth after inhaler use?
   a. "Rinsing my mouth after using the inhaler will help improve the absorption of the medication."
   b. "Rinsing my mouth will prevent the corticosteroid from reaching my lungs effectively."
   c. "Rinsing my mouth will help decrease the side effects of the corticosteroid on my throat."
   d. "Rinsing my mouth can reduce the risk of developing oral thrush from the corticosteroid."

35. A patient admitted for a lower GI bleed has become increasingly pale and confused. Their blood pressure is 85/50, heart rate 114, and pulse oximetry 90%. Which of the following orders should be prioritized?
    a. Administer IV normal saline at 100 ml/hr.
    b. Draw serum hemoglobin and hematocrit levels.
    c. Administer emergent blood.
    d. Perform an abdominal CT scan.

36. The nurse is caring for a patient on an aggressive course of chemotherapy for colon cancer. The patient is experiencing grade-three side effects related to pain and nutrition status. The nurse believes that the patient would benefit from a consult with the palliative care team. What is the best way to explain to this patient what palliative care is?
    a. Palliative care is an expert interdisciplinary team that works alongside your treatment team to improve quality of life and relieve the suffering that comes with complex medical problems.
    b. The palliative care team works closely with terminally ill patients and their families to maximize quality of life and minimize suffering at the end of life.
    c. The palliative care team is made of experts who work to improve your quality of life and reduce suffering. They take over when you and your doctor decide to minimize or stop curative treatment.
    d. The palliative care team is made of specially trained nurses and nutritionists who will help manage your side effects while your doctors continue treatment.

37. Which patient is at greatest risk for hospital-acquired pneumonia?
    a. A patient on high-flow nasal oxygen
    b. A patient who is heavily sedated and intubated
    c. A patient on non-invasive positive-pressure ventilation (NIPPV)
    d. A patient who is intubated and minimally sedated

38. Which of the following is an example of providing culturally competent care for a patient of Asian descent?
    a. Use a professional interpreter for all communication.
    b. Maintain eye contact to make them feel comfortable.
    c. Reassure the patient that their healthcare team will make the best decisions for them.
    d. Encourage the patient's family members to participate in the patient's care and decision-making.

39. Which of the following interventions should the nurse implement to promote comfort and relaxation during the end of life?
    a. Administer pain medication as needed.
    b. Encourage the patient to eat their regular diet.
    c. Limit visitors and keep the room dark to reduce stimulation.
    d. Help the patient participate in daily physical activity.

40. Delirium may affect patients in the hospital and can result in increased mortality. What interventions should be avoided to help reduce the occurrence of delirium?
    a. Use the television or radio.
    b. Cluster care to provide less disturbance.
    c. Control pain and discomfort.
    d. Maintain sleep/wake cycle, provide reorientation, and have sensory aids present.

41. Which of the following is a common precursor to *Clostridium difficile* (*C. diff*) infection?
    a. Illicit drug use
    b. GERD
    c. Poor handwashing
    d. Antibiotic use

42. Which of the following is a clinical manifestation of diabetes mellitus?
    a. Hematuria
    b. Polyuria
    c. Oliguria
    d. Hemoptysis

43. The nurse is part of the quality improvement team at their hospital. Which of the following actions by the nurse demonstrates systems thinking?
    a. Identify underlying factors that are contributing to errors.
    b. Collect data on individual staff members' performance.
    c. Implement new protocols to reduce errors.
    d. Determine which staff members are responsible for errors.

44. A patient is recovering from an interventional cardiac catheterization in which a stent was placed in a coronary artery. Which medication would the nurse expect to administer post-procedure to this patient?
    a. Antiplatelet agent
    b. Beta-blocker
    c. Calcium channel blocker
    d. Diuretic

45. Which of the following findings would the nurse expect to find in a patient diagnosed with diabetic ketoacidosis?
    a. Hyperventilation
    b. Oliguria
    c. Hypoglycemia
    d. Hypoventilation

46. Which of the following is a risk factor for potentially developing dementia?
    a. Frequent infections
    b. Increasing age
    c. Being male
    d. Hypotension

47. A nurse is taking care of a college-age student who has recently started taking an antidepressant. Which of the following side effects should the nurse monitor for?
    a. Fever
    b. Rash
    c. Hallucinations
    d. Suicidal ideation

48. The nurse is caring for a patient with stage 3 pressure injuries in various stages of healing. The nurse should encourage the patient to eat which kind of diet?
    a. A diet high in protein and total calories
    b. A diet low in protein and high in fiber
    c. A low-calorie diet to reduce the patient's weight
    d. A low-residue diet

49. Nurses are responsible for which of the following elements of informed consent?
    a. Identification of alternatives to the planned procedure
    b. Description of associated risks and benefits
    c. Explanation of the planned procedure or diagnostic test
    d. Assessment of the patient's understanding of the information that is provided

50. The nurse is doing an admission assessment with a patient who speaks Farsi. The patient speaks some English but is not fluent. The patient's husband is fluent in English and says that he will translate for her. What is the best response by the nurse?
    a. "Thank you. That will be very convenient, and I appreciate your help."
    b. "It's better if we speak English. I think she'll be able to understand, and I want her to be able to reply to me directly."
    c. "I'm concerned that you might not be able to translate the complex medical terms I'm going to be using, so I think we should use a translator."
    d. "The hospital does not allow me to use family members as translators. We will use an approved translator, but you are more than welcome to participate."

51. The nurse is caring for a 62-year-old patient who suddenly complains of palpitations. The ECG reveals AFib with a rapid ventricular response (RVR). The nurse knows that immediate medical intervention is critical to prevent which of the following complications?
    a. MI
    b. Stroke
    c. Angina
    d. Hypertension

52. Which of the following statements is consistent with the major premise of the Synergy Model?
    a. Family participation in patient care improves outcomes.
    b. The model is based on the condition of patients and the function of the nursing staff.
    c. The model only relates to critical care environments.
    d. Synergy is said to exist when the environment and nursing competencies are consistent with the needs of the patient and the patient's family.

261

53. The nurse is caring for a patient who is on the first postoperative day following an open CABG surgery. Which of the following complications is the nurse most likely to encounter during the immediate postoperative period?
   a. Hypotension
   b. Thrombocytopenia
   c. AFib
   d. Transient ischemic attack

54. The nurse is caring for a 62-year-old patient with COPD who was admitted for acute respiratory failure. The nurse understands that acute respiratory failure is characterized by which of the following?
   a. Severe hypoxemia with normal or low carbon dioxide levels
   b. Severe hypoxemia with elevated carbon dioxide levels
   c. Mild hypoxemia with normal or low carbon dioxide levels
   d. Mild hypoxemia with elevated carbon dioxide levels

55. Which of the following adverse effects should the nurse prioritize when monitoring a patient receiving opioid analgesics for a broken tibia?
   a. Constipation
   b. Respiratory depression
   c. Nausea
   d. Sedation

56. At which level of the caring practices continuum identified in the Synergy Model is death initially viewed as an acceptable patient outcome?
   a. Level 1
   b. Level 2
   c. Level 3
   d. Death is considered as an acceptable outcome at all levels of caring practice.

57. The nurse is running a root cause analysis of a medication error that occurred at the hospital. Which of the following actions by the nurse indicates the use of systems thinking for this cause analysis?
   a. Monitor the nurse that made the error during their shift.
   b. Identify and address all the factors that contributed to the medication error.
   c. Implement a double-check system for medication administration.
   d. Notify the nurse manager.

58. A 40-year-old patient is admitted to the progressive care unit with severe asthma exacerbation. Which of the following medications should the nurse anticipate administering as a first-line treatment?
   a. Corticosteroids
   b. Long-acting beta-agonists
   c. Anticholinergic agents
   d. Short-acting beta-agonists

59. What is the most appropriate nursing intervention for a patient who speaks a different language?
   a. Use a professional interpreter.
   b. Use a family member to interpret, as they know the patient best.
   c. Speak slowly and loudly to help the patient understand.
   d. Provide the patient with written instructions in their language.

60. Which of the following would be the most appropriate action the nurse could take to help facilitate continuous learning for a patient that has just received a colostomy?
    a. Provide diagrams and written instructions on how to apply the appliance.
    b. Show a video on colostomy care to the patient.
    c. Demonstrate colostomy care to the patient and allow them to practice on a mannequin.
    d. Have the patient participate in a colostomy support group.

61. Which of the following should the nurse prioritize when providing education about breastfeeding to expectant parents?
    a. The use of pre-recorded video demonstration
    b. The use of practice dolls
    c. The use of written step-by-step instructions
    d. The use of verbal discussion

62. The nurse is caring for a 55-year-old patient who is suspected of having the flu. The patient presented with symptoms of fever, body aches, cough, and fatigue. The patient also mentions receiving the flu vaccine last year and asks the nurse why they still got the flu. Which of the following statements is the most appropriate response by the nurse?
    a. "The flu vaccine is 100% effective in preventing the flu, so it's unusual that you still got infected."
    b. "The flu vaccine is not 100% effective, so it's possible that you were still able to contract the virus."
    c. "It's possible that you were exposed to a different strain of the flu virus that wasn't covered by last year's vaccine."
    d. "It takes a couple of weeks for the flu vaccine to provide full protection, so you may have been exposed before it took effect."

63. A 55-year-old patient with COPD and respiratory failure has been receiving mechanical ventilation for the past week. The healthcare team decides to initiate a weaning trial to assess the patient's readiness for extubation. During the weaning trial, the patient exhibits increased work of breathing, decreased oxygen saturation, and increased respiratory rate. The nurse recognizes that these findings suggest which of the following?
    a. Respiratory distress and the need for continued mechanical ventilation
    b. Successful weaning from mechanical ventilation
    c. Normal physiological response during the weaning process
    d. Ineffective breathing pattern due to anxiety

64. A 68-year-old patient with a history of chronic pain is admitted to the progressive care unit. The nurse notes the patient's respiratory rate is 6 breaths per minute and the patient is difficult to arouse. The nurse suspects respiratory depression. Which of the following actions should the nurse prioritize?
    a. Administering naloxone
    b. Assisting with endotracheal intubation
    c. Providing supplemental oxygen
    d. Assessing the patient's level of consciousness

65. A 62-year-old patient is admitted to the progressive care unit with acute respiratory distress syndrome (ARDS). Which of the following is a characteristic feature of ARDS?
   a. Rapid onset of wheezing and dyspnea
   b. Elevated carbon dioxide levels and respiratory acidosis
   c. Diffuse alveolar damage and impaired gas exchange
   d. Hyperinflation of the lungs and increased residual volume

66. The nurse is caring for a patient who identifies as transgender. Which of the following interventions is the most appropriate?
   a. Avoid using pronouns when addressing the patient.
   b. Use gender-neutral terms when addressing the patient.
   c. Use the patient's chosen name and pronouns.
   d. Encourage the patient to speak with their provider regarding transitioning.

67. How can the nurse apply systems thinking when caring for a patient who has a chronic illness?
   a. Identifying all the physical systems involved in the patient's chronic illness
   b. Focusing on the patient's psychosocial needs
   c. Implementing disease-specific interventions for the patient
   d. Coordinating with several healthcare providers and specialists for their treatment plan

68. When caring for a patient with Methicillin-resistant Staphylococcus aureus (MRSA), what type of precautions should the nurse implement?
   a. Airborne precautions
   b. Standard precautions
   c. Droplet precautions
   d. Contact precautions

69. A 58-year-old patient with a history of hypertension presents with severe, sudden-onset chest pain that radiates to the back. The doctor suspects a dissecting aortic aneurysm. Which diagnostic test is most used to confirm this diagnosis?
   a. Echocardiogram
   b. Chest X-ray
   c. CT scan
   d. ECG

70. The nurse is caring for a patient who is non-English-speaking and is having a difficult time communicating with the healthcare team. Which action should the nurse take as an advocate for this patient?
   a. Ask another nurse who speaks the patient's language to help with communication.
   b. Have a family member of the patient come in to translate.
   c. Use a translation app to speak with the patient.
   d. Document the communication difficulties in the patient's chart.

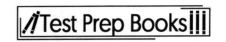

71. A patient with end-stage renal disease is receiving discharge education from the nurse. Which of the following statements by the patient indicates an understanding of following a low-phosphorus diet?
    a. "For breakfast I should try to eat oatmeal or bran."
    b. "Drinking milk daily will help strengthen my bones on this diet."
    c. "Incorporating white rice is okay for this diet."
    d. "I should eat more beans and lentils to help my digestive system."

72. An elderly man presents in the emergency department with complaints of difficulty walking and feeling unsteady when walking. He reports that he is afraid that he is going to fall and has had a few near falls this month. The nurse assesses the patient and notes that the patient has a stooped posture and shuffling gait. Which of the following gait disorders does the nurse suspect the patient may have?
    a. Myasthenia Gravis
    b. Parkinson's Disease
    c. Multiple Sclerosis
    d. Duchenne Muscular Dystrophy

73. A patient is admitted due to dehydration and an electrolyte imbalance due to prolonged diarrhea. The patient has a markedly elevated creatinine level. The physician has ordered a CT of the patient's abdomen with contrast to diagnose possible causes of the patient's diarrhea. Which of the following interventions is best for this patient?
    a. Request an order for an MRI instead of a CT.
    b. Request an order for IV fluids following the CT.
    c. Request an order for an antidiarrheal medication.
    d. Request an order for an x-ray instead of a CT.

74. A 68-year-old patient with a history of uncontrolled hypertension is admitted to the progressive care unit following an episode of chest pain at home. On admission, the patient's blood pressure is recorded at 220/120 mm Hg. Despite the administration of IV antihypertensives, the patient's blood pressure remains significantly elevated and is accompanied by worsening dyspnea and chest discomfort. The nurse should prepare for which of the following potential complications in this patient?
    a. MI
    b. Cardiac arrest
    c. Pulmonary embolism (PE)
    d. Acute renal failure

75. The nurse is caring for a 72-year-old patient with acute heart failure. The patient's blood pressure is 90/60 mm Hg, heart rate is 110 BPM, and oxygen saturation is 88%. Which of the following interventions should be the nurse's first priority?
    a. Start supplemental oxygen.
    b. Administer diuretics as ordered.
    c. Administer a beta-blocker.
    d. Increase IV fluids.

76. A 65-year-old patient who recently suffered a severe MI is now showing signs of cardiogenic shock, including hypotension and tachycardia. The doctor has prescribed dobutamine. What is the primary reason for administering this medication?
   a. To improve renal perfusion
   b. To reduce preload and afterload
   c. To increase myocardial oxygen demand
   d. To increase cardiac output

77. The nurse is caring for a patient who was admitted to the progressive care unit yesterday after arriving at the emergency department with signs and symptoms of a myocardial infarction (MI). The nurse is reviewing the patient's chart and notes that on arrival, the patient's electrocardiogram (ECG) showed ST-segment elevation. Which of the following statements best describes the key pathophysiological difference between ST-elevation myocardial infarction (STEMI) and non-STEMI (NSTEMI)?
   a. STEMI is associated with complete occlusion of a coronary artery, whereas NSTEMI is associated with partial occlusion.
   b. NSTEMI is more severe and has a higher mortality rate than STEMI.
   c. STEMI is characterized by elevated troponin levels, and NSTEMI is not.
   d. STEMI involves ST-segment elevation on the ECG, and NSTEMI does not.

78. A 58-year-old patient is admitted to the progressive care unit following a pneumonectomy for lung cancer. The nurse is assessing the patient and notes absent breath sounds on the right side, tracheal deviation to the right, and decreased chest expansion on the right side. The nurse recognizes these findings as suggestive of which of the following complications?
   a. Pneumothorax
   b. Hemothorax
   c. Atelectasis
   d. Empyema

79. The nurse is responsible for implementing new evidence-based practices at the hospital. Which of the following actions by the nurse is most important in implementing these practices at the hospital?
   a. Hanging posters on evidence-based practices in the break room
   b. Testing the evidence-based practices first and collecting data on their effectiveness
   c. Collaborating with the healthcare team and staff to share evidence-based practices that will be implemented
   d. Providing handouts to the staff on the new practices

80. The nurse is caring for a 58-year-old postoperative patient following a diagnosis of STEMI two days ago. Which of the following surgical procedures did this patient most likely have?
   a. Coronary artery bypass graft (CABG) surgery
   b. Aortic valve replacement
   c. Carotid endarterectomy
   d. Percutaneous coronary intervention (PCI)

81. Which body system will exhibit the most obvious effects of a state of hyperosmolar hyperglycemic nonketotic syndrome (HHNK)?
    a. Neurologic
    b. Cardiac
    c. Endocrine
    d. Pulmonary

82. The nurse is managing a patient who is experiencing anaphylactic shock. The nurse has just administered emergent intramuscular epinephrine. What medication(s) should the nurse prepare to administer next?
    a. Acetaminophen PO
    b. Diphenhydramine and methylprednisolone IV push
    c. 0.9% normal saline continuous infusion
    d. Oxygen 10 L/min by non-rebreather mask

83. A patient who fell at home is admitted to the progressive care unit with a subdural hematoma. What symptoms is the patient likely experiencing?
    a. Headache, hypertension, tachycardia
    b. Drowsiness, confusion, agitation
    c. Headache, hypotension, vision loss
    d. Sudden severe headache, loss of consciousness, double vision

84. The nurse is caring for a 62-year-old patient with a history of type 2 diabetes and uncontrolled hypertension. The patient has been prescribed a regimen of hydrochlorothiazide and lisinopril. What is the primary reason these medications were chosen for this patient?
    a. To reduce the risk of kidney damage associated with diabetes and hypertension
    b. To improve blood glucose control
    c. To treat potential cardiac arrhythmias
    d. To decrease the patient's risk of developing atherosclerosis

85. A patient is undergoing a bedside electroencephalogram (EEG) for new onset seizure activity. What is the most important intervention for the nurse during this test?
    a. Assess neurological status during EEG.
    b. Ensure patient is adequately sedated.
    c. Ensure patient is given anxiolytic.
    d. Avoid nursing care during the EEG.

86. The nurse is caring for a 60-year-old patient with a history of pulmonary hypertension who has been admitted with worsening dyspnea on exertion and fatigue. Which of the following is a characteristic finding in pulmonary hypertension?
    a. Elevated pulmonary artery wedge pressure (PAWP)
    b. Decreased pulmonary vascular resistance
    c. Right ventricular hypertrophy
    d. Increased left ventricular ejection fraction

87. A 45-year-old patient is admitted to the progressive care unit following a TBI. The patient has a decreased level of consciousness and requires close monitoring. The nurse recognizes that a decreased level of consciousness can lead to respiratory depression due to which of the following mechanisms?
    a. Increased stimulation of the respiratory centers in the brain stem
    b. Activation of the sympathetic nervous system, causing bronchodilation
    c. Depressed responsiveness of the respiratory centers in the brain stem
    d. Increased production of surfactant in the alveoli

88. Which of the following is a precursor to acute kidney injury?
    a. Having a solitary kidney
    b. A diagnosis of sepsis
    c. Excessive intake of sugary drinks
    d. Age less than 65 years

89. Hyperglycemia can potentially lead to what issue for patients with diabetes?
    a. Retinal detachment
    b. Secondary infections
    c. Dysphagia
    d. Hyperactivity

90. A nurse is providing discharge education to a 65-year-old patient diagnosed with chronic heart failure. The nurse emphasizes the importance of recognizing the signs of an acute exacerbation. Which of the following signs should the nurse include in the discussion?
    a. Decreased urination
    b. Weight loss
    c. Increased shortness of breath, particularly at night
    d. Decreased swelling in lower extremities

91. The nurse is caring for a patient who has had an adverse reaction to a medication. Which of the following actions by the nurse is an example of clinical inquiry?
    a. Research potential causes and interventions for the adverse reaction.
    b. Document the adverse reaction in the patient's medical record.
    c. Notify the adverse reaction to the patient's healthcare provider.
    d. Reference medication administration guidelines for further information.

92. The nurse is assessing a patient with COPD. Which of the following pulse oximetry reading ranges would the nurse anticipate for this patient?
    a. 85–90%
    b. 88–92%
    c. 92–95%
    d. 95–98%

93. The nurse is caring for a patient diagnosed with AFib. Which medication would the nurse anticipate administering to this patient to help manage the arrhythmia?
    a. Hydrochlorothiazide
    b. Metoprolol
    c. Digoxin
    d. Warfarin

268

94. The nurse works in a community health clinic. Which of the following actions by the nurse aims to improve healthcare services to underserved communities?
    a. Implement a COVID-19 vaccination program for the clinic's staff.
    b. Provide health education sessions for clinic patients.
    c. Hang informational posters in the clinic.
    d. Collaborate with local religious organizations to organize health fairs.

95. A patient admitted to the neurology unit after a hemorrhagic stroke is now complaining of a severe headache along with nausea. The nurse knows that she should assess for which of the following potential complications based on the patient's symptoms?
    a. Aphasia
    b. Hemiplegia
    c. Seizures
    d. Increased intracranial pressure

96. The nurse is caring for a 59-year-old female patient with a severe headache, confusion, and blurred vision. Her blood pressure is 230/115 mm Hg, and IV nitroprusside is initiated. The nurse should closely monitor for which of the following when administering this medication?
    a. Hyperkalemia
    b. Hypotension
    c. Bradycardia
    d. Hyperglycemia

97. Which of the following is NOT an expected finding following an esophagogastroduodenoscopy (EGD)?
    a. Somnolence
    b. Sore throat
    c. Melena
    d. Nausea

98. The nurse is caring for a patient with an upper GI bleed. Which of the following would be the nurse's priority and initial intervention?
    a. Draw blood for complete blood count (CBC).
    b. Administer IV fluids.
    c. Administer oral proton pump inhibitors (PPIs).
    d. Provide the patient with an immediate blood transfusion.

99. A 65-year-old patient is scheduled to undergo a video-assisted thoracic surgery (VATS) for the resection of a lung nodule. The nurse is providing preoperative education to the patient. Which of the following statements made by the patient indicates understanding of the surgical procedure?
    a. "I will have a large incision made in my chest for the surgery."
    b. "The surgeon will use a scope and small incisions to perform the surgery."
    c. "I will be placed on a heart-lung machine during the surgery."
    d. "The surgery will involve the removal of the entire lung."

100. Which of the following is a potential complication of liver failure?
   a. Hepatic encephalopathy
   b. Glomerulonephritis
   c. Hepatitis B
   d. Fatty liver disease

101. The nurse is caring for a pediatric patient with sickle cell anemia who is currently going through a sickle cell crisis. He is experiencing pain in his hands and feet and appears short of breath and tired. What is the primary intervention the nurse should take in caring for her patient experiencing a sickle cell crisis?
   a. Apply ice packs to areas of pain.
   b. Administer both oral and intravenous fluids.
   c. Encourage the patient to exercise for 30 minutes.
   d. Administer intravenous immunoglobulin (IVIG) to boost the immune system.

102. Which of the following patients has the highest risk of developing a catheter-associated urinary tract infection (CAUTI)?
   a. An 80-year-old male who recently underwent orthopedic surgery for a broken leg and has a catheter in place
   b. A 50-year-old woman with urinary incontinence who has a catheter in place
   c. A 30-year-old male with a history of recurrent urinary tract infections who has a catheter in place
   d. A 55-year-old female with a history of hypotension who has a catheter in place

103. Which of the following statements by the new graduate nurse indicates an understanding of how to manage a patient having a tonic-clonic seizure?
   a. "I will put a spoon in the patient's mouth to hold their tongue down and prevent them from choking."
   b. "I will hold the patient down so that he does not injure himself during the seizure."
   c. "I will time the seizure for emergency medical services."
   d. "I will perform mouth-to-mouth breathing to assist the patient in maintaining oxygenation."

104. Which of the following laboratory results would be an expected finding in a patient with end-stage renal disease (ESRD)?
   a. Creatinine 2.5 mg/dl
   b. Potassium 6.3 mEq/l
   c. Calcium 12.5 mg/dl
   d. Troponin 1.5 ng/ml

105. A nurse is preparing to discharge an elderly patient after their hospital stay. The patient tells the nurse that they are worried about managing their medications on their own at home. Which of the following actions should the nurse leader take?
   a. Provide the patient with written instructions for their medications.
   b. Coordinate a home health nurse to visit the patient after their discharge.
   c. Discuss the patient's concerns with the healthcare team to develop a plan of care.
   d. Ask one of the patient's family members to take control of medications for the patient at home.

106. Which of the following research articles should the nurse utilize to conduct a literature review?
    a. Qualitative studies
    b. Expert opinions
    c. Case studies
    d. Randomized control trials

107. The nurse hears one of her patients yelling from their room. Upon entry, she notices that the patient is on the floor after having a suspected fall. Which of the following interventions should the nurse take FIRST?
    a. Notify the physician.
    b. Put the patient on fall precautions.
    c. Check for injuries.
    d. Assess the patient's level of consciousness.

108. How could a healthcare institution successfully support diversity?
    a. Requiring all employees to speak a second language
    b. Providing mandatory cultural sensitivity training for all managers
    c. Offering alternative food services
    d. Providing alternative solutions to all patient requests

109. The nurse is caring for a patient with vancomycin-resistant enterococcus (VRE). Which transmission-prevention practices are appropriate for this patient?
    a. Handwashing with soap and water only and restriction of visitors
    b. Handwashing with soap and water or alcohol-based sanitizer and meticulous disinfection of surfaces
    c. Droplet precautions and daily disinfection of surfaces
    d. None. VRE is not transmissible to others.

110. The nurse is caring for a 40-year-old patient diagnosed with dilated cardiomyopathy. The patient asks why they experience breathlessness during mild exertion. What is the best explanation for this?
    a. The heart is unable to pump blood efficiently, leading to fluid buildup in the lungs.
    b. There is a decrease in the oxygen-carrying capacity of the blood.
    c. The respiratory muscles are weakened due to the disease process.
    d. There is an obstruction to the outflow of blood from the heart.

111. The dialysis nurse is caring for a patient with chronic kidney disease. Which of the following should the nurse consider when caring for a patient receiving hemodialysis?
    a. Monitoring the patient's respiratory status
    b. Providing the patient with high potassium, sodium, and phosphoric-containing foods
    c. Monitoring the patient's blood pressure
    d. Encouraging the patient to consider a kidney transplant

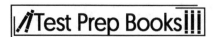

112. The nurse is caring for a 70-year-old female patient who has a history of rheumatic fever during her childhood. She now reports a history of fatigue and shortness of breath on exertion. An echocardiogram reveals stenosis and regurgitation of the mitral valve. These findings are most consistent with which of the following conditions?
   a. Mitral valve prolapse
   b. Aortic stenosis
   c. Mitral valve disease
   d. Tricuspid regurgitation

113. The nurse is caring for a 55-year-old patient who was diagnosed with unstable angina after presenting to the emergency department with intermittent chest pain that occurs at rest and is not relieved by nitroglycerin. Which of the following risks should the nurse recognize as most closely associated with unstable angina?
   a. Increased risk of sudden cardiac death
   b. Higher likelihood of developing heart failure
   c. Increased risk of developing AFib
   d. Increased risk of progression to MI

114. The nurse is caring for a patient who suddenly presents with hypotension, muffled heart sounds, and jugular venous distension. The nurse suspects cardiac tamponade. Which of the following is another clinical sign of this condition?
   a. Normal pulse pressure
   b. Pulsus paradoxus
   c. Widened pulse pressure
   d. Positive Homan's sign

115. The nurse is performing a respiratory assessment and notes decreased breath sounds, asymmetrical chest expansion, and tracheal deviation to the unaffected side. The nurse recognizes these findings as suggestive of which of the following pleural space complications?
   a. Pneumothorax
   b. Hemothorax
   c. Pleural effusion
   d. Chylothorax

116. A patient presents with a rapid, deep breathing pattern, a blood glucose level of 425, an anion gap of 14, and a blood pH of 7.25. Which of the following disorders does the nurse suspect?
   a. Diabetic ketoacidosis
   b. Diabetes insipidus
   c. Myxedema coma
   d. Hyperosmolar hyperglycemic state

117. The nurse enters the patient's room to obtain vital signs. Upon their interaction, the patient becomes increasingly agitated and aggressive. Which of the following interventions should the nurse implement?
   a. Quietly leave the patient's room and return when they are calm.
   b. Offer a diversional activity using a calm tone.
   c. Administer Haldol to the patient.
   d. Let the patient know that this behavior is not tolerated.

118. A 50-year-old male patient in the progressive care unit with a history of uncontrolled hypertension is observed to be restless and anxious. His blood pressure readings over the past 24 hours have ranged from 185/95 mm Hg to 210/110 mm Hg. The patient reports a severe headache and has been complaining of blurred vision. Recognizing these signs and symptoms, the nurse understands that the patient may be experiencing which of the following conditions?
   a. Hypertensive urgency
   b. Hypertensive emergency
   c. Acute heart failure
   d. Acute stroke

119. The National Institutes of Health Stroke Scale (NIHSS) is commonly used to assess the severity of strokes and is used for continuing to monitor any changes in patient condition. A patient who recently suffered an ischemic stroke has a NIHSS stroke scale score of 27. What is the severity of the patient's stroke?
   a. Severe stroke
   b. Moderate stroke
   c. Mild stroke
   d. Transient ischemic attack (TIA)

120. The nurse is caring for a patient with a respiratory condition who is experiencing impaired gas exchange and respiratory distress. Which of the following characteristics would indicate acute respiratory failure rather than chronic respiratory failure?
   a. Gradual onset of symptoms
   b. History of long-term oxygen therapy (LTOT)
   c. Normal arterial blood gas (ABG) values
   d. Severe hypoxemia and hypercapnia

121. The nurse is caring for a 72-year-old patient with a history of hypertension, hyperlipidemia, and atrial fibrillation (AFib) who was admitted to the progressive care unit after presenting to the emergency department with chest pain, shortness of breath, and diaphoresis. The patient was diagnosed with NSTEMI and the use of fibrinolytic therapy was considered. The nurse questions why fibrinolytic therapy was considered based on the patient's presentation. Which of the following statements best explains why fibrinolytics would NOT be indicated for this patient?
   a. Fibrinolytics are contraindicated in patients with a history of AFib.
   b. Fibrinolytics are not effective in patients with elevated troponin levels.
   c. Fibrinolytics are primarily used for patients with STEMI.
   d. Fibrinolytics increase the risk of hemorrhagic complications in patients with NSTEMI.

122. A patient is receiving discharge teaching from his nurse after having a laparoscopic gastric banding surgery. Which of the following statements by the patient indicates an understanding of his diet during the recovery period?
   a. "I am able to eat solid foods after 72 hours."
   b. "I am allowed to have carbonated beverages to help settle my stomach."
   c. "I should only eat clear broths for two to three weeks."
   d. "I can resume my regular diet as soon as I feel better."

273

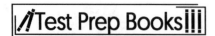

123. Which of the following clinical manifestations indicates a possible lower GI bleed?
    a. Hematochezia
    b. Hematemesis
    c. Melena
    d. Diarrhea

124. A patient is admitted to the progressive care unit complaining of severe diarrhea. The patient reports she recently completed a course of clindamycin. Which personal protective equipment (PPE) should staff wear while caring for this patient?
    a. Gloves
    b. Gloves and gown
    c. Gloves, gown, and eyewear
    d. Gloves, gown, and N95

125. A patient presents with jaundice, dark urine, and fatigue—characteristic signs of hemolytic anemia. What laboratory value would explain the cause of the patient's clinical manifestations?
    a. Elevated sodium levels
    b. Increased red blood cell levels
    c. Decreased white blood cell levels
    d. Elevated bilirubin levels

126. A patient who is admitted for a small bowel obstruction is awaiting surgery in the morning. The patient suddenly complains of increased abdominal pain and vomiting despite antiemetic use. Which intervention should the nurse do first?
    a. Request an order for nasogastric tube placement.
    b. Request an order for abdominal CT.
    c. Prepare the patient for an EGD.
    d. Request an order for additional antiemetics.

127. The nurse is caring for a patient that has recently had a stroke. The patient is having difficulties with communication. Which of the following actions by the nurse would be an example of caring practice?
    a. Use nonverbal communication to show empathy and support.
    b. Restrict visitors to prevent excessive stimulation.
    c. Speak to the patient in a slow and loud voice.
    d. Pretend that the patient is speaking normally.

128. What is the most effective intervention to prevent a surgical site infection (SSI)?
    a. Administering prophylactic antibiotics prior to surgery
    b. Maintaining a sterile technique during surgery
    c. Performing hand hygiene before and after patient contact
    d. Drawing a complete blood count on the patient prior to surgery

129. A pediatric patient is feeling anxious about their upcoming surgery. Which of the following actions by the nurse indicates caring and compassionate care?
    a. Decrease the child's involvement in their healthcare decision-making to decrease anxiety.
    b. Explain to the child that they do not have anything to worry about and that it will be okay.
    c. Listen to the child's concerns and provide age-appropriate explanations.
    d. Utilize diversion techniques to decrease the child's anxiety.

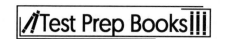

130. A 56-year-old patient on postoperative day two following a minimally invasive direct coronary artery bypass (MIDCAB) complains of localized chest pain and shortness of breath. On examination, the nurse notes reduced breath sounds on the left side and dullness to percussion. What does the nurse suspect based on these findings?
   a. MI
   b. Atelectasis
   c. Pneumothorax
   d. Pleural effusion

131. A patient with pancreatitis in the progressive care unit is found to be tachycardic and hypotensive. The patient is visibly in pain and states that the pain is scored 10/10. What should be the nurse's priority intervention?
   a. Administer fluid resuscitation.
   b. Administer oral pain medication.
   c. Administer intravenous pain medication.
   d. Administer antibiotics that are due now.

132. Which of the following medications would be administered to a patient with an influenza infection?
   a. Amoxicillin
   b. Fluconazole
   c. Oseltamivir
   d. Doxorubicin

133. A 55-year-old male patient with a history of pneumonia presents with a persistent cough, shortness of breath, chest pain, and a high-grade fever. On physical examination, decreased breath sounds are auscultated on the affected side, and there is dullness to percussion. A chest x-ray reveals fluid collection with the presence of pus in the pleural space. Which of the following diagnoses should the nurse anticipate?
   a. Pneumothorax
   b. Hemothorax
   c. Empyema
   d. Pleural effusion

134. A nurse is caring for a patient with a history of alcohol abuse who has been diagnosed with acute pancreatitis. Upon assessment of the patient, the nurse notes that they are disoriented and confused and that their level of consciousness is fluctuating. Which of the following is most likely the cause of the patient's delirium?
   a. Medication side effects
   b. Infection from pancreatitis
   c. Hypoxia
   d. Alcohol withdrawal

135. A patient with a terminal illness discloses to their nurse that they would like to transfer to hospice care. Which of the following actions by the nurse is the most appropriate and an example of compassionate care?
    a. Withhold all medical interventions and focus on comfort measures only.
    b. Avoid discussing the patient's prognosis and continue care per the provider's orders.
    c. Provide emotional support to the patient.
    d. Meet with the healthcare team and the patient to create a palliative care plan.

136. The nurse is caring for a patient with a chronic illness who sees healthcare professionals across several specialties. Which of the following actions by the nurse is an example of interdisciplinary collaboration?
    a. Notifying the patient's primary care provider of the patient's health history
    b. Sharing the patient's test results with all involved healthcare professionals
    c. Helping schedule follow-up appointments for the patient with several specialists
    d. Keeping the patient's medical information private

137. Which of the following actions should the nurse take to prevent central-line associated bloodstream infection (CLABSI) when caring for a patient with a peripherally inserted central catheter (PICC)?
    a. Change the dressing every 24 hours.
    b. Use the same infusion tubing for all medications.
    c. Perform hand hygiene before and after handling the line.
    d. Use a clean technique during dressing changes.

138. The nurse is preparing to administer gabapentin to her patient that suffers from chronic pain due to arthritis. What should the nurse monitor in this patient after administering gabapentin?
    a. Hyperactivity
    b. Sedation
    c. Tachycardia
    d. Constipation

139. The nurse is preparing a patient for a diagnostic cardiac catheterization. Which of the following instructions should the nurse give the patient before the procedure?
    a. The patient will be put under general anesthesia.
    b. The patient should fast for 24 hours before the procedure.
    c. The patient might feel a warm sensation when the dye is injected.
    d. The patient will need to stay in the hospital for a week following the procedure.

140. The nurse is preparing a presentation to give to a group of nursing students on the importance of preventing CAUTIs. Which statement correctly represents the impact of CAUTIs in the hospital setting?
    a. Approximately 50% of hospitalized patients receive urinary catheters during their admission.
    b. Medicare will reimburse the hospital for only half the cost of a CAUTI.
    c. About three-quarters of UTIs acquired in the hospital are related to urinary catheters.
    d. The longer a patient has a urinary catheter, the lower their risk of CAUTI.

141. What is the priority nursing action when treating a patient who is experiencing signs of anaphylactic shock?
    a. Ensure a patent airway and IV access.
    b. Administer intramuscular epinephrine.
    c. Administer aggressive intravenous fluids.
    d. Call the MET.

142. A patient with type 2 diabetes mellitus is admitted for elevated blood glucose and altered mental status. The patient's serum blood glucose level is 854. Based on the following arterial blood gas, which initial intervention does the nurse expect?
Arterial blood gas results:
   - pH 7.36
   - PaO2 78 mmHg
   - PaCO2 34 mmHg
   - HCO3 23 mEq/L

    a. Sodium bicarbonate drip
    b. Isotonic saline bolus
    c. Subcutaneous insulin
    d. Hypertonic saline drip

143. The oncoming nurse is taking care of a patient on intravenous antibiotics. When she checks the medication bag and compares it to the order in the patient's EMAR, she notices that the dose is incorrect. Which of the following actions would be appropriate for the nurse to take?
    a. Administer an additional bag of antibiotics to compensate for the incorrect dose.
    b. Notify the healthcare provider and pharmacy of the error.
    c. Allow the current antibiotic to finish infusing and redraw a complete blood count (CBC).
    d. Inform the patient and their family about the medication error.

144. The nurse is caring for a 55-year-old patient with a history of hypertrophic cardiomyopathy (HCM). The patient has no history of hypertension or other cardiovascular diseases. The nurse recognizes that one potential risk associated with HCM is sudden cardiac death. Which of the following is a typical finding in HCM that could lead to this outcome?
    a. Myocardial ischemia due to narrowed coronary arteries
    b. Disorganized myocardial architecture and abnormal diastolic function
    c. Reduced cardiac output due to ventricular dilation
    d. Severe mitral valve regurgitation, leading to heart failure

145. The nurse is caring for a 73-year-old patient with a history of diabetes mellitus and hyperlipidemia who was admitted to the progressive care unit after presenting to the emergency department with complaints of nausea, lightheadedness, and mild indigestion. Upon further testing, the patient was diagnosed with STEMI, and the primary nurse is curious about the patient's atypical presentation of an MI. In which of the following patient populations is a silent MI more likely to occur?
    a. Patients with a history of gastrointestinal disorders
    b. Patients with a history of diabetes mellitus
    c. Patients with a history of thyroid disorders
    d. Patients with a history of asthma

146. The family member of a patient receiving palliative care tells the nurse that the patient is losing a lot of weight and has very low energy. Which of the following responses is most appropriate by the nurse?
   a. "We don't usually intervene at this stage as this is part of the dying process."
   b. "Let's assess their nutritional status and identify any contributing factors."
   c. "We should encourage the patient to eat more to maintain weight."
   d. "I will start intravenous fluids to help maintain the client's weight."

147. The nurse observes a break in sterility by the doctor placing a central line. Which action should the nurse take?
   a. Discuss the break in sterile procedure with the doctor after the procedure is complete.
   b. Immediately alert the doctor to the break in sterility and assist with correction and resumption of sterile procedure.
   c. Continue to assist with the procedure but notify the charge nurse so that a safety report can be made.
   d. Nothing. It won't affect the safety of the procedure, and the patient needs the line quickly.

148. The nurse is caring for a patient diagnosed with cardiac tamponade. What is the definitive treatment for this condition?
   a. Administration of vasopressors
   b. Cardiac catheterization
   c. Pericardiocentesis
   d. Cardiopulmonary resuscitation (CPR)

149. The nurse is holding an informational group for parents about childhood immunizations. Which of the following teaching methods would be the most effective to facilitate learning for the parents?
   a. Hand out copies of the childhood immunization schedule.
   b. Have a group discussion on common immunization concerns and misconceptions.
   c. Show an informational video on the importance of childhood immunizations.
   d. Teach parents how to administer the immunizations.

150. A 75-year-old patient with right lower lobe pneumonia is being treated with antibiotics. As the nurse is administering medications, she notices that the patient appears to be taking a long time to swallow their pills. The patient then begins coughing after taking the medication. What intervention should be the nurse's priority?
   a. Crush medications and put them in pudding.
   b. Administer oxygen.
   c. Perform a bedside swallow evaluation.
   d. Give the patient more to drink.

Answer Key and Explanations #2

1. D: This response best respects and addresses the patient's concern (pain) while also educating the patient about the risks of leaving the catheter in. Choice *A* is incorrect because the catheter should not remain in place longer than necessary. Choice *B* is incorrect because removal of the catheter is already part of postoperative order sets, and the timing of removal is firmly within the nurse's scope of practice. Choice *C* is incorrect because, while it may be correct, this response does not acknowledge the patient's valid concerns about pain, nor does it explain the importance of removing the catheter.

2. B: The patient described in Choice *B* is *most* likely to be developing sepsis because they have both the most risk factors (advanced age and pneumonia) and the most clinical signs (systolic BP <90, temperature <36 °C, and altered mentation). Choice *A* is incorrect because, with the exception of a slightly elevated respiratory rate, this patient's vital signs are within normal limits. The elevated respiratory rate may be related to pain. Choice *C* is incorrect because elevated blood pressure is not an early sign of sepsis, and the elevated temperature can be attributed to possible SSI. While this patient is at risk of sepsis, their signs point more toward localized SSI. Choice *D* is incorrect because this patient's vital signs are within normal limits. However, they are at risk of sepsis due to their immunosuppressive medications.

3. A: Collaborating with a wound care specialist, such as a wound-ostomy nurse, can allow for appropriate wound care that will increase the likelihood of positive outcomes for the patient. The nurse may collaborate with the patient care assistant to help during wound dressing procedures but would not solely collaborate with them, making Choice *B* incorrect. Although notifying the primary care provider may be important to keep them up to date with the patient's health, a wound specialist would be the best to collaborate with, making Choice *C* incorrect. Nutrition is very helpful with wound healing so consulting and working with a dietician may be helpful; however, since the wound is more complex, wound care should be managed first, making Choice *D* incorrect.

4. D: The best initial treatment for a patient who has decreased level of consciousness and hypoglycemia is IV D50, Choice *D*. Choice *A* is incorrect because orange juice or any other oral route of glucose supplementation would be contraindicated in a patient who is confused or unconscious, as they are at increased risk of aspiration. Choice *B* is incorrect because IM glucagon may be indicated if there is no IV access available, but this route is much slower to increase the patient's blood glucose. Choice *C* is incorrect because while an IV D5W drip may be indicated to maintain the patient's blood sugar at a therapeutic level after initial resuscitation, it would not likely be a sufficient dose to quickly recover their glucose and prevent hypoglycemic coma initially.

5. A: Patients with acute kidney injury are prone to retaining fluid because their kidneys are unable to filter effectively. The nurse needs to obtain daily weights at the same time every day with the patient wearing the same clothing to determine if the patient is retaining fluid. Administering intravenous spironolactone is inappropriate because spironolactone, although a diuretic, spares potassium. This can cause complications in patients with acute kidney injury who already are unable to filter electrolytes, making Choice *B* incorrect. Encouraging increased fluids is also inappropriate because the patient may be on a fluid restriction since they are prone to retaining fluid, making Choice *C* incorrect. Choice *D* is also incorrect because cyclosporine is an immunosuppressive drug that is not used in acute kidney injury. Cyclosporine is a nephrotoxic drug, which can cause damage to the kidneys.

6. B: AMI can significantly compromise the pumping ability of the heart, leading to cardiogenic shock, a state in which the heart fails to supply enough blood to the organs. COPD, Choice *A*; pneumonia, Choice *C*; and asthma, Choice *D*, can cause shortness of breath, but they do not typically result in cardiogenic shock.

7. A: An endocrinologist specializes in the management of hormonal disorders, including diabetes, and should be consulted to create an improved treatment plan for the patient. A gastroenterologist is a doctor that specializes in disorders of the gastrointestinal tract. They would not be consulted for this patient, making Choice *B* incorrect. Although consulting a dietician may be helpful as a part of the treatment plan for this patient, it is not the best choice in this case, making Choice *C* incorrect. Choice *D* is also incorrect because a urologist specializes in disorders that affect the urinary tract, which is unrelated to the pathophysiology of diabetes.

8. B: A history of DVT is a significant risk factor for the development of PE. DVT occurs when a blood clot forms in the deep veins, typically in the legs. If this clot dislodges and travels to the pulmonary arteries, it can cause a PE. Patients with a history of DVT are at an increased risk of developing a PE. Choice *A* is a general risk factor for various health conditions but not specifically for a PE. Choice *C* is a respiratory condition that can lead to other pulmonary complications, but it is not a direct risk factor for a PE. Choice *D* falls within the normal range and is not a specific risk factor for a PE.

9. B: Since the complication is unexpected, the nurse should reference literature to gather evidence-based information on the surgery and potential adverse effects. This can help her collaborate with the interdisciplinary team to create an effective plan of care for the patient. Discussing the complication with the surgeon should certainly occur, but it is not the best option to help the patient, especially if the surgeon is unaware of this type of complication. This makes Choice *A* incorrect. The complication should be documented in the patient's medical record, but it is not the best choice the nurse can make to help the patient, making Choice *C* incorrect. The charge nurse should also be notified of the complication, but this is not the best choice the nurse can make to help the patient, making Choice *D* incorrect.

10. C: Providing chest physiotherapy is an appropriate nursing intervention to promote effective airway clearance in a patient with pneumonia. Chest physiotherapy involves various techniques, such as percussion, vibration, and postural drainage, to help mobilize and remove secretions from the lungs. Choice *A* is primarily used to relieve bronchospasm in conditions such as asthma and COPD. Choice *B* helps to improve lung volumes and prevent atelectasis but may not be sufficient for airway clearance in pneumonia. Choice *D* is an invasive procedure reserved for patients with a compromised airway or excessive secretions.

11. D: Pulmonary hypertension is characterized by increased pulmonary vascular resistance due to vasoconstriction and remodeling of pulmonary arterioles. These changes in the pulmonary vasculature result in elevated pressure within the pulmonary arteries, leading to right ventricular hypertrophy and eventual right heart failure. Choices *A*, *B*, and *C* do not accurately describe the pathophysiology of pulmonary hypertension.

12. D: TAVR is a minimally invasive procedure to replace the aortic valve, but it carries a risk of causing a stroke due to the potential for dislodging aortic plaque or valve tissue that can embolize to the brain. Acute kidney injury, Choice *A*, could occur due to contrast-induced nephropathy if contrast was used during the procedure, but it's not as directly related to the procedure as stroke. Pericardial effusion, Choice *B,* and aortic dissection, Choice *C,* are not common complications of TAVR.

280

13. C: Having the group participate in a discussion regarding their personal asthma triggers and experiences will help enhance the education based on the group's experiences. Although Choices *A, B,* and *D* may be helpful, discussing personal experiences may be more beneficial overall to understanding how asthma triggers can be managed.

14. B: This patient is experiencing hypoglycemia, or low blood sugar. Hypoglycemia can become serious or even life-threatening, leading to possible coma or death if untreated. The most important action the nurse can take for a patient experiencing hypoglycemia is to administer 15 mg of a fast-acting carbohydrate such as candy, fruit juice, or soda. The nurse should recheck the patient's blood sugar in 15 minutes and should see improvement. Having the patient sit down and take deep breaths may be beneficial if they are feeling anxious, but it is not the primary step in managing hypoglycemia, making Choice *A* incorrect. It would not be appropriate to administer insulin to an individual who is experiencing hypoglycemia because insulin lowers blood sugar, making Choice *C* incorrect. This would not be safe for an individual already experiencing low blood sugar. Choice *D* is incorrect because the nurse should administer a fast-acting carbohydrate per mouth if the person is alert. If unconscious and hypoglycemic, the nurse can administer IM glucagon.

15. B: Ischemic stroke is a stroke caused by a disruption of blood and oxygen flow to the brain, typically caused by a blood clot or narrowed vessel. Diabetes, smoking, and hypertension all increase the risk for ischemic strokes because they can contribute to blood clots and stenosis of arteries. Hypolipidemia is not a precursor to stroke, but hyperlipidemia is, making Choice *B* correct for this question. Hyperlipidemia, also known as high cholesterol, can lead to fatty plaque buildup in vessels, which also contributes to potential blood clots and vessel narrowing or stenosis.

16. B: Implementing lung-protective ventilation strategies is a key component in the management of severe ARDS. Lung-protective ventilation involves using lower tidal volumes, maintaining PEEP, and avoiding high plateau pressures to minimize ventilator-induced lung injury. Choice *A* is not recommended as a routine therapy for ARDS. Choice *C* may be used to support oxygenation, but it does not address the underlying lung injury. Choice *D* may be considered in certain situations, such as fluid overload, but it is not a primary intervention for ARDS management.

17. C: Postoperative patients, particularly those who have undergone an AAA repair, are at risk for ischemia due to the clamp and unclamp procedure during surgery. Decreased sensation and movement in the legs could suggest spinal cord ischemia, which is a serious complication. Absent bowel sounds, Choice *A*, could indicate paralytic ileus, which is common after surgery and typically resolves on its own. Mild incisional pain, Choice *B*, is expected after surgery and can be managed with appropriate pain medication. A urine output of 50 mL/hr, Choice *D*, is within the normal range and does not raise immediate concern.

18. B: Pericarditis primarily presents with chest pain that improves when leaning forward. Pulsus paradoxus, Choice *A*, is associated with cardiac tamponade; peripheral edema, Choice *C*, is a common symptom of heart failure; and wheezing, Choice *D*, is more indicative of respiratory conditions such as asthma and COPD.

19. D: The correct answer is Choice *D*, status epilepticus. Status epilepticus is a state in which seizures recur before the patient has a return to baseline mentation. Choices *A* and *C* are incorrect. Tonic-clonic seizures were previously known as grand-mal seizures. These terms do not describe recurrent seizures.

20. B: Performing thoracentesis is a priority intervention in managing a large pleural effusion. Thoracentesis involves the insertion of a needle or catheter into the pleural space to drain the fluid. It helps relieve symptoms such as dyspnea and improves lung function. Choice *A* may be considered if the effusion is due to CHF, but the primary intervention is to remove the accumulated fluid. Choice *C* may be beneficial in improving oxygenation, but it does not address the underlying issue of fluid accumulation. Choice *D* would be indicated if the pleural effusion is associated with infection, but it also does not address the underlying issue.

21. A: The healthcare team should closely monitor liver function during administration of pirfenidone, making Choice *A* correct. ALT, AST, and bilirubin are the main components of a liver function lab panel. GFT, serum creatinine, and BUN are kidney function tests; glucose, sodium, and potassium are components of a CMP which assess basic metabolic function; PT and INR assess the ability and timeliness of clotting formation.

22. B: The presence of myocardial cell death is the most helpful pathophysiological difference in differentiating between NSTEMI and unstable angina. In NSTEMI, myocardial cell death occurs due to partial occlusion of the coronary artery, leading to elevated troponin levels. In contrast, unstable angina does not involve myocardial cell death, and troponin levels remain normal. Choices *A*, *C*, and *D* are not specific enough to differentiate between NSTEMI and unstable angina because these factors can vary between individuals and do not provide a clear distinction between the two conditions.

23. C: The nurse should conduct a root cause analysis to determine the reasons for increased readmission rates prior to taking any interventions. This will then allow the nurse to collaborate with other healthcare professionals to decrease readmission rates. Choice *A* is helpful but does not address the root cause. Choice *B* is also helpful, but this cannot be done until the root cause is addressed. Choice *D* is also incorrect as the nurse does not know whether the cause of readmissions is due to medication compliance. However, this is an important idea to discuss during discharge teaching.

24. C: The primary goal of treatment for OSA is to provide CPAP therapy. CPAP helps keep the airway open during sleep by delivering a constant flow of pressurized air. It prevents airway collapse and maintains adequate oxygenation. Although Choices *A* and *B* may be beneficial in managing OSA, they are not the primary goals of treatment. Choice *D* is contraindicated in OSA because it can further relax the upper airway muscles and worsen the obstruction.

25. A: A normal potassium level ranges from 3.5-5.3 mEq/L. A value of 7.0 mEq/L indicates hyperkalemia, which can present as muscle weakness, and most commonly, cardiac arrhythmia. A value of 7.0 mEq/L indicates hyperkalemia, which can present as muscle weakness, and most commonly, cardiac arrhythmia. Choice *B* is incorrect as hyperreflexia is a clinical manifestation of hypocalcemia, or calcium levels below 8.5 mEq/dL. Choice *C* is incorrect as nausea and vomiting commonly present in patients with hyponatremia, or sodium levels less than 135 mEq/dL. Mental status changes are common in patients experiencing hypernatremia, or sodium levels greater than 145 mEq/dL, which makes Choice *D* also incorrect.

26. B: Knowing that the patient is on antihypertensive medication, the nurse should first assess for overuse of prescription diuretics, which can cause hypokalemia. Choice *A* is incorrect because illicit drug use should not be the first assumption in this case; additionally, searching a patient's belongings is invasive and requires permission. Choice *C* is incorrect because hypermagnesemia would appear on the patient's metabolic panel and does not necessarily correlate with hypokalemia. Choice *D* is incorrect because, though some patients with acute leukemia will have hypokalemia, the more probable cause with this patient is overuse of diuretics.

27. D: IV thiamine should be initiated as soon as Wernicke Encephalopathy is suspected. Choice *A* is incorrect because treatment with IV thiamine should not be delayed while waiting on lab results. In particular, thyroid studies often take an extended time to complete. Choice *B* is incorrect because, while IV fluid hydration may be indicated, IV thiamine is the priority action. Choice *C* is incorrect because IV magnesium does not counteract Wernicke Encephalopathy.

28. C: Focal seizures are a type of seizure that occurs in one localized area in the brain. Manifestations of the seizure depend on where in the brain the seizure is occurring. Typically, common clinical manifestations include changes in senses and automatisms. Automatisms are repetitive movements such as lip-smacking or chewing. Choices *A, B,* and *D* are incorrect as these are clinical manifestations of tonic-clonic seizures.

29. A: *Staphylococcus aureus* is the most common cause of infective endocarditis. *Clostridium difficile*, Choice *B*; *Pseudomonas aeruginosa*, Choice *C*; and *Streptococcus pneumoniae*, Choice *D*, are not typically associated with infective endocarditis. *Clostridium difficile* is a bacterium that causes gastrointestinal infections, *Pseudomonas aeruginosa* is commonly associated with nosocomial infections, and *Streptococcus pneumoniae* is more commonly associated with pneumonia and meningitis.

30. A: Iron deficiency anemia is a type of anemia typically caused by a low intake of iron in one's diet. Symptoms of iron-deficiency anemia include an inflamed and sore tongue, fatigue, brittle and spoon-shaped nails, dizziness, weakness, and cold hands or feet. Low iron levels cause the tongue to become reddened and painful because there is a lack of oxygen being received in the area. Choice *B* is incorrect as low iron levels would lead to increased fatigue and weakness due to the decreased oxygenation occurring in the body. Choice *C* is also incorrect as iron deficiency may cause increased heart rate, or tachycardia, due to the body attempting to compensate for low oxygen levels in the blood. Choice *D* is also incorrect because fingernail clubbing is a clinical manifestation of chronic obstructive pulmonary disorders. As mentioned above, iron-deficiency anemia leads to brittle and spoon-shaped nails due to malnutrition.

31. C: Coumadin, also known as warfarin, is an anticoagulant medication that prevents blood clots. Its mechanism of action is through interference with the synthesis of vitamin K-dependent clotting factors, which are important factors needed for blood to clot. Coumadin can be prescribed to prevent or even treat conditions including deep vein thrombosis or pulmonary embolism. Prothrombin time (PT) is the laboratory test used to measure how long it takes for blood to clot. Even though platelets are important in the clotting process, it does not indicate the effectiveness of Coumadin therapy. Instead, it is better at assessing the risk or possibility of bleeding or clotting disorders, making Choice *A* incorrect. Choice *B* is also incorrect because Coumadin does not have any effect on hemoglobin, or red blood cell count. Activated partial thromboplastin time (aPTT) is a test that can monitor the effectiveness of heparin therapy, another type of anticoagulant medication, making Choice *D* incorrect.

32. D: Diabetic ketoacidosis occurs in diabetic patients that cannot produce enough insulin and do not have control of their blood sugars. Since there is not enough glucose available for cellular use, the body breaks down fats in an attempt to get energy from another source. When the liver breaks down fat, the metabolic byproduct is ketone bodies which can be seen in the urine and blood. Positive nitrites and leukocytes in the urine are an indication of a possible urinary tract infection—not diabetic ketoacidosis—making Choices A and B incorrect. Positive bilirubin in the urine can indicate a possible liver condition, making Choice C incorrect.

33. D: A bedridden and immobile patient is at risk of developing pressure injuries. For this reason, the nurse should turn and reposition the patient every two hours to alleviate the pressure on the patient's bony prominences since they are unable to reposition themselves. Although assisting the patient to perform range of motion exercises is helpful, it is not the primary intervention, making Choice A incorrect. Choice B is incorrect because compression stockings are not necessary in this case unless the patient is at a higher risk for deep vein thrombosis. Administering pain medication is also important but not the primary intervention for this immobile patient, making Choice C incorrect. It is far more important to ensure that the patient does not develop pressure sores because that can lead to further complications such as infections.

34. D: Corticosteroids can increase the risk of developing oral thrush, a fungal infection in the mouth, because they can disrupt the natural balance of microorganisms. Rinsing the mouth with water after inhaler use helps to remove any residual medication and reduce the risk of oral thrush. Choice A is incorrect because rinsing the mouth does not affect the absorption of the medication in the lungs. Choice B is incorrect because rinsing the mouth does not prevent the corticosteroid from reaching the lungs effectively. Choice C is incorrect because rinsing the mouth primarily helps reduce the risk of developing oral side effects rather than decreasing throat-related side effects.

35. C: Based on this patient's presentation and vitals, they are most likely going into hypovolemic shock. Until the cause of the bleeding can be stopped, the priority intervention is to increase the patient's blood volume. Ideally, this will be done with blood transfusion. If this cannot be obtained fast enough, the care team may start with isotonic crystalloids until blood transfusion is possible. Choice A, administering IV normal saline at 100 ml/hr, is incorrect; the rate of fluid administration is not quick enough for fluid resuscitation. Choice B, drawing serum hemoglobin and hematocrit levels, and Choice D, performing an abdominal CT scan, are incorrect; laboratory tests and diagnostic imaging should be a part of the secondary or tertiary assessment. These are not priority over restoring the patient's circulation.

36. A: Choice A provides the patient with the most complete understanding of palliative care, informing them that palliative care works alongside curative care, that it is an interdisciplinary team, and that they are experts in relieving suffering and improving quality of life. Choice B is incorrect because it suggests that palliative care is only for terminally ill or end-of-life patients. Choice C is incorrect because, while palliative care sometimes assumes care for end-of-life patients, palliative care often works in concert with curative care. Choice D is incorrect because palliative medicine includes many types of care providers, including medical doctors.

37. B: Intubation puts a patient at greater risk for hospital-acquired pneumonia. Compared to minimal sedation, heavy sedation puts the intubated patient at greatest risk for hospital-acquired pneumonia. Choices A and C are incorrect because a non-intubated patient is at lower risk of hospital-acquired pneumonia than an intubated patient. Choice D is incorrect because evidence shows that minimizing sedation leads to a lower risk of hospital-acquired pneumonia (as does earlier extubation).

38. D: In Asian cultures, family plays an important part in decision-making, especially when it comes to health. Allowing the patient's family members to participate in the patient's care and decision-making is the most culturally competent option as it will make the patient feel more comfortable with the care that they receive. Using a professional interpreter for communication may be helpful if the patient speaks another language, but this was not stated in the question, making Choice A incorrect. Choice B is incorrect as Asian culture views prolonged eye contact as rude and disrespectful. Choice C is incorrect also as the patient's healthcare team would not make the decisions for the patient. The patient is involved in the decision-making process of their care.

39. A: One of the most important parts of end-of-life care is pain control to ensure comfort. The appropriate intervention for this patient is to administer pain medication as needed. Choices B, C, and D are all incorrect. Encouraging the patient to eat their regular diet may cause discomfort since the body is naturally shutting down, so this should be avoided. When patients no longer want to eat or drink, they may eat ice chips to help with any dryness or oral discomfort. The dying process is emotional; therefore, preventing visitors from being with the patient may cause additional stress which goes against maintaining comfort for the dying patient. Since the body is naturally shutting down, the patient is not expected to participate in physical activity, and they may not have enough energy to do so. Making them do so would be inappropriate at this stage.

40. A: The correct choice is Choice A. Television/radio or other noises may further agitate the patient. Any disturbing noise should be eliminated if possible. Choices B, C, and D are all appropriate interventions for a patient experiencing delirium.

41. D: A *Clostridium difficile* (*C. diff*) infection is an infection of the gastrointestinal system caused by the *Clostridium difficile* bacteria. It leads to frequent diarrhea, abdominal cramping, dehydration, and nausea. The most common cause of *C. diff* is antibiotic use, especially for an extended period of time. Treatment of *C. diff* includes antibiotics such as vancomycin. Choice A is incorrect as illicit drug use does not directly correlate to the development of a *C. diff* infection. GERD may cause similar symptoms to *C. diff* but having GERD does not lead to the development of *C. diff*, making Choice B incorrect. Poor handwashing can spread *C. diff* but doesn't necessarily lead to its development, making Choice C incorrect.

42. B: Diabetes mellitus is a set of disorders that result in increased blood sugar levels in the body (hyperglycemia), also known as glucose. Glucose provides energy for the body, especially for our muscles, tissues, and the brain. When there is too much glucose in the blood, or hyperglycemia, there can be several symptoms that develop. The most common clinical manifestations of diabetes mellitus can be categorized as the "three Ps" or "the three polys"—polyuria, polydipsia, and polyphagia. These terms represent large increases in urination, thirst, and appetite. Choice A is incorrect as hematuria, or blood in the urine, is not typically associated with diabetes mellitus. Hematuria is typically seen with kidney disease, injury, or infection. Choice C is also incorrect as oliguria, or low urine output, occurs in patients with kidney disease or injury. Oliguria may also occur when a person is dehydrated or as a side effect of medications. Hemoptysis, or coughing up blood, is not a clinical manifestation of diabetes mellitus. It is typically caused by several different types of pulmonary conditions such as pneumonia, tuberculosis, or pulmonary embolism. This makes Choice D incorrect.

43. A: By identifying the underlying factors that are contributing to errors, the nurse is taking a systems approach. This action allows the nurse to determine weaknesses and how to improve them. Collecting data on the performance of individual staff members does not account for factors that may be causing them to have such performances, making Choice B incorrect. Choice C is also incorrect since the nurse

285

needs to understand the root cause of errors prior to implementing new protocols. Protocols should be tailored to the cause. Choice *D* is also incorrect as this doesn't solve why the errors are occurring.

44. A: Interventional cardiac catheterization involves both diagnostic aspects and therapeutic procedures (e.g., angioplasty, stenting) to treat blockages or structural abnormalities that are found during the procedure. In this scenario, the nurse would expect to administer an antiplatelet agent after coronary artery stent placement to prevent the formation of blood clots. Antiplatelet medications, such as aspirin or P2Y12 inhibitors (e.g., clopidogrel), are commonly prescribed in this setting to reduce the risk of stent thrombosis and subsequent cardiovascular events. Beta-blockers, Choice *B*, are commonly used for the management of hypertension, arrhythmias, and certain heart conditions, but they are not directly related to the post-procedural care of coronary artery stent placement. Similarly, calcium channel blockers, Choice *C*, are often used for blood pressure control and the management of certain cardiac conditions, but they are not specifically indicated for post-stent placement care. Diuretics, Choice *D*, may be used for the management of fluid overload in some cardiac conditions, but they are not directly related to stent placement.

45. A: When a person has diabetic ketoacidosis, their blood becomes acidic. In an effort to compensate for the strongly acidic environment, the respiratory system will eliminate excess carbon dioxide through rapid and shallow respirations known as Kussmaul respirations. Oliguria, or low urine output, does not occur in patients with diabetic ketoacidosis. In fact, they experience polyuria, or increased urine output. This is because the kidneys will excrete any excess glucose in the body. This pulls fluid with it and leads to increased urination, making Choice *B* incorrect. Patients with diabetic ketoacidosis experience blood sugars at or above 300 mg/dL, an indication of hyperglycemia. This makes Choice *C* incorrect. As mentioned above, patients with diabetic ketoacidosis experience hyperventilation in the form of Kussmaul respirations, not hypoventilation, making Choice *D* also incorrect.

46. B: The biggest risk factor for the development of dementia is increasing age. In fact, once over 65 years of age, a person's risk for developing dementia doubles every five years. Frequent infections are not considered a risk factor for dementia, making Choice *A* incorrect. Choices *C* and *D* are also incorrect because research has shown that being female and having hypertension may increase an individual's risk of developing dementia, not being male or having hypotension.

47. D: Suicidal thoughts or ideation is a potential side effect of many antidepressants, specifically in the beginning stages of treatment. Research has shown that the risk for suicidal ideation is higher in people less than 25 years old who have just recently started antidepressant therapy. The nurse should monitor for this side effect for this patient because of their age. Fever, rash, and hallucinations are not side effects of antidepressants, making Choices *A, B,* and *C* incorrect.

48. A: High protein and total calories are important to support the catabolic state often present during wound healing. Choice *B* is incorrect because the patient should be consuming increased protein. Choice *C* is incorrect because the patient needs high caloric intake to support wound healing. Choice *D* is incorrect because a low-residue diet will not affect wound healing and may contribute to constipation.

49. D: While the physician is legally responsible for satisfying all elements of informed consent, nurses are ethically responsible for assessing the patient's ability to process and understand the implications of informed consent. Nurses protect the patient's autonomy by raising these questions and concerns. The remaining elements of informed consent are required of the physician, rather than the nurses.

50. D: Bilingual family members should not be used for translation of nursing communication. However, they should be respected and included in the conversation. Choice *A* is incorrect because the husband should not be relied upon as a translator. Choice *B* is incorrect because the patient is not fluent in English and may not be able to express herself fully. Choice *C* is incorrect because it is disrespectful to the husband and does not convey that use of a hospital-approved translator is required.

51. B: Patients with AFib have a disrupted atrial rhythm, which can lead to the pooling and clotting of blood in the atria. If a clot dislodges and travels to the brain, it can cause a stroke. Although AFib can exacerbate underlying heart disease and potentially increase the risk for MI, Choice *A*; angina, Choice *C*; or hypertension, Choice *D*, these complications are less immediate and less directly related to AFib than stroke.

52. D: The major premise of the Synergy Model states that synergy—optimum health—can only be achieved when agency resources and nursing competencies are congruent with the patient's needs. Family participation in the patient's care may improve outcomes, however, the synergy is related to the patient–nurse–healthcare agency triad.

53. C: After CABG surgery, the nurse is most likely to encounter AFib because it is a common postoperative cardiac arrhythmia. Hypotension, Choice *A*, can occur but is generally well-managed with fluid and medication adjustments. Thrombocytopenia, Choice *B*, can occur due to heparin administration or platelet consumption during cardiopulmonary bypass, but it is not as frequently observed as AFib. Transient ischemic attack, Choice *D*, is not common in the immediate postoperative period of CABG surgery.

54. B: Acute respiratory failure is characterized by severe hypoxemia (low oxygen levels) and hypercapnia (elevated carbon dioxide levels). It typically occurs in patients with underlying lung diseases such as COPD, in which impaired gas exchange leads to inadequate oxygenation and retention of carbon dioxide. Choices *A*, *C*, and *D* are incorrect because they do not reflect the characteristic features of acute respiratory failure.

55. B: Opioid analgesics cause several side effects including constipation, respiratory depression, nausea, and sedation among many others. The most important adverse effect the nurse should monitor for is respiratory depression, as opioids depress the central nervous system. The nurse should monitor respiratory rate, pattern, and depth as well as oxygen saturation levels. If severe respiratory depression occurs, it can become fatal. Choices *A, C,* and *D* are all incorrect because they are not the priority adverse effects the nurse should monitor when administering opioid analgesics.

56. B: The nurse at the second level of clinical practice continuum understands that the patient's death may be an acceptable outcome based on the knowledge accumulated through engagement with the patient and family and expert assessment of the patient's progress. The level 1 nurse understands that the patient may possibly die, but the nurse does not comprehend that the death is inevitable or acceptable. According to the Synergy Model, experienced nurses possess skills in managing end-of-life care, which benefits both the patient and the family. This special caring practice not only acknowledges death as an acceptable outcome but consists of a plan of care to achieve that outcome in the best way possible. According to the model, death is initially viewed as an acceptable outcome at the second level of caring practices.

57. B: Systems thinking involves understanding the multiple factors that contribute to an event. The nurse should consider all of the potential factors that contributed to the medication error as part of her root cause analysis. Choice *A* is incorrect since focusing on the nurse who made the error does not provide further explanation as to why it happened or how it can be prevented. Choice *C* is incorrect as this should already be in place and is part of the rights of medication administration. The nurse manager should already be aware of the event, making Choice *D* incorrect.

58. D: Short-acting beta-agonists are the first-line treatment for bronchodilation in acute asthma exacerbations. They provide rapid relief of bronchospasm by stimulating beta-2 adrenergic receptors in the airways. Choices *A*, *B*, and *C* may also be used in the management of asthma, but they are not the initial bronchodilator therapy. Corticosteroids help reduce airway inflammation and are commonly used in combination with short-acting beta-agonists. Long-acting beta-agonists and anticholinergic agents have a longer onset of action and are typically used for maintenance therapy in asthma.

59. A: Using a professional interpreter is important to provide safe and effective care for the patient. The professional interpreter is trained in medical terminology to help explain medical conditions. Using a family member to interpret is not the best choice as they can be biased and may withhold information if they do not want the patient to know everything that is happening medically. Not only this, but family members may not fully understand medical terminology. This makes Choice *B* incorrect. Choice *C* is incorrect because this will not help the patient's understanding. Choice *D* is also incorrect as they may not be able to read or write in their own language, and they also may not understand medical terminology.

60. D: Although all options may be useful in helping the patient feel more comfortable with their colostomy, having the patient participate in a colostomy support group will help the patient learn more than just how to apply and remove the colostomy appliance. The patient can learn the struggles of other people with colostomies and how they manage them in their daily lives. Choices *A*, *B*, and *C* should be implemented to help the patient understand how to care for their ostomy, but having the support group will provide a different level of support and insight for the patient.

61. B: The most effective method to educate families and facilitate learning is utilizing practice dolls and mannequins. This allows those who are learning to gain hands-on experience so they can be comfortable on their own. Although playing a pre-recorded video demonstration may be helpful, it is not the best choice because it does not allow the expectant parents to have hands-on practice, making Choice *A* incorrect. Providing written step-by-step instructions may be helpful as a reference, but it isn't the most effective way to facilitate learning, making Choice *C* incorrect. This is also true for Choice *D*, making it also incorrect.

62. C: The most appropriate response by the nurse is to explain that it is possible the patient was exposed to a different strain of the flu virus that wasn't covered by last year's vaccine. Influenza viruses can change and mutate over time, resulting in new strains that may not be fully protected by previous vaccinations. Choice *A* is incorrect because the flu vaccine is not 100% effective in preventing the flu. Choice *B* is incorrect because it wrongly implies that contracting the virus despite the vaccine is a common occurrence, which can lead to misunderstanding and reduced vaccine compliance. Choice *D* is incorrect because it does not address the possibility of exposure to a different strain of the virus and focuses on the timing of vaccine effectiveness, which is not relevant in this case.

63. A: The patient's increased work of breathing, decreased oxygen saturation, and increased respiratory rate during the weaning trial indicate respiratory distress and the need for continued mechanical ventilation. These findings suggest that the patient is not yet ready to be extubated and requires ongoing support from the ventilator. Successful weaning from mechanical ventilation is characterized by stable vital signs, improved gas exchange, and minimal or no signs of respiratory distress. Choices *B* and *C* are incorrect because the patient's symptoms do not suggest a successful weaning or normal physiological response. Choice *D* is incorrect because the patient's respiratory distress is likely related to the physiological challenges of weaning rather than anxiety.

64. B: Assisting with endotracheal intubation is the priority action for a patient with severe respiratory depression. Endotracheal intubation provides a secure airway and allows for mechanical ventilation to support adequate oxygenation and ventilation. Choice *A* is not appropriate in this scenario because there is no indication or suspicion of opioid-induced respiratory depression. Choice *C* may help improve oxygenation temporarily but does not address the underlying respiratory depression. Choice *D* is important but should not delay the initiation of interventions to secure the airway and support ventilation.

65. C: Diffuse alveolar damage and impaired gas exchange are characteristic features of ARDS. The condition is characterized by widespread inflammation and injury to the alveoli, leading to impaired oxygenation and ventilation. Choice *A* may occur in conditions such as asthma, but it is not specific to ARDS. Choice *B* is more commonly associated with respiratory failure rather than ARDS. Choice *D* is characteristic of obstructive lung diseases such as COPD, not ARDS.

66. C: The nurse should use the patient's chosen name and pronouns to respectfully address them. Choice *A* is incorrect as avoiding using pronouns can make the nurse-patient interaction awkward and nontherapeutic, causing unnecessary stress for the patient. Choice *B* is also incorrect as this may be dismissive of the patient's gender identity. Choice *D* is also incorrect because this does not assist the current interaction with the patient.

67. D: Systems thinking involves utilizing several interconnected components to provide a holistic approach to a patient's care. This includes considering their social, psychological, and physical needs, not just the physical needs of the patient. The nurse should coordinate with several healthcare professionals who can help the patient meet their various needs. Choice *A* is incorrect since limiting the identification to only physical systems and issues is not holistic. Choice *B* is incorrect as this also only focuses on one aspect of their treatment plan. Although implementing disease-specific interventions for the patient may be helpful, these interventions fail to acknowledge the psychological and social factors that the patient experiences. This makes Choice *C* incorrect.

68. D: MRSA is an antibiotic-resistant bacteria that is spread through physical contact. Contact precautions include a gown and gloves. Choices *A, B,* and *C* are all incorrect because MRSA is not an airborne disease and is not spread through droplets. Contact precautions are more effective in preventing the spread of MRSA than standard precautions.

69. C: CT scan is the preferred method for diagnosing an aortic dissection due to its accuracy and rapid results. An echocardiogram, Choice *A*, may be used if a CT scan isn't available, but it has lower sensitivity. A chest x-ray, Choice *B*, may appear normal in cases in which the aortic dissection is small or localized or if the dissection is limited to the descending aorta; therefore, it is not a reliable diagnostic method. Furthermore, in the early stages of an aortic dissection or shortly after symptom onset, there may not have been sufficient time for significant changes or complications to manifest on a chest x-ray. An ECG, Choice *D*, is typically used to rule out an MI, which can mimic an aortic dissection, but is not the correct diagnostic test for this condition.

70. A: The nurse should facilitate effective communication between the patient and the healthcare team. The nurse can coordinate with another nurse on their unit who speaks the patient's language to assist in communication or utilize interpreter services within the hospital. Choice *B* is incorrect as having a family member may be helpful, but there could be difficulty explaining medical terms if the family member doesn't understand themselves. Using a translation app is a possibility, but it can cause miscommunication because sometimes words and phrases are not translated correctly, making Choice *C* incorrect. Documenting the communication difficulties in the patient's chart has no effect on facilitating effective communication between the patient and the healthcare team, making Choice *D* incorrect.

71. C: Patients with chronic kidney disease and end-stage renal disease are unable to remove phosphorus, sodium, and potassium through their kidneys. These patients should avoid high phosphorus, sodium, and potassium diets. High levels of phosphorus can cause the weakening of the bones, as phosphorus binds to calcium and removes it from the body. White rice is a low-phosphorus food and is okay for the patient with end-stage renal disease to eat. Choices *A, B,* and *D* are all incorrect because these foods are high in phosphorus.

72. B: The patient's symptoms and clinical manifestations align with that of Parkinson's Disease. Parkinson's Disease is a neurodegenerative disorder that alters movement. These patients have a stooped posture and shuffling gait but also have difficulty initiating movements and stopping them. These patients also experience tremors and postural instability, putting them at increased risk for falls. Choice *A* is incorrect as Myasthenia Gravis is an autoimmune disorder that affects the signaling between nerve cells and muscles. This condition leads to muscle weakness and fatigue, ptosis, and difficulty chewing or smiling. Choice *C* is also incorrect because Multiple Sclerosis is an autoimmune disease that affects the central nervous system, leading to disruptions in nerve function. Common symptoms include numbness and tingling in the limbs and face, blurred or double vision, weakness, and fatigue. Choice *D* is also incorrect as Duchenne Muscular Dystrophy is a genetic disorder that affects the muscles and begins to appear in boys between ages two and five. Symptoms of this disorder include toe walking, enlarged calf muscles, weakness, and muscle wasting.

73. B: CT contrast can cause harm to a patient's kidneys. The patient may have an acute kidney injury at this time due to dehydration. However, it is likely that the benefits of finding the cause of the diarrhea may outweigh the risks of receiving CT contrast. Therefore, the patient should receive IV fluids following CT contrast administration to decrease the potential harm of the contrast on the kidneys. Choice *A*, requesting an order for an MRI instead of a CT, is incorrect; while an MRI may be an option if CT is not, it will likely cause a delay in diagnosis and care, and if the MRI requires contrast, this will not reduce the risk of kidney injury. Choice *C*, requesting an order for an antidiarrheal medication, is incorrect; it may be inappropriate to administer antidiarrheal medications prior to knowing the cause of the diarrhea. Choice *D*, requesting an order for an x-ray instead of a CT, is incorrect; an x-ray will not likely provide sufficient diagnostic imaging for this patient.

74. A: This patient's uncontrolled hypertension, coupled with chest pain and worsening dyspnea, is highly suggestive of MI, especially because the symptoms have persisted despite attempts to lower the blood pressure. Although cardiac arrest, Choice *B*, could be a potential outcome if the MI is not treated, it's not an immediate complication. PE, Choice *C*, typically presents with sudden-onset chest pain and

290

dyspnea but is less likely given the patient's history and the absence of other common risk factors. Acute renal failure, Choice *D,* could be a potential complication of uncontrolled hypertension over time, but it would not explain the patient's acute chest pain.

75. A: When a patient with acute heart failure presents with hypoxia (indicated by the low oxygen saturation), the first intervention should be to improve oxygenation. Diuretics, Choice *B,* could help decrease fluid overload but should only be administered after ensuring adequate oxygenation. Administering a beta-blocker, Choice *C,* is not appropriate in ADHF and could exacerbate the condition. Increasing IV fluids, Choice *D,* would typically worsen heart failure.

76. D: The primary reason for administering dobutamine in this situation is to increase cardiac output. Dobutamine is a positive inotrope that enhances the force of the heart's contractions, leading to an improved pumping capacity and subsequently increasing cardiac output. In the context of cardiogenic shock, in which the heart's ability to supply adequate blood flow to the organs is compromised, increasing cardiac output is crucial for improving tissue perfusion and supporting vital organ function. Improving renal perfusion, Choice *A,* may be an indirect effect of increasing cardiac output because better cardiac function can enhance blood flow to the kidneys. However, the primary goal of administering dobutamine is to enhance cardiac output rather than directly targeting renal perfusion. Reducing preload and afterload, Choice *B,* is typically accomplished using other medication classes, such as diuretics (for reducing preload) and vasodilators (for reducing afterload), which work by different mechanisms than dobutamine. Increasing myocardial oxygen demand, Choice *C,* is not a desirable effect in the context of a compromised heart because it could potentially worsen ischemia and further damage cardiac tissue.

77. A: The key pathophysiological difference between STEMI and NSTEMI is the extent of coronary artery occlusion. STEMI occurs when a coronary artery is completely blocked, leading to more extensive myocardial damage. In contrast, NSTEMI results from partial occlusion of a coronary artery, leading to a smaller area of myocardial damage. Both STEMI and NSTEMI are associated with elevated troponin levels, and STEMI is typically more severe than NSTEMI; therefore, Choices *B* and *C* are incorrect. Although Choice *D* is a true statement, it describes an ECG manifestation rather than the underlying pathophysiology; therefore, it is also incorrect.

78. C: The findings of absent breath sounds on the right side, tracheal deviation to the right, and decreased chest expansion on the right side are suggestive of atelectasis, which is a common complication after pneumonectomy. Atelectasis refers to the collapse or closure of lung tissue, leading to reduced ventilation and decreased breath sounds. Choices *A, B,* and *D* do not accurately describe this patient's presentation.

79. C: When implementing new evidence-based practices, it is important to educate the staff on what the practice is, why it is being implemented, and how to follow it. This will allow for a more seamless transition into practice. Choice *A* is incorrect as simply hanging posters about the new practices in the break room has little to no effect on applying them to clinical practice. Most staff members may overlook them and not pay attention. Choice *B* is incorrect because these practices have already been proven to have positive outcomes. They do not need to be tested by the nurse individually prior to implementation. Choice *D* is also incorrect as the staff members need hands-on education about these practices with explanations.

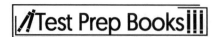

80. D: PCI is the most appropriate and preferred surgical intervention for a patient diagnosed with STEMI. PCI, also known as angioplasty with stenting, is a minimally invasive procedure used to open the blocked coronary artery and restore blood flow to the affected myocardial tissue. Choice *A* may be considered in select cases of STEMI with complex coronary anatomy or when PCI is not feasible, but it is not the first-line treatment. Choices *B* and *C* are not relevant to the management of STEMI because they address different cardiovascular issues.

81. A: The most obvious effects of the super-concentrated blood that are characteristic of HHNK will appear neurologically. Confusion, seizures, coma, stroke-like syndromes, dizziness, and drowsiness are all neurological symptoms that appear in HHNK. The other systems of the body, such as cardiac, endocrine, and pulmonary may be affected but are not directly associated with the usual symptomology of HHNK.

82. B: Antihistamines and steroids would be the next priority. Both medications work to correct the systemic symptoms of anaphylaxis. Choice *A* is incorrect because acetaminophen PO will not be effective and the patient should not receive anything by mouth. Choices *C* and *D* are incorrect because neither normal saline nor oxygen will control the systemic symptoms of anaphylaxis, so they are not priority steps after epinephrine.

83. B: The correct choice is Choice *B*. Patients with a subdural hematoma typically present with drowsiness and are confused with agitation. Choice *A* is incorrect. Hypertension and tachycardia are not symptoms of subdural hematoma. Choice *C* is also incorrect. While headache and hypotension can occur with subdural hematoma, vision loss is not a symptom. Choice *D* is also incorrect. The symptoms of sudden severe headache, loss of consciousness, and double vision are typically seen in subarachnoid hemorrhage.

84. A: Hydrochlorothiazide is a diuretic that reduces blood pressure by helping the body eliminate excess sodium and water, and lisinopril is an ACE inhibitor that also lowers blood pressure and can have a specific protective effect on the kidneys in patients with diabetes. Improving blood glucose control, Choice *B,* is not the main action of these medications. Treating potential cardiac arrhythmias, Choice *C*, and decreasing the risk of developing atherosclerosis, Choice *D*, are also not the primary reasons for choosing these particular medications.

85. D: The correct choice is Choice *D*. Choice *A* is incorrect because the nurse should avoid performing any nursing functions during the EEG. In fact, the patient should have minimal stimulation for the most accurate data. Choices *B* and *C* are both incorrect. It is best for the patient to be free from any medications that may affect mentation and therefore alter the results of the EEG. If the patient is given any of these types of medication, the EEG tech should be made aware.

86. C: Right ventricular hypertrophy is a characteristic finding in pulmonary hypertension. Pulmonary hypertension is characterized by elevated pressure in the pulmonary arteries, leading to increased workload on the right ventricle and subsequent hypertrophy. Choice *A* is a characteristic of left-sided heart failure. Choice *B* is incorrect because pulmonary hypertension is associated with increased pulmonary vascular resistance, not decreased resistance. Choice *D* is indicative of improved systolic function of the left ventricle and is not typically seen in pulmonary hypertension.

87. C: A decreased level of consciousness can lead to respiratory depression due to the depressed responsiveness of the respiratory centers in the brain stem. The brain stem contains the respiratory

292

centers responsible for regulating breathing. When the level of consciousness is reduced, such as in cases of head injury or sedation, the brain stem's ability to respond to changes in oxygen and carbon dioxide levels may be impaired, resulting in decreased respiratory drive and subsequent respiratory depression. Choice A is incorrect because increased stimulation of the respiratory centers in the brain stem would typically lead to increased respiratory drive, not depression. Choice B is unrelated to the respiratory centers and pertains to sympathetic nervous system activity. Choice D is incorrect because surfactant production is not directly influenced by the level of consciousness.

88. B: Acute kidney injury (AKI) is characterized by a sudden decrease in renal function or kidney failure. It typically has a short onset of a few hours or days. There are several risk factors that may lead to AKI, but one of the primary precursors is severe infection or sepsis. Sepsis can affect the cardiovascular system, causing reduced blood flow throughout the body. If the kidneys do not receive enough blood and oxygen, the kidney tissue becomes injured, leading to several other complications. Having a solitary kidney does not predispose a person to acute kidney injury, unless that solitary kidney has been affected detrimentally, making Choice A incorrect. While an excessive intake of sugary drinks may irritate the bladder and cause an increased risk of a urinary tract infection, consuming sugary drinks does not directly correlate with acute kidney injury, making Choice C incorrect. Choice D is incorrect because an older age, especially over 65 years, is a risk factor for AKI, not younger.

89. B: Hyperglycemia, or increased blood sugar, is known to decrease the effectiveness of the body's immune system. As a result, patients with uncontrolled hyperglycemia are prone to secondary infections. Although hyperglycemia can affect the nerves of the eyes and cause blurred vision, there is no direct correlation between hyperglycemia and retinal detachment, making Choice A incorrect. Dysphagia, or difficulty swallowing, is not caused by hyperglycemia. Dysphagia is caused by damage to the nervous system or oral and esophageal cancers; therefore, Choice C is incorrect. Hyperglycemia can lead to severe fatigue, not hyperactivity, making Choice D also incorrect.

90. C: Exacerbations of chronic heart failure are often characterized by increased shortness of breath, especially when lying down (orthopnea or paroxysmal nocturnal dyspnea), due to fluid accumulation in the lungs. Although decreased urination, Choice A, may occur due to reduced renal perfusion, it is not a primary sign of an acute exacerbation. Weight loss, Choice B, and decreased swelling in lower extremities, Choice D, are typically signs of improved, not worsening, heart failure.

91. A: The nurse should research and gather evidence to better understand the adverse reaction, its possible causes, and ways to prevent and manage it. This is an example of clinical inquiry. Documenting the adverse reaction in the patient's medical record is important but is not an example of clinical inquiry, making Choice B incorrect. Notifying the healthcare provider of the reaction is necessary but also is not an example of clinical inquiry, making Choice C incorrect. Choice D is incorrect since this would only provide information about how to administer the medication and would not provide answers on what caused the adverse reaction and how to prevent or manage it.

92. B: For a patient with COPD, the nurse would anticipate a pulse oximetry reading range of 88–92%. This range takes into account the impaired gas exchange and reduced oxygen saturation often seen in COPD. Choice A would indicate lower oxygen levels and potential hypoxemia. Although Choices C and D would be considered within the normal range, these higher levels are less likely to be seen in patients with COPD due to their underlying respiratory condition.

93. B: In the management of AFib, metoprolol is commonly used as a medication to help control the heart rate. AFib is characterized by irregular and often rapid heart rhythms, and beta-blockers such as metoprolol are effective in slowing down the heart rate. Hydrochlorothiazide, Choice *A*, is a diuretic primarily used for managing hypertension and reducing fluid volume. Digoxin, Choice *C*, is a medication that can be used to control heart rate, but it is generally reserved for specific cases. Warfarin, Choice *D*, is an anticoagulant medication used to prevent blood clot formation in patients with AFib to reduce the risk of stroke. However, the primary focus in this question is on medication for heart rate control, making metoprolol the most appropriate choice.

94. D: This option can help with outreach to underserved communities since the fairs will be held outside of the clinic. Choice *A* does not have any benefit to the underserved communities, making this choice incorrect. Choice *B* is also incorrect as this only benefits the clinic's patients and not underserved communities that may not receive regular healthcare. Choice *C* is incorrect as this also does not provide appropriate outreach to individuals outside of the clinic.

95. D: Nausea and severe headache are signs of increased intracranial pressure (ICP) in patients diagnosed with hemorrhagic stroke. Increased ICP can lead to life-threatening complications including brain herniation and even death. Although aphasia, hemiplegia, and seizures are also potential complications of a patient who has had a hemorrhagic stroke, they are not related to the symptoms the patient described. This makes Choices *A, B,* and *C* incorrect.

96. B: Nitroprusside is a potent vasodilator used in hypertensive emergencies to rapidly decrease blood pressure. When administering nitroprusside, the nurse should closely monitor for hypotension as a potential side effect. The medication's primary action is to reduce blood pressure, and excessive lowering of blood pressure can lead to inadequate perfusion to vital organs. Choices *A, C,* and *D* are not the priority for the nurse to monitor when administering nitroprusside.

97. C: Melena, Choice *C*, is a possible sign of GI bleeding, which could be an adverse complication of the EGD. This finding should be reported to the physician immediately. Choice *A*, somnolence, Choice *B*, sore throat, and Choice *D*, nausea, are all expected findings following an EGD.

98. B: An upper GI bleed is typically caused by esophagitis or gastritis, esophageal varices, or even cancer. It typically presents as a melena or hematemesis, and sometimes both. Melena is a dark and tarry stool, and hematemesis is vomiting coffee ground-like substances. Due to the increased fluid loss, it is essential that fluids are replaced to maintain blood pressure to support continuous perfusion to the patient's vital organs. Although drawing blood for a CBC, administering proton pump inhibitors, and providing the patient with a blood transfusion may also be done for a patient with a GI bleed, the nurse's first intervention is making sure that the patient is normovolemic, or has enough blood volume. This makes Choices *A, C,* and *D* incorrect.

99. B: VATS is a type of minimally invasive thoracic surgery that involves the use of a scope and small incisions to perform the procedure. This technique allows for a less invasive approach than traditional open surgery. Choice *A* is incorrect because minimally invasive surgery does not involve a large incision. Choice *C* is incorrect because the use of a heart-lung machine, or cardiopulmonary bypass, is not typically required for thoracic procedures and is more commonly used in open-heart surgeries in which the heart itself needs to be temporarily bypassed. Choice *D* is incorrect because minimally invasive thoracic surgery typically involves the removal of a portion of the lung rather than the entire lung, which is also indicated in the question.

100. A: Liver failure has several causes ranging from autoimmune disorders to toxins or viruses. In chronic and severe liver failure, there is an increased risk for hepatic encephalopathy, a neurological disorder that is usually temporary. It is characterized by four stages, beginning with mild confusion and agitation and eventually leading up to a coma. Treatment includes the administration of lactulose and antibiotics. Glomerulonephritis is characterized by damage to the filtering mechanisms of the kidneys, usually caused by an immune response. It affects an entirely different organ; therefore, Choice *B* is incorrect. Hepatitis B is a liver infection that can potentially lead to liver failure, making Choice *C* incorrect. Hepatitis B is not a complication of liver failure. Fatty liver disease can also lead to liver damage, especially in severe cases, but it is not a complication of liver failure itself. This makes Choice *D* incorrect.

101. B: Sickle cell disease is an inherited blood disorder characterized by red blood cells that have a sickle shape. The sickle shape causes less oxygen to be carried. Not only this, but the sickled red blood cells can clump together and block blood vessels. This can lead to a sickle cell crisis, causing severe pain, swelling in the extremities, and anemia. Providing adequate hydration can help slow or prevent the sickled cells from clumping together, allowing for blood to flow easier, which leads to decreased pain and improved oxygenation. Applying ice packs to areas of pain should never be done for patients with sickle cell as they decrease circulation and lead to worsening pain, making Choice *A* incorrect. Warm packs are recommended as an alternative. Although exercise is important—especially for those with sickle cell to help prevent clumping of red blood cells—increased physical activity during a crisis can actually cause more pain due to the lack of oxygen being carried in the blood, making Choice *C* incorrect. Choice *D* is incorrect as sickle cell anemia is not related to immune function. Administering intravenous immunoglobulin would not be indicated for this patient; rather, intravenous immunoglobulin is used for autoimmune and infectious diseases such as Kawasaki disease and lymphocytic lymphoma.

102. C: Patients with a history of recurrent urinary tract infections have a higher risk of developing CAUTI due to the presence of bacteria that congregates in the urinary tract. Although those who have urinary incontinence also have a higher risk for CAUTI, having a history of recurrent urinary tract infections is a stronger risk factor for the development of CAUTI, making Choice *B* incorrect. Choices *A* and *D* are both incorrect because neither a broken leg nor hypotension necessarily leads to an increased risk for CAUTI.

103. C: When a person is having a seizure, it is important to time the length of the seizure as seizures extending beyond five minutes or more will typically need medication to stop. It is not recommended to put anything in a person's mouth who is having a seizure because this can cause choking, making Choice *A* incorrect. When a person is having a seizure, their movements and body should not be held down. This can cause more injuries and make the person aggressive or agitated because of possible confusion. This makes Choice *B* incorrect. Providing mouth-to-mouth breathing for a patient during a seizure is not recommended because the person's chest will stiffen during the seizure. When the seizure stops, the person should resume breathing normally, making Choice *D* incorrect.

104. D: Blood pressure medications like Choice *D*, lisinopril, should be held prior to dialysis because they can lower the patient's blood pressure that will likely lower even more during dialysis. This can cause hemodynamic instability. Choice *A*, risperidone, Choice *B*, levothyroxine, and Choice *C*, carbidopa-levodopa, are incorrect because all of these medications are generally time-sensitive, require a strict administration schedule, and are considered safe to give with dialysis.

105. C: Since the patient is expressing concerns about life at home after discharge, the nurse must advocate for the patient and coordinate with their healthcare team to create a plan of care that addresses the patient's concerns and promotes their safety and health well after discharge. If the nurse discharges the patient without addressing their concerns, it can potentially harm the patient and violate ethical principles. Although providing written instructions for the patient on when to take their medications and what they are for may be helpful, it is not the best choice to address their concerns, making Choice *A* incorrect. Coordinating a home health nurse to visit the patient after discharge may be helpful, but before this, the healthcare team needs to determine the needs of the patient, making Choice *B* incorrect. Choice *D* is also incorrect as the nurse should not pass the responsibility onto the family of the patient.

106. D: Randomized control trials are the best piece of evidence to use when evaluating the effectiveness of interventions or treatments. Since participants are randomly assigned to different interventions or control groups, determining cause-and-effect relationships between interventions and outcomes is more accurate than other types of research. Qualitative studies are not the best primary source of evidence since they have a potential for bias and have limited generalizability, making Choice *A* incorrect. Choice *B* is also incorrect as this does not provide evidence-based findings and may also have a potential for bias. Choice *C* is incorrect as these findings aren't generalizable to larger populations since they may not be widely representative of such populations.

107. D: When a patient falls, the first action the nurse should take is to assess their level of consciousness to help determine the patient's neurological status and potential injuries. If the patient is unconscious, they may have sustained a head injury that may need immediate attention. Choices *A, B,* and *C* are all appropriate interventions, but they are not the first intervention the nurse should take in this case, making them incorrect.

108. C: The institution can support diversity by providing resources that satisfy cultural practices, such as dietary rules. Institutions also may provide interpreters, information sessions for employees, and accommodations for religious observances. Under normal circumstances, requiring employees to speak a second language would severely limit the pool of eligible employees and would not be an effective strategy. Educational programs should be provided for all employees and should not be limited to supervisory staff. Offering alternative solutions to all requests for accommodation could be viewed as paternalistic and culturally insensitive. The institution is required to consider ways to satisfy all reasonable patient requests.

109. B: Handwashing with an alcohol-based sanitizer or soap and water is appropriate for preventing transmission of VRE. VRE can last up to seven days on surfaces, so meticulous disinfection is warranted. Choice *A* is incorrect because, while handwashing with soap and water only is necessary for a patient with *Clostridium difficile*, it is not necessary for a patient with VRE. Choice *C* is incorrect because VRE is not transmitted by droplets, and high-use surfaces should be cleaned more than once per day. Choice *D* is incorrect because VRE is a highly transmissible infection to which hospitalized patients are uniquely vulnerable.

110. A: Dilated cardiomyopathy is characterized by the enlargement and weakening of the left ventricle, the primary pumping chamber of the heart, leading to a reduced ability to effectively pump blood. This can lead to fluid buildup in the lungs, causing shortness of breath, especially during exertion. Decreased oxygen-carrying capacity, Choice *B;* weakening of respiratory muscles, Choice *C;* and outflow obstruction, Choice *D,* are not the primary reasons for breathlessness in dilated cardiomyopathy.

111. C: Hemodialysis is used for patients with chronic kidney disease that may not be able to receive a kidney transplant. The kidneys of these patients are unable to filter waste through their kidneys. In hemodialysis, blood is removed from the patient, filtered through what is called a dialysis membrane, and returned to the patient. Due to the large amount of blood that is out of the body at one time, it is important to make sure that blood pressures are assessed throughout the dialysis process to ensure that the patient does not experience hypotension or disequilibrium syndrome. Although monitoring respiratory status may be important in other areas of nursing, it is not a priority in dialysis care, making Choice *A* incorrect. Patients who are undergoing dialysis should avoid foods with high potassium, sodium, and phosphor levels because dialysis alters the electrolyte levels within the blood. High levels of these electrolytes can potentially become dangerous, making Choice *B* incorrect. Choice *D* is also incorrect because kidney transplants may not be an option for many patients—the nurse should not discuss this with the patient at this time.

112. C: This patient's history of rheumatic fever, along with symptoms of fatigue and shortness of breath on exertion and echocardiographic findings of mitral stenosis and regurgitation, is most consistent with rheumatic heart disease affecting the mitral valve. Mitral valve prolapse, Choice *A*, is typically asymptomatic and would not explain the patient's symptoms. Aortic stenosis, Choice *B*, would not explain the findings on the echocardiogram. Tricuspid regurgitation, Choice *D*, would also not explain the echocardiogram findings, which are specific to the mitral valve.

113. D: Unstable angina is associated with an increased risk of progression to MI. This is due to the fact that unstable angina typically results from a partially occluded coronary artery, which can progress to myocardial ischemia and MI. Choices *A*, *B*, and *C* are not as closely associated with unstable angina.

114. B: The patient's presentation of hypotension, muffled heart sounds, and jugular venous distension are consistent with cardiac tamponade. However, to further confirm the diagnosis, the nurse should assess for pulsus paradoxus, which is a classic finding in cardiac tamponade. Pulsus paradoxus is caused by the exaggerated decrease in blood pressure during inspiration due to the impaired cardiac filling caused by the pericardial effusion. Cardiac tamponade is also characterized by a narrowed pulse pressure due to compromised ventricular filling, making Choices *A* and *C* incorrect. A positive Homan's sign, Choice *D*, is unrelated to cardiac tamponade and is associated with DVT.

115. A: The findings of decreased breath sounds, asymmetrical chest expansion, and tracheal deviation to the unaffected side are suggestive of a pneumothorax. A pneumothorax occurs when air accumulates in the pleural cavity, leading to lung collapse and the associated clinical manifestations. Choices *B*, *C*, and *D* do not accurately describe this patient's symptoms.

116. A: Diabetic ketoacidosis is diagnosed with an elevated blood glucose and ketoacidosis, which is presenting with an acidotic pH and elevated anion gap. The patient in diabetic ketoacidosis will likely attempt to compensate for acidosis with a Kussmaul breathing pattern, which allows the body to expel excess carbon dioxide more quickly. Choice *D* is incorrect; a patient with hyperosmolar hyperglycemic state will have elevated blood glucose with acidosis. Choice *B* is incorrect because a patient with diabetes insipidus will have increased urine output and is less likely to have changes to blood glucose. Choice *C* is incorrect because a patient with myxedema coma may be hypoglycemic.

117. B: For patients experiencing aggression and agitation, it is best to divert their attention while maintaining a calm tone to prevent escalation of the situation. Choice *A* is incorrect because leaving their room may cause increased frustration. Administering Haldol, an antipsychotic drug, to the patient

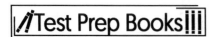

is unwarranted in this situation. Haldol is typically used in psychiatric emergencies for people experiencing psychosis, making Choice C incorrect. Choice D is also incorrect as this statement may escalate their behavior.

118. B: This patient's significantly elevated blood pressure in combination with their signs/symptoms suggests a hypertensive emergency, which requires immediate blood pressure reduction. Hypertensive urgency, Choice A, is characterized by significantly elevated blood pressure without signs of organ damage. Acute heart failure, Choice C, and acute stroke, Choice D, could be potential complications of a hypertensive emergency but do not fully explain this patient's symptoms and findings.

119. A: Choice A is correct. The NIHSS ranges from 0 to 42. Any score above 20 indicates a severe stroke with a poor prognosis for the patient. Choice B is incorrect. A moderate stroke score is 16-20. Choice C is also incorrect. A mild stroke score on the NIHSS is 1-4. Choice D is also incorrect. This patient suffered a significant stroke, not a TIA.

120. D: Severe hypoxemia and hypercapnia would indicate acute respiratory failure rather than chronic respiratory failure. Acute respiratory failure is characterized by a sudden and severe impairment of gas exchange, resulting in low levels of oxygen (hypoxemia) and high levels of carbon dioxide (hypercapnia) in the blood. Choices A and B are more associated with chronic respiratory failure. Choice C is incorrect; normal ABG values would not be expected in either acute or chronic respiratory failure because both conditions result in abnormal gas exchange, leading to altered ABG values.

121. C: Fibrinolytic therapy, also known as thrombolytic therapy, is primarily used for patients with STEMI, which is characterized by complete occlusion of a coronary artery. In these cases, fibrinolytics help dissolve the clot and restore blood flow to the affected myocardial tissue. NSTEMI, on the other hand, is associated with partial occlusion of a coronary artery, and the use of fibrinolytics is not indicated for this condition. Instead, treatment focuses on antiplatelet therapy, anticoagulation, and possible PCI to reduce the risk of further ischemia and myocardial damage. Choices A, B, and D are incorrect because they do not accurately describe the primary reason for not using fibrinolytics in NSTEMI cases.

122. C: Gastric banding surgery is a type of bariatric surgery that separates the stomach into two different pouches to help restrict food intake for those who suffer from obesity. It is a reversible surgery. It is important for the nurse to educate the patient on following a liquid or puree-only diet for the first two to four weeks to help the stomach heal and reduce complications. Clear broths are an example of what the patient may eat during these first few weeks. Choice A is incorrect as any solid food eaten too prematurely can cause irritation and discomfort to the stomach, increasing the risk for complications. Choice B is also incorrect because carbonated beverages can cause additional discomfort and irritation. Not only this, but carbonated beverages will not provide the adequate nutrition needed to recover. Returning to the patient's regular diet as soon as he or she feels better is not recommended, making Choice D incorrect. Resuming a regular diet too soon may cause complications.

123. A: A lower GI bleed is typically caused by hemorrhoids or anal fissures, diverticulosis, colon polyps, and even cancers of the colon or anus. Because the bleeding is in the lower portion of the GI tract, the blood typically presents as frank red blood with the passage of stools, known as hematochezia. Choices B and C are incorrect because they are associated with an upper GI bleed. Hematemesis is the vomiting of blood, especially vomit that appears "coffee ground-like." Melena is dark and tarry stools that may appear black in color. Choice *D* is also incorrect as diarrhea can have several causes and does not directly indicate the potential for a lower GI bleed.

124. B: Patients who have been on antibiotics and are having diarrhea are at increased likelihood of having *Clostridium difficile* (*C. diff*) and should be placed on contact isolation. This means that all staff should wear gloves and a gown when performing patient care, and they should thoroughly wash their hands after patient care is complete. Choice *A*, gloves, would not be sufficient, as the bacteria may come in contact with staff clothing. Choices *C* and *D* would be acceptable, but eyewear and masks are not generally required for contact isolation.

125. D: Hemolytic anemia is caused by the destruction of red blood cells (RBCs). There are several potential factors that can cause RBCs to become destroyed or hemolyzed. Some of these include infections, medications, toxins, physical trauma, and inherited disorders. As red blood cells are destroyed, the yellow pigment known as bilirubin is produced. Elevated levels of bilirubin can lead to jaundice—the yellowing of the skin and sclera—dark urine, and even fatigue. This makes Choice *A* incorrect as elevated sodium levels are not related to hemolytic anemia, and clinical manifestations of elevated sodium levels include excessive thirst, oliguria, muscle twitching, and even seizures. Choice *B* is incorrect because increased red blood cell levels do not have a direct correlation with increased levels of bilirubin, only the destruction of red blood cells. Choice *C* is also incorrect as white blood cells do not have a direct correlation with bilirubin.

126. A: Worsening abdominal pain and nausea/vomiting in the patient with a small bowel obstruction indicate a need for gastric decompression, which can be done with NG tube placement, Choice *A*. Choice *B*, requesting an order for abdominal CT, may potentially be indicated to rule out a worsening condition, but it is not priority. Choice *C*, preparing the patient for an EGD, is not indicated for a small bowel obstruction, nor will it assist with the worsening abdominal pain and vomiting. Choice *D*, requesting an order for additional antiemetics, may help the patient with their discomfort if they have not yet reached the maximum dose of antiemetics, but it will not treat the underlying cause of their symptoms.

127. A: Patients who have difficulties with communication may exhibit frustration. The nurse should show empathy and support through nonverbal communication, which can include therapeutic touch, smile, or nodding for reassurance. Choice *B* is incorrect as restricting visitors reduces the patient's social support and can cause unnecessary distress. Choice *C* is also incorrect because even though the patient has communication difficulties, they do not have hearing difficulties; therefore, the nurse should not change how she speaks to the patient because they still understand what she is saying. Choice *D* is also incorrect since pretending like the patient is speaking normally and failing to acknowledge the difficulty can cause even more distress to the patient.

128. A: The most effective intervention to prevent a surgical site infection (SSI) in a patient is to administer prophylactic antibiotics before surgery. Choices *B* and *C* are also appropriate interventions, but they are not the most effective. Choice *D*, drawing labs prior to surgery, may be necessary to determine patient stability, but this intervention does not directly prevent SSI.

129. C: The nurse should acknowledge the child's feelings and address their concerns to provide caring and compassionate care. By explaining things in a way that the child can understand, their anxiety may decrease. Choice *A* is incorrect as this may cause increased anxiety since the child might not have any idea of what is going on. Choice *B* is also incorrect as this doesn't represent compassionate and therapeutic care—it does not address the child's concerns. Choice *D*, utilizing diversion techniques, may

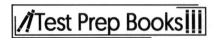

Answer Key and Explanations #2

be helpful to decrease the child's anxiety temporarily, but it will not address the root cause of their anxiety regarding the surgery.

130. D: The patient's symptoms and physical examination findings (localized chest pain, shortness of breath, reduced breath sounds, and dullness to percussion) are most consistent with a pleural effusion, or fluid accumulation in the pleural space. An MI, Choice *A*, would typically present with more severe chest pain and systemic symptoms. Atelectasis, Choice *B*, could cause similar symptoms but is less likely given the lack of common risk factors (such as recent surgery or immobility). A pneumothorax, Choice *C*, would typically present with sudden-onset dyspnea and potentially severe chest pain and would be less likely to cause dullness to percussion.

131. A: The correct choice is Choice *A*, fluid resuscitation. Acute pancreatitis causes significant hypovolemia from vomiting and inflammation. This results in hypotension and tachycardia. Choices *B* and *C* are both incorrect. Giving pain medication will likely result in further hypotension. Choice *D*, administering due antibiotics, is also incorrect. While antibiotics should be given on time, fluid resuscitation is the priority intervention.

132. C: Patients with the influenza virus may be given oseltamivir, an antiviral, which can help improve and treat symptoms. It should be administered within 48 hours of symptom onset to have the best efficacy. Amoxicillin would not be administered because it is an antibiotic that is solely used to treat bacterial infections, making Choice *A* incorrect. Choice *B* is also incorrect because fluconazole is an antifungal medication that is used to treat fungal infections. Doxorubicin would not be administered to a patient with influenza either, as this drug is a chemotherapy drug used to slow the growth of cancer cells, making Choice *D* incorrect.

133. C: In this case, the patient's symptoms and physical examination findings are consistent with empyema. Choice *A* refers to the accumulation of air in the pleural space, leading to lung collapse, which does not align with the patient's presentation. Choice *B* involves the presence of blood in the pleural space, which is not indicated in this patient. Choice *D* also involves fluid in the pleural space, but it does not necessarily involve the presence of pus.

134. D: The most likely cause for the patient's delirium is their alcohol withdrawal since being admitted into the hospital. Common symptoms of alcohol withdrawal include tremors, anxiety, sweating, increased heart rate, delirium, and, in severe cases, seizures. Although Choices *A, B,* and *C* can all potentially cause delirium, they are not the most likely cause in this situation.

135. D: Respecting a patient's preferences and goals is an important part of compassionate care, especially for those who have been diagnosed with a terminal illness. The nurse should collaborate with the patient's healthcare team as well as the patient to create a palliative care plan that supports the patient's goals. This allows the promotion of dignity and comfort during the dying process. Choice *A* is incorrect as the nurse would not solely make this decision. It is a decision that is made by the patient and healthcare team together. Choice *B* is also incorrect as this ignores the patient's ultimate wishes. Providing emotional support to the patient is certainly helpful, especially during the dying process, but it is not the only or most important action that can be taken, making Choice *C* incorrect.

136. B: Interdisciplinary collaboration requires open and timely communication between healthcare providers. The nurse should share pertinent test results with the members of the patient's healthcare team so that their care plan is well-rounded. Choice *A* is incorrect as the primary care provider would

300

already have a record of the patient's health history. Choice C is incorrect as simply making appointments with the patient's specialists does not constitute collaboration. Choice D is also incorrect because keeping the patient's medical information private and excluding their healthcare team from this information would not lead to any benefit for the patient.

137. C: It is important to perform hand hygiene before and after handling the PICC because handwashing is the most effective way to prevent the spread of germs. Choice A is incorrect as changing the dressing every 24 hours is unnecessary and may cause an even further risk of infection. Dressings should be changed every five to seven days, or when they are visibly soiled. Choice B is incorrect because using the same infusion tubing for all medications increases the risk of contamination – infusion tubing can be used for up to three days as long as it is the same medication. Choice D is incorrect as a sterile technique should be used during dressing changes.

138. B: Gabapentin is an anticonvulsant and nerve pain medication that is used frequently for patients who have chronic pain. Some of the major side effects include fatigue, dizziness, nausea, vomiting, and diarrhea. The nurse should make sure that the patient is not heavily sedated to the point of danger because if the patient attempts to ambulate, they may fall and become injured. Choice A is incorrect because gabapentin does not cause hyperactivity but instead fatigue and tiredness. Choices C and D are also incorrect because gabapentin is known to cause bradycardia and diarrhea, not tachycardia or constipation.

139. C: Before a diagnostic cardiac catheterization, the patient should be informed that they might feel a warm sensation when the dye is injected. This is because a contrast dye is used during the procedure to visualize the coronary arteries. Although the patient may receive sedation or local anesthesia for the procedure, general anesthesia, Choice A, is not typically required for a diagnostic cardiac catheterization. Fasting for 24 hours, Choice B, is not necessary for this procedure, and it is important to clarify the specific fasting instructions with the patient based on the hospital's protocol. Choice D is incorrect because patients are typically discharged the same day following a cardiac catheterization unless the patient has underlying conditions that would require additional monitoring.

140. C: This is the only correct statement. According to the CDC, "Among UTIs acquired in the hospital, approximately 75% are associated with a urinary catheter." Choice A is incorrect because, according to the CDC, about 15-25% of patients receive a urinary catheter in the hospital. Choice B is incorrect because the Centers for Medicare and Medicaid Services do not reimburse any of the cost for a hospital-acquired CAUTI. Choice D is incorrect because the longer a patient has a urinary catheter, the *higher* their risk of developing a CAUTI.

141. B: If a patient is experiencing signs of anaphylactic shock, they should receive intramuscular epinephrine as quickly as possible. Any delay in administration risks obstruction of the airway. Choice A is incorrect because the time taken to ensure IV access may allow shock to worsen and obstruct the patient's airway. Choice C is incorrect because this is the priority intervention for hypovolemic shock; epinephrine is the priority for the patient with anaphylactic shock. Choice D is incorrect because, while the nurse should delegate this task to a member of the healthcare team, it is not the priority action.

142. B: Choice B, isotonic fluids, are generally the standard of care for this situation, with some patients requiring hypotonic fluids to manage electrolyte imbalances. The patient is presenting with signs of hyperosmolar hyperglycemic state (HHS). This is distinguished from diabetic ketoacidosis, a blood glucose that is typically much higher. HHS usually presents in patients with type 2 diabetes who are experiencing dehydration rather than insulin deficiency. Initial treatment involves fluid resuscitation in order to decrease the patient's high serum glucose levels. Choice *A* is incorrect; a sodium bicarbonate drip is not indicated, as the patient is not acidotic and sodium bicarbonate levels are expected. Choice *C* is incorrect; depending on the patient's response to the fluids, they may then receive insulin either via IV drip or subcutaneously. Choice *D*, hypertonic saline, is unlikely to be used as well, as it may increase the patient's hyperosmolar state.

143. B: The nurse should take action to address the medication error and prevent harm to the patient. By notifying the healthcare provider and the pharmacy of the error, the situation can be fixed promptly. Administering an additional bag of antibiotics to compensate for the incorrect dose would not be ethical and may cause more harm to the patient, making Choice *A* incorrect. Allowing the current antibiotic to finish infusing and redrawing blood tests is also not appropriate. Depending on the dose the patient receives, this could cause additional harm, making Choice *C* incorrect. Not only this, but the nurse cannot administer an additional bag unless prescribed by the healthcare provider. Informing the patient and their family about the medication error is an important action, but it is not the first action the nurse should take to prevent further harm to the patient, making Choice *D* incorrect also.

144. B: HCM is characterized by the abnormal thickening of the heart muscle, which can lead to disorganization of myocardial architecture and abnormal diastolic function. This abnormal structure and function can disrupt the heart's normal electrical pathways and cause life-threatening arrhythmias, leading to sudden cardiac death. Myocardial ischemia, Choice *A*; reduced cardiac output due to ventricular dilation, Choice *C*; and severe mitral valve regurgitation, Choice *D*, can occur in various heart conditions, but they are not typical findings in HCM.

145. B: Silent MIs refer to cases in which the patient does not experience the typical chest pain or other classic symptoms of a heart attack. Instead, they may present with atypical symptoms or no symptoms at all. This phenomenon is more common in patients with diabetes mellitus due to diabetic neuropathy, which can affect the nerves responsible for transmitting pain signals. In addition, older adults and men may also be at a higher risk. Choices *A*, *C*, and *D* are not specifically associated with an increased likelihood of experiencing a silent MI.

146. B: The most appropriate response from the nurse is to discuss reviewing the patient's nutritional status and any contributing factors to their weight loss, which can include nausea or difficulty swallowing. It would be counterintuitive and unsafe to have a patient eat solids if they are having difficulty swallowing. Choice *A* is incorrect as the nurse should collaborate with the multidisciplinary team to determine a plan of care for nutrition, energy levels, and quality of life during the dying process. However, it is true that at the end stages of life, patients become weaker and lose interest in consuming food compared to previous stages. Choice *C* is also incorrect because having a patient eat at the end of the dying process may cause additional discomfort and decrease the quality of life. Choice *D* is also incorrect because the additional fluids administered may cause edema and discomfort for the patient, again decreasing the quality of life.

147. B: Sterile procedure during central line placement is a critical step in preventing a CLABSI. Even if it causes delay or inconvenience, the nurse must advocate for patient safety by helping the team resume the sterility of the procedure. Choices *A*, *C*, and *D* are incorrect because inaction or action taken after the procedure is complete fails to protect the patient from potential harm from nonsterile placement of the central line.

148. C: Pericardiocentesis is the definitive treatment for cardiac tamponade. In this procedure, a needle or catheter is inserted into the pericardial sac to drain the accumulated fluid, relieving the pressure on the heart. Administration of vasopressors, Choice *A*, may temporarily increase blood pressure, but it does not address the underlying issue of fluid accumulation around the heart. Cardiac catheterization, Choice *B*, is a diagnostic procedure that may provide information about the underlying cause of cardiac tamponade, but it is not the definitive treatment. CPR, Choice *D*, is a life-saving procedure performed during cardiac arrest and is not specific to treating cardiac tamponade.

149. B: There are a lot of concerns and misconceptions related to childhood immunizations. Having a group discussion will allow the nurse to answer questions and debunk misconceptions so parents can leave the informational group with better knowledge. Choice *A* would not be helpful as parents do not need to know the immunizations needed for their children; this is something that their primary care provider will monitor. The role of the parents is to bring their children for routine well-child and immunization visits. Choice *C* is also incorrect as this may not answer the parents' concerns. An informational video may be helpful to incorporate within the group, but it shouldn't be the only component. Choice *D* is incorrect since parents are not allowed to administer immunizations.

150. C: The correct answer is Choice *C*. The patient may be aspirating, as evidenced by a right lower lobe pneumonia, difficulty swallowing, and coughing after intake. A bedside swallow evaluation should be performed to determine if it is safe to eat or drink or if a speech therapy consult needs to be placed. Choice *A* is incorrect. It should be determined if it is safe to eat or drink before giving the patient anything by mouth. Choice *B* is incorrect. Based on the information presented there is no indication of hypoxia. Choice *D* is also incorrect. Giving more liquids may cause the patient to aspirate.

PCCN Practice Test #3

To keep the size of this book manageable, save paper, and provide a digital test-taking experience, the 3rd practice test can be found online. Scan the QR code or go to this link to access it:

testprepbooks.com/bonus/pccn

The first time you access the tests, you will need to register as a "new user" and verify your email address.

If you have any issues, please email support@testprepbooks.com.

Dear PCCN Test Taker,

Thank you for purchasing this study guide for your PCCN exam. We hope that we exceeded your expectations.

Our goal in creating this study guide was to cover all of the topics that you will see on the test. We also strove to make our practice questions as similar as possible to what you will encounter on test day. With that being said, if you found something that you feel was not up to your standards, please send us an email and let us know.

We have study guides in a wide variety of fields. If you're interested in one, try searching for it on Amazon or send us an email.

Thanks Again and Happy Testing!
Product Development Team
info@studyguideteam.com

FREE Test Taking Tips Video/DVD Offer

To better serve you, we created videos covering test taking tips that we want to give you for FREE. **These videos cover world-class tips that will help you succeed on your test.**

We just ask that you send us feedback about this product. Please let us know what you thought about it—whether good, bad, or indifferent.

To get your **FREE videos**, you can use the QR code below or email freevideos@studyguideteam.com with "Free Videos" in the subject line and the following information in the body of the email:

      a. The title of your product

      b. Your product rating on a scale of 1-5, with 5 being the highest

      c. Your feedback about the product

If you have any questions or concerns, please don't hesitate to contact us at info@studyguideteam.com.

Thank you!